Calamity and Re

MW01036283

~~HHHO~~ Chapter 1

Calamity and Reform in China

• • • • •

State, Rural Society, and Institutional Change Since the Great Leap Famine

Dali L. Yang

• • • • •

Stanford University Press
Stanford, California

Stanford University Press
Stanford, California
© 1996 by the Board of Trustees of the
Leland Stanford Junior University
Printed in the United States of America

CIP data are at the end of the book.

To the memory of
L., Y. H. K., and C. Y. Z.
and
the millions of Chinese who died in the Great Leap Famine

*The major advances in civilization are
processes which all but wreck the societies
in which they occur.*

—Alfred North Whitehead,
Symbolism

· · ● · ·

Preface

Of the numerous political traumas that have afflicted twentieth-century China, the Great Leap Forward and the Cultural Revolution stand out. The tribulations of the Cultural Revolution are well known not only because this upheaval resulted in much violence and profound disillusionment but also because most victims of the Cultural Revolution—including deposed party bureaucrats and members of the intelligentsia—survived, returned to power, and were articulate enough to tell their side of the story. As a result, the Cultural Revolution has been the subject of shelves of books and tens of thousands of articles.

The Great Leap Forward led to at least as much human suffering as did the Cultural Revolution, far more if one measures suffering by the number of people who died. Demographers estimate that the Great Leap Famine of 1959–61 resulted in 30 million deaths, making it the worst famine in human history. Yet both in China and abroad the Great Leap Famine has received meager attention and has been the focus of only a small number of scholarly publications, mostly academic articles scattered here and there. This lack of attention is partly because victims of the Great Leap Famine were chiefly farmers, who were likely to remain inarticulate even if they survived. It is also partly because, with rare exceptions, archives on the Great Leap Famine remain tightly guarded. After all, many members of the current elite in China played a part in that inglorious era and have no interest in displaying their own dirty linen.

Born during the baby boom that followed on the heels of the Great Leap

Famine, I grew up in the Chinese countryside (Shandong province) and learned the popular lore surrounding the famine. Throughout my childhood and youth, an indelible image was repeatedly etched onto my mind. Every winter, especially around Spring Festival (a Chinese holiday season comparable to Christmas in the West), farmers from northern Shandong came to my area to beg. Individually or in pairs (typically an adult leading a child), they asked for morsels of food, moving from one house to the next and one village to another. While people in my area were hardly prosperous at that time, the "visitors" rarely left empty-handed, receiving a couple of dumplings or a piece of corn or wheat bread each time. In those bygone days, the scene described here, and others more heart wrenching, were probably repeated hundreds of thousands of times a day in China.

It was not until I was in college that I began to understand the wider ramifications of my personal experience, especially against the official textbook emphasis on bountiful harvests and the wise leadership of the Communist Party. In the meantime, widespread seasonal begging had largely become a thing of the past under the reforms. Yet my memory of that period has continued to shape my intellectual agenda. While this volume, as a work of social science, was conceived as a step toward redressing the imbalance of scholarly attention to the Great Leap Famine and its historical implications, it is also fundamentally the outcome of a personal journey that began with handing out morsels of food to unexpected visitors and an intense curiosity about how we come to be what we are.

In my effort to understand the dynamics of change in China, I have drawn on Chinese documents that were previously classified and have placed particular emphasis on provincial variations in policy implementation. After an overview of the progression toward the Great Leap Forward in the 1950's, I provide what I believe is a rigorous and counterintuitive explanation of the patterns of the Great Leap Famine by emphasizing not only the role of the Chinese leadership but also the incentives induced by the political structure that resulted from the Communist conquest.

But the Great Leap Famine is intellectually interesting both because it was one of the worst tragedies in human history and because it furnished the crucial historical motives for dismantling the rural collective institutional structure in post-Mao China. As I will demonstrate, the patterns of rural reform in China, epitomized by the introduction of the household responsibility system, were linked to the history of the Great Leap Famine, as well as to political geography. Those areas that suffered more during the famine or were farther from Beijing, the political center, were also more likely to spearhead the introduction of household farming. Because the rural reforms provided the breakthrough that launched China into the reform era, the dynamics of the latter cannot be fully appreciated without paying attention to the Great Leap Famine, though it occurred two decades earlier.

By tracing the causal patterns leading from revolution to famine and then to reform, this book explains much about how and why the Chinese revolution self-destructed. While standard interpretations of the causes of rural reform emphasize the impact of the Cultural Revolution and the role of leaders such as Deng Xiaoping, I suggest that these two factors, alone or together, are inadequate to explain what happened. The rise of rural reform was effected not just by the words and actions of such prominent leaders as Deng Xiaoping, as the conventional literature would have us believe, but also by the initiative of tens of millions of ordinary Chinese who had not the slightest idea of producing reform but did it anyway in response to the Great Leap Famine. By debunking official Chinese rhetoric (and derivative scholarly writings) christening Deng Xiaoping the chief architect of China's reforms, this study underscores the crucial need for scholars of China to go beyond official discourse and seek independent answers that emphasize both agency and historical structure, as well as contingency.

Most social science cannot perform controlled experiments but must work with historical evidence that suffers from all sorts of imperfections. These challenges to rigorous research are further compounded by the various roadblocks to archival access, especially in authoritarian political regimes such as China's. (This book was written mostly in 1990–92, when social science fieldwork in China was particularly suspect.) Even as I send the manuscript to press, I am keenly aware how much it might be improved were I to have systematic access to the vast provincial archives in China that remain off-limits. At the least, I could give more voice to the victims of the Great Leap Famine than I have been able to. Thus, my book remains a midterm report on rethinking historical change in an extraordinarily complex era of Chinese history. Ever the optimist, I cherish the hope that I will one day have the opportunity to work in those archives along with scholars from other disciplines.

In one of his last published works, the great French historian Fernand Braudel asked a question that students of historical change are inevitably drawn to at one time or another: "Can we say that [history] limits—note that I do not say eliminates—both men's freedom and their responsibility?" In an apparent swipe at Marx, the doyen of the *Annales* school answered that "men do not make history, rather it is history above all that makes men and thereby absolves them from blame."[1]

Millions of Chinese families, including my own, have many reasons to disagree with Braudel as they look back at such traumatic events as the Great Leap Famine and the Cultural Revolution. It is easy to become morally outraged as one examines the consequences of policies made by China's leaders, however well intentioned and historically constrained they might have been, in launching the myriad political movements that x • *Preface*

brought so much suffering to the very people they claimed to represent and serve.

The fundamental purpose of this study, however, is not to offer historical judgment, though some readers may use my findings for that purpose. Instead, I hope to offer readers a more rigorous dissection of the dynamics of change, from the causes of the Great Leap Famine to the origins of post-Mao reforms and beyond. Indeed, in writing this volume I was more sustained by a deepening appreciation of societal rejuvenation than driven by a macabre desire to ferret out the dirty secrets of history. Despite the social science terms and statistical calculations used to make the argument more exact and the causal linkages better specified, there is no hiding the fact that this is a volume about hope, renewal, and regeneration, and about the role played by both elites and humble peasants in shaping the path of history. If after reading this book, the reader feels that he or she has learned something about why China never ceases to fascinate and amaze, I will be gratified.

It is impossible to name all the people who have helped me acquire the mental fortitude and scholarly skills to write this book. I owe a very deep debt of gratitude to them all but can only single out a few of them in these pages.

I would like to offer my most sincere thanks to a number of teachers and friends who made it possible for me to make the transition from industrial engineering to political science: the late Professor Cheng Yuzheng; Professor Zhong Tianju, who gave me refuge when I became a victim of Chinese bureaucratic corruption; Professor Mel Gurtov, who welcomed me into political science and assisted me in many ways; and Bart Singletary and Elizabeth Ducy.

My greatest debts while working on this volume are to my teacher-advisers in graduate school: David Bachman, Henry S. Bienen, and Lynn T. White III. Each read through drafts of the manuscript with meticulous care and offered constructive comments, wise counsel, and moral support as I groped for my own voice. My special thanks go to David for leading me through the maze of graduate school and to Professor Robert Gilpin for his insistence on social *science*.

The University of Chicago has proved an ideal environment for revising the manuscript. I am most grateful to John Mearsheimer, Bernard Silberman, and Norman Nie for easing my transition to Chicago and making my stay fruitful. In a variety of settings, many of my colleagues, especially David Laitin and Bernard Silberman, provided stimulating comments, which forced me to rethink the issues with which I am intellectually engaged. William L. Parish, Lucian Pye, Thomas P. Bernstein, and Joseph Fewsmith deserve many thanks for reading through the entire manuscript and offering extensive comments. Kunal Bhaumik read through the manuscript from the perspective of a college student and offered useful suggestions. Ben Klemens provided efficient research support while I worked on the final revision. Lorraine Dwelle was of immense help in 101 ways.

For helpful discussions on statistical inferences, I am grateful to Gregory Chow, D. Gale Johnson, John Londregon, William Parish, Pei Minxin, Yair Mundlak, George Tolley, Theodore Schultz, and participants at the Agricultural Economics Workshop of the University of Chicago. Robin Hogarth kindly discussed with me the psychological arguments embedded in this study. Daniel Kelliher, Nicholas Lardy, Kenneth Lieberthal, Kevin O'Brien, and Brantly Womack commented on an earlier version of Chapters 2 and 3 when I presented them at the annual meetings of the Association for Asian Studies and the Midwest Political Science Association. I also benefited from the constructive comments offered by seminar participants at the University of Missouri, as well as at Cornell, Duke, and Princeton Universities. I would like to thank Benedict Anderson, Robert Bates, Thad Brown, Sherman Cochran, Donald Horowitz, Vivienne Shue, Sydney Tarrow, Tang Tsou, and Paul Wallace for questions and encouragement. Paul David, Edward Friedman, Timothy Guinnane, Barry Naughton, Jean C. Oi, Louis Putterman, Andrew Watson, Tyrene White, and Christine Wong shared with me their own writings.

I am indebted to the following teachers and friends for their support and friendship over the years: Nancy Bermeo, Xiaonong Cheng, Lowell Dittmer, Jameson Doig, Fred Greenstein, Mildred Kalmus, Atul Kohli, Kesuke Iida, Samuel Kim, David Lampton, Kenneth Oye, Arthur Waldron, Wang Xiaoyi, and Xiaowei Yu. In one way or another, my fellow graduate students shared my journey and constituted an immediate circle of comfort: a partial list includes Thomas Banchoff, Thomas Drohan, Andrew Farkas, Arie Kacowicz, Solomon Karmel, London Kirkendall, Paul Lewis, Cheng Li, Thomas Moore, Thomas Nimick, and Kate Zhou.

In writing this volume, I have drawn upon my personal experience in rural China, interviews, and, most important, documentary sources. I wish to thank the excellent support I have received from the staff of the Gest Oriental Library and Far Eastern Collections at Princeton University, especially Martin Heijdra; they made me feel at home. Since I moved to Chicago, I have also become indebted to the staff of the East Asia Library, especially Wen-Pai Tai and Barbara Banks. Shiwei Chen, Li Li, Ruan Ming, as well as others, provided me with a number of useful sources and saved me much time. I would also like to acknowledge the services of the cooperative librarians of the Library of Congress, and the libraries at Yale University, Columbia University, the Harvard Yen-ching Institute, and the Hoover Institution. Muriel Bell and Amy Klatzkin of Stanford University Press shepherded this manuscript through the publishing process, and Mark Jacobs copyedited the manuscript with expert care.

The research for this volume was made possible by generous financial support from a number of institutions. The Princeton University Graduate School awarded me a fellowship as well as a Charlotte Elizabeth Procter Honorific Fellowship. The Center of International Studies, then directed by Henry Bienen, and the Council on Regional Studies, chaired by Ezra Suleiman, provided grants for summer research. The Mellon Seminar on Comparisons of Socialism, directed by Gilbert Rozman, and the Center for Modern China funded my research on rural enterprise policy. At the University of Chicago, my research has been supported by grants from the Social Sciences Divisional Research Fund and the Committee on Chinese Studies.

My parents and parents-in-law, as well as other members of my extended family, tolerated my long absences and were a constant source of moral support. My two daughters were born while I wrote this book. They have greatly enriched my life and provided the balance I needed. Last, but certainly not least, my greatest thanks go to my wife, Ling. To put it simply, I could not have made it without her dedication and support.

D.L.Y.

Contents

Figures

. . ● . .

Tables

· · **·** · ·

A Note on Translation, Transliteration, Names, and Measures

All translations are by the author unless otherwise indicated. *Pinyin* is used for the transliteration of Chinese terms. With the exception of Chinese writers who published in English and presented their names in Western fashion, Chinese personal names in the text appear in Chinese form, with surname preceding given name.

1 *mu* = ⅙ acre
1 *jin* = 1.1 pounds; 1 *dan* = 100 *jin*
1 *li* = ½ kilometer = 0.31 mile

PEOPLE'S REPUBLIC OF
CHINA

AFGHANISTAN

PAKISTAN

XINJIANG

Urumqi

GANSU

QINGHAI

Xining

TIBET

NEPAL

Lhasa

SICHUAN

BHUTAN

BANGLADESH

INDIA

Kunmi

YUNNAN

BURMA

BAY OF BENGAL

LAOS

THAILAND

The Great Leap Famine, the Rise of Reform, and the Cognitive Basis of Institutional Change

The prevailing interpretations of the rise of rural reform in China are dominated by conceptions or hypotheses emphasizing the traumatic legacy of the Cultural Revolution and the role or "plans" of revisionist leadership. Both are obviously relevant to our understanding of the political economy of change in China. Yet, as I hope to demonstrate in this study, these conventional hypotheses essentially miss the target as causal explanations of the rise of rural reforms in China. The central thesis of the present study, to summarize drastically, is that the key to understanding the rise of rural reforms in China and the interactive relationship between state and rural society that went with them lies in the Great Leap Famine of 1959–61, the worst in human history. The patterns of the famine were in turn accounted for by the interaction between the Chinese leadership and certain structural features of the political system generated by the communist takeover. In other words, the dramatic victory of the communists over the Guomindang (i.e., nationalists) unfortunately also produced the structural conditions for the Great Leap. But out of the ruins of the Great Leap Famine arose the incentives for political innovation or reform. The delineation of reform patterns thus requires an understanding of both structural conditions and political entrepreneurship. The path and political dialectics of reform in China were embedded in history, a very specific history.

The analytical results of a study of China's rural institutional transformation not only permit us to gain a better understanding of the dynamics of change in China but also provide an important case for understanding the role played by beliefs and cognitive biases in the political economy of institutional change. Whereas it is commonly assumed that political actors' cognitive limitations tend to produce path-dependent and incremental institutional change, the Chinese case provides striking evidence that drastic changes in belief, such as the profound disenchantment with rural people's communes, can lead to the rupture of institutional evolution.

In the rest of this introduction, I first discuss the political significance of rural decollectivization and then review the conventional perspectives on the rise of China's rural reforms. Next I indicate the alternative argument to be elaborated in this book and explicate several general terms I use. This is followed by a general discussion of the impact of human cognitive limitations on the nature of institutional change, which I will use as the framework for analysis. I end with an overview of the research approach adopted in this study, as well as a preview of the rest of the book.

The Political Significance of Decollectivization

Less than a decade after the death of Mao Zedong in 1976, the Chinese people's commune system, a hallmark of Maoist egalitarianism and self-reliance, had been dismantled. Collective land came under the management of individual households through the household responsibility system. Once bound to the collectives like serfs, hundreds of millions of Chinese peasants regained their residual claims over the harvest and could again engage in sideline businesses, commerce, and private industry. Individual initiative, rather than collective mobilization, became the new order of the day in the rural economy.[1] In the words of a leading student of China's rural economy, a peaceful revolution had occurred in rural China.[2]

The decollectivization of rural communes ushered in an era of reforms in China.[3] Not only did decollectivization contribute to the surprisingly rapid growth of agriculture in the early 1980's, but, by releasing underemployed laborers from agriculture, it has also fueled the dramatic expansion of rural industry.[4] Decollectivization in China had important economic consequences, but it was also of fundamental political significance. The transformation from collective agriculture to household farming, whose significance for China's rural residents was analogous to the demise of feudalism in Europe, concerns one basic constitutional issue in the organization of society: Who has control over a person's labor and has residual claims to its product?

To be sure, self-proclaimed doctrinal heirs to Marx, from Stalin to Mao and beyond, have professed their faith in agricultural collectives by alleging economies of scale or size. In reality, the decision to collectivize in Marxist regimes was largely made on political and social grounds, especially in the name of combating the power of landlords and rich peasants and of harnessing the potential of individualistic peasants for the common good.[5] Instead of fulfilling those grandiose promises, however, collectivization brought state domination of rural society, the regimentation of peasant life, and "the gratuitous sacrifice of the flesh and blood of live human beings upon the altar of idealized abstractions."[6] What was originally billed as a worker-peasant alliance under the leadership of the Communist Party inevitably degenerated into a party-state dictatorship over needs.[7]

In light of the party-state's domination of society, one cannot help asking how and why decollectivization took place at all, when the same Communist Party remained in power, as intent on preserving its dictatorship as ever? For, unlike Eastern Europe at the end of the 1980's, when the "Autumn of the People" in 1989 seemed unstoppable, China in the late 1970's and early 1980's had just emerged from the nightmarish Cultural Revolution and was neither experiencing nor expecting epoch-making reforms such as the dismantlement of the people's communes.[8] Setbacks and problems notwithstanding, the commune system had by then been entrenched for about two decades. One had every reason to expect it to last into the foreseeable future as one of Chairman Mao's legacies. As Vivienne Shue pointed out in 1986: "Ten years ago one would have been thought lunatic to suggest that Chinese peasants would be urged by their government to abandon collective cultivation for family farming."[9] Indeed, in the words of Andrew Watson, another leading scholar on rural China: "It is unlikely that those supporting household contracting could have predicted both the way in which the collectives would disappear and what that would mean for the structure of the rural economy as a whole."[10]

In fact, decollectivization occurred in China with surprising rapidity and apparent success, generating momentum for further reforms in other spheres of China's political economy.[11] Hence it is warranted to take decollectivization, or the introduction of household-based farming, as a critical case in an effort to understand the political economy of China's reforms.[12] The central question posed here is: What were the causes and causal mechanisms of decollectivization in rural China? Because of the political nature of decollectivization, I hope the answers to this question will shed light not only on the processes of reform but also on the interactive relationship between state and rural society, the role of leaders at both local and central levels, and theories of institutional change.

The Rise of China's Reforms: Two Conventional Explanations

I shall now briefly survey the two complementary explanations of China's reform movement. While one suggests that the destruction caused by the

Cultural Revolution laid the basis for the reform movement, the other states that Deng Xiaoping or the reformist faction headed by Deng was responsible for launching the rapid changes. I shall refer to these two explanations as the Cultural Revolution thesis and the leadership thesis; they are not mutually exclusive. Both are popular among those Chinese as well as Western scholars writing on China.[13] Indeed, so widely accepted are the two theses that scholars in the West routinely refer to them without attribution.

The Cultural Revolution and Reform

According to the first thesis, the Cultural Revolution initiated by Mao "led to domestic turmoil and brought catastrophe to the Party, the state and the whole people."[14] In the words of leading government economist Xue Muqiao: "After 1976 everyone recognized that there had been 10 years of catastrophe, that the national economy was already on the edge of collapse."[15] Hence the lessons from the Cultural Revolution "were a most [sic] painful." In consequence, the Third Plenary Session of the Eleventh Party Central Committee held in December 1978 "was a turning point of far-reaching significance in the history of the Party.... It began to rectify in earnest the 'leftist' mistakes [committed] before and during the 'Cultural Revolution.'"[16] Thus the Cultural Revolution is believed by many Chinese as having "made the 'second revolution' inevitable. Without those 'ten calamitous years,' they say, there would have been no sea change in China."[17] Western scholarship has largely mirrored the Chinese pattern of argument regarding the legacies of the Cultural Revolution. For Ezra Vogel, "The suffering of the Cultural Revolution, and the horrible awareness that so many lives were ruined, has become a catalyst for change."[18] The prominent political scientist Lucian Pye concurred. He believed that "the current reforms and the open-door policies could never have come about except for the trauma" of the Cultural Revolution.[19] For Pye, the Cultural Revolution was perhaps "the traumatic equivalent of what the other Confucian societies experienced from war."[20] In the words of economist Robert M. Field, "Countless thousands suffered untold hardships, and the experience changed their attitudes profoundly."[21] Thus, in the editors' introduction to the highly acclaimed volume *The Political Economy of Reform in Post-Mao China*, Elizabeth Perry and Christine Wong write:

The origins of the reforms are found in the combination of poor economic performance and disruptive political upheavals resulting from the Cultural Revolution and its aftermath. . . . The seeds of the current drive for reform were planted during the tumultuous Central Revolution decade, but did not germinate until the death of Mao Zedong and the arrest of the gang of four in the autumn of 1976.[22]

Similarly, sociologist Mark Lupher concluded that "the major unintended consequence of power restructuring during the Cultural Revolution was the unleashing of processes of localism, economic decentralization, and marketization which culminated in the reforms of the post-Mao period."[23] In short, as two economists put it, "The impetus for reform . . . arose in the Cultural Revolution period."[24]

Leaders and Reform

While the Cultural Revolution thesis stresses the influence of the past on the present, the leadership thesis emphasizes the role of China's leaders, especially that of Deng Xiaoping, in initiating the reform movement. In so doing, this thesis joins a growing literature on the political economy of reform in developing countries by arguing that policy elites are important determinants of reform.[25]

For consumers of China's official propaganda, this second thesis is a familiar one, especially in the aftermath of the crisis of 1989. Assessment of reform has invariably meant praise for Deng Xiaoping, who is referred to as the "general architect of reforms" (*zong shejishi*). It is no surprise that Deng's thought has replaced Mao Zedong's to become "the strategic thinking for contemporary China."[26]

Western scholarship has likewise paid careful attention to the important role played by Deng Xiaoping and his colleagues. Deng's writings are scrutinized, and his myriad roles are carefully analyzed.[27] Unlike Chinese writers on the subject, however, scholars in the West have tended to focus on how Deng Xiaoping outmaneuvered his political rivals to secure the adoption of a reform program in the late 1970's and after.[28]

Generally, Western scholarship dates "the decisive break point" of reform to the December 1978 Third Plenum, when "the process of change in China initiated by Deng Xiaoping and his political and ideological supporters began to gather momentum."[29] As Harry Harding put it in his critically acclaimed volume, *China's Second Revolution,*

> The reforms have been the result of extraordinary political engineering by a coalition of reform-minded leaders led by Deng Xiaoping. That coalition used Deng's personal prestige, as well as the unresolved grievances of the Cultural Revolution (1966–76), to push Mao's immediate successor, Hua Guofeng, off the political stage and begin a massive restaffing and restructuring of the Party and state bureaucracies, leading to a large-scale program of political and economic reform.[30]

This "great man" model of reform has been extended to the decollectivization of agricultural production, which Harding termed "the most notable reform in the rural sector." He pointed out that "this policy has been only one of a series of measures, implemented sequentially since the late 1970's, that have been *designed* to improve rural productivity and increase agricultural output."[31] Similarly, Roderick MacFarquhar writes eloquently in the authoritative Cambridge History of China: "Teng [Deng] turned back the clock, dismantling the commune system set up during the Great Leap Forward in 1958, returning control over production to the farm family for the first time since land reform in the early 1950's."[32] As Vivienne Shue reminded us in the aftermath of the Tiananmen crackdown of 1989,

The Deng Xiaoping who approved moving against the students in Tiananmen Square is the same Deng Xiaoping, after all, who was responsible for initiating China's early and audacious moves away from the irrationalities of Soviet-style central planning as well as from the phony politics of China's early-1970s' ultra-left socialism. It was Deng Xiaoping who, insisting on the pragmatic separation of politics from economics, authored the first several acts in the drama of the Chinese reforms.[33]

The emphasis on reform from above and the indispensability of leadership has led to a search for the strategy, blueprint, or plan for reform. Consequently, discussions of reform are frequently cast in terms of "model," "program," "design," "script," and "political engineering."[34] As Anne Thurston writes, "The first step in [Deng's] ambitious plan [to quadruple the 1978 GNP] was the decollectivization of agriculture."[35]

An Alternative Explanation: The Great Leap Famine and the Rise of Reform

Both the Cultural Revolution and the leadership theses make some sense, logically and empirically. The chaos of the Cultural Revolution certainly led to a lot of suffering among the intelligentsia as well as members of the party machine (most notably Liu Shaoqi and Deng Xiaoping). The internal exile of Deng Xiaoping and numerous other officials, intellectuals, and urban youths evidently led them to reflect more on the fate of their nation and grow more in touch with the lives of ordinary people, especially peasants living in abject poverty. That experience probably gave the reform movement greater momentum.

Yet those two explanations provide only partial and even misleading answers to the question of why China adopted reforms. The Cultural Revolution was, after all, chiefly urban (though I hasten to add that many rural areas, especially suburban counties, were affected), yet the early breakthrough of the reform movement occurred not in urban areas but in rural China, with decollectivization. Chronologically, the Cultural Revolution immediately preceded the launching of reform, but I shall contend that it was not the most important historical event that compelled peasants and local cadres to risk political disapproval and adopt reform. The Great Leap Famine of 1959–61 was.

Similarly, one could overemphasize the role of leaders, which immediately raises the counterfactual question of whether China would have pursued reform without Deng Xiaoping. Moreover, even when good architects are available for transforming a major sociopolitical institution, they are rarely adequate to the task by themselves and still need the cooperation of others. Put another way, if a leader or the leadership was so effective in one thing (such as decollectivization), why was it not equally effective in other areas (such as anticorruption or urban reform)? Apparently something else was involved. That something else was the sociopolitical basis of reform and the forces behind it.[36] Using previously classified Chinese materials, as well as the tools of statistical analysis, I shall argue that the Great Leap Famine changed the outlook of peasants and basic-level cadres and provided the incentives for peasants allied with those cadres to seek institutional change in some areas. This combination of leadership *and* social forces *in the context of the Great Leap Famine* made for a broad movement such as the decollectivization of agriculture. The lack of one or the other would have probably resulted in paralysis and gridlock.

In short, I do not deny that political entrepreneurs and the legacy of the Cultural Revolution contributed to the eventual success of China's reforms. What I contend is that these two theses cannot account for why reform started in rural China or specify the causal mechanisms that led to such an outcome; indeed, one wonders whether the widespread acceptance of these two arguments has in a sense impeded the search for more precise answers. By using multiple case studies and statistical tests, I suggest that the reforms may best be regarded as the outcome of interaction or struggle between state and peasants, mediated by local and regional leaders and fundamentally conditioned by the Great Leap Famine, which delegitimated collective institutions in rural China. In short, the reintroduction of household farming will be interpreted as the outcome of a historically grounded political struggle between the state and the peasant.

Reform, the Rural Economy, and Peasants: Defining the Terms

In the rest of this volume, the singular "reform" is used, arbitrarily, to refer to the adoption of the household responsibility system; the spectrum of measures commonly referred to as reform in the Chinese context will be termed "reforms."

A few comments on the term "peasant" are now in order. Whether in English or in Chinese, the term evokes ambivalence. Chinese politicians, including prominent members of the democracy movement, routinely deploy the phrase "small peasant economy" (*xiaonong jingji*) to refer, with disdain and a sense of helplessness, to the constraints on China's democratic development or other signs of progress by what they consider a backward peasant population.[37] A small minority of the Chinese elite has nevertheless begun to adopt more neutral terms such as "rural resident" (*xiangmin*), heralding a shift in rhetoric and attitude.[38] The national newspaper oriented to rural residents now renders its English masthead *Farmers' Daily* rather than the former *Peasant Daily*.

In English, a peasant is a member of a class of persons "tilling the soil as small landowners or as laborers."[39] In contrast, I follow the established practice in Chinese and Western publications on China and use "peasant" to denote anyone who lives in the Chinese countryside, as demarcated by the household registration system—a system of birth-ascribed stratification with caste-like features.[40] A Chinese peasant so referred to may not work the soil at all. In fact, crop production now accounts for less than half of the gross rural output. As many as 100 million of the rural population work in rural industry, construction, commerce, and other nonfarm occupations.[41] Nevertheless, Chinese publications routinely refer to rural businessmen and industrial entrepreneurs as peasant businessmen and peasant entrepreneurs. Clearly, while the peasants remain, it would be misleading to speak of the peasantry as a coherent group, because of the diversity of the rural population.

Like other members of society, such as cadres and workers, peasants are goal directed, "capable of acquiring well-grounded beliefs about their natural and social environment" and "capable of comparing the costs and benefits of various actions."[42] In other words, Chinese peasants respond to the structure of incentives established through the interaction and struggle between the state and peasants. In the oft-quoted words of Theodore Schultz: "Incentives to guide and reward farmers are a critical component. Once there are investment opportunities and efficient incentives, farmers will turn sand into gold."[43] Generally speaking, peasants pursue their interests not as atomistic individuals but as members of corporate bodies such as households and rural enterprises and, for most of the period covered in this volume, as reluctant members of production teams and brigades. Their economic dependence on these basic-level units "creates solidarity and vested interests in [them], and rivalry with other nearby units," inhibiting horizontal cooperation on irrigation and other tasks.[44]

Because the state is both the dominant political actor and the largest supplier for and purchaser from the agricultural economy, its impact on the lives of peasants cannot be overestimated. A growing body of literature has probed into urban-rural cleavages in developing societies and the reasons for policies that favor urban interests at the expense of rural dwellers.[45] On the one hand, urban dwellers are more educated and are close to each other and to state power centers. They are more easily organized to threaten people in positions of power. On the other, rural dwellers often live in scattered villages and are, comparatively speaking, poorly edu-

cated and hard to organize. Governments routinely use violence to fore-
stall the mobilization of rural populations against government policies
and employ their control of credit, inputs, and markets to manipulate
peasant support. Nevertheless, while peasant revolutions and large-scale
rebellions are relatively rare in the contemporary world, under special circumstances, peasants allied with members of the elite in nondemocratic
polities can still have a major effect on policy.

I am not the first to claim that peasants played a role in China's rural
reforms. Numerous Chinese scholars and commentators have already
done so.[46] Similarly, a number of Western scholars have also pointed to the
role of peasant initiatives in rural reforms, but they fail to systematically
link the Great Leap Famine with the reform initiatives and thus answer
the why part of the question.[47] As I stated, this study will suggest that it
was the complex interactions between state and rural society in the context
of the Great Leap Famine that determined the patterns of reform.

The Analytical Framework:
Cognitive Biases and Institutional Change

There is no need to belabor the importance of studying institutions and
institutional change. Douglass North and many others have already made
the case that studies of institutional change are indispensable to a better
understanding of divergent economic performance in different countries.[48]
Moreover, most institutional arrangements are not purely economic but
have important implications for the scope and substance of individual
freedom and happiness.

In the rest of the introduction, I suggest that the dramatic shifts in China's rural institutions cry out for understanding beyond the rational choice
approach to institutional change, which takes preferences and motivations
as exogenous. Instead, the motivations and preferences for making choices
evolve through time and are forged in historical circumstances. By looking
at institutional change from the perspective of human cognitive biases and
limitations, I suggest that institutional change is not merely incremental
but may also be episodic. The Chinese case provides a powerful example
that may be examined in light of the cognitive approach to institutional
change.

The Conventional Approach to Institutional Change

Institutions embody informal constraints, such as taboos and conventions, and formal rules, such as constitutions and laws, as well as the enforcement characteristics of both. As the rules of the game in a society,
they give structure to human interaction by reducing the uncertainty

faced by human beings. They define and limit the choices of individuals, shaping the performance of societies and economies over time.[49]

It is beyond the scope of this study to attempt a survey of the ever-growing literature on institutions and institutional change.[50] There is little doubt, however, that the economic or rational choice approach to institutional change, with its emphasis on rational individuals pursuing self-interest, has in recent years become conventional. This is partly because economic reforms in socialist and former socialist countries have highlighted the urgent need for new institutions suited to a market economy and partly because more and more economists have recognized the importance of institutions to economic performance and have brought their analytical skills to this subject.

Earlier works by economists, including Theodore Schultz, Vernon Ruttan and Yujiro Hayami, and Douglass North, adopted the efficiency view of institutions. On this view, changes in relative prices and technological opportunities introduce disequilibrium in existing institutional arrangements by creating profitable new opportunities for individuals and groups in society. These individuals and groups, referred to as the institutional entrepreneurs, will seek to bring about institutional changes when the benefits of undertaking such changes exceed the costs, leading to improvements in economic efficiency.[51]

While theoretically elegant, the efficiency view of institutions has in recent years come under critical scrutiny.[52] One leading critic has been Douglass North himself, who now recognizes that the persistence of inefficient institutions calls the efficiency view into question. In a series of recent publications, North has offered a revised framework for analyzing institutional change.[53] In that framework, fundamental changes in relative prices remain "the most important source" of institutional change.[54] But, in contrast to the tenets of neoclassical economics, changes in preferences or tastes also assume importance in institutional change. In North's words, "The motivation of the actors is more complicated (and their preferences less stable) than assumed in received theory. . . . Individuals make choices based on subjectively derived models that diverge among individuals."[55] The abandonment of the efficiency view of institutions leads North to conclude that institutional changes are not only incremental but also path dependent. Moreover, North pays attention to the political framework within which institutions develop. He recognizes that it is the polity that "specifies and enforces the property rights of the economic marketplace," going so far as to mention "the priority of political rules."[56]

Human Cognitive Limitations and Institutional Path Dependence

Throughout his 1990 book, North emphasized that "the single most important point about institutional change, which must be grasped if we are to begin to get a handle on the subject, is that institutional change is overwhelmingly incremental."[57] Moreover, as Stinchcombe and others have long argued, institutions as the embodiment of social technology are also path dependent; once established, they tend to persist over long periods of time.[58]

For North, the incremental and path-dependent nature of institutional change lies in the ideologies or subjective perceptions (mental models, theories) held by institutional entrepreneurs. The processing of incomplete information through imperfect subjective models can result in persistently inefficient paths being taken.[59] As Brian Arthur has argued, "Humans systematically underexplore less-known alternatives, so that learning may sometimes lock in to an inferior choice when payoffs to choices are closely clustered, random, and difficult to discriminate among."[60]

Yet North has been rather vague about the mechanisms leading from people's subjective perceptions to the choice of institutions. His definition of ideology or subjective perceptions suggests that his emphasis is on the substantive content in people's minds rather than the cognitive processes by which humans process information.[61] Indeed, North appears to be frustrated by the intractability of people's perceptions to his analytical framework, commenting that "improved understanding of institutional change requires greater understanding than we now possess of just what makes ideas and ideologies catch hold."[62]

To appreciate the importance of the human cognitive limitations to understanding institutional change, I turn to recent developments in cognitive psychology. For cognitive psychologists, people's behavior is largely determined by the way in which they select, code, store, and retrieve information. In contrast to the rationality assumption stipulated by rational choice, the cognitive information-processing approach recognizes that human information-processing abilities are limited, and that coping with complexity and uncertainty is central to human decision making.[63] Consequently people use various intuitive implements of mental economy to cope with the world.

The intuitive implements comprise "knowledge structures" and "judgmental heuristics."[64] Knowledge structures are made of abstracted knowledge such as beliefs, theories, propositions, and schemas.[65] They provide the individual with a framework for defining and interpreting data or stimuli quickly and, for the most part, accurately. Judgmental heuristics are cognitive strategies employed by people to reduce complex inferential tasks to simple judgmental operations. Two heuristics receiving much attention, especially in the influential work of Kahneman and Tversky, are the representativeness heuristic and the availability heuristic. An individual employs the former to reduce many inferential tasks to what are essentially simple similarity judgments and the latter to make judgments of frequency, probability, and causality.[66] Furthermore, individuals also make sense of data in terms of their salience and vividness.[67]

The adoption of the general strategies of human inference that are drastically summarized above makes for mental efficiency but also entails costs in the form of inferential errors or failures.[68] These inferential shortcomings are summed up by Nisbett and Ross as the underutilization of normatively appropriate strategies and overutilization of more primitive intuitive strategies.[69] One major cognitive tendency that may cause inferential failures is the perseverance of beliefs, which Francis Bacon pithily described in *The New Organon* (1620):

> The human understanding when it has once adopted an opinion . . . draws all things else to support and agree with it. And though there be a greater number and weight of instances to be found on the other side, yet these it either neglects and despises, or else by some distinction sets aside and rejects, in order that by this great and pernicious predetermination the authority of its former conclusions may remain inviolate.[70]

Modern psychological research has uncovered abundant evidence about the persistence of belief. As Anderson and others conclude, "People often cling to their beliefs to a considerably greater extent than is logically or normatively warranted."[71] Regardless of the ideas and ideologies that already exist, the very manner by which humans process information leads them to continue with their existing beliefs and favor the status quo.

Moreover, the bias for what one already possesses goes beyond beliefs and has been found in other settings and given other names in a growing literature on the borderline of economics and psychology. This literature directs its attention at phenomena variously called endowment effect, status quo bias, and loss aversion.[72] It has been found that people tend to adhere to status quo choices more frequently than the rational choice model would predict. Instead of the stable preference order stipulated by the rational choice model, these findings suggest that one's preference order depends on the current reference level, that is, the status quo.

The implications of these psychological phenomena for institutional change become apparent from the definition of institutions as human constructs in which social knowledge and beliefs are embedded.[73] Since our cognitive structures, in which attitudes and supporting beliefs are embedded, are resistant to change and tend to persist, the institutions that embody social knowledge and beliefs will also tend to be resistant to change. As Samuelson and Zeckhauser pointed out, rational models that ignore the status quo tend to predict "greater instability than is observed in the world."[74] In reality, once established, institutions tend to persist and be path dependent because the people who construct the institutions tend to cling to the status quo.

Cognitive Biases and Institutional Change

North denies that institutional change can be truly discontinuous owing to the embeddedness and great tenacity of informal constraints in societies and cultures. For North, discontinuous change in formal rules "has some features in common with discontinuous evolutionary changes," and "its most striking feature is that it is seldom as discontinuous as it appears on the surface."[75]

Yet studies by paleontologists suggest that mass extinctions, the equivalent of discontinuous change, are "more frequent, rapid, devastating in magnitude, and distinctively different in effect than we formerly imagined." They can "derail, undo, and reorient whatever might be accumulating during the 'normal' time between."[76] Hence North's evolutionary analogy is at best inappropriate. Whether North's argument about discontinuous change can be sustained depends on how one defines and measures fundamental institutional change and on empirical investigation. In reality, North's argument against discontinuity appears to be intended for institutional systems or frameworks only. He allows that parts of an institutional system, such as formal rules, may be changed overnight as a consequence of wars, revolutions, conquest, or natural disasters.

Such abrupt institutional changes should not be trivialized but are worthy of explanation. To do so, we need to return to the cognitive basis of institutional change. For, while beliefs tend to persist and people tend to favor the status quo, it is also evident that beliefs do change, leading to institutional shifts. The cognitive limitations exhibited by humans are not so deep-seated that they are impervious to change.

Here again psychologists have produced studies that indicate the conditions under which people's preferences and behavior are likely to be influenced. Generally speaking, vivid evidence has a disproportionate influence on personally relevant and important choices, that is, our beliefs.[77] A piece of information is vivid and likely to attract and hold our attention, excite our imagination, and be remembered when it is (*a*) emotionally interesting, (*b*) concrete and imagery provoking, and (*c*) proximate in a sensory, temporal, or spatial way. And, of course, information that is more likely to be remembered is also more likely to be retrieved and affect people's inferences and behavior.[78] More concretely, a major crisis is very likely to reshape a person's beliefs. It is common sense that Americans who grew up during the Great Depression are more careful in managing their finances than those who grew up in the booming 1950's and 1960's.

While our beliefs and the cognitive process we use to reinforce our beliefs lead to the choice of suboptimal institutions and to institutional path dependence, over time these cognitive limitations and biases would also tend to lead people to misinterpret the world, make faulty decisions, and have consequences that sharply diverge from the preferences of the decision makers, even in the absence of exogenous events such as natural disasters. Such consequences may from time to time reach a crisis and generate pressures for a long-standing belief or decision to be changed.[79] The more extensive and profound the adjustment of belief in a society is, the more likely that the path of institutional change will be interrupted and redirected.

In short, human cognitive limitations account for not only institutional path dependence but also change, since they were imperfect by definition (which is also why I have eschewed the word "learning"). At any time, there may be many ideas floating around in the polity on how to constitute institutions, but only certain ideas are incorporated into real institutions, and these in turn tend to become path dependent.[80] Crisis, by exposing the vulnerability of existing institutions and reshaping actors' motivations and preferences, pushes the actors to choose from among alternative options. As Stinchcombe has long argued, organizations and institutions of a given type tend to be established in spurts and their structures, once established, tend to persist over a long time, till new crises bring about a new spurt of institutional reconfiguration.[81] It appears that the very notion of path dependence calls for the opposite notion of path rupture.

This cognitive feature of institutional change has not been lost on reformers. In order to mobilize opinion and arouse action, they tend to use the rhetoric of crisis and danger and emphasize the risks of inaction.[82] One need only mention such topics as the health care crisis, the budget crisis, and on and on.

The Great Leap Famine, Belief Adjustment, and Institutional Change

Like the Cultural Revolution, the Great Leap Famine was a watershed in the history of modern China. Earlier studies of the Great Leap legacy, such as the perceptive works of Richard Baum and Roderick Mac-Farquhar, emphasized how the Great Leap debacle exacerbated the cleavages within the Chinese leadership, thereby contributing to the outbreak of the Cultural Revolution.[83] Here I consider the causal linkages between the Great Leap Famine and the subsequent decollectivization of rural China, whose scope rivaled the demise of feudalism in Europe but occurred in just a few years' time.

I begin by asking the puzzling question why the Chinese leadership continued to push for more and more collectivization in the 1950's even though it had produced few of the benefits the leadership desired. I suggest the answer lies in the Chinese leadership's continuing belief in the superiority of collectivization.

Because the Great Leap Famine resulted from the people's communes movement during the Great Leap Forward, it is expected that the famine produced significant belief adjustment in the population, thus giving rise to demands for rural institutional change (i.e., decollectivization). We might also expect that the degree of belief adjustment varied in the population according to how close a person was to the famine and, furthermore, that people in those areas more severely affected by the famine would also tend to become more committed to institutional change. These hypotheses, adjusted for a number of other important variables, will be operationalized and tested using data from Chinese provinces.

Research Strategy

My research strategy is to seek to explain variations in the incidence of famine and the adoption of household farming in China's provinces—each of which is as large as a medium-sized nation-state—by combining inductive case studies with quantitative statistical analysis.[84]

The rationale for this combination is simple. Social science theorizing must focus on the construction and reconstruction of the causal mechanism—the process by which one variable influences another.[85] The significance of the search for mechanisms has been discussed by Jon Elster:

> The distinctive feature of a mechanism is not that it can be universally applied to predict and control social events, but that it embodies a causal chain that is sufficiently general and precise to enable us to locate it in widely different settings. It is less than a theory, but a great deal more than a description, since it can serve as a model for understanding other cases not yet encountered.[86]

Yet, while single case studies frequently get mired in mind-boggling detail and ad-hoc explanations, correlations do not indicate causality and cannot substitute for the causal story. Moreover, cross-national comparisons frequently raise eyebrows about whether the units or countries, such as India and Singapore, are legitimately comparable.[87] It is hoped that the combinations of qualitative and quantitative research methods will allow me to stand on surer ground in offering causal explanations of historical events and processes through a rigorous examination of differences in variables among the Chinese provinces. Not only are the Chinese provinces far more homogenous and comparable units than nation-states, but the collectivization-decollectivization process in China occurred under virtually "laboratory" conditions, in that throughout this period China was largely closed off to the rest of the world and interaction between the Chinese provinces was minimal. The use of quantitative data for practically all Chinese provincial units also allows me to avoid the problem of selection bias that often afflicts case studies of a single province.[88]

Causal explanations do not have to lose touch with historical detail by offering lawlike and overextended generalizations.[89] A number of recent studies have effectively demonstrated such a possibility by dealing with topics ranging from comparative responses to economic crises in advanced industrial countries (Peter Gourevitch), revolution and rebellion in the early modern world (Jack Goldstone), to the origins of democracy and autocracy in early modern Europe (Brian Downing). It is my belief that history and social science can be complementary. As Nobel Laureate

Robert Solow put it, what we ought to look for are "models contingent on society's circumstances—on the historical context, you might say—and not a single monolithic model for all seasons."[90] By paying attention to antecedent and circumstantial historical conditions faced by the players (peasants, local cadres, and central leaders), as well as their contextually based choices, I hope to be able to account for the particular sequence of events that led from social revolution to the Great Leap Famine and then to the rise of reform in China.

Apart from the concluding chapter, which revisits the main findings of this study, the rest of this volume will proceed diachronically. Chapter 1, intended for readers who do not have a specialized knowledge of contemporary China, gives an overview of the events leading to the Great Leap Forward and introduces data on the differential effect of the Great Leap Famine on China's provinces. Chapter 2 tackles the thorny question of what caused the Great Leap Famine. The first half of this chapter offers a historical account of the events leading to the Lushan conference of 1959 and suggests that the worst of the Great Leap Famine could probably have been avoided but for the confrontation between Mao and Defense Minister Peng Dehuai. In the second half, a systematic effort is made to understand how certain structural forces within the Chinese political system accounted for the differential effect of the famine among the provinces and what the causal mechanisms leading to the famine were.

The next four chapters examine the legacy of the Great Leap Famine for rural policy and institutional change through the post-Mao reforms. Chapter 3 draws on hitherto-classified Chinese documents and details the divergence between official policies and peasant behavior in the aftermath of the Great Leap Famine. Put simply, in reaction to the famine, about 30 percent of rural China's basic units adopted household-based farming without central approval. It took the central government nearly two years and a major political movement (the socialist education campaign) to clamp down on household-based farming. In contrast to conventional argument, however, this chapter again pays attention to contingency and suggests that Mao was extremely close to formally adopting household contracting in agriculture in July 1962 and only decided against it at the last minute.

In spite of the suppression of household farming in the early 1960's, the political legacy of the Great Leap Famine lived on. In Chapter 4, in contrast to the conventional emphasis on the deleterious effect of agrarian radicalism, I suggest that the famine accounts for a number of important rural policies during the Cultural Revolution. In other words, an understanding of rural policy must be made with reference to both the legacy of the famine and the impact of agrarian radicalism.

Chapters 5 and 6 seek to establish the causal linkages between the famine and the rise of rural reform, as signified by the introduction of the household responsibility system in the late 1970's and early 1980's. Chapter 5 begins with a discussion of the leadership cleavages that provided the window of opportunity for local initiatives. It then offers a quantitative assessment of the structural incentives for rural reform. It is found that two variables—the severity of the Great Leap Famine and the physical distance from Beijing (which is really a proxy for party control)—account for nearly half the variations in the provincial propensity for reform. Chapter 6 then turns to a detailed discussion of the political struggles over the adoption of the household responsibility system in the late 1970's and early 1980's. It argues that the rise of rural reform in post-Mao China may best be viewed as the result of an interaction between state and peasant that was mediated by local and regional leaders and fundamentally conditioned by the incentive structures shaped by the famine and the opening up of political space.

I devote Chapters 7 and 8 to a thematic overview of the evolution of state-rural society relations under the reforms. Together, these two chapters underscore the need to go beyond a simple dichotomy between state and society and again point to the haphazard nature of various central policies under the reforms. Yet rural China is not simply an object to be shaped by outside forces. For the Chinese leadership, rural China presents both formidable challenges and exceptional opportunities.

The concluding chapter takes another look at the momentous consequences of the Great Leap Famine. It points again to the political nature of institutional change and how that change has been better elucidated by cognitive psychology. A brief comparison with the Great Irish Famine highlights the path dependency of historical transformation in China. I conclude the chapter with a few reflections on Chinese development over the latter half of the twentieth century.

● ● ● PART I ● ● ●

Context

$$\cdots\bullet\ 1\ \bullet\cdots$$

The Path to Disaster

People do not make choices in a vacuum. To understand why China abandoned collective agriculture and went back to household farming, I shall begin with an overview of how it got into collective agriculture and eventually people's communes in the first place.[1] My emphasis here will be on the relationship between collectivization and agricultural performance.[2] When efforts to build agricultural cooperatives brought no appreciable increase in agricultural production, the Chinese leadership, led by Mao Zedong, decided to launch the people's communes movement during the Great Leap Forward. Instead of utopia, the Great Leap precipitated the worst famine in human history and thus provided the underlying impetus for agricultural decollectivization.

From Land Reform to Collectivization

The Chinese Communist Party (CCP) came to power in 1949 with the express goal of "transforming a backward agrarian nation into a civilized and progressive industrial nation" and building socialism in China.[3] To achieve this goal, the CCP, during the 1949–57 period, adopted the Stalinist development model, which emphasized investment in industries, especially heavy industry. The rural sector would provide the savings for industrial investment and raw materials for light industry.[4]

Yet such savings were at best meager in China. Whereas per-capita grain output in the Soviet Union was 480 kilograms in 1928, the figure for China was a mere 220 kilograms in 1952 and 256 kilograms in 1957 (the last year of China's First Five-Year Plan), below "self-sufficiency."[5] It became necessary for China "to mount a development program for agriculture, even as concurrent steps were being taken to enforce collection."[6]

Because of its commitment to industry and the limited resources it commanded, the Chinese leadership invested only minimally in agriculture while paying lip service to its importance. Indeed, the patterns of central budgetary allocations since the CCP came to power indicate that the Chinese leadership increased agricultural investment as a proportion of the central budget only when necessary and when other low-cost measures were exhausted.[7] During the First Five-Year Plan (1953–57), even though the rural sector produced more than half of the income and employed more than 80 percent of the labor force, it received less than 8 percent of the total state investment, in contrast to more than 52 percent for industry.[8] Rural development had to rely on institutional transformation. In the words of Li Fuchun, vice-premier and chairman of the powerful State Planning Commission:

Socialist industrialization demands that the scattered and backward mode of production in agriculture be changed to a collective and advanced mode of production, that more grain and industrial crops be produced on the basis of collectivization and mechanization. . . . If they are to shake off poverty and suffering once and for all, the broad masses of peasants must give up the way of small-scale production which they followed for so long in the past, and take to the new way of collectivized and mechanized socialist agriculture.[9]

The process of rural transformation began with land reform—the confiscation and redistribution of landlord-held land and other property (farm implements, draught animals, grain, and houses).[10] Through land reform, the CCP destroyed the old elite, economically, politically, and oftentimes physically, and also built up its credibility and support in the rest of rural society—support that the CCP could now tap with its network of local political activists. By the fall of 1952, land reform, mostly conducted during the agricultural slack seasons, had been completed in areas occupied by over 90 percent of the rural population. About 43 percent of China's cultivated land was redistributed to about 60 percent of the poorer peasants. While peasants were encouraged to form mutual aid teams, which pooled labor, they retained ownership of land and other productive assets.

Yet private farming was not to be, despite the population's longing for normalcy and the desire of rural cadres to return to individual farming.[11] Instead, in tandem with the socialist transformation of industry and commerce (including the imposition of unified procurement and sale of grain), rural China was led, in overlapping phases, onto the path of collectiviza-

TABLE 1

Number of Rural Institutions in China, 1950–59

(year-end figures, in thousands)

Year	Mutual aid groups		APCs		Advanced APCs		People's communes	
1950	2,724	(4.2)	18[a]	(10.4)	1[a]	(32)	—	
1951	4,675	(5.0)	129[a]	(12.3)	1[a]	(30)	—	
1952	8,026	(5.7)	4	(15.7)	10[a]	(184)	—	
1953	7,450	(6.1)	15	(18.1)	15[a]	(137)	—	
1954	9,931	(6.9)	114	(20.0)	0.2	(59)	—	
1955	7,147	(8.5)	633	(26.7)	0.5	(76)	—	
1956	85	(12.3)	216	(48.2)	540	(199)	—	
1957	—		36	(44.5)	753	(157)	—	
1958	—		—		—		23.63	(5,443)
1959	—		—		—		25.45	(5,008)

SOURCE: *ZGNYNJ 1980*, p. 4.
  NOTE: Figures in parentheses are the average number of households in each organizational unit.
  Dash = not applicable.
  [a]Actual numbers rather than in thousands.

tion. By the end of 1957, over 97 percent of all peasant households had been organized into agricultural producers' cooperatives (APCs), including nearly 93.7 percent in higher-stage APCs, or full collectives, and 3.7 percent in lower-stage APCs.[12] The average higher-stage APC had 157 households, a huge jump from the household-based production that had prevailed at the beginning of the decade (see Table 1). Under both the lower- and higher-stage APCs, productive property and the division of the harvest came under the control of the collective.[13] Unlike in the lower-stage APC, however, the peasant in the much larger higher-stage APC received no dividend from his contribution of productive property; he or she received payment according to labor only.

Collectivization and Agricultural Performance

Marxist-Leninist regimes influenced by Stalinism have usually made rural collectivization a major ideological goal, rationalized by considerations of production efficiency.[14] However, rather than the promised "liberation of productive forces" in China, collectivization campaigns over the 1953–57 period failed to energize agricultural growth.[15]

Table 2 lists China's grain output for 1949–57.[16] The land reform period (1950–52) coincided with spurts of agricultural growth and a significant improvement in the standard of living of the average peasant.[17] Major agricultural indicators such as grain and cotton outputs, the number of draught animals and pigs, had by 1952 reached or exceeded the best levels of the prewar years (the mid-1930's).[18]

TABLE 2
Grain Output, 1949–57

Year	Grain output (10,000 tons)	Percentage change	Per capita (kg)	Per *mu* (kg)
1949	11,318		208.95	
1950	13,213	16.74%	239.38	
1951	14,369	8.75	255.22	
1952	16,392	14.08	285.17	88.14
1953	16,683	1.78	283.74	87.83
1954	16,952	1.61	281.29	87.61
1955	18,394	8.51	299.26	94.44
1956	19,275	4.79	306.79	94.25
1957	19,505	1.19	301.69	97.31

SOURCE: *ZGTJNJ 1983*, pp. 103, 154–55, 158–59.

Growth rates slowed dramatically beginning in 1953, when collectivization began nationwide. Instead of the double-digit growth rates of the 1950–52 period, grain output grew by 3.55 percent per year on average from 1953 to 1957. Owing to rapid population growth, per-capita grain output increased by a mere 1.13 percent annually. I now consider each of the collectivization campaigns of the period.

Winter 1952–53: Small "Rash Advance," Many Ripples

In connection with a rural party rectification that started in fall 1952 and lavish official praise for Soviet collective agriculture in November (the Sino-Soviet Friendship Month), a mutual aid–cooperativization craze spread across the country.[19] Localities vied with each other to hastily organize more mutual aid groups and bigger agricultural producers' cooperatives. Local cadres in many places put much political and economic pressure on peasants to contribute their property—land, farm implements, draught animals, and sometimes even wood reserved for coffins—to the cooperative with meager compensation. By the end of 1952, the number of mutual aid teams more than doubled, to over 8 million, from 1951. The number of lower-level APCs grew from 129 in 1951 to 3,634 in 1952, and there were now ten higher-level APCs compared with just one a year earlier.[20] All these numbers appear to have grown substantially by spring 1953.

The significance of the campaign lies not only in the number of new APCs—indeed, that number was quite small in terms of both China's size and developments in the next few years—but also in the violation of the social pact between state and peasant that existed during land reform. During land reform, the state had mobilized rural support by promising to guarantee private property after land reform (land to the tiller). Peasants were led to believe that, after the redistribution of land and productive property through land reform, it would be business as usual; they would continue with the dream of "building up a family fortune" (*fa jia zhi fu*) in a private small-peasant economy.[21]

That dream was shattered for a relatively small number of peasants in winter 1952–53. For many more, the still-limited cooperativization campaign brought great uncertainty and must have served as a stern warning about private ownership. A report by the Rural Work Department pointed out that "peasants were disturbed." They "feared 'communization,' 'socialization,' and 'showing their wealth.'"[22] In certain areas peasants killed draught and domestic animals and cut down trees in order to avoid their being made collective property. In many places, farm work, as well as sideline businesses, was neglected, because peasants, especially middle ones, had little incentive to work.[23]

These problems came to the attention of the CCP's Rural Work Department (headed by Deng Zihui), formed in February 1953. In early March, leaders of the department reported the problems to the Central Committee, headed by Chairman Mao Zedong. As a result of this meeting, the committee immediately issued a series of directives, including at least one drafted by Mao himself, in an attempt to "check impetuosity and rash advance."[24] The directives called for scaling down the targets of collectivization, emphasized the need for agricultural policy to suit the special characteristics of the peasant economy, and made spring planting the top priority of the moment.[25] In the words of Mao, "Agricultural production is the overriding task in the countryside; to it all other tasks play a supporting role. Any assignment or method of work that hinders the production of the peasants must be avoided." Pointing out that the Chinese agricultural economy remained "basically a scattered small peasant economy," Mao warned that any plan or assignment that disregarded this fundamental reality "is bound to be unworkable and is certain to evoke peasant opposition and alienate our Party from the peasant masses who constitute over 80 percent of our population. This can be very dangerous indeed."[26]

The directives led to a moderation of the pace of collectivization. In some areas, cooperatives were dismantled or scaled down. In North China, 36 percent of the 9,283 APCs were dissolved into mutual aid groups. About one-tenth of the members withdrew from the remaining APCs. Complaints about commandeered property were also dealt with.[27] Nevertheless, 15,053 lower APCs and 15 higher APCs still remained at the end of 1953, compared with 3,634 lower APCs a year earlier.[28]

As the Chinese leadership recognized, the brief collectivization "fever" hurt agricultural growth, especially the summer wheat harvest. In spite of the remedial measures and average weather, grain output grew by less than 2 percent in 1953, owing to a reduction in the summer wheat harvest, a far cry from the double-digit growth rates of the previous three years. Moreover, as the data in Table 2 indicate, that growth was the result *not* of increased productivity but of an expansion of acreage under cultivation. In fact, the output of both grain and cotton per *mu* (land productivity) declined in 1953.

November 1953–January 1955:
Market Restriction and Collectivization

The lull of 1953 did not last long. By fall 1953, the Chinese leadership was facing a grain crisis that was the result of the unsatisfactory summer harvest and rapidly growing urban consumption. Grain prices on local markets shot up while state grain stocks shrank. Attributing the crisis to "the contradiction between socialist elements and capitalist elements,"[29] the leadership, under the stewardship of Vice-Premier Chen Yun, decided to implement a state system for the procurement (through compulsory deliveries at state-set prices) and rationing of grain beginning in November even though they anticipated that the program would undermine production initiatives and probably cause local rebellions.[30]

By equating "spontaneous peasant forces" with "capitalist elements," the leadership underscored the need to speed up socialist collectivization in tandem with the efforts to import Soviet technology and central-planning practices.[31] Collectivization was deemed a crucial measure in increasing agricultural output, and it would facilitate the CCP's control over rural production and thus extraction of resources from rural areas. In talks to leaders of the Rural Work Department in October and November 1953, Mao Zedong pointed out that "it is at once imperative and possible to develop agricultural producers' cooperatives" and urged people to "go for a medium-sized or big cooperative wherever possible." For Mao, "Peasants working on their own cannot raise production to any great extent; therefore we must promote mutual aid and cooperation. If socialism does not occupy the rural positions, capitalism inevitably will." Therefore, Mao argued, "there must be a transition from individual ownership to collective ownership, to socialism."[32]

Regional leaders attending the Third Conference on Rural Mutual Aid and Cooperation fully supported Mao's call and criticized their own "undue caution" in the spring.[33] They returned to the provinces in November 1953 to launch what would later be known as the 1954 cooperative campaign, which lasted till January 1955.[34] Instead of beefing up the development of mutual aid teams, as in winter 1952–53, the new campaign shifted its emphasis to the development of agricultural producers' cooperatives.

By late November 1953, the context for collectivization had changed from the previous winter's, for there was now an intense campaign to procure grain from peasants. The Central China region fielded 3.3 million cadres and activists. Shanxi province alone mobilized 1.3 million people to extract grain, with each person being responsible for two-and-a-half households, on average.[35] In the absence of detailed regulations on procuring grain, it was not unusual for local cadres, in their eagerness to fulfill and over-fulfill goals passed down from above, to resort to "commandism" and illegal methods, including physical torture, to force peasants to surrender their grain at state-determined prices.[36] As a result, in the 1953 grain year (April 1953–March 1954), gross procurement of grain came to 47.46 million tons, 14.2 million tons (or 42 percent) more than in 1952. This represented 28.4 percent of total production, a 40 percent increase over the 1952 ratio. In the 1954 grain year, despite a dismal summer harvest, the percentage further rose to 30.6 percent.[37]

The cooperativization campaign a year earlier and the grain procurement campaign made it clear to peasants that they were not safe from arbitrary expropriations (which effectively devalued their property), even though they legally owned their land and other assets. In the meantime, the state used a host of institutions, including credit cooperatives as well as supply and marketing cooperatives, increasingly to restrict the private economic opportunities of richer peasants and channel economic resources to the cooperative sector.[38] The incentives were beginning to turn against those who remained outside the collectives.

In this context, local cadres and activists were urged to spearhead the collectivization of rural China at the end of 1953. Drawn mostly from the ranks of poor peasants, these activists and cadres were also the main beneficiaries of the transformation they were bringing about, making them a powerful interest group for change.[39] Eager to demonstrate their political zeal, they became preoccupied with the establishment of cooperatives with "high-level forms" and in greater numbers. The result was a collectivization drive that dwarfed what occurred in winter 1952–53 in intensity and damage, as the newly created cooperatives were beset with problems of poor planning and bad leadership. By the end of 1954, there were 993,100 mutual aid teams, 114,165 lower-level APCs, and 201 higher-level APCs; altogether they enrolled 60.3 percent of all rural households (up from 39.5 percent at the end of 1953).[40]

These figures mask the reality of peasant resistance, however. Excessive grain procurement and poor management of the cooperatives led peasants, including youth league members, to complain that they did not have enough to eat and were tired from overwork. Fearing that their property might disappear overnight with little compensation, some peasants rushed to sell or kill their draught and domestic animals and decreased their investment in land.[41] According to Deng Zihui, riots by peasants demanding redress occurred in every Chinese province.[42] An investigating group sent by the CCP Secretariat to Zhejiang province found in spring 1955 that "more than 60 mass [food] riots had occurred in 15 counties (over 1,000 townships) [of the province]. . . . In one township in Kaihu county, more than ten people died of starvation recently and some of the masses had swollen faces from eating tree roots."[43] Peasants commented that "the Communist Party has suddenly turned hostile" (*bian le lian*).[44] As a CCP Central Committee document put it: "The situation in many a locality is serious, as peasants have killed pigs and oxen, are not keen on collecting fertilizers, are not actively preparing for spring ploughing, or have a low morale for production. There were resistance and sabotage by a small number of rich peasants and other bad elements, but, generally speaking, it was in the nature of a warning by peasant masses, especially middle peasants; they are expressing their dissatisfaction with the various Party and government policies in the countryside."[45] In the words of Mao Zedong, "The peasants were disgruntled, and there were a lot of complaints both inside and outside the Party."[46]

In the end, the disruption of collectivization, overzealous procurement, and bad summer weather were enough to make agricultural production in 1954 an almost exact repeat of 1953. Cotton production again declined by more than 9 percent (despite an increase in the relative price of cotton vis-à-vis grain). Grain output grew by 1.6 percent, but this was again due to increased acreage rather than improvement in productivity.

January–October 1955: A Year of Consolidation

The rapid growth in the number of cooperatives and the chaos that surrounded it, including the widespread complaints of hunger, prompted Deng Zihui, director of the Rural Work Department, to initiate a series of measures to bring the rural situation under control with the approval of China's top leaders (Mao Zedong, Liu Shaoqi, and Zhou Enlai).[47] The concerns of the Chinese leadership were clearly reflected in the titles of three directives: "Notice on the Rectification and Consolidation of Agricultural Producers' Cooperatives (January 10, 1955)," "Emergency Directive Regarding the Vigorous Protection of Farm Animals (January 15, 1955)," and "Emergency Directive on Swiftly Making Arrangements for the Purchase and Marketing of Grain to Calm Peasants' Feelings for Production (March 3, 1955)."

The central aim of the directives was to create incentives for peasants to produce. As one directive put it: "Peasants are realistic. If they think increased production will not benefit themselves, they will not be enthusiastic about production. . . . Therefore, all rural work measures must be centered on the development of production, must be beneficial to production and to giving play to peasants' enthusiasm for production."[48]

A two-pronged approach was adopted by the leadership. First, the collectivization drive would pause and consolidate, if necessary by reducing the number of APCs, especially in provinces that had overambitious targets (including Shandong, Henan, Hebei, and Zhejiang).[49] The slogan, summarized by Mao, was "pause, contraction, and development" (*ting, suo, fa*); and the emphasis in the spring of 1955 was clearly on pause and contraction rather than development. Peasants who wanted to withdraw from APCs were permitted to do so. Draught animals brought into APCs were to be fairly priced. By the end of July 1955, some 20,000 APCs had been dismantled (though this was far below the number expected by Liu Shaoqi and Deng Zihui). Some 650,000 APCs survived the consolidation.[50]

Second, a "three-fix policy" was introduced into grain procurement to reassure peasants about the state's claims on them.[51] Under this scheme, quotas for grain procurement and sales for each township were set each year prior to spring ploughing on the basis of projected grain output. These quotas were then allocated to peasant households. The compulsory procurement quotas for 1955 were fixed for three years, thus assuring peasants that if they produced more, they could keep more, in contrast to what had happened in 1953 and 1954. Peasants immediately praised these changes.[52]

The policy adjustments appeared to have the desired effect. Grain output expanded by 8.5 percent in 1955, with grain output per *mu* gaining by just under 10 percent. After a two-year slump, cotton output shot up by 43.5 percent. Even when we take account of the recovery effect after two years of stagnation, 1955 was a significant improvement over 1953–54.

Late 1955–57: The "Socialist High Tide"

The fall crops of 1955 had barely been harvested when another wave of collectivization, now known as the "socialist high tide," was kicked off by Mao in his speech of July 31, 1955.[53] The launching of this "tide" has been interpreted by China scholars as a clear indication of Chairman Mao's "vexing propensity to change his position suddenly."[54] On the basis of a reading of recent Chinese writings on this period, however, it appears that Mao was probably more consistent than has been generally believed. In March 1955, Mao came up with the slogan of "pause, contraction, and development" to guide the party's policy on cooperatives. He apparently intended consolidation and development to go hand in hand. Thus, when in April 1955 Deng Zihui and others were busy dealing with the chaotic situation in Zhejiang province (15,000 APCs were dissolved by July), Mao warned of a singular emphasis on contraction: "Don't repeat the 1953 error of dissolving large numbers of cooperatives or [you will] have to make self-criticism again." For some unknown reason, this "warning" was not relayed to lower levels at the time.[55] Instead, the policy of consolidation remained the official line through July.

Mao continued to push for development.[56] At the end of April, Mao told Li Xiannian, Deng Zihui, and others that the peasants desired "freedom" and that some 30 percent of the cadres reflected the interests of middle peasants and were not in favor of building socialism. He thus indicated the need to combat these interests and to push collectivization forward.[57] On May 17, at a meeting of provincial party secretaries, Mao zeroed in on combatting pessimism. In reiterating the policy of pause, contraction, and development, he emphasized development.[58] While Deng Zihui believed that certain conditions, such as the training of cadres, had to be met before cooperatives could be built, Mao was convinced that peasants desired to follow the socialist road because they did not have much land and were not prosperous. For Mao, it was strategic for the party to exploit the peasant enthusiasm for change and speed up the socialist transformation of agriculture.[59]

Yet, when the Second Session of the First National People's Congress (NPC), held July 5–30, convened to ratify the First Five-Year Plan, it was the conservative vision of the Rural Work Development that was officially ratified. The plan stipulated that about one-third of the peasant households would join lower-level APCs by 1957.[60]

Mao probably felt that his message had fallen on deaf ears, but he had prepared well for the occasion. First, in addition to sending his guards to find out the situation in their hometowns, he had just made an investigative trip in June and was confident of his own understanding of the nature, interests, and sentiments of China's peasants. Second, after he returned from his trip, Mao read through the document files of the Rural Work Department and came to the conclusion that Deng Zihui's thinking was leaning to the Right (i.e., too conservative).[61] Thus, on July 31, 1955, the day after the NPC session adjourned, Mao addressed a conference of provincial party secretaries to lobby for his own position.[62] Mao criticized the Rural Work Department, headed by Deng, for having carried out "a wrong policy," especially in regard to cooperativization work in Zhejiang, and, instead, offered his own more upbeat assessment. According to Mao, "The majority of the peasants are enthusiastic about taking the socialist road," and "the high tide of the social transformation of cooperativization in the countryside is already evident in some areas and will soon engulf the whole country." Arguing that the leadership had lagged behind the mass movement, Mao called on members of the audience to "throw in our lot with the members and cadres of the cooperatives and the cadres of the county, districts, and townships and not thwart their enthusiasm."

Mao continued to pursue his own agenda following the July meeting. In October 1955, at the Sixth Plenum (Enlarged) of the Seventh CCP Central Committee, he argued that the policy of contraction "reflected the demands of the bourgeois class and the spontaneous capitalist forces in the countryside." In his concluding speech to the plenum, he linked the debate on rural cooperativization to class struggle and stated that the debate concerned "whether the Party's general line was completely correct."[63] Again

Mao prevailed, and the plenum approved "The Resolution on Agricultural Cooperativization," which endorsed Mao's assessment and concluded that Deng Zihui had committed the error of "right opportunism."[64]

Mao's speeches clearly signaled to provincial and local leaders that he preferred advance to consolidation in agricultural collectivization and that this was to be a political litmus test. Given Mao's preeminent position in the tightly knit and hierarchic Chinese polity, provincial leaders quickly jumped on Mao's bandwagon in order to become members of the winning coalition.[65] In August 1955, they revised the targets for collectivization significantly upward.[66] In January 1956, a twelve-year program for agriculture was adopted by the Politburo, chaired by Mao; the targets of the program for the 1960's were so ambitious that they would remain unfulfilled until the 1980's.

In a fundamental sense, Mao correctly gauged the wish of local cadres and poor peasants for further transformation. For cadres of cooperatives, transition from the lower-level cooperative to the high-level cooperative would simplify their managerial tasks; they would no longer have to calculate both dividends from property contribution and work points for labor and would concentrate on labor distribution alone. For peasants, as mentioned above, a series of policies adopted had made entrance to a cooperative virtually the only option.[67] The government's pledge that 90 percent of collectivized peasants would increase their incomes every year was also an enticement.[68] Peasants wanted to join collectives *not* because they were convinced of the inherent superiority of collective production, but because the potential alternatives, such as individual farming, were being closed to them.

Indeed, the high tide of collectivization exceeded even Mao's most optimistic expectations, as well as the various provincial forecasts.[69] By the end of October, the number of APCs had reached 1.28 million, nearly doubling the end-of-June figure of 650,000. By the end of 1955, 63.3 percent of rural households had enrolled in 1.9 million APCs (the October resolution had called for 70 percent of the households to join by spring 1957).[70] The rapid growth of the movement made Mao rewrite the preface for a book to be titled "How to Build APCs" and compelled him to change its title to *Socialist Upsurge in China's Countryside*. The "upsurge" continued into 1956. By the end of 1956, 96.3 percent of all rural households had joined APCs, with 87.8 percent in higher-level APCs; many of the peasants jumped into higher-level APCs without going through lower-level APCs or even mutual aid teams.[71] (In Mao's report of July 31, 1955, the target date for the completion of socialist transformation of agriculture was 1960 or later.)

As in previous cooperativization campaigns, the upsurge of 1956 unleashed a host of administrative excesses but failed to bring about large increases in agricultural growth. While grain output grew a respectable

4.8 percent in 1956 (partly because statistical collections were strengthened under collectivization), it expanded by a mere 1.2 percent in 1957 (see Table 2).[72] Cotton output did somewhat better; it declined by 4.8 percent in 1956 but recovered the following year. The number of draught animals (*yichu*) declined by 3.56 million head between 1954 and 1957 and dropped further during the Great Leap Forward.[73]

Even more disappointing to peasants was the decline in their incomes despite official promises to the contrary.[74] An analysis by the Rural Work Department estimated that between 10 and 20 percent of APC members saw their incomes decline. Most of these were formerly well-to-do peasants, handicraftsmen, and commercial peddlers. Some areas fared especially badly. In Guangxi, natural disasters, combined with mismanagement on the part of regional leaders, produced a major famine in 1956.[75] In Anhui, the mortality rate jumped from 11.80 per thousand in 1955 to 14.25 per thousand in 1956.[76]

The excesses of the 1956 upsurge prompted peasants to demand redress. By fall 1956, official estimates were that some 20 percent of all members sought to withdraw from cooperatives, especially in Guangdong, Henan, Jiangsu, Anhui, Zhejiang, Jiangxi, Beijing, Shandong, Shaanxi, Hebei, and Liaoning.[77] The number of peasants making appeals to higher authorities for help (*shangfang*) also increased significantly by spring 1957. Meanwhile, peasants tried to withhold agricultural products from state procurement so that they could get a better price in rural markets. In a significant number of localities across the country, the practice of contracting out labor tasks or agricultural output to households began, occasioning a public discussion on the importance of using household contracting to resolve contradictions in cooperatives.[78] Interestingly, according to the Chinese sociologist Lu Xueyi, the practice was first adopted by more developed areas, such as Jiangjin in Sichuan and Wenzhou in Zhejiang, in response to management problems that had accompanied the establishment of agricultural cooperatives.[79] To anticipate my argument, household contracting was widely adopted by 1962 in response to the Great Leap Famine and replaced collective agricultural production by the 1980's.

To counter the pressures from below, the leadership launched, in connection with the antirightist campaign, a rural socialist education movement in the fall of 1957. This movement clamped down especially hard on the well-to-do peasants who wanted to withdraw from the collectives and put a lid on "deviant" behavior such as household contracting.[80] Meanwhile, the State Council sought to prohibit the sale of major agricultural products such as grain and cotton in rural markets, though with limited success.[81]

In sum, the 1953–57 period saw the socialist transformation of China's countryside. As can be seen from the index of gross agricultural output in Table 3, agricultural growth zigzagged during this period because of the

TABLE 3

Indexes of Gross Output Value of Agriculture and Industry, 1950–57

(by year)

	1950	1951	1952	1953	1954	1955	1956	1957
Agriculture	117.8	109.4	115.2	103.1	103.4	107.6	105.0	103.6
Industry	136.4	138.2	129.9	130.3	116.3	105.6	128.1	111.5

SOURCE: *ZGTJNJ 1983*, p. 18.
NOTE: Based on comparable prices, with the preceding year as the base year.

disruptions caused by collectivization. The highest output growth rate in agriculture was achieved in 1955, when the cooperatives were undergoing consolidation and the "three-fix policy" in grain procurement improved the incentives for peasant agricultural production. Overall, spurts of collectivization (including imposition of the unified purchase and marketing of grain at the end of 1953) appeared to have led to downturns in agricultural growth. Fundamentally, as the economist Nicholas Lardy put it, "The collectivization campaign of 1955–56 did not provide even a partial solution to China's agrarian problems."[82]

The Great Leap Forward and Famine

By 1957, the last year of the Five-Year Plan, agriculture had risen to the top of the agenda in discussions by leaders on formulating a development strategy for the Second Five-Year Plan and after. At the Third Plenum of the Eighth Central Committee (September 20–October 9, 1957), Chen Yun put the problem of agriculture starkly. Population growth and growing urban employment posed "a sharp contradiction" for the supply of grain and cloth. During the First Five-Year Plan the state directed the bulk of the investment to industry and transport, while agricultural development was forced to rely on institutional change, namely, collectivization. Chen warned that "collectivization merely created the conditions for agricultural development but could *not* fundamentally solve the problem." "If [we] do not pay attention to agricultural development during the second five-year plan period (1958–62), but instead wait until the third five-year plan, it will be too late. [We] will be in a tense situation for the next fifteen years."[83]

The Third Plenum marked the beginning of the Great Leap Forward. It reauthorized the ambitious Twelve-Year Program for Agriculture as well as a series of innovative, but cautious, measures, developed under the supervision of Chen Yun, to reform industrial management, commerce, financial management (decentralization), and agricultural production. Yet the vision that emerged after the plenum was not Chen's balanced-growth strategy, but one premised on mass mobilization, rapid expansion, leaping forward, and, before long, utopia.[84] In his closing speech of October 9, Mao acknowledged the need for the simultaneous development of industry and agriculture but reaffirmed the priority of heavy industry. Mao criticized Zhou Enlai and Chen Yun's efforts to oppose rash advance and balance the economy in 1956 and called for giving emphasis to "doing things with greater and faster results."[85] As the days wore on, the attacks would be further escalated, especially during the Second Session of the Eighth CCP Congress in May 1958, when Zhou Enlai, Chen Yun, Bo Yibo, and Li Xiannian made self-criticisms.[86] The entire party, indeed, the whole country, was to unite behind the Great Leap Forward; dissenting voices were not to be heard, especially in the context of the ongoing antirightist campaign, which would claim more than 550,000 victims by 1958.

Symbolic of the Great Leap Forward's launch and of the desire for "doing things with greater and faster results" was Mao's Moscow announcement on November 18, 1957, that China would overtake Britain in the production of steel and other products in fifteen years. Contrary to previous speculation that Mao made the commitment "on his personal initiative,"[87] a highly reliable Chinese volume recently revealed that Mao did so with the prior approval of his colleagues in Beijing.[88] This indicates that the beginning of the Great Leap Forward was more collective "fever" than Chairman Mao's own brainchild. As Deng Xiaoping put it in a talk with certain members of the Central Committee in 1980: "Comrade Mao [Zedong] got carried away when we launched the Great Leap Forward, but didn't the rest of us go along with him? Neither Comrade Liu Shaoqi nor Comrade Zhou Enlai nor I for that matter objected to it, and Comrade Chen Yun didn't say anything either."[89]

As the Great Leap Forward progressed, the timetable for catching up with Great Britain and then the United States was repeatedly shortened. On New Year's Eve, a *People's Daily* editorial reiterated the call to catch up with Great Britain in fifteen years and the United States in twenty to thirty years. By the Second Session of the Eighth CCP Congress in May 1958, the time needed had been reduced to seven and fifteen years, respectively. In June, Mao agreed with Bo Yibo (vice-premier and head of the State Economic Commission) that only two to three years were needed for China to catch up with Great Britain. On September 5, 1958, speaking at the supreme state conference, Mao proposed that China would basically catch up with Great Britain the very next year.[90]

The frequent changes in the timetable were symptomatic of the Great Leap, which, in retrospect, was fantasy incarnate. There were in fact even more exaggerated targets, also frequently revised upward, for steel, grain, cotton, and other products.[91] Any semblance of serious planning was abandoned. The virtual shutdown of the state statistical system at the time would in any case have ensured chaos.

It required herculean efforts to meet even remotely the announced targets. Thus it is not surprising that the state budget went into the red on a vast scale during the Great Leap (Table 4). Investment in both agriculture and heavy industry increased in absolute terms. In proportional terms, however, most of the increased investment went into heavy industry; in 1958, it accounted for 56 percent of the state capital investment, up from about 38 percent in 1956. Even while China sought to distance itself from the Soviet style of development, the Chinese investment pattern during the leap showed a preference for heavy industry that would make diehard Soviet planners blush (Table 5).

If printing money were not enough, the CCP, through its corps of cadres and activists, mobilized labor using "human wave" tactics to undertake water conservation and to build and operate backyard iron and steel furnaces, leading one Western commentator to refer to the Great Leap For-

TABLE 4

Deficit Financing During the Great Leap Forward

(*in billions of yuan*)

Year	Gross revenue	Gross expenditure	Balance	
			Amount	As percentage of gross revenue
1957	31.02	30.42	+0.60	1.93%
1958	38.76	40.94	−2.18	−5.62
1959	48.71	55.29	−6.58	−13.51
1960	57.23	65.41	−8.18	−14.29
1961	35.61	36.70	−1.09	−3.06
1962	31.36	30.53	+0.83	2.65

SOURCE: *ZGTJNJ 1983*, p. 445.

TABLE 5

Sectoral Investment in China Before and During the Great Leap Forward

Year	Amount of investment (billion yuan)			Share of total investment[a] (%)		
	Agriculture	Light industry	Heavy industry	Agriculture	Light industry	Heavy industry
1956	1.19	0.94	5.88	7.7%	6.1%	37.8%
1957	1.19	1.10	6.14	8.3	7.7	42.8
1958	2.63	2.18	15.12	9.8	8.1	56.2
1959	3.29	2.31	18.58	9.4	6.6	53.1
1960	4.52	2.09	20.87	11.6	5.4	53.7
1961	1.70	0.77	6.91	13.3	6.1	54.2
1962	1.44	0.32	3.69	20.2	4.4	51.8
1963	2.26	0.36	4.56	23.0	3.7	46.4

SOURCE: State Statistical Bureau, *Zhongguo guding zichan touzi tongji ziliao 1950–1985* (China Fixed Asset Investment Statistics, 1950–1987), p. 97.

[a]Besides agriculture and light and heavy industries, total investment also includes items such as construction (not shown here); hence the percentages here add up to less than 100 percent.

ward as "the policy of permanent mobilization of the Chinese masses."[92] The mobilization was backed up by coercion. Anyone who voiced doubts about the projected goals was immediately suspect and subjected to intense political pressures. In Henan's Xiping county, more than 10,000 people were persecuted in connection with the county's totally unrealistic wheat output figures. Of these, 7,000 could not stand the abuse and ran away, while over 300 people were persecuted to death.[93] Similar, if milder, pressures were felt throughout the country.

In the winter of 1957–58 more than 100 million peasants were mobilized to build large-scale water conservation projects. The scale of the projects prompted Mao to suggest in March 1958 that smaller APCs be combined into bigger ones—the better to deal with such projects—to build local factories, and to anticipate the scale economies of mechanized agriculture to be introduced in the future. The Central Committee duly approved the proposal, and a document was issued in early April. Numerous big collectives soon appeared in various guises. Praised in the media, those big collectives were emulated by other localities. When Mao endorsed the name "people's commune" in early August, it was taken up immediately and the number of people's communes snowballed. In Henan, the transition to people's communes was "completed" by the end of August. Its 38,473 APCs (each with about 260 households) were converted into 1,378 giant people's communes, each with over 7,200 households.[94]

Other provinces quickly followed suit, especially after an enlarged Politburo meeting held in Beidaihe, a seaside resort, in August 1958 called for the establishment of communes amid an intense confrontation between the mainland and Taiwan.[95] By the end of October, even the slowest of the provinces, Yunnan, had made the transition. By November 1, some 26,500 people's communes, accounting for 99.1 percent of all rural households, had been "built" throughout the country, each averaging 4,756 households.[96] The entire rural labor force was mobilized to work with great intensity in the fields and other collective work.[97] In the words of one contemporary Western observer: "There were communal messhalls, communal kitchens, communal labor, communal indoctrination and hortatory meetings—in fact a form of communal living totally different in its incidence from the family and village way of life."[98]

Such "super speed" was evident in other spheres as well: 21.9 million state workers—twice the size of the industrial labor force in 1957—were recruited to support the expansion of industry and construction in 1958.[99] Of the 21.9 million, about 10 million came from the rural labor force. In addition, an unknown, but perhaps far greater, number of peasants were mobilized to build local industries.[100] The siphoning off of labor led to neglect of agricultural work, sometimes leaving harvested grain to rot in the field.

In the meantime, wild claims about grain output were made by local

fire winds

leaders.[101] Provincial party committees put tremendous pressure on directors of provincial statistical bureaus to report higher numbers to the center.[102] The sum of these numbers, even if only 70 percent true, would make China the land of plenty. Thus the *People's Daily* was able to declare joyfully on September 10, 1958: "With the overcoming of the reactionary conservatism and the collapse of the old conventions in agricultural techniques, agricultural production takes a Great Leap Forward. The yields increase by 100 percent, by several hundred percent, by 1,000 percent and by several thousand percent."[103]

Instead of checking the accuracy of the various wild claims, the Chinese leadership were the first to concoct the make-believe world of abundance. While Deng Zihui lost influence over policy matters, the front man for guiding the Great Leap was Tan Zhenlin, who became a Politburo member in May 1958. When wild claims began to surface, Tan disregarded critics and believed that these claims reflected the morale of the masses. For Tan, "Morale should be boosted, not dampened." While initially still cautious, soon Tan began to urge the removal of rightist conservatives—those who doubted the leap's achievements—and to advance exaggerated claims of his own. He thought that a locality had reached communist utopia when the average commune per-capita income reached 100 yuan per year. When Shanghai leader Ke Qingshi suggested that "everyone could eat to his stomach's content" for free in commune mess halls, Tan enthusiastically endorsed Ke and propagated all-you-can-eat practices in meetings around the country.[104]

While rural commune mess halls were encouraged to supply food for free, state grain procurement was sharply increased on the basis of forecast output, since the logical conclusion from the output claims was that China had solved its grain problem.[105] By the spring of 1959, however, many communes, caught between higher procurement and free supply, had exhausted their grain reserves. Production plummeted and famine began to appear, especially in areas that had pursued the Great Leap Forward with great intensity. However utopian the intentions behind the Great Leap might have been, in contrast to Stalin's "war from above," it pushed China into the throes of a great depression and a devastating famine.

Before the Chinese authorities released population data for the Great Leap Forward, Western opinion on the leap's impact was sharply divided, with some asserting no famine, or few deaths despite a famine, and others arguing that a major famine had occurred.[106] The release of official data easily settled this argument.[107] What demographic experts now argue about is the extent of the catastrophe, not whether it occurred. Ansley J. Coale estimated that China saw excess deaths of 16.5 million over 1958–61, in contrast to an estimate of 23 million by John Aird as well as Peng Xizhe, and 29.5 million by Ashton, Hill, Piazza, and Zeitz. Using a simple extrapolation, the Chinese scholar Cong Jin came up with a figure of 40 million (including both excess deaths and reduction in birth).[108] Judith

Banister derived a similar range of figures for excess deaths. Assuming that without the Great Leap the 1957 death rate of 10.8 per 1,000 was maintained in 1958–61, the official data implied 15 million excess deaths; assuming underreporting of deaths in 1957 as well as in all the famine years, her computer reconstruction results in an estimated 30 million excess deaths during 1958–61.[109] And the total demographic impact (in absolute terms) of the Great Leap dwarfed that of the Soviet collectivization of 1929–33 by more than three to one.[110] One scholar suggested that "the 1958–61 famine must rank as the largest in human history."[111]

From Table 6, we can see that the provinces of Anhui, Guizhou, Qing-

TABLE 6

Mortality Rates in China, 1956–62

(per 1,000 population)

	1956	1957	1958	1959	1960	1961	1962	Average 1956–58	High[a]	Difference[b]	Percentage change
China	11.4	10.8	12.0	14.6	25.4	14.2	10.0	11.4	25.4	14.0	122.8%
Tianjin	8.8	9.4	8.7	9.9	10.3	9.9	7.4	9.0	10.3	1.3	14.9
Shanxi	11.6	12.7	11.7	12.8	14.2	12.2	11.3	12.0	14.2	2.2	18.3
Shaanxi	9.9	10.3	11.0	12.7	12.3	8.7	9.4	10.4	12.7	2.3	22.1
Shanghai	6.8	6.0	5.9	6.9	6.8	7.7	7.3	6.2	7.7	1.5	23.5
Inner Mongolia	7.9	10.5	7.9	11.0	9.5	8.8	9.0	8.8	11.0	2.2	25.5
Zhejiang	9.5	9.3	9.2	10.8	11.9	9.8	8.6	9.3	11.9	2.6	27.5
Heilongjiang	10.1	10.5	9.2	12.8	10.5	11.1	8.6	9.9	12.8	2.9	28.9
Ningxia	10.6	11.1	15.0	15.8	13.9	10.7	8.5	12.2	15.8	3.6	29.2
Beijing	7.7	8.2	8.1	9.6	9.2	10.8	8.7	8.0	10.8	2.8	35.0
Xinjiang	13.9	13.9	13.9	18.8			9.7	13.9	18.8	4.9	35.3
Jiangxi	12.5	11.5	11.3	13.0	16.1	11.5	11.0	11.8	16.1	4.3	36.8
Hebei	11.3	11.3	10.3	12.3	15.8	13.6	9.1	11.0	15.8	4.8	44.1
Yunnan	15.2	16.3	21.6	18.0	26.3	11.9	10.9	17.7	26.3	8.6	48.6
Jilin	7.5	9.1	9.1	13.4	10.1	12.1	10.0	8.6	13.4	4.8	56.4
Guangdong	11.2	8.4	9.1	11.7	15.1	10.7	9.3	9.6	15.1	5.5	57.8
Jiangsu	13.0	10.3	9.4	14.6	18.4	13.4	10.4	10.9	18.4	7.5	68.8
Shandong	12.1	12.1	12.8	18.2	23.6	18.5	12.4	12.3	23.6	11.3	91.4
Fujian	8.4	7.9	7.5	7.9	15.3	11.9	8.3	7.9	15.3	7.4	92.9
Hubei	10.9	9.6	9.6	14.5	21.2	9.2	8.8	10.0	21.2	11.2	111.3
Liaoning	6.6	9.4	8.8	11.8	11.5	17.5	8.5	8.3	17.5	9.2	111.7
Guangxi	12.5	12.4	11.7	17.5	29.5	19.5	10.3	12.2	29.5	17.3	141.8
Hunan	11.5	10.4	11.7	13.0	29.4	17.5	10.4	11.2	29.4	18.2	162.5
Gansu	10.8	11.3	21.1	17.4	41.3	11.5	8.2	14.4	41.3	26.9	186.8
Henan	14.0	11.8	12.7	14.1	39.6	10.2	8.0	12.8	39.6	26.8	208.6
Sichuan	10.4	12.1	25.2	47.0	54.0	29.4	14.6	15.9	54.0	38.1	239.6
Qinghai	9.4	10.4	13.0	16.6	40.7	11.7	5.4	10.9	40.7	29.8	272.3
Guizhou	13.0	12.4	15.3	20.3	52.3	23.3	11.6	13.6	52.3	38.7	285.5
Anhui	14.3	9.1	12.4	16.7	68.6	8.1	8.2	11.9	68.6	56.7	474.9

SOURCE: See Appendix.

NOTE: Data for Tibet were not collected for this period. The figures for Xinjiang over 1956–58 are the average for the 1955–58 period.

[a]The highest mortality rate for the 1959–62 period.

[b]The difference between the highest mortality rate and the average for the 1956–58 period.

hai, Sichuan, Henan, Gansu, Hunan, and Guangxi saw their mortality rates increase the most during this period. While urban dwellers as well as soldiers also suffered, mostly from reductions in food rations, the Great Leap Famine was predominantly and emphatically rural.[112] Not surprisingly, as Sen has indicated in other contexts, the grain producers became the famine's main victims.[113] Later in this volume, I will relate the severity of the famine to the propensity for reforms in China's provinces.

The Great Leap Famine and the Social Basis for Change

While China had regularly experienced famine before the CCP came to power,[114] it appears that the average Chinese unmistakably linked the famine of 1958–61 with the Great Leap Forward and its associated policies, including communization.[115]

In urban areas, Lindqvist reported in 1961 that "there is not much left now of the spontaneous enthusiasm witnessed by earlier observers, but there is instead more perception and awareness."[116] In the army, whose recruits come mostly from rural areas, the impact of the famine raised a warning signal for the military leadership. One report indicated that one or more people had died from the famine in about 10 percent of the families of soldiers.[117] Wang Dongxing, head of the elite guard unit 8341, reported at the end of 1960 that, between January and October 1960, of the 193 members of one typical company under his command, 154, or 79.8 percent, received letters from their families "informing them of disaster in their villages, of the death of relatives or relatives suffering from disease, and of difficulties in life." According to Wang, "The ideological conditions in these Army units are still complicated. It will be very dangerous if this trend is not corrected in time but allowed to develop."[118]

If urban residents and army recruits were "disturbed," their rural brethren bore the brunt of the famine and its aftermath. In Anhui's Fengyang county (pop. 481,000 in 1980), some 380,000 people died and 120,000 fled in this period.[119] In the Xiaogang production team of Fengyang's Liyuan commune, which was to lead the retreat from collectivization in the post-Mao period, all but one family was forced to flee the area.[120]

In the struggle for survival, rural public security deteriorated, and, as a secret document issued by the General Political Department of the People's Liberation Army put it, "counterrevolutionary and destructive activities have become rampant," particularly in those areas worst affected by the famine (such as Henan and Shandong).[121] It was not unusual for militia commanders to turn predatory, "seizing grain, beating and cursing the people, raping their women, barring the roads and openly robbing the people."[122]

The desolation, even some eight years after the famine, was described with poignancy by the dissident Wei Jingsheng, who escaped to Anhui in 1968 to avoid arrest during the Cultural Revolution:

One day I went with a relative to visit another village. On the way we passed an uninhabited village. The houses stood open to the sky. Their roofs had rotted and grass had grown within their walls. The disorder of the wild grass within contrasted with the neat rows of the paddy fields outside. I asked my relative why the houses had not been pulled down to make way for rice fields. He replied: "Those houses belong to people. How can they be torn down without their approval?"

"But no one is living here!"

"Of course no one is living here. Most of the villagers died of starvation when the wind of communization blew, except for a few who went off to beg for food and never returned. But people said that surely some would return, so their houses were left standing while their land was given to others to till. Many years have passed and no one has come back. I am afraid that no one ever will."[123]

More fundamentally, one might suggest, the famine produced a sea change in peasant attitudes toward collective institutions. In the words of one confidential CCP inspection report: "For a long time the masses have lost interest in [collective] production. They have lost faith in the future. They say they would rather be dogs somewhere else than people here."[124] Again, in the words of Wei Jingsheng, "Now I often heard peasants talk about [the Great Leap Forward]. The official explanation of the three years of hardship which followed the Great Leap Forward was that they were caused by nature. But the peasants told me that the hardship was the work of men who had pursued disastrous policies."[125] In other words, the lesson was not lost on peasants and local cadres alike that collectivization and then communization had led to a hell, not the heaven promised by China's leaders and trumpeted in writings by China's intellectuals.[126]

Conclusion

In his study of revolutionary messianism in medieval and Reformation Europe, Norman Cohn suggested that both the subterranean fanaticism in medieval society as well as the major fanaticisms in the contemporary world were rooted in what he summed up as "a boundless, millennial promise made with boundless, prophet-like conviction to a number of rootless and desperate men in the midst of a society where traditional norms and relationships were disintegrating."[127]

Though abstracted from a different context, Cohn's statement seems to capture much of what occurred during the Great Leap Forward. Throughout this chapter, I have emphasized how collectivization disrupted agricultural production. Yet top Chinese leaders, especially Mao, appear to have started with a firm belief in the economic virtues of agricultural collectivization. Drawing on the CCP's enormous revolutionary charisma and facilitated by what Avery Goldstein termed a bandwagon polity, Mao and his colleagues were able to tap into the energies of tens of millions of Chinese to launch the millenarian Great Leap Forward.

Mao's agrarian vision reached its zenith in the fervor of the Great Leap, only to be cast into the valleys of deep anguish. However well-intentioned Mao and his colleagues might have been in initiating the Great Leap Forward, they evidently shared the blame for causing the worst famine in world history.[128] The road to hell, as a common saying puts it, is paved with good intentions. The next chapter probes into the causal mechanisms leading to the Great Leap Famine.

··· 2 ···

The Political Economy of
the Great Leap Famine

The Communists are good, but all these people are dead.
—A grandmother's comment
during the Great Leap Famine

The tragic irony of great famines is that countries suffering from them are frequently exporting food at the same time. Evidently these famines are not caused simply by crop failures.[1] One reason for using the term the "Great Leap Famine" throughout this book is to convey and underscore the political nature of the calamity that befell millions of Chinese.

In this chapter, I seek to go beneath the surface and uncover the mechanisms that caused the Great Leap Famine. The first two sections give a historical narrative of the interactions between center and localities and among the elite up to the Lushan conference of 1959 and suggest that, in hindsight, much of the worst of the Great Leap Famine could have been avoided had the adjustment of spring 1959 been continued. Instead, an unexpected confrontation between Mao Zedong and Defense Minister Peng Dehuai during the conference unleashed a dramatic political reversal that severely aggravated the incipient famine. These two sections thus focus on agency and contingency as explanations for the Great Leap Famine.

In the rest of the chapter, the structural causes of the famine are explored. Contrary to recent studies, it is argued here that the famine is better understood as a tragedy of the commons; one crucial institutional link between Great Leap radicalism and starvation was the commune mess hall. In addition, the leadership failed to take timely remedial measures, as evidenced by the fact that China was a net exporter of one million metric tons of grain in 1960, a year in which the Chinese population saw a net loss of ten million people. Through an examination of the patterns of commune mess hall participation and relative famine severity, it is suggested that certain structural features of the Chinese political system accounted for the differential incidence of the Great Leap Famine.

The First Retreat: Before the Lushan Conference

As the high tide of the people's communes movement swept across China from August to October 1958, tensions rose dramatically within the state administrative apparatuses and between cadres and peasants. For the Chinese leadership, the first sign of a major problem was its decreasing ability to supply grain. The government's grain ledger went into the red sharply soon after the launch of the Great Leap Forward. When we compare the four months of July–October 1958 with the same period in 1957, state grain procurement decreased by 4.4 million tons while domestic sales and exports increased by 2.6 million tons. As a result, by the end of October, the amount of state grain reserves had been reduced by some 7 million tons. Provincial authorities tried hard to "import" grain from outside their provinces, even as they proudly forecast record grain harvests.[2] Local procurement was also stepped up. Eventually total grain procurement for the 1958 grain year (April 1958–March 1959) amounted to 58.76 million tons, 22.3 percent more than in 1957.[3]

Meanwhile, problems of implementation and cadre style—officially to be known as the "five winds or five styles" (the "communist wind" [*gongchanfeng*], commandism [*mingling zhuyi*], blind direction of production [*xiazhihui shengchan*], boastfulness [*fukua*], and cadre privilege seeking [*ganbu teshu*])—provoked peasants into individual, but widespread, resistance, especially in light of the intensifying grain procurement drives. Peasants sought to avoid the various communal activities by such actions as cooking at home and taking their children away from poorly run kindergartens. Production brigades and teams hid grain and other resources from the commune level. There were also cases of sabotage. In extreme cases, such as in areas of Shandong, peasants looted grain in order to survive. In Guangdong, where Tao Zhu and Zhao Ziyang were organizing drives to force peasants to surrender concealed grain,[4] residents on the Guangdong-Hunan border stormed into Hunan to seize grain in early 1959.[5] According to Jürgen Domes, who surveyed the Chinese provincial press of November–December 1958, local riots also occurred in Hubei, Hunan, Jiangxi, Gansu, Sichuan and Qinghai.[6] Six of the provinces mentioned here would be counted among the eleven most severely distressed provinces of the Great Leap (see Table 6).[7]

In this context, the leadership, led by Mao Zedong himself, gradually introduced a series of policies to alleviate the various problems and deal with the impending crisis from the end of 1958 to the summer of 1959. In the meantime, peasants and local cadres in many areas confronted the crisis through practices that were not officially sanctioned, leading to the first major adoption of household contracting in agricultural production. These two streams of action are discussed separately below.

Adjustment from Above

Through a variety of publications for internal consumption, including highly restricted bulletins such as *Internal Reference (Neibu cankao)*, *Economic News (Jingji xiaoxi)*, and *Bulletin of Assorted News (Lingxun)*,[8] China's leaders were apparently apprised of the various problems as they unfolded. Mao's speech to the Wuchang conference on November 23, 1958, for example, showed that he knew the incidence of false reports about outputs made by local cadres.[9] It is also known that two days later Mao read a report from Yunnan on the incidence of hunger-related edema in no. 145 of *Trends in Propaganda and Education (Xuanjiao dongtai)*, an internal publication, and wrote a comment titled "A Lesson."[10] Moreover, both during the leap and in the next few years, Mao repeatedly sent his secretaries and bodyguards to undertake local investigations for him.[11]

Partly on the basis of these reports, Mao, during the Zhengzhou (Henan) and Wuchang (Hubei) meetings of November–December 1958, became the first national leader to suggest that extreme haste was probably doing more harm than good, censuring Chen Boda for proposing to abolish commodity exchange (markets).[12] The "Resolution on Several Problems of People's Communes," approved by the Sixth Plenum of the Eighth Central Committee, stipulated that the houses, quilts, furniture, and savings of peasants were private property and should not be confiscated. Commune members might also keep small farm implements and small domestic animals, and even undertake minor sidelines. Within this context, a number of provinces undertook limited adjustment. Guangdong, for example, issued the "Directive on the Rectification and Consolidation of People's Communes" on December 20, 1958.[13]

As of the end of 1958, there was no indication that the leadership thought the problems with the people's communes movement were major ones. Mao's speech of December 9, 1958, to the Sixth Plenum mentioned that only a small minority of the cadres made false reports.[14] Thus the small adjustments were accompanied by renewed calls for yet another Great Leap in 1959. The "Resolution" again endorsed the commune mess halls and the supply system. The target for grain output in 1959 that emerged from these meetings remained the impossible 525 million tons (the 1957 output was 195.05 million tons).

As adjustments (or rectification) in communes were made, more problems were reported. To Mao's credit, by the end of February 1959, he had come to realize that the major problem with the communes was that of egalitarianism (*yiping erdiao*, as the practice would later be known), that is, the equalization of income and distribution within the commune and the transfer of property and labor from production brigades, teams, and households, with little or no compensation. Egalitarian practices undermined peasant initiative and frequently caused peasants to kill their domestic animals rather than surrender them. As Mao put it in a conversation with a number of prefectural secretaries in Henan province: "It is now unreasonable for us to equalize poor and rich brigades, and poor and rich villages. This is plunder, this is robbery."[15] During his visit to Hubei in spring 1959, when some local cadres suggested to him that peasants were hiding their grain from the state, Mao commented: "I would be happy if peasants really have hidden grain. I am afraid they have nothing to hide!"[16]

In a number of talks delivered to the second Zhengzhou conference (February 17–March 5), Mao again admitted that state-peasant relations were quite tense and dealt extensively with the problem of egalitarianism.[17] Mao's solution, accepted by the conference, was to adhere to the principle of "three-level accounting, with the brigade as the basic accounting unit." In other words, while ownership and management powers were vested in the three levels of commune, brigade, and team, the production brigade, which was about the size of the former higher-level APC, became the principal unit of ownership. Income differences would be legitimate both among brigades and among peasant households.[18] In April, an enlarged Politburo conference held in Shanghai further specified that the team become the unit for production contracting and possess certain rights of ownership and management.[19]

Mao not only initiated the adjustment in early 1959 but also supervised its implementation. On March 9, 15, 17, and 29, respectively, he wrote four letters to provincial party first secretaries urging them to carry out the decisions of the Zhengzhou conference.[20] By early April, at the Seventh Plenum of the CCP Central Committee, the Zhengzhou decisions were incorporated into a document entitled "Eighteen Problems Concerning the People's Communes."[21] Furthermore, in contrast to the Zhengzhou conference, it was decided, again upon Mao's initiative, to settle accounts within communes and thus make communes return, or compensate for, property and funds requisitioned from lower-level units. Nevertheless, the high grain-output target remained unchanged, as was the people's commune supply system, which the above-mentioned document insisted "must be continued" because it allegedly "conformed to the demands of most peasants and had their support."[22] By this time, the perplexed Mao realized that he underestimated the complexity of managing the economy when he rushed into economic management in 1957. At the end of June, Mao openly admitted that the main lesson from the Great Leap was the lack of balance and that Chen Yun, the doyen of balanced economic development, was correct in putting people's livelihood ahead of investment.[23] Indeed, Chen, who had been out of the limelight in 1958, was allowed to play a major role in economic policy-making in the spring of 1959.[24]

In mid-April, the Chinese economy clearly showed signs of a major crisis. A spring famine occurred in parts of at least ten provinces, and the state grain reserves (and other products) were further drawn upon to feed a greatly expanded urban population and were in danger of being depleted.[25] Consumer goods were scarce in both urban and rural markets. More fundamentally, peasants lost confidence. As a research group from the Institute of Economics of the Chinese Academy of Sciences discovered during fieldwork in Hebei's Changli county in April (the "Changli Report"), peasants doubted that they would profit from the fruits of their labor at harvesttime in 1959. They believed the bulk of what they produced would be taken away from them anyway, as had happened in 1958. In consequence, they reported to work but put little effort into it.[26] As much as 30 percent of the acreage of the spring crops lacked base fertilizer.[27]

In this context, both Mao Zedong and Chen Yun came up with a policy of limited retrenchment in the next few months. Mao's initiative took the form of a letter (dated April 29) addressed to cadres at all levels, down to the head of a production team. He discussed a variety of agricultural issues and most emphatically urged cadres to report realistic output figures and disregard the exceedingly high targets coming from above. For Mao, the most important criterion at the moment was "the possibility of realization," or actual production.[28] Chen Yun's policy platform, which apparently had Mao's blessing, was expressed in a letter (April 30) addressed to members of the Central Finance and Economy Small Group, the highest formal economic authority in China. Chen Yun believed that China had not solved the grain problem. He called for supplementing the collective economy by allowing peasants to raise pigs and other small animals and giving them private plots for this purpose to increase the supply of nonstaple goods. The more than ten million extra workers recruited for factory work from rural areas in 1958 were to be sent back to reduce urban demand.[29]

Simply put, the measures adopted by the leadership over the next two months or so for dealing with the crisis were for improving peasant incentives for agricultural production while ensuring urban stability. The rural policies were fundamentally those that had been advocated by Deng Zihui in 1956–57. They include the following actions:[30]

May 7: Prompted by the realization that the acreage of summer crops was reduced by more than 110 million *mu*, the Central Committee (CC) issued "Five Emergency Directives Concerning Agriculture." Among its provisions, the document called on party first secretaries at various levels to make agriculture the focus of their work in May and June. Chen Yun's idea on raising pigs was incorporated with the provision that persons raising pigs for the collective should be given fodder and time. This was designed to stop the rapid decline in the number of pigs, the major source of meat for rural as well as urban dwellers. The system of private plots (*ziliudi*, literally land retained for individual cultivation) was to be reinstated. As in the regulations of the higher-level APCs, the size of the private plots was set at 5 percent of the total acreage.

May 25: CC issued directive ordering a temporary suspension of "account-settling" in communes. Called for total concentration on agricultural production.

May 26: CC issued directive on the distribution of the summer harvest in people's communes. Stipulated that 60 percent of the income be distributed to commune members and that 90 percent of the members see their incomes increase.[31] Production units (brigades and teams) should contract for production output, labor, and costs, with rewards and penalties specified. Called for consolidation of commune mess halls.

May 26: CC issued emergency directive on the supply of edible oils. Because of dwindling stocks, CC decided to "stop supplies to *rural* areas in order to guarantee the needs of urban dwellers, export, industry, and service trades" (emphasis added).

June 1: CC issued emergency directive on vigorously curtailing economic demand. Called for reducing by eight to ten million the number of workers in enterprises belonging to the county and above; the target of reduction was the ten million–plus temporary and contract workers recruited from rural areas.

June 11: CC issued directive concerning certain noncollective activities by commune members, including ownership of private animals and private plots, as in directive of May 7. Called on county people's councils to publicize these provisions.

In short, those measures indicate the urgency of the problems as well as the limits of official action and its urban bias. Above all, as the directive of June 11 made clear, the small "private matters" now being permitted officially were within the context of big collectives (*da jiti zhong de xiao siyou*) and could not be equated with the "development of capitalism."[32] They were necessary for the sake of relieving production difficulties. But the Chinese leadership apparently thought that these difficulties were temporary and saw no need to change the basic structure of the commune or question the existence of commune mess halls. For Mao, once the temporary difficulties were relieved, the people's communes movement would regain its momentum.

The messages from the center were transmitted through documents and regional meetings, which were then relayed to lower levels. In May 1959, for example, there was an agricultural conference of nine provincial units. At the conference, Tan Zhenlin, who became a vice-premier in April, criticized the practices of communization, cadre boasting, and the censure and demotion of people expressing caution (*ba baiqi*). He also criticized himself for propagating "eating to one's stomach's content for free" and other radical messages.[33]

Initiatives from Below

Provincial responses to the centrally authorized adjustment in early 1959 varied widely.[34] At one end of the spectrum were Sichuan and Henan, where provincial leaders continued to push for radical agrarian policies precisely because central leaders placed severe limits on the retrenchment. In Sichuan the provincial leadership, led by Li Jingquan, blocked the relay of Mao's April 29 letter to grass-roots levels. These provincial officials feared Mao's letter would undermine their own authority with lower-level cadres and peasants. While Mao called for close planting of crops, they advocated extremely close planting, with no regard to natural conditions, and put great pressure on lower-level cadres to follow *their* orders.[35] Mao had called for giving certain rights to the production team, but Sichuan insisted that the production brigade be the basic accounting unit.[36] This insistence on radical policies appears to have aggravated the famine in Sichuan. In 1959, agriculture-rich Sichuan led the nation by a wide margin with a mortality rate of 47 per 1,000. In Henan, especially Xinyang Prefecture, regional officials influenced by provincial first party secretary Wu Zhipu pressured village cadres to exaggerate production figures and increase procurement. As in Sichuan, the result was calamitous.[37]

At the other end of the policy spectrum, and probably more common, were provinces that undertook initiatives that exceeded the mandate from the center. We may recall that the focus of the centrally led adjustment of spring 1959 was on ownership. Instead of commune ownership, the Chinese leadership decided to adopt a "three-level ownership, with the brigade as the foundation." The production team would also have partial ownership rights and enter into contract relations with the production brigade for labor, output, and costs through a practice known as big contracting (*dabaogan*). A share of the output above the set target would go to the brigade and the rest to the team as "reward." Any costs saved would be the team's.

Rather than sticking to the letter of the official document, many localities went further than the center permitted. Unfortunately, in contrast to two years later, contemporary documents that have become available so far do not allow us to specify the exact scope of such activities in 1959 except to indicate the types of such activities and to elucidate their political dynamics with reference to selected provinces.

On the basis of a reading of contemporary documents, it appears that the most prevalent form of local initiative in the spring and summer of 1959 was to make the production team, rather than the production brigade (as decreed by the center), the de facto accounting unit.[38] Also widespread—and something that went much further than central policy—was the delegation of decisions over agricultural production to households or to work groups within the production team (*shengchan xiaodui*).[39] The practice of household contracting of outputs (*baochan daohu*) had previously surfaced in 1957 in response to management problems from collectivization, but it was soon displaced by the Great Leap Forward.[40] In spring 1959, household contracting reemerged and began to spread in rural China. Peasants reportedly commented that "the people's communes were not as good as the higher-level APCs; the higher-level APCs were not as good as the lower-level APCs."[41] They called for delegating authority over land, draught animals, farm implements, and grain to the household, with household contracting for output.

The record suggests that areas in Henan and Anhui, the two most visible pacesetters during the Great Leap in building communes and irrigation works, respectively, were also the leaders in adopting household contracting in spring 1959. What is especially interesting in Anhui and Henan was the interaction between local leadership and peasants that fueled the turn to household contracting and, in the process, appeared to cause a split in the provincial leadership. Not only did many peasants adopt household contracting on their own, but cadres, including some at the prefectural and even provincial levels, supported and spread the practice, for which they soon paid dearly with their careers.

In Xinxiang prefecture of Henan, first secretary Geng Qichang, an alternate member of the provincial party committee, spearheaded the adoption of household contracting. Geng argued that collectivization had deprived peasants of their freedom and disrupted production. During commune rectification in May 1959, he called for flexibility in mess-hall operations and advocated contracting agricultural work to the household (*baogong daohu*). Each worker would be assigned responsibility for a piece of land with a set output target, and he or she would be rewarded for output above the contracted amount (70–90 percent of the above-quota amount). Moreover, production brigades that were too big (with more than 50 households) were to be broken up. All these measures, Geng emphasized, "were for the long term; they will not change this year, next year, or for several years." Under his leadership, more than 60 percent of the production brigades in Xinxiang adopted household-based production, with some simply dividing up land among the households. Similarly, Wang Huizhi, the second secretary of Luoyang prefecture, also advocated this method of contracting work and production to the household, with reward and penalty based on production, and no change for three years. In Luoyang, over 800 production groups adopted household contracting and more than 100 communal mess halls were dismantled in a very short period of time.[42]

The style of household contracting varied across regions. In Gansu, one production brigade adopted household contracting of output and assigned land and farm animals and implements to households according to labor. Other brigades contracted all or most of the agricultural labor to the household, thus largely obviating the need for communal labor.[43] In Jiangsu, household contracting was centered on either particular crops or agricultural work. In some areas of Jiangsu, all agricultural labor was contracted to the household. In a small number of areas, output for all or some of the crops was contracted to the household.[44] Indeed, local residents sometimes deliberately adopted names that avoided the politically sensitive word "contracting" (*bao*), such as "fixing land to the household, with above-quota output for reward" (*dingtian daohu, chaochan jiangli*). Needless to say, the more complex description was in reality still household contracting.[45]

Finally, commune mess halls were widely dismantled, even though central leaders continued to praise their superiority. As mentioned earlier, a central directive of May 26, 1959, called for consolidating commune mess halls. While the directive stipulated that commune mess halls not be dismantled indiscriminately, it nevertheless stated that participation should be voluntary. Moreover, various forms of commune mess halls should be permitted. For those peasants who did not want to eat in commune mess halls, they were to be allowed to keep their grain rations.[46] Once peasants gained access to their grain rations, they preferred to cook and eat at home; consequently, commune mess halls began to disappear throughout the country. By fall 1959, only a small portion of the original number of commune mess halls remained in Gansu and Xinjiang. In Shanxi, only 20 percent of the rural population still ate in them.[47] Like the adoption of household contracting, the dismantlement of commune mess halls also had the support of local officials. When Zhang Kaifan, an Anhui provincial secretary, visited Wuwei county in early July 1959, he realized that the mess halls should no longer be continued. On July 9, during a visit to Wangfu production brigade of Xinmin commune, he declared in front of cadres and peasants that peasants could now return to their own houses to cook and ordered the county secretary to carry this out that very night. By July 15, 1959, over 6,000 public mess halls had been dismantled in Wuwei.[48]

The Lushan Conference and the Suppression of
Household Contracting

By approximately the middle of June 1959, Mao Zedong most likely thought that the deteriorating situation had been brought under control by the adoption of adjustment measures. In a remark that highlights how Mao—who had grown up in a farming family—had lost touch with reality, he could not understand why the working class did not have meat, chicken, duck, and eggs to eat.[49] In response to Mao's remark, the sycophant Premier Zhou Enlai and his subordinates at the State Council immediately adopted special measures to improve the supply of these products in urban areas. The temporary improvement in urban supply only served to encourage Mao to think that the various problems had been solved. Therefore, an enlarged Politburo conference was scheduled for July at the mountain resort Lushan in Jiangxi province so that China's senior leaders could reassess the situation and draw the appropriate lessons in a relaxed setting.[50]

The Lushan conference began with participants talking about the great achievements as well as problems of the leap. The basic tone of the conference was to reaffirm the leap while conceding that there were problems, especially those of economic imbalance. On agriculture, Mao mentioned in talks that preceded the Politburo meeting that the three-fix policy had to be resurrected owing to the demand of rural residents. Under this policy, each production brigade and production team was to be assigned fixed targets for grain output, procurement, and sales for a period of three years. The production team would become a semi-accounting unit. Rural primary markets were to be revived.[51] While Mao continued to support the communal mess halls, he was evidently ready for relative moderation concerning agriculture.

Instead of thrashing out a policy of moderation, the Lushan conference took a sharp turn to the Left with Defense Minister Peng Dehuai's letter to Mao of July 14. While Peng reiterated that the Great Leap had made undoubted achievements, the purpose of his letter was to call for a more systematic and sober assessment of the leap than had been offered at the conference so far. For Peng, problems with the Great Leap had strained relations between workers and peasants, and between different social strata in both urban and rural areas. The problems were political in nature. He attributed the leftist errors of the leap to "petty-bourgeois fanaticism" (*xiao zichanjieji kuangrexing*) and argued that "putting politics in command cannot substitute for either economic laws or the concrete measures of economic work."[52] As it turned out, these and other comments by Peng touched a raw nerve and provoked Mao into a decisive counterattack.[53] In a dramatic confrontation that fused elements of power, policy, and person-

ality, Mao, with all the major leaders attending the conference on his bandwagon, branded Peng Dehuai and his supporters "right opportunists."[54]
It was alleged that Peng and his supporters belonged to an "anti-party
clique headed by Peng Dehuai."[55] Zhang Kaifan of Anhui was referred to
as a representative of right opportunists in provincial committees. "Their
present guiding principle of anti-socialism is to oppose the Great Leap
Forward, and oppose the people's communes," Mao asserted.[56] Thus Mao
issued his verdict to those cadres who advocated household contracting
or the dismantlement of commune mess halls.

On August 7, the Central Committee issued a directive on combating
rightism,[57] launching another witch hunt that extended from the top
leadership down to the production brigades throughout China, condemn-
ing cadres such as Zhang Kaifan to two decades of political persecution.
Altogether, more than three million people became political targets in
China.[58] In every production brigade, one or more people, usually cadres
or richer peasants, were singled out for criticism as antisocialist. But the
assault was not limited to persons; even the Chinese language had to
adjust. On August 22, 1959, the Jiangsu provincial party committee decreed that the phrase "household contracting" should, as a rule, no longer
be used in order to avoid confusing the masses. Instead, one should say
"fixing tasks" (*ding*) or "production responsibility system" (*shengchan
zerenzhi*).[59]

A media campaign against household contracting and related practices also followed the Lushan conference. Perhaps the severest attack
came toward the end of 1959 when a *People's Daily* special commentary
suggested that household contracting or its variants had already been
adopted in Hebei, Henan, and other provinces. The commentary asserted
that household contracting was extremely retrogressive and reactionary.
Areas that had adopted the practice not only suffered losses in production, but also seriously harmed the economy, politics, and ideology.[60] As a
result, the "poisonous weeds" of household contracts, or going it alone
(*dan'gan*), "must be completely rooted, burned, without leaving a trace of
it!" In contrast, the forces of collective production should be vigorously
strengthened.[61]

Amid the blast against right opportunism, the leap was revived.[62] Mao
averred that people's communes and public mess halls "had deep social
and economic roots" and could not be blown away by a gust of wind. For
him, the Great Leap Forward and the people's communes followed a historical trend.[63] A major document of the CCP Central Committee and the
State Council likewise beamed: "The present situation is excellent and extremely beneficial for vigorously building waterworks; the general line [of
the party] shines ever brighter; and the superiority of the people's communes is displayed ever more prominently."[64]

In fact, Mao and his colleagues could not have been more wrong, and their poor judgment produced terrible consequences. Investment, especially in heavy industry, was again increased. While state employment had been reduced by 5.07 million workers by the end of August 1959, 5.36 million were added between September and year's end, more than offsetting earlier reductions.[65] And, as in the winter of 1957–58, the central authorities called for a step-up in building large-scale waterworks, further exacerbating the rural labor shortage and hurting poorly fed peasants.[66]

Even more disastrous were the policies of grain procurement and institutional transition. Based on impossibly high grain-output forecasts, grain procurement accounted for as much as 39.7 percent of the estimated actual output for the 1959 grain year (April 1959–March 1960) and 35.6 percent for 1960.[67] In early 1960, a nationwide effort to change from brigade-based ownership to commune-based ownership was launched to speed up the transition to communism.[68] Under the pretext of developing community enterprises and other public projects, various levels of government, especially communes, freely requisitioned property (such as land, houses, grain, farm implements) and labor from lower levels in a recrudescence of communization, exaggeration, and commandism.[69] To add insult to injury, while being stripped of what they had, peasants were forced to work harder for less; communes and brigades were urged to retain more of income as savings. Many of the communal mess halls that had closed in spring 1959 were reopened under official pressure, often providing nothing but watery gruel. Poorly fed, peasants were forced to work longer hours in intense work campaigns.[70] These practices deprived peasants of what little they had left and of incentives to produce for the future. Output plummeted.

As rural residents were still reeling from the effects of the 1958 leap, the renewed campaign severely aggravated the already desperate rural situation and unquestionably added to the death toll. The consequence was shocking: China's population suffered a net loss of ten million people in 1960, making it the worst year of the Great Leap Famine.[71]

In conclusion, as can be seen from Table 6, China's mortality rate increased from 12 per 1,000 in 1958 to 14.6 per 1,000 in 1959 (the latter figure obviously reflected the immediate impact of the Lushan confrontation). While this was a significant increase, it was a far cry from the 1960 figure of 25.4 per 1,000. The historical narrative presented above suggests that the worst consequences of the Great Leap Famine, especially the disastrous population loss that occurred in 1960, could have been avoided had the Lushan conference turned out as originally intended by Mao. There should be little doubt that neither Mao nor Peng Dehuai wanted the famine to intensify, but their confrontation led to that, making the Great Leap Famine a result of contingency and all the more senseless and tragic.[72]

That account also highlights the fact that agricultural policies in the aftermath of the Lushan confrontation had again become highly politicized as central leaders joined Mao's bandwagon. As I will discuss in the next section, those politics, combined with various radical measures adopted in communes, proved a recipe for disaster.

Explaining the Great Leap Famine

In spite of the enormity of the Great Leap Famine, no satisfactory explanation for it has been produced that is both theoretically rigorous and empirically sound. In this section, I first discuss Justin Lin's recently advanced explanation of the agricultural crisis of 1959–61 and then offer an alternative explanation focusing on the commune mess hall as a principal institution through which starvation and famine were caused. I also draw on provincial data to explore the patterns of mess-hall participation and suggest that those patterns reflected what will be termed the politics of loyalty compensation in a highly constrained and hierarchic political system characterized by a low degree of functional differentiation.

The Commune Mess Hall and the Tragedy of the Commons

In a seminal article published in 1990, Justin Lin offered a simple, yet systemic, explanation of both the agricultural crisis of 1959–61 and the changes in agricultural productivity in China from the 1950's to the 1980's.[73] According to Lin, conventional explanations, which focused on bad weather, poor policies, and bad management in the collectives and the incentive problems associated with the unwieldly size of the communes, covered only secondary causes of the crisis, because they could not explain the patterns of agricultural productivity changes from the 1950's to the 1980's. Instead, Lin argued that "the collapse in 1959–61 was *mainly* caused by the deprivation of the right to withdraw from a collective in the fall of 1958. This switch in the form of organization, from a game theory point of view, changed the nature of a collective from a repeated game to a one-time game."[74] He claimed his hypothesis was confirmed after producing estimates that showed that productivity during the period of the production team was lower than during both the voluntary cooperative period of the 1950's and the household farm period of the late 1970's and beyond.

The Lin study has given rise to a vigorous debate about the impact of Chinese agricultural organization, on both theoretical and empirical grounds.[75] For my purpose, however, Lin dealt with changes in agricultural productivity but *not* with the causes of the famine. In the rest of this chapter I offer and test an explanation that seeks to specify the mechanisms that caused starvation in the people's communes. It is argued here that the commune mess hall both epitomized the frenzied commune system of the Great Leap and provided a crucial institutional link to the depletion of grain and thus starvation and famine. In other words, the Great Leap Famine was a tragedy of the commons in a world of scarcity.

The tragedy of the commons may be summarized as follows.[76] With a pasture of limited size open to all, each rational herdsman will seek to increase the size of his herd as much as possible. As a result of everyone's seeking to do the same, however, overgrazing occurs and leads to the ruin of the commons.[77] In the real world, constraints such as norms, conventions, and contracts serve to temper individually rational behavior that tends toward suboptimal outcomes.

As has been discussed in Chapter 1, the essence of what actually occurred in the people's communes of the Great Leap Forward was the pooling of the resources of individuals and lower-level cooperatives without adequate compensation, namely, the re-creation of a sort of commons in each commune that severed effort and reward. As Minquan Liu points out, "For a while, around 60–70%, and in some places as high as 80%, of a collective's income was distributed freely or according to needs."[78]

As the embodiment of the commune spirit and life, the mess hall epitomized the commune system of the Great Leap and constituted the crucial link to the tragedy of the commons.[79] Under a millenarian illusion of abundance, regional leaders such as Ke Qingshi and Tan Zhenlin urged in late 1958 that peasants be allowed to eat as much as they liked for free. In other words, instead of prescribing rules and conventions that mitigated the sort of behavior causing the tragedy of the commons, Chinese leaders called for behavior that would hasten the demise of the communes.

As can be expected, where the commune mess hall was established, free supplies led to excessive food consumption. In some communes three months' supply of grain was consumed in a mere two weeks.[80] Given the limited grain supply each commune had, there was soon a grain shortage. Unless the mess hall was closed or significantly and quickly scaled down (if we assume that outside assistance was extremely limited), shortage in turn led to starvation and famine in the commune. Moreover, the diminishing amount of food available further contributed to the collapse of production incentives in commune work. In the words of one production team leader, "However we shout, however hard we knock at the bell, [commune members] will still not appear for work."[81] In consequence, land was neglected and desolation set in.

While in spring 1959 famine had occurred in parts of at least ten provinces, it appeared that the worst of the Great Leap Famine could still have been avoided in mid-1959 owing to the excellent harvest in 1958, which provided some cushion, the adjustment measures adopted in spring 1959, the relatively short time communes had been in existence, and the less-than-universal adoption of commune mess halls (many of which were also scaled down at this time). Unfortunately, the impact of Lushan led to a "second leap" and renewed efforts to set up commune mess halls. Below, I first examine the patterns of mess-hall participation during this second leap and then explore their relationship to famine severity in 1960, the worst year of the Great Leap Famine.

Patterns of Mess-Hall Participation

The Lushan conference of 1959 led to an anti–right opportunist campaign, and as a result agricultural policy became extremely politicized. With the closure of political debate and the numerous signals calling for a continued Great Leap Forward, cadres rushed to jump on the bandwagon to demonstrate their loyalty and activism. As Goldstein suggests: "The reasonable choice, especially for those who had displayed prior doubts regarding the wisdom of the Great Leap or had cooperated with the mild retrenchment of early 1959, was to dispel political suspicions of right opportunism by enthusiastically backing the revival of leaping at its most ambitious."[82] The symbol of leap radicalism was the all-you-can-eat communal mess hall, which local cadres across the country rushed to build or rebuild in their communes. By the end of 1959, nearly 400 million people, or 72.6 percent of the total rural population, were forced to eat in 391,900 commune mess halls, with each mess hall catering to just over 1,000 people.[83]

Although it was in political favor, the mess hall was nevertheless not mandated by the political center as of late 1959. Local leaders could still refrain from establishing mess halls if they were willing to withstand some political pressure. Thus it is useful to examine the regional variations in mess-hall participation rate, that is, the percentage of rural population eating in commune mess halls in each province, for 1959 (year-end figures).[84] As can be seen from Table 7, these varied from over 90 percent for Henan, Hunan, Sichuan, Yunnan, Guizhou, and Anhui to under 50 percent for Inner Mongolia, Liaoning, Heilongjiang, Jilin, Qinghai, Shandong, and Gansu.[85]

What accounted for the regional variation in mess-hall participation rate? To begin with, differences in provincial leadership apparently had some effect on the variations in provincial radicalism. Moreover, the patterns of provincial radicalism were significantly related to variations in levels of economic development and the effect of what I term the politics of loyalty compensation.

Variations in Provincial Leadership. Anyone familiar with the turbulent history of the period would immediately recognize that the seven provinces that had the highest mess-hall participation rates (Shanghai is not in the table) either were under the influence of the four most prominent and zealous leaders of the time or had just gone through a political purge.

Falling into the latter category was Hunan, where former Party Secre-

TABLE 7
Data Used in Analyses of the Patterns of the Great Leap Famine

	Party[a] (%)	Income57[b] (yuan)	Mess hall[c] (%)	Death[d] (%)	Mort60[e] (per 1,000)
Shanxi	2.92%	146	70.6%	18.33%	14.2
Shaanxi	1.15	124	60.8	22.12	12.3
Inner Mongolia	1.78	164	16.7	25.48	9.5
Zhejiang	0.78	136	81.6	27.50	18.8
Heilongjiang	1.38	261	26.5	28.86	10.5
Ningxia		120	52.9	29.16	13.9
Xinjiang	1.27	246	85.1	35.25	18.8
Jiangxi	1.39	136	61.0	36.83	16.1
Hebei	3.14	128	74.4	44.07	15.8
Yunnan	0.98	108	96.5	48.59	26.3
Jilin	1.62	175	29.4	56.42	10.1
Guangdong	0.93	155	77.6	57.84	15.1
Jiangsu	1.37	118	56.0	68.81	18.4
Shandong	2.14	101	35.5	91.35	23.6
Fujian	1.06	143	67.2	92.86	15.3
Hubei	0.77	146	68.2	111.30	21.2
Liaoning	1.75	304	23.0	111.69	11.5
Guangxi	0.85	87	81.0	141.80	29.5
Hunan	0.80	113	97.6	162.50	29.4
Gansu	1.54	122	47.7	186.81	41.3
Henan	1.08	98	97.8	208.57	39.6
Sichuan	0.71	104	96.7	239.62	54.0
Qinghai	1.04	166	29.9	272.26	40.7
Guizhou	0.86	87	92.6	285.50	52.3
Anhui	0.83	119	90.5	474.86	68.6
Mean	1.34	144	64.7	115.14	25.1
Std. Deviation	0.64	54	26.0	111.00	15.8

SOURCE: See Appendix.
[a] Percentage of population who were CCP members as of mid-1956. Ningxia was included in Gansu.
[b] Per-capita national income by province in 1957.
[c] Percentage of population in commune mess halls at the end of 1959.
[d] Percentage increase in mortality rate = (highest mortality rate during 1959–62 − average mortality rate for 1956–58) ÷ average mortality rate for 1956–58.
[e] Mortality rate in 1960.

tary Zhou Xiaozhou was removed from his post for expressing doubts about the Great Leap in sympathy with Peng Dehuai during the Lushan conference. The new provincial leadership under Zhang Pinghua (appointed in September 1959) perhaps felt a greater urge to demonstrate its political enthusiasm. By September 30, 1959, the Hunan Rural Work Department had drawn up a plan for commune rectification, which called for "a mass movement to safeguard the Party's general line, the Great Leap Forward, and the people's commune movement." In early October, the Hunan leadership began the rectification. Hungry peasants labored during daytime and still had to attend meetings on commune rectification in the evenings. The party center in Beijing loved the Hunan plan and urged all provinces to launch similar efforts.[86]

All six other provinces came under the influence of the four recognizably most fanatical regional leaders of the time. Shanghai was in the grips of Ke Qingshi, a leading evil genius of the Great Leap.[87] In Anhui and Henan, the two Great Leap zealots Zeng Xisheng and Wu Zhipu led the clampdown on people such as Zhang Kaifan. Wu Zhipu took revenge on those who assigned individual families full responsibility for providing labor and for production.[88] Lower-level cadres, including Geng Qichang and Wang Huizhi, who had promoted policies that improved peasant incentives for work, were severely attacked as right opportunists and roundly criticized in party rectification meetings held throughout the province.[89]

Sichuan, Guizhou, and Yunnan were in the southwestern region. Li Jingquan, the top leader in the southwest and provincial secretary of Sichuan, had in spring 1959, before the Lushan conference, blocked the center's messages for adjustment. Convinced of his political uprightness, Li now pushed for leap-style policies with even greater enthusiasm.[90] Li also aggressively transferred grain away from Sichuan (2.5 million tons in 1960) to the center.[91] Whereas other provinces were making the production team the basic rural accounting unit, the Sichuan leadership insisted on staying at the production brigade level and also urged localities to prepare for transitions to commune-level accounting. Whereas the center called for returning private plots to peasants, the Sichuan leadership decided that "it is not necessary to reinstate private plots." Moreover, while some other provinces had begun to dismantle commune mess halls, Li Jingquan emphasized that "commune mess halls are the heart of the people's communes" and insisted on retaining them.[92] In this context and under tremendous political pressure, leaders in Yunnan and Guizhou probably felt that they had to keep up with Li Jingquan. In Guizhou, for example, the provincial leadership had been relatively cautious and conservative in adopting radical policies earlier in the Leap.[93] Yet, in the aftermath of the Lushan conference, perhaps to compensate for past caution, the provincial leadership in Guizhou focused on the development of mess halls. A report by the Guizhou provincial party committee of February 24, 1960, launched a drive to make mess halls larger (at least doubling their size) and to abolish private plots and turn them over to the mess halls. The latter measure effectively cut off the private sources of food for peasants and forced them to stay with the mess halls.[94] The central leadership, especially Mao, so loved the Guizhou program for consolidating and further developing public mess halls that they exhorted the entire nation to emulate Guizhou.[95]

The Politics of Loyalty Compensation. The millenarian atmosphere that infused the Great Leap, as well as the nature and administrative implications of the bandwagon polity, leads us to two hypotheses. First, people in less-developed areas were more likely to adopt radical policies such as commune mess halls in order to leapfrog the more developed areas.

Hypothesis 1: The eagerness with which a province adopted commune mess halls during the Great Leap Forward was negatively related to the province's level of economic development.

Second, given the tightly constrained political structure and the administrative consequences of bandwagon politics, as discussed by Avery Goldstein, it is hypothesized that the phenomenon of what I refer to as loyalty compensation will result as subordinates vie to demonstrate their loyalty to the political center by trying to become "more Catholic than the pope." Therefore, among lower-level elites seeking career advancement, those who were close to joining the party would likely be more zealous than those who were party members and already possessed the right political credentials. By extension, it is also expected that those areas with fewer party members (on a per-capita basis) would also be more likely to adopt radical measures than those areas that had more party members; generally, this meant that those areas that were taken over later by the Chinese Communist Party would likely be more radical than the old revolutionary areas with impeccable revolutionary pedigrees.

Hypothesis 2: The degree of agrarian radicalism in a province was negatively related to the density of party members in the province. In other words, the lower the density of party membership in a province, the more likely the province was to engage in radical programs such as building commune mess halls.

The data used to test these two hypotheses are presented in Table 7.[96] Excluding Tibet (for which data were not available) and the three urban centers (Beijing, Shanghai, and Tianjin), I obtain the following regression results, which confirm my hypotheses (Table 8).[97] The adjusted R^2 (0.4109) indicates that the two variables combined explain just over 41 percent of the variations in the mess-hall participation rate.

TABLE 8
Determinants of Mess-Hall Participation Rate

Mess hall participation rate	Coefficient	Standard error	t	$p > |t|$
log(*Density of party membership*)	− 24.42943	10.79219	− 2.264	0.034
log(*Income level*)	− 37.85905	13.73514	− 2.756	0.012
Constant	256.5436	67.13794	3.821	0.001

NOTE: Number of observations = 24
F(2, 21) = 9.02
$p > F = 0.0015$
$R^2 = 0.4622$
Adj. $R^2 = 0.4109$

In Figures 1 and 2, the relationships among the three variables are graphed so that even readers with no statistical training may easily recognize the patterns called for by the hypotheses. From Figure 1, for example, we can see that as the percentage of population who were party members increases, the mess-hall participation rate (i.e., percentage of rural population who ate in commune mess halls) declines steeply. Interestingly, two dots representing Shanxi and Hebei respectively on the upper right-hand corner apparently depart from this general pattern; in

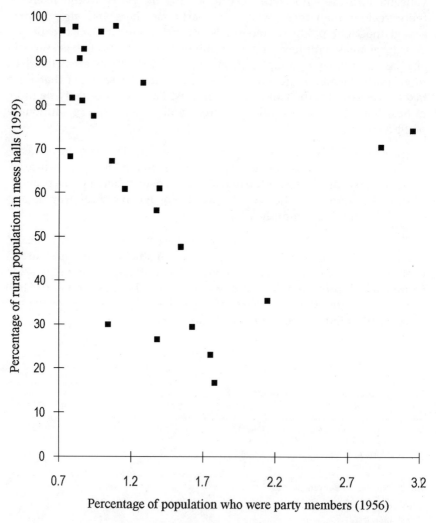

Fig. 1. Density of party membership and commune mess-hall participation rate

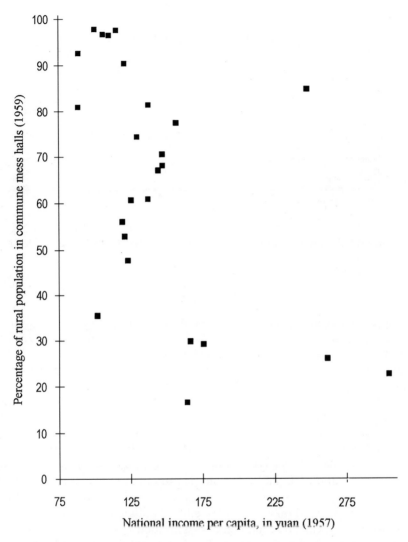

Fig. 2. Level of economic development and commune mess-hall participation rate

statistical terms, these two provinces—which are the two provinces that are closest to Beijing—are the outliers. Removing Hebei and Shanxi from the sample, I reanalyze the relationship between the density of party membership and mess-hall participation rate. From the regression results shown in Table 9, we see that the adjusted R^2 rises to an impressive 0.59, indicating that density of party membership alone explains 59 percent of the variations in the commune mess-hall participation rate. When I add in

Relationship Between Density of Party Membership and Mess-Hall Participation Rate
(*Shanxi and Hebei excluded*)

Mess hall participation rate	Coefficient	Standard error	t	$p>\|t\|$
log(*Density of party membership*)	−54.99549	9.82467	−5.598	0.000
Constant	129.6901	12.24033	10.595	0.000

NOTE: Number of observations = 22
   $F(1, 20) = 31.33$
   $p>F = 0.0000$
   $R^2 = 0.6104$
   Adj. $R^2 = 0.5909$

the data on the level of development, the adjusted R^2 increases further to 0.67 (details not shown here).[98]

Patterns of Famine Severity

On the basis of my earlier discussion of the tragedy of the commons centering on the commune mess halls, it is expected that those provinces that had more people eating in mess halls at the end of 1959 would also suffer more severely in 1960, the worst year of the Great Leap Famine.[99] This pattern can be seen from Figure 3, which shows that the provincial mortality rate for 1960 rises as the commune mess-hall participation rate for the end of 1959 increases. Regression analyses similarly yield a positive relationship between these two variables; with both variables logged, the adjusted R^2 equals 0.2595 ($N = 25$, coefficient = 0.5968, standard error = 0.1946, $p = 0.005$). In the context of the earlier discussions about the role of provincial and regional leaders in the pursuit of radical measures such as commune mess halls and about the administrative consequences of the bandwagon polity, it may be concluded that millions of Chinese peasants paid for the radicalism of their leaders with their lives.

So far in this empirical examination, my emphasis has been on the specific mechanisms causing the Great Leap Famine, focusing on the link between the patterns of commune mess-hall participation at the end of 1959 and the patterns of population mortality in 1960. In other words, the commune mess-hall participation rate has been used as the variable representing the degree of Great Leap radicalism. Likewise, the patterns of mortality for 1960 were used to approximate the degree of famine severity in China's provinces.

As an alternative measure of the above thesis, the relative famine severity for a province may be defined as the percentage of increase in mortality rate between the prefamine years and the highest mortality rate dur-

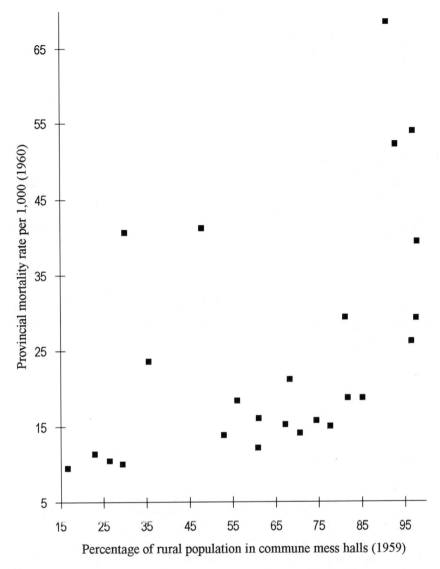

Fig. 3. Mess-hall participation rate and provincial mortality rate

ing the Great Leap Famine.[100] Using the average mortality rate for 1956–58 as the prefamine mortality so as to minimize the effect of year-to-year fluctuations, we have the following formula:

Relative Famine Severity = (highest mortality rate during 1959–61 − average mortality rate for 1956–58) ÷ average mortality rate for 1956–58.

TABLE 10
Determinants of Relative Severity of Famine

Famine severity	Coefficient	Standard error	t	$p > \lvert t \rvert$
log(*Density of party membership*)	−.9036625	.4293553	−2.105	0.048
log(*Income level*)	−.7786404	.5464369	−1.425	0.169
Constant	8.395647	2.671007	3.143	0.005

NOTE: Number of observations = 24
F(2, 21) = 4.53
$p > F$ = 0.0232
R^2 = 0.3012
Adj. R^2 = 0.2347

Given my original hypotheses about the impact of the bandwagon polity and the level of economic development, it is expected that (1) the density of party membership would in general be negatively related to relative famine severity and (2) a province's level of development before the famine would also be negatively related to relative famine severity. In the latter case, a province that had started from a lower economic level would more easily drop below the starvation point. In theory, a poor province could have received assistance from the rest of the country to alleviate its plight. But even when such assistance was available, it was unlikely to be timely enough to alter the hypothesis, because the Great Leap Forward put strong emphasis on self-reliance, because each provincial leadership had boasted that the province could produce much more grain than needed in the first place, and because the Great Leap had caused much disruption to transportation. In reality, with the exception of major urban centers, most provinces were left to cope with the famine on their own, as will be discussed later.

In Table 7, the data on relative famine severity appear in the column labeled "Death."[101] They ranged from a low of 18.33 percent in Shanxi to a whopping 474.86 percent for Anhui. The regression results on the determinants of relative famine severity are presented in Table 10.[102] To my surprise, only the relationship between density of party membership and relative famine severity is confirmed, and no statistically significant relationship between level of development and relative famine severity is found.[103] This finding is important because it highlights the fact that the Great Leap Famine was rooted in politics rather than nature. Given the bad policies initiated by the top leaders, the structure of political incentives accounted for the differential rates of adoption of commune mess halls, which in turn led to differences in famine severity among the provinces.

State Grain Policy and the Great Leap Famine

So far I have focused on the commune mess hall as a major institutional mechanism linking political incentives in the Chinese polity with the exhaustion of local grain supplies and ultimately famine. Yet even when food in a locality was exhausted, one could still follow Sen's argument and ask why that locality did not receive timely and adequate relief and what went awry.[104] This question is particularly appropriate for China, because the imperial dynasties had a tradition of famine relief (albeit not always effective) and because the leadership in Communist China espoused a rhetoric of "serving the people."

To begin with, it is now generally recognized that the campaign atmosphere of the Great Leap, the intense political pressures on and competition among local party officials, and the extensive disruption of the statistical system led to extreme exaggerations in reporting agricultural output. In consequence, the official estimate of the 1958 grain harvest, at 375 million tons, was up more than 92 percent from the actual 1957 output of 195 million tons.[105] This illusion of superabundance had a number of consequences. First, it led planners to shift land from grain to economic crops, such as cotton, sugarcane, and beets, and divert huge numbers of agricultural laborers into industrial sectors, fueling state demand for procured grain from the countryside. Second, it prompted the Chinese leadership, especially Zhou Enlai, to speed up grain exports to secure more foreign currency to repay debts to the Soviet Union and to purchase capital goods needed for industrialization. Finally, the illusion of superabundance made the adoption of the commune mess halls seem rational at the time. All these changes, of course, contributed to the rapid exhaustion of grain supplies.

It should not be difficult to establish that the Chinese leadership, including those in the State Council, were culpably negligent in unleashing and encouraging the Great Leap fervor.[106] It is also clear that events at the Lushan conference of 1959 led to a drastic reversal in the countryside. The Sino-Soviet split in 1960 likewise diverted attention from domestic issues. Nevertheless, I want to suggest here briefly that those who were in charge of grain production and distribution, particularly Zhou Enlai, failed to take timely action even though they had become aware of China's worsening grain situation by 1959.

Over the 1958–61 period, the state consistently allocated more grain for consumption than it received. As a result, balancing the grain ledger became externally difficult. For the first quarter of 1959, the state planned to allocate and transfer about 4.1 million tons of grain but was only able to mobilize 2.1 million tons. The situation only became worse with each passing day. By mid-1960 grain stored in state warehouses along transport trunk lines was near depletion, and major cities such as Beijing, Tianjin, and Shanghai were barely making ends meet.[107] These problems persisted throughout this period, and one wonders why Zhou Enlai, who, as the country's top administrator, oversaw the Ministry of Food and thus had to confront the disastrous impact of the Great Leap head on, was so slow to respond and propose changes in rural policy. The least Zhou could have done was to investigate the rural situation carefully. But he did not appear to pay serious attention to the rural situation until the latter half of 1960.[108]

Instead, under Zhou, China's grain exports (net amount) rose from 1.88 million tons in 1957 to 3.25 million tons in 1958 and 4.74 million tons in 1959. Even in 1960, when the country suffered a net population loss of ten million people, China's net grain export still reached one million metric tons—enough to save the lives of four million people.[109]

Zhou's preoccupation with supplying grain for the urban population and for exports most likely contributed to the excessive procurement which burdened China's peasants. In late 1960, the State Council Finance and Commerce Office concluded that the amount of excessive procurement taken by the state was on the order of ten million tons.[110] Largely as a result of excessive procurement, the amount of grain for each rural resident was reduced from 294.5 kilograms in 1957 to 214.5 kilograms in 1960. Each resident on average consumed less than half a kilogram of grain (about one pound) per day during 1960–61. The number of draft animals was reduced by over 17 percent, from 83.82 million in 1957 to 69.49 million in 1961, and the number of pigs by 50.5 percent.[111]

Conclusion

A causal explanation of the Great Leap Famine must take into consideration agency and structure, as well as contingency. This chapter suggests that, while the adjustments of spring 1959 were limited, the worst of the famine could probably have been avoided had the Chinese leadership persisted with the limited retrenchment. Unfortunately, the Lushan confrontation between Mao and Peng Dehuai—a remarkably fortuitous event—led Mao and those who supported him politically to reaffirm their commitment to the Great Leap in public.[112] Thus Peng's questioning did what Agamemnon had done when he asked whether the Greeks should abandon the siege of Troy. The difference is that Agamemnon intended to persuade the Greeks to stay and fight, while Peng sought to quench, rather than stoke, the fires of the Great Leap. Arrow's explanation of the Greek commitment to the siege of Troy is equally appropriate for understanding the Chinese leadership's commitment to the Great Leap in the aftermath of the Lushan conference:

Some commitments are to purposes which involve much sacrifice and very great depth of involvement. A commitment to a war or a revolution or to religion is typically one that is very hard to reverse, even if conditions have changed from the time when the thing started. Even if experience has shown the unexpectedly undesirable consequences of a commitment, the past may continue to rule the present.

It is this thinking which I think gives rise to the greatest tragedies of history, this sense of commitment to a past purpose which reinforces the original agreement precisely at a time when experience has shown that it must be reversed.[113]

A well-intentioned act by Peng led to an outcome that was completely contrary to original intentions.[114]

The political implications of the Lushan conference help explain the tragedy but do not reveal the mechanisms leading to widespread famine, which must be sought in more proximate causes. My discussion suggests that the Great Leap Famine is better understood as a tragedy of the commons. Unlike the original parable, which would unfold over a relatively long period of time, the commons of the Great Leap—the commune mess hall—was the product of a frenzied political campaign, which in turn led to a famine of unprecedented rapidity and magnitude. That the Chinese government under Premier Zhou Enlai continued to push for grain exports even in 1960 only served to aggravate the famine.

The patterns of mess-hall participation and relative famine severity reveal that the famine reflected not only the role of top leaders but also certain fundamental structural factors in China's political system that resulted from the dramatic Communist takeover. These factors constituted what Goldstein has christened the bandwagon polity. In this polity, subordinates sought to outshine each other, carrying central policies to excess. As a result, the statistical analyses support the counterintuitive hypothesis that those provinces with relatively fewer Communist Party members pushed for more radical measures, such as the commune mess hall, and thus suffered more severely from the famine.

Yet, as this volume seeks to document, the Great Leap Famine also proved a critical juncture for innovation in China's political economy. Some inkling of this dynamic aspect of change could already be seen in spring 1959, when certain localities adopted initiatives that pushed beyond what was permitted by the center. In the next chapter, I shall document how in the immediate aftermath of the Great Leap Famine central-local interactions led to a remarkable liberalization in rural China.

PART II

Catastrophe and Reform

··· 3 ···

The Great Leap Famine and Rural Liberalization

Throughout late 1959 and the spring of 1960, China's leaders pushed for a second Great Leap and appeared oblivious to the deepening crisis they were precipitating in rural areas. The *People's Daily*, for example, began 1960 with a front-page editorial entitled "Looking Forward to the Sixties," which averred that "we are not only full of confidence about the continuing and even better leap forward of 1960, we are also full of confidence about continuing the leap through the 1960s." Later editorials similarly combined exhortation and promise: "We Must Continue to Leap Forward, We Will Continue to Leap Forward" (March 31), "Strive to Implement the National Agricultural Development Outline Two to Three Years Ahead of Schedule" (April 12). Documents issued by the central leadership were equally out of touch with the utter misery then engulfing rural China. Of the cluster of four Central Committee directives on rural affairs issued May 15, only one—on guaranteeing enough manpower for agriculture—may be regarded as addressing an important cause of the famine.[1] The three other directives called for a campaign against corruption, waste, and bureaucratism in rural areas, for combining work with leisure so as to ensure continuation of the Great Leap Forward, and for guaranteeing increased income for 90 percent of commune members.[2]

The renewal of the Great Leap campaign in rural areas centered on upgrading collective organization to production brigade or even commune level accounting and reestablishing commune mess halls. The former was heavily pushed by commune cadres and again led to the widespread req-

TABLE 11

Percentage of Rural Population Eating in
Commune Mess Halls in Eight Provinces

Province	December 1959	February 1960
Henan	97.8%	99.0%
Hebei	74.7	86.1
Shanxi	70.6	81.0
Gansu	47.7	63.3
Shandong	35.5	55.4
Heilongjiang	26.5	40.0
Liaoning	23.0	33.0
Jilin	29.4	29.4
Unweighted average	50.6%	60.9%

SOURCE: *NJZWH*, 2: 292, 297.

uisition of property from peasant households and lower-level rural organizations (especially the production team). Because Peng Dehuai, Zhang
Wentian, and Zhou Xiaozhou had criticized the commune mess hall during the Lushan conference, many local authorities now regarded the commune mess hall as a political litmus test during the anti–right opportunism campaign. As was mentioned in Chapter 2, nearly 400 million people,
or 72.6 percent of the total rural population, ate in commune mess halls at
the end of 1959.[3] On the basis of information from eight provinces, the
mess-hall participation rate increased further over the next few months
(Table 11). A Central Committee document issued in March 1960 called on
the country to make 80 percent of the rural population eat in commune
mess halls.[4]

While central leaders promoted another Great Leap, provincial reports
to the center during early 1960 pointed to the recurrence of problems such
as the "communization wind" that had led to similar difficulties in 1958,
as well as cases of grain overconsumption in commune mess halls and of
famine.[5] In light of the savage attack during the Lushan conference on
leaders who held more moderate views, however, it was politically dangerous for a provincial official to be a bearer of bad news. Thus it is not
surprising that the provincial reports invariably portrayed the problems
as isolated ones within generally favorable circumstances. Central leaders
such as Mao responded by calling for an immediate redress of these "serious problems." But Mao seemed to have regarded them as routine and
easily correctable and apparently failed to generalize beyond these cases.[6]

By the summer, however, there was no ignoring the deepening disaster.
Perhaps the most important indicator of disaster was the depletion or near
depletion of grain reserves in major industrial areas such as Beijing, Tianjin,
Shanghai, and Liaoning at the end of May. Efforts to replenish the reserves
with supplies from other provinces were frustrated, because these provinces were also in desperate need of grain. China's leaders, including Mao,

were shocked by what was happening. Mao's librarian recalled that Mao had rarely been as depressed as in the summer of 1960. He spoke little and sometimes sat for long stretches of time, gazing at nothing.[7] Ever the mandarin administrator, Zhou Enlai started to spend enormous amounts of time supervising the balancing of grain supplies in China at this time.

This chapter details the struggle over rural policy as China grappled with the crisis brought on by the Great Leap Forward. Its message is a simple one. The Great Leap Famine shook people's faith in the new people's communes. It not only forced the Chinese leadership to adopt remedial measures but also compelled peasants and basic-level cadres to seek unofficial avenues for survival. While the adjustment policies emanating from the center were doubtless important, the orientation of rural policy during and immediately after these famine years was also shaped by peasants and basic-level cadres bent on self-preservation. As a result, household contracting, a practice that had surfaced in 1956–57 and would later again be deemed inimical to collective interests, was widely adopted throughout the country *without* central approval in the early 1960's. In many places it persisted into the mid-1960's despite state efforts to crack down.

While the Great Leap Famine set the structural incentives for change, we should again pay attention to agency and contingency. Most interesting, on the basis of research materials that have recently become available, this chapter concludes that Mao himself was close to permitting the nationwide adoption of household contracting in summer 1962. As in the discussion of the adjustments of 1959, I shall first detail the retrenchment policies adopted by the Chinese leadership and then document the flourishing of local initiatives linking effort with reward, notably household contracting of agricultural production. This is followed by an examination of the elite debate over household contracting in 1962. The outcome of the elite interaction shaped rural policy until the post-Mao reforms.

The Second Retreat by the Chinese Leadership

Faced with economic depression and a deteriorating relationship with the Soviet Union, the Party Central Committee convened a work conference at Beidaihe (a seaside resort) from July 5 to August 10, 1960, to discuss the twin problems. (It was during the conference—in late July—that Khrushchev terminated various cooperative agreements with China and began the rapid withdrawal of Soviet technical experts.) While a year earlier Mao championed the transition from a brigade-based to a commune-based rural economy in three-to-five years' time, he now insisted that the brigade-based economy not change for at least five years. Moreover, commune members were to be given some private plots for vegetables and so forth and allowed to have domestic animals. On the issue of mess halls, Mao pointed out that the earlier Central Committee approval of the Guizhou report on developing mess halls was flawed and should be corrected.[8]

The directive on agriculture produced by the meeting acknowledged the "seriousness of the present grain difficulties," but it did *not* follow up on the issue of private plots and animals.[9] In fact, in the context of the intensifying Sino-Soviet conflict, the directive emphasized that "the three red banners—the Party's general line of socialist construction, the Great Leap Forward, and the people's communes—have unlimited vitality" and stressed that the "present political and economic situation is good." Peasants were urged to do a good job running commune mess halls.[10] Meanwhile, the directive called for a shift in development priorities to grain production. The scale of waterworks was to be reduced and labor shifted to agriculture (even school-age youths were called upon to work half a day). Support of grain production was "not just the responsibility of the agriculture departments, but the common responsibility of all departments, the whole party and whole people."[11] By the end of August, China's economic policy had come under the rubric of "adjustment, consolidation, improvement, and filling out" (*tiaozheng, gonggu, tigao, chongshi*), a slogan coined by Li Fuchun and Zhou Enlai.

By emphasizing grain production, yet still praising the communes and commune mess halls, the Beidaihe directive on agriculture appears to have sent a mixed message to rural local cadres. Still smarting from the campaign against right opportunism, many of these cadres appear to have taken the tone of political stridency more seriously than intended. In particular, the communist wind of "one, equalization, two, transfer" (*yiping erdiao*) continued to blow in many areas, and land set aside for peasant cultivation (*ziliudi*) was still being made collective. One outstanding example of such abuses was Tonghaikou commune in Hubei's Mianyang county: 41 county-level organizations and 25 commune-level enterprises made outright requisitions from production brigades and teams, which in turn preyed on peasants, taking property ranging from land and houses to sickles and chopsticks. A rough estimate put the value of houses, oxen, farm implements, and furniture that were torn down, killed, or damaged at between 50 and 100 yuan per person, then about one to two years' cash income for each peasant.[12]

Given the mixed message conveyed by the Beidaihe directive, the situation in each province in the fall of 1960 appears to have depended on the initiatives of the provincial leadership. In fact, as early as late February 1960, before China's central leadership had recognized the seriousness of the rural situation in the post-Lushan period, the Guangdong provincial leadership, headed by Tao Zhu and Zhao Ziyang, issued a directive on several problems in the operation of rural people's communes. It put a strict limit on the number of communes that could experiment with commune-level accounting and emphasized that premature transition would violate objective conditions. It also cautioned against developing the commune-controlled economy at the expense of the brigades and called for a "cool head" in rural work.[13]

In August 1960, following the Beidaihe directive, a number of provinces, including Guangxi, Hubei, and Guangdong, issued directives on rural policy that called for contractual relationships between production brigades and teams. Remarkably, the Guangxi directive gave a higher priority to the peasants' grain rations than state procurement if the two came into conflict and called for allocating the officially permitted maximum amount of land in private plots.[14] In Guangdong, the newly issued stipulations called for an end to the communist wind and for giving peasants some "small liberties." Tao Zhu reportedly stated: "We should not be afraid of spontaneous [societal] forces. We now have too little spontaneity and too much control."[15] In the Hubei directive, the emphasis was on the rights of the production team to manage agricultural production and assign work and rewards to small groups (*zuoyezu*) on the basis of labor, land, and work quality; this contrasted with the central emphasis on the production brigade.[16] At least in Hubei, work teams were sent into communes to rectify mistakes in areas such as Mianyang county.[17]

Despite their variations, these provincial documents and perhaps others were routinely approved by the Central Committee headed by Mao for distribution to other provincial authorities as reference.[18] As a result, Mao and the central leadership were cast in the role of reacting to provincial initiatives rather than as initiators in the fall of 1960.[19] (I will provide more evidence of the divergence between central policy and local practice in the next section.)

Yet China's leaders at the center could not afford to sit quietly. While the Beidaihe meeting was being held, a work team from the Shandong provincial committee was investigating the situation in Tuanwan brigade in Jimo county. It was found that in the five months of January–May 1960, 159 people, or 5.19 percent of the brigade's population, died of famine or famine-related diseases and 380 people (12.39 percent) still suffered from edema as of July. During the same five-month period, 42 percent of the brigade's draft animals died or were killed.[20] On August 3, 1960, the investigation report was distributed within the province by the provincial leadership and was also reported to the center for the record.[21]

The Shandong experience was not isolated. In the summer and early fall of 1960, secret telegrams began to come in from the provinces, especially Henan and Gansu, which reported on the tragic turn of events. Part of the Henan report to the Central Committee reads:

Between winter 1958 and spring 1960, very bad situations developed in about 30 percent of the province, especially Xinyang prefecture, resulting in extremely serious circumstances. . . . According to recent statistics, between October 1959 and October 1960, more than 1.9 million people had died [of starvation] in the province. Xinyang alone accounted for over one million. It is estimated that when the problems are thoroughly exposed, the total number of deaths in the province will exceed two million.[22]

Thus by the end of October, the Chinese leadership clearly knew of the tragedies still in the making, though they did not explicitly refer to them in official documents until early December.[23] All these developments prompted Mao to direct Zhou Enlai to oversee the writing of the famous emergency letter of November 3, 1960 (alternatively known as the Twelve Articles), to party leaders at all levels (including the production team).[24] After the usual nod to the excellent overall situation, the letter hit the nail on the head with an attack on the "communist wind" of "one, equalization [of income], and two, transfer [of property]." Since the end of 1958, only some areas had corrected the mistake of blowing the "communist wind"; most areas, however, had failed to do so or had reverted to such abusive practices after the Lushan conference of 1959, thereby "doing serious damage to productive forces in agriculture." This necessitated the systematic resurrection of the policies of spring 1959. In the people's commune system, the production brigade was the foundation, but the production team also had certain rights and could enter into contractual relationships with the brigade in agricultural production. Moreover, peasants should be given small plots to cultivate on their own (limited to 5 percent of the total acreage). The mistakes of "equalization and transfer" should be resolutely opposed and completely rectified.

The emergency letter inherited the limitations of the 1959 policies, however. It called for continuing the military-style supply system and insisted on operating commune mess halls. Grain rations for peasants would go directly to commune mess halls, thereby binding peasants to collective dining (and, frequently, collective hunger). Menacingly, in an accompanying directive distributed only to provincial-level authorities, the center warned against "rightist mistakes" but ordered provincial leaders "*not* to alert lower-level cadres and the masses to the task of fighting rightism in the beginning." Instead, provincial authorities were instructed to "launch counterattacks" against rightism at appropriate moments in the future.[25] Thus the center, led by Mao, had already placed a political shackle on the adoption of more free-wheeling practices even while it called on provincial leaders to be the first to "make the determination" to "rectify errors."[26]

These limitations notwithstanding, as the extent of rural devastation became ever clearer, the policy emphasis of the moment was clearly on rectification. The situation was especially bad in Henan's Xinyang prefecture. In Chayashan commune of Suiping county, one of China's earliest communes in 1958, 10 percent of the total population and up to 30 percent in some production brigades had died of starvation by the end of 1960. The rest of Xinyang prefecture was similarly wrecked by radical practices.[27] Putting on the best face, a Central Work conference held from December 24, 1960, to January 13, 1961, in preparation for the Ninth Plenum (January 14–18 and chaired by Mao) of the Eighth Central Committee conceded that 20 percent of all rural units had serious problems—the euphemism for famine-related deaths—and were in need of rectification (zhengfeng zhengshe) so as to purge the "rotten elements." The heightened sense of urgency led the center to raise the upper limit of the amount of land that could be set aside for private cultivation to 7 percent of the total (up from 5 percent) and to allocate 2.5 billion yuan to help local authorities compensate for goods and property that were requisitioned and damaged during the leap.[28] To ensure a steady supply for urban areas when free-market prices were sharply higher, the center also approved Chen Yun's plan to increase the purchase prices for agricultural products beginning with the summer harvest of 1961. Actual procurement prices rose 25 percent for grain, 26 percent for pigs, 37 percent for poultry, and 13 percent for oils.[29] Meanwhile, the Chinese leadership swallowed its pride and began to import grain from abroad.[30]

A sobered Mao spoke on both January 13 and 18 and set the tone for the two meetings.[31] He called for on-the-spot investigations to unearth the real conditions in grass-roots units and urged cadres at all levels to do so. He declared that 1961 should become the year for seeking truth from facts.[32] Shortly after the Ninth Plenum, Mao left Beijing for the south. He also sent three of his secretaries, each heading a group, to Zhejiang, Hunan, and Guangdong for grass-roots investigations.[33]

As a result of these investigations and his own talks with local leaders, Mao found that the emergency letter of November 3, 1960, had only solved the problem of "requisitions" from lower to higher levels and did not resolve the problem of egalitarianism among production teams within a production brigade and among peasants within a team.[34] Toward the end of February 1961 (and contrary to previous studies of the period),[35] Mao Zedong took up a suggestion made by his secretary Tian Jiaying and organized the drafting of what would be known as the Sixty Articles.[36] This document, officially known as the "Work Regulations on Rural Communes," was intended to enshrine the various changes that had been made in rural policy in a more authoritative form than the emergency letter of November 1960 and thus give peasants greater confidence in official policy. A draft of the document was discussed and approved at the Central Work conference of March 15–23 (held in Guangzhou and attended by Mao and his senior colleagues) for wide discussion and trial implementation.[37]

The draft version of the Sixty Articles defined the nature and management structure of the people's communes in detail.[38] The production brigade was still the basis, or the basic accounting unit, of the commune system, and it was analogous to the former higher-level APC in size; but the production team had its rights in managing production within the team, and commune members were entitled to have private plots. However, production teams were still urged to maintain public mess halls as long as they could.

For Mao, the Guangzhou conference was a milestone not only because it produced the draft Sixty Articles but also because it was the first serious effort by China's central leaders to discuss and deal with the agricultural crisis since the establishment of people's communes.[39] A sense of realism permeated the meetings, and Zhou Enlai reemphasized the importance of seeking truth from facts.[40] Judging by Mao's comments at the conference, it appeared that he was very much in the mood for compromise, because he feared that the policy changes coming from the center could be too little, too late, as indeed they were.[41] Commenting on reports from Shandong and Guangdong, he recognized the tensions between team production and brigade ownership and distribution. He was willing to make the production team the basic accounting unit of the commune system. Nevertheless, his motion to do this was not approved at the conference probably because Mao wanted to give his colleagues more time to change their minds and did not push hard for the motion at this time.[42]

The Guangzhou conference was followed by more field investigations by Mao's own teams. In late spring and early summer, Mao's senior colleagues Liu Shaoqi, Zhou Enlai, Zhu De, Deng Xiaoping, Chen Yun, Tan Zhenlin, Peng Zhen, and Tao Zhu went on their own field trips as well, as did various ministerial leaders.[43] They quickly recognized the political dangers of the famine. Vice-Premier Tan Zhenlin, who went to Henan's Qiliying, a star of the Great Leap, concluded: "The masses now doubt and distrust our Party's principles and policies. The rural economy is in paralysis and lacks leadership." "The essence of the leftist errors in rural work was to rob the peasant and expropriate the laborer. . . . Such errors are extremely dangerous and their continuation will ruin the revolution."[44]

Before long, most investigators had correctly concluded that the public mess hall and the supply system associated with it were at the root of hunger and malnutrition in rural areas. As a report submitted by Hu Qiaomu on April 14, 1961, pointed out: "Judging by the reactions of the masses, most mess halls have actually become obstacles to the development of production and a tangled knot [geda] in Party-mass relations. We therefore believe that the sooner this problem is resolved, the better."[45] Liu Shaoqi, Zhou Enlai, and Zhu De concurred in their written or oral reports to Mao in early May.[46] The mess halls were not only wasteful but also inconvenient to peasant families. Even on rainy days, peasants had to walk a considerable distance to share the same poorly cooked meals at mess halls. The elderly and children received no special treatment. In contrast, the health of rural residents improved when they were allowed to cook and eat at home. In a letter to Mao dated May 9, 1961, Marshall Zhu De reported that the incidence of edema dropped by 40–50 percent in eastern Henan after peasants were allowed to eat in their own homes.[47]

While these investigations were under way, Mao maintained close contact with his colleagues. Even though the mess halls and the supply system were his favorite institutions, he now bowed to reality and supported his colleagues in experimenting with the dismantlement of mess halls, as Zhou Enlai did in one Hebei locality.[48] In Hunan, Liu Shaoqi did the same but on a grander scale. In concert with the provincial leadership, he acted upon the complaints of peasants and closed down the public mess halls in Tianhua brigade and Huaminglou commune, two communities he visited. Their respective counties (Changsha and Ningxiang) followed suit. Soon mess halls were closed throughout the province.[49]

On the basis of these investigations and experiments, the Chinese leadership revised the draft Sixty Articles at a Central Work conference held from May 21 to June 12, 1961, in Beijing.[50] The only major change concerned the mess halls and the supply system. In the revised draft, all grain rations were to be distributed to peasants directly rather than channeled to the mess halls. Peasants "totally decided" whether they wanted to set up a mess hall in the production team (Art. 36). In other words, they were free to dismantle it now! Moreover, while in the draft Sixty Articles peasants were entitled to a set amount of income (supply) whether they worked or not, all income would now be distributed on the basis of work done. On June 15, the revised draft of the Sixty Articles was issued for trial implementation. Four days later, the Central Committee issued a decision calling for the resolute correction of the error of egalitarianism and "requisitionism" (*pingdiao*) and for compensating lower levels for earlier requisitions.[51]

Interestingly, the directive accompanying the Sixty Articles also called for a reassessment of the verdicts (such as being declared rightists) that had been meted out to cadres and party members in the past few years. It stipulated that henceforth struggles against either rightism or leftism would not touch cadres engaged in production or the masses.[52] In Guangdong, 31.5 percent of the cadres who suffered political persecution between 1958 and 1960 saw their verdicts reversed.[53] To the people specified in the directive, this signaled a political cease fire and thus a limited suspension of the rules of the political game that had been played so far. Production, rather than political purity, was the overriding concern when survival was at stake. In this sense, the accompanying document may have served to encourage lower-level cadres and peasants to engage in practices not sanctioned by the center.

The implementation of the revised draft of the Sixty Articles and other policies that accompanied it led to the rapid downsizing of rural organizations from communes to production teams. The numbers of these rural units correspondingly increased. An August 1961 survey by the CC Rural Work Department found that the number of communes had increased from the original 25,204 to 55,628 (more than doubling), the number of production brigades from 483,814 to 708,912, and the number of production teams from 2,988,168 to 4,549,474.[54] These institutional changes helped stabilize the rural situation and stem the slide in agricultural production.

On September 27, 1961, Mao convened a discussion meeting in Hebei's Handan to canvass opinions on what the rural basic accounting unit should be. On September 29, he wrote to members of the Politburo standing committee and others concerned and clearly stated that the basic accounting unit ought to be the production team rather than the production brigade. He wrote that "the serious problem of egalitarianism in our agriculture has not been completely solved by now."[55] The Sixty Articles lacked a provision on this. On October 7, 1961, the Central Committee issued a directive that called on every county to select one or two production brigades as experimental subjects to try out the idea of making production teams the basic accounting unit.[56] In implementing this practice, production teams became even smaller, reverting to the size of the former lower-level APCs, with between 20 and 30 households to every team.[57] The 7,000-cadre meeting (January 11–February 7, 1962) decided that this would not be changed for at least 30 years, which simply meant a long time.[58]

To sum up, beginning in late 1960, the Chinese leadership began to deal with the adverse consequences of the Lushan conference. By the fall of 1961, Mao Zedong himself had proposed that the basic accounting unit be the (downsized) production team. In the context of the strident official rhetoric about the superiority of the people's communes over other forms of rural organization, this was a significant retreat and permitted China's rural population to breathe.

In hindsight, however, the retreat must be taken for what it was: both belated and saddled with weaknesses. The leadership still insisted on retaining the rhetoric and framework of people's communes, which, according to the Sixty Articles, would combine the functions of party and government. The communes possessed substantial power over their constituent parts—the production brigades and production teams. The reach of the state in rural China was, despite the retreat forced by the famine, still far greater than it was before the Great Leap Forward.

Our assessment of the official policies should also be made with a view to what the people in rural China wanted. Horrified by the disastrous consequences of the Great Leap and in spite of the severe political attacks against rightism following the Lushan conference, the rural population, in its struggle for survival, preferred to return the organization of agricultural production to the household level. Put simply, the Great Leap Famine sowed the seeds for the breakup of the commune system. As a result, a tug of war ensued around 1961 between the Chinese leadership, seeking to balance growth and equity, and the rural population, seeking to control its own destiny.

The Struggle from Below and the Spread of Household Responsibility

Despite the heavy political pressure to carry on the Great Leap in early 1960, isolated instances of individual peasant cultivation began to emerge. In Suxian county of northern Anhui, a farmer in his seventies named Liu Qinglan had to take care of his tuberculosis-ridden son and could not participate in collective labor. Probably seeing the collective disaster in the making, the farmer pleaded with the commune that he did not want to impose burdens on the collective and asked the commune's permission to head into the hills in 1960. The farmer was granted permission and opened up sixteen *mu* of hilly land for cultivation. By harvest time, the farmer not only had enough to feed his family but also handed over 900 kilograms of grain to the commune while a famine swept across rural Anhui. The stark contrast between the old farmer's self-sufficiency and the collective's failure allegedly inspired local cadres to contract strips of land to individual households for cultivation.[59]

The peasants' demand for household cultivation was not confined to Suxian but could also be found in Quanshu and other areas in Anhui province. More generally, peasants earnestly called for restructuring the management of communes and linking work with reward.[60] These demands amid the ravages of famine probably weighed heavily on the mind of Zeng Xisheng.

Zeng Xisheng had been the party boss in Anhui province since the early 1950's. During the leap, Zeng led Anhui in a competition with neighboring Henan; while Henan excelled in establishing bigger communes, Anhui led in the drive to build backyard steel furnaces. Zeng was certainly in the limelight during the 1958–60 period. He was host to China's top leaders, including Mao Zedong, Zhou Enlai, and Deng Xiaoping, during their visits to Anhui. His articles on water conservation, backyard steel furnaces, antirightism, and people's communes appeared in the *People's Daily* and *Red Flag*, the two most important party publications.[61] Zeng's ardent pursuit of the Great Leap undoubtedly contributed to making Anhui the worst-off province in China during the famine. In 1960 alone, Anhui's population was reduced by nearly 7 percent.

The severe famine and the cries for change by peasants and local cadres caused Zeng to reflect on what was happening and change his outlook.[62] In early fall 1960, he suggested that agricultural production be contracted to teams, and the provincial leadership issued a set of ten regulations on commune management in late August, authorizing the assignment of production tasks to small groups within production teams.[63] When in February 1961 he heard the story of Liu Qinglan, he was very impressed and proposed at a meeting of the provincial party secretariat that individual households be assigned responsibility for agricultural output.[64] Subsequently the provincial leadership reviewed the positive results from several localities that had tried output contracting and on March 6 sanctioned assigning responsibility for plots of land to peasant households.[65]

In doing so, the Anhui leaders were clearly taking advantage of the easier political atmosphere following the Ninth Plenum of the Eighth Central Committee, but this did not obscure the fact that they acted without central approval and were taking political risks. In a politically cautious move, they named the new practice "responsibility plots or responsibility land" (*zeren tian*), in order to distinguish it from the practice of "contracting output to the household" (*baochan daohu*) that had been under political attack since the Lushan conference of 1959.[66] Future detractors of the Anhui practice would nevertheless point out that the two appellations represented virtually the same practice.

In writing about the provincial decision in the next-to-last paragraph, I deliberately chose the word "sanction." The Anhui leaders were not starting a new practice on their own, but merely approving of activities that had already been adopted by a sizable portion of the rural population. The official approval on the part of the provincial leadership, however, certainly helped the practice spread. Thus it was not surprising that by March 20, barely two weeks after the provincial decision, 39.2 percent of all production teams in Anhui had already adopted the *zeren tian* responsibility system. A sizable portion of the rural population appear to have interpreted the *zeren tian* as "contracting output to the household" or simply "dividing up land."[67]

While the *zeren tian* spread in Anhui, Zeng Xisheng went to Guangzhou and sought the approval of central leaders at the Central Work conference held in Guangzhou.[68] He advocated its adoption at one or more of the conference group meetings but was immediately greeted with hostile criticisms of the practice as just a version of household contracting (*baochan daohu*). After all, the draft Sixty Articles produced by the Guangzhou conference still insisted on communal mess halls and only made the production brigade the basic unit in people's communes; mention of making the household assume responsibility for agricultural production amounted to political heresy.

At first Mao urged Zeng Xisheng to try the *zeren tian* out in order to boost production. Zeng relayed Mao's message back to Anhui, greatly helping *zeren tian* spread. A few days later, however, word came from Mao that the *zeren tian* could only be tried on a small scale.[69] Unsure of the political verdict on the *zeren tian*, Zeng took a two-pronged strategy on March 20. He telephoned colleagues at the Anhui Provincial Party Committee to call for an immediate suspension of the *zeren tian* policy. Meanwhile, he sent a letter to Mao Zedong, Liu Shaoqi, Zhou Enlai, Deng Xiaoping, and others and sought their understanding and approval. In the letter, he conceded that the *zeren tian* had certain similarities to the practice of contracting output to the household. Yet, Zeng asserted, the Anhui leadership had not simply accepted the peasants' demand to divide up land among individual households. Instead, Anhui "had absorbed some of the good points [of contracting output to the household] while stipulating measures to guard against its [politically] bad side." Specifically, the province had emphasized "five unifications" (*wu tongyi*) to counteract the disintegrative effect of household contracting. Major farmwork such as planting rice and harvesting was still undertaken collectively, and the distribution of the portion of the output specified in contracts was also handled at the brigade level. Only field management was left to individual households. More important, the *zeren tian* system, by linking effort with reward, spurred peasant enthusiasm, improved work quality, and ensured increases in output of as much as 10 percent.[70]

After the Guangzhou conference, the central leaders busied themselves with field investigations in an effort to improve the draft Sixty Articles. There appears to have been no formal response from the central leadership to Zeng's letter. With neither central endorsement nor disapproval, the *zeren tian* remained in political limbo. In an act of self-protection, the Anhui Provincial Committee sent the center a report on April 27, 1961. The report argued that the *zeren tian* was neither "contracting output to the household" nor simply "dividing up land" and that it was in complete accordance with the provisions for responsibility in production in the Sixty Articles.[71] By late July, in yet another more systematic report to the center by the Anhui leadership, the *zeren tian* was redefined as a responsibility system for field management (*lianjian guanli zerenzhi*). The Anhui leadership was clearly seeking both to cover itself politically and to justify what was going on in the countryside. This report incorporated the central arguments of Zeng's March 20 letter and the April 27 report. Its central aim was to explain that Anhui had not adopted household contracting or even individual farming. While individuals took responsibility for field management, the collective economy remained; it "still owned the land, draft animals, and large farm tools." To be sure, there were problems, such as concealment of output and negligence by cadres, but the system did not violate socialist principles and was a form of collective management.[72] In the same month, Mao traveled through Anhui, and Zeng Xisheng reported to him on Anhui's rural policies. Without specifically mentioning *zeren*

tian, Mao nevertheless indicated that Zeng and his colleagues might promote the responsibility system if they believed the system were correct.
Moreover, Mao stated that loaning land to peasants was "a good plan"
and argued that the amount of private plots should be more than 5 percent
of the total and might even reach 10 percent.[73]

Despite Zeng's earlier call for suspending it, the *zeren tian* had continued to spread in the province. By late July 1961, 66.5 percent of Anhui's
production teams had adopted the *zeren tian*. Mao's encouragement in July
prompted the Anhui leadership to promote the practice vigorously. By
fall, 85.4 percent of the production teams had adopted the *zeren tian*. Yet
Anhui was not alone. Similar practices could also be found in other parts
of the country, usually under different appellations, including allocating
land according to labor (*anlao fentian*), contracting output to the household, or allocating "grain ration" land (*fen kouliangtian*), a plot large
enough for subsistence. Even some areas of Hunan, Mao's native province,
had adopted household contracting in various forms by as early as March
1961, even though Xiangtan and Changsha (where Mao grew up and
worked, respectively, in his early days and which were now under the
leadership of Hua Guofeng) continued to hold out against household contracting at this time.[74] On August 26, the Hunan leadership went further
with the decision that production brigades and teams should loan peasants collective land that might otherwise lie idle during the winter season.[75] As a report by the Central Committee's Rural Work Department put
it in August 1961, in areas severely affected by the Great Leap Forward, "a
sizable proportion of the cadres and peasants have lost their confidence in
collective production." In consequence, household contracting in agriculture had become "widespread, and had been found in almost every province, municipality, and autonomous region." Peasants commemorated the
de facto return of land to them (*tudi huanjia*) with firecrackers and drums
and gongs. In some places, collective production had been so disrupted
and cadres so weak that it had become difficult to resume collective agricultural production; some other teams existed only because team members had been realigned according to kinship ties.[76]

The Debate over Household Contracting

The rapid spread of the various forms of household farming raised the
ideological antennae of some members of China's top leadership, most noticeably Mao Zedong. By fall 1961, Mao proposed lowering the basic accounting unit in people's communes from the production brigade to the
production team. For him, this institutional change would resolve the
problem of excessive equalization among teams, improve peasant incentives, and yet preserve the fundamental element of collectivism. Growth

had to be combined with a concern for equality. Therefore, while team accounting was officially propagated, the Central Committee called for carrying out socialist education in rural areas in a directive issued on November 13, 1961. Targeted at "the ideological problems that still existed among peasant masses and rural cadres," the directive categorically declared that, of the activities such as contracting output to the household and individual farming, "none is in keeping with the principles of socialist collective economy. They are therefore incorrect" and need to be rectified. For peasants, their "only correct way out [of the present difficulties] was to rely on the development of collective economy." The egregious winds of exaggeration, communization, and blind commandism, it was pointed out, should be distinguished from the genuine commune system.[77]

Because of Zeng Xisheng's role as leading advocate for the *zeren tian*, Mao sought him out in December 1961 and asked him whether it was time to change, since production had started to revive. Zeng responded by arguing that the *zeren tian* should be continued for a while longer, since peasants had just started to benefit from the practice. When Mao did not give a clear-cut indication of his views, Zeng apparently took this as tacit approval and planned on continuing to promote the *zeren tian* in 1962.[78] Instead, Mao had decided that Zeng not only had gone too far in promoting the *zeren tian* but was also politically disobedient. At the enlarged Central Work conference (7,000-cadre conference, January 11–February 7, 1962), both Mao and Liu Shaoqi indicated their own responsibility for the errors that had occurred during the Great Leap, but both also put on brave faces to emphasize that the achievements were greater and that China had become stronger because of the lessons learnt.[79] Yet Zeng Xisheng came under severe attack not only for his ill-fated enthusiasm for leftist practices in 1958 but, more important, for his continual advocacy of the responsibility system. He was stripped of his post as Anhui's top leader.[80]

On March 20, 1962, the reconstituted Anhui leadership dutifully produced a resolution that blamed the provincial committee headed by Zeng Xisheng for committing the political mistake of encouraging the spread of the *zeren tian*. Unlike in previous provincial documents, the *zeren tian* system was now equated with contracting output to the household (*baochan daohu*). While the measure was necessary during the worst days of the famine, it nevertheless encouraged peasants to pursue individual farming, led cadres to focus on their contracted land at the expense of their cadre duties, increased income disparities, reduced the collective's economic power, and affected state procurement. Thus the *zeren tian* was said to have "catered to the spontaneous capitalist tendencies of peasants" and "did not accord with the principles of socialism."[81] According to the notice accompanying the provincial resolution, the *zeren tian* was "wrong in [political] orientation" and "must be resolutely and completely rectified."[82]

Yet despite disapproval from China's top leadership, most noticeably

Mao, individual farming and household contracting under various guises continued to spread throughout China in the spring and summer of 1962.[83] In a report to Mao Zedong and the Central Committee dated May 24, 1962, Deng Zihui, vice-premier and director of the Rural Work Department, pointed out that peasants still "do not have trust in the Party's policies." As of late May 1962 about 20 percent of all rural households in China had adopted individual farming under various guises. "If effective measures are not taken," Deng warned, "the phenomenon of individual farming will develop further in the winter and next spring and threaten to undermine the consolidation of the people's commune system."[84] By summer 1962, Mao's secretary Tian Jiaying revealed, the corresponding figure had risen to about 30 percent, and the practice of household-based agriculture was still spreading.[85]

Deng Zihui's statement was corroborated by local cases. In Anhui, the provincial resolution cited earlier freely admitted that only about 20 percent of the commune members wanted to stop the *zeren tian* system; they were mostly cadres, Communist Party and youth league members, activists, and households that lacked labor or skills—in other words, people who would benefit from income sharing.[86] In Guizhou province, despite objections from the provincial authorities, land had been contracted to the household in 25 percent of the areas by late September 1961.[87]

In an invaluable survey of cadres in Guangxi conducted in early 1962, it was found that about 25 percent of the cadres at the commune level or below were inclined toward the division of land among peasant households, household contracting for output quotas, and the restoration of independent farming.[88] In an ironic twist on the party's general line, some local cadres said that their "general line" was independent farming (*dan'gan*). For many cadres, household-based independent farming simplified management, saved operational costs, and spurred peasant enthusiasm. Privately managed land produced more than the collective land. Household farming was the only way to overcome egalitarianism and rejuvenate the countryside.

The survey revealed that the proportion of cadres who favored independent farming varied with local economic conditions and with cadre rank. In areas with relatively good economic conditions, 15 percent of the cadres believed in and encouraged independent farming, in contrast to 60 percent in areas that were devastated by the leap. In Liucheng county, one of the worst-hit areas in Guangxi, 272, or 65.2 percent, of the 417 cadres who took part in the county's three-level cadre meeting favored independent farming. While 20 percent of the commune party secretaries favored this, 48 percent of the members of commune party committees did so. The percentage was even higher among basic-level cadres in production brigades and teams. In a number of areas in Guangxi, a relatively high proportion of production teams had adopted household-based farming.

Of the 1,867 production teams in Longsheng county, 790 (42.3 percent) had adopted household contracting. In Sanjiang county, a survey indicated that 15.3 percent of the teams adopted household contracting and 8.4 percent practiced small work-group contracting. In a certain Gaoming commune, 56.2 percent of the production teams had already divided the land up in favor of individual farming.[89]

The popular preference for household contracting and similar practices was also indicated by the appeals in their favor after the Anhui leadership issued its resolution against household contracting.[90] Perhaps the most celebrated and interesting of such appeals was a report addressed to Mao Zedong by Qian Rangneng, a cadre in the propaganda department of the Taihu county Party Committee in Anhui.[91] At great risk to his own career, Qian said the provincial resolution had to be refuted because the *zeren tian* practice "was pioneered by peasants and suited the inexorable develop-mental trend of rural productive forces." To prove his point, Qian sup-plied detailed data on the county. By the end of 1960, it had been devas-tated by the leap. A high percentage of the surviving peasants suffered from edema and lacked agricultural assets.[92] In March 1961, over 90 per-cent of the production teams in the county adopted the *zeren tian*, which immediately began to bring the county back to life. Peasants "showed an enthusiasm that I have not seen in ten years," wrote Qian. Despite a severe drought and then flood in 1961, agricultural output increased dramati-cally from the trough of 1960. Women of child-bearing age were again able to bear children. For Qian, the *zeren tian* "was the most effective measure for combating egalitarianism among peasants." Because individual peas-ants still fulfilled the state grain-procurement quotas and supplied the production brigade with public accumulation savings (*gonggong jilei*), the *zeren tian* system was socialist in nature.

In contrast, hearing of the impending rectification of the *zeren tian*, peasants refrained from investing in and caring for the land. Such "pas-sive resistance," Qian warned, "is especially stubborn and difficult to overcome." Contrary to the provincial leadership's assertions, Qian re-vealed that most peasants were against the provincial resolution. While the leadership stated that a majority of the peasants would favor rectifi-cation, Qian mentioned that the county's own surveys indicated that at least 80 percent, perhaps 90 percent, of the peasants wanted the *zeren tian* preserved.[93] Qian thus begged Chairman Mao to send people to Taihu county to investigate.

Qian's report would eventually be circulated by Mao in early August, but as an example of incorrect political thinking. In contrast, Wu Nianci (party secretary of Fuli district in Anhui's Suxian county) fared better when he wrote Deng Zihui to plead the case for the *zeren tian* in April.[94] Before the leap, Deng had already been interested in measures to link work effort with reward.[95] However, after he was criticized for committing the error of "right opportunism" by Mao in 1955, Deng had to be doubly cautious. He dispatched three work teams to different areas in Anhui to see whether the *zeren tian* was a form of collective management and whether it could be transplanted to areas outside Anhui. By July, he was satisfied that both could be done.[96] In a number of talks delivered in June and July, Deng Zihui elaborated on his views that China's peasants had suffered chiefly because of problems in the workings of government. While he said that it would be wrong to set aside as much as 40–50 percent of the land as private plots, as some localities had done, he believed a figure of 20 percent (the figure as of late May 1962) posed no danger to collective ownership. Dearest to Deng's heart was introducing responsibility into farm work, such as by contracting field management to individual households. In late June, Deng Zihui decided to support the *zeren tian* system by submitting a report on Anhui to the Beidaihe Central Work conference, which began on July 25, 1962.[97]

Chinese Leaders and Household Contracting in 1962

Deng Zihui was not alone among the senior policymakers in expressing support for household contracting. After the 7,000-cadre conference, Mao asked his secretary Tian Jiaying to head an investigation team (divided into three groups) to Hunan in late March 1962. The three groups went, respectively, to Shaoshan (Mao's birthplace), Daping production brigade (or Tangjiatuo, hometown of Mao's grandparents), and Tanzichong production brigade (Liu Shaoqi's birthplace)—areas that fell under the jurisdiction of Hua Guofeng and were among the slowest in adopting liberal agricultural practices.[98] By late March 1962, these localities had only closed the mess halls and adopted team accounting. Yet, to the surprise of the investigation team members, "peasants generally demanded household contracting of output and distributing land to the household," especially in Shaoshan and Daping. They debated with members of the investigation team by enumerating the many advantages of household contracting and pointing to the problems that had afflicted the collective economy since the push for people's communes. While Tian Jiaying had opposed household contracting and Anhui's *zeren tian* during the Guangzhou conference in spring 1961, he was now persuaded that household contracting was the way to go in agriculture.[99]

Shortly thereafter, Tian Jiaying reported the findings of his team to a number of senior leaders, with his endorsement of household contracting. After he made an initial report to Mao in Shanghai in June 1962, Mao reportedly commented: "We should follow the mass line, but sometimes we cannot totally follow the masses, we cannot agree with them in the case of contracting output to the household."[100] When Deng Zihui reported to

Mao at the end of June and advocated the adoption of the *zeren tian*, Mao also disagreed.

In contrast to Mao, Chen Yun, perhaps the only senior leader who did not openly endorse the Great Leap Forward, praised Tian's report for its "clear-cut stand."[101] Tian Jiaying also reported to Liu Shaoqi and Deng Xiaoping, two of Mao's comrades-in-arms in launching the Great Leap Forward. Both had since changed their minds, however. Liu Shaoqi, in particular, needed no further prodding. He interrupted Tian Jiaying's report by saying that "the situation has now become clear" and that household contracting was indeed needed. Deng Xiaoping and a number of other central leaders also agreed with Tian that household contracting be allowed to coexist with other forms of agrarian organizations.[102] "What the masses prefer should be adopted, even if this means legalizing what is illegal," Deng argued. On a number of occasions during June and July, Deng Xiaoping quoted an adage—which has since become closely linked with his name—that the color of the cat made no difference as long as it caught mice.[103]

The shifting attitudes at the center were reflected in a small-scale central work conference held in May 1962.[104] It was attended by Liu Shaoqi, Zhou Enlai, Chen Yun, and Deng Xiaoping while Mao was away from Beijing. At this conference, Tian Jiaying called for criticizing leftist tendencies. Participants were generally in favor of legalizing "contracting output to the household."[105] Even when a meeting of the Central Committee Secretariat heard a report on the controversial issue of *zeren tian* in Anhui from the East China regional leadership in late June, supporters and detractors of the practice were about evenly divided.[106]

Mao Wavers

In the meantime, Mao was also moving toward permitting contracting agricultural production to the household, as indicated by his interaction with Wang Renzhong and Tao Zhu in summer 1962. This development started when Mao heard a report from Wang Renzhong on the rural investigations Wang and Tao had undertaken in Guangxi's Longsheng county.[107]

Wang and Tao visited two small production teams located deep in the mountains on June 6–7, 1962. Partly because farmland was scattered in this isolated area, the few households belonging to the two teams did not endure the many excesses of the Great Leap and go hungry while the nation was in the throes of famine. Most interesting to Tao and Wang, reward was linked to labor input in the two teams. The arrangement was largely what Tao Zhu had promoted in some areas of Guangdong beginning in 1961. Both Tao Zhu and Wang Renzhong went to Guangxi predisposed toward some sort of production responsibility system in agriculture. After seeing Longsheng, they became convinced that they had found the formula for success in agriculture.

On his way back from Longsheng, Wang Renzhong reported to Mao, whose special train happened to be staying near Hunan's Changsha. Wang stated that he and Tao Zhu were in favor of giving peasant households the responsibility for managing pieces of land. Under this arrangement, the collective organized plowing and seeding; households assumed responsibility for production and were rewarded according to the contracted output. If total exceeded contracted output, the peasant household retained the surplus. Mao responded: "Yes, it's contracting output to the household, not dividing up land for individual farming."[108] Mao carefully distinguished between household contracting and individual farming; he was willing to condone the former in collectives, especially for peasants isolated in mountainous areas, but was strongly against the latter.

Encouraged by Mao, Tao Zhu and Wang Renzhong submitted to the Central Committee a report on rural organizational practices in Longsheng (hence the Longsheng report).[109] In contrast to Tian Jiaying, who matter of factly stated that household contracting would inevitably spread, Tao Zhu and Wang Renzhong put their emphasis on consolidating the collective economy. They started with the following upbeat assessment:[110] "Agricultural production in Longsheng county has shown marked improvement this year [1962] in comparison with last year. This indicates that the absolute majority of cadres and masses wish to follow the road of socialism, and want to improve production and raise their living standards. This is consistent with the Party's requirements."[111]

Only then did the report concede that the problems of the past few years had undermined agricultural production and lowered people's living standards. As a result, some peasants' faith in socialism was "temporarily shaken," leading to a resurgence of individual farming. Nevertheless, the report concluded that the percentage of teams that had adopted individual farming—30–40 percent—was far less than the original estimate of 60–70 percent.[112] Moreover, on the nature of rural organizations it was important not to make hasty judgments that might prove counterproductive. For example, the division of labor responsibilities within a collective demonstrated the superiority of the collective economy and should not be regarded as disguised individual farming. Fundamentally, superior collective production depended on a system of responsibility.

The report ended with an extensive discussion of the principles for consolidating the collective economy. It stated that peasant participation in the collective economy should be voluntary. The party should not use rigid administrative orders to force those households that engaged in individual farming back into the collective. Instead, various authorities should strive to build up a group of successful production teams to demonstrate the superiority of the collective economy and "persuade peasants to follow us voluntarily." The collective economy could only be consolidated if it competed successfully against individual farming. Therefore, the party should not be afraid if even 10 percent of the rural households continued to engage in individual farming for some time to come: "The socialist road is in accordance with peasant interests. And peasants will surely follow us."[113]

In short, the Longsheng report not only advocated the adoption of various forms of individual responsibility within collectives but also justified the continued existence of individual farming as a necessary evil. In the meantime, the report seemingly promised that in time, under the leadership of the Communist Party, peasants would willingly join the collective economy.

The upbeat tone of the Longsheng report reflected Mao's own position at the time, which he had formed after hearing from numerous regional and local officials during his extensive travels in central and southwest China in the past few months. As will be discussed below, Mao apparently liked the Longsheng report on first reading it.

Once Mao returned to Beijing, however, he was surrounded by senior colleagues who believed that China's situation was far worse than he had realized and demanded extraordinary responses such as the official adoption of household contracting in rural policy.[114] Two of the people who requested to see him were Chen Yun and Mao's secretary Tian Jiaying. Knowing that the majority of China's senior leaders supported household contracting, Tian Jiaying sought to convince Mao, who had not made clear his position on household contracting. During his meeting with Mao, Tian Jiaying had a chance to give a more systematic report on his Hunan findings than he had done in Shanghai. Tian pointed out that 30 percent of all peasants had already adopted household contracting throughout the country without central approval and more were likely to follow. He counseled that it would therefore be better if the center gave its official blessing to household contracting in order to claim leadership over these hitherto unauthorized developments.[115] Eventually, Tian conceded, as many as 40 percent of all peasants might engage in household-based agriculture, with the rest in semicollective and collective arrangements. Of course, Tian pointed out, the adoption of household contracting would be a tactical measure; peasants would again be urged to promote the collective economy when rural production recovered.[116]

On the night of July 9, Chen Yun talked with Mao for over an hour and suggested that individuals be allowed greater initiative in rural production in order to deal with the difficulties facing agricultural production. Because the minutes of the meeting are unavailable, we do not know the exact wording of Chen's oral report. He certainly championed the adoption of household contracting as the solution to China's rural problems, though he later denied that he had also called for adopting individual farming.[117]

Mao made no direct comment on the political acceptability of household contracting during these two meetings, though he did ask Tian a politically loaded question: "Are you in favor of a predominantly collective or predominantly private economy?" (Tian was too flabbergasted to answer.) The day after meeting Chen Yun, however, Mao was reportedly livid at Chen and apparently believed Chen was calling for dividing up land among peasants for individual farming (*fentian dan'gan*). He severely criticized such a policy option, pointing out that it would undermine the rural collective economy, lead to the dismantlement of people's communes, and was Chinese-style revisionism.[118] Now that the rural economy had stabilized and begun to recover, Mao was concerned about preserving elements of the collective economy.

Around this time, Mao also reportedly chastised Liu Shaoqi for not holding out against Chen Yun when Chen advocated individual farming among senior leaders. (Typical of the epigone, Liu would immediately redefine himself and support Mao's position.)[119] Mao also criticized Tian Jiaying for using his time to promote household contracting and individual farming rather than to revise the Sixty Articles. Instead of Tian, Mao entrusted Chen Boda to draft a Central Committee decision on consolidating the collective economy and further developing agriculture.[120]

Mao nevertheless did not close the door on household contracting. Speaking on July 20, Mao indicated that politically he would rather not see the widespread adoption of household contracting. However, he was also willing to tolerate household contracting if peasants demanded it: "If some [peasants] insist on practicing household contracting, [we] should not adopt a rough attitude toward them."[121] Two days later, on July 22, 1962, Mao instructed that the Tao-Wang report be distributed for discussion to participants at the Beidaihe Central Work conference—convened in preparation for the Tenth Plenum of the Tenth Central Committee—and to cadres down to the prefectural level. He also made the following comment on the report: "The analysis in this document is Marxist; the suggestions that followed the analysis are also Marxist."[122]

That comment indicates that Mao strongly endorsed the Tao-Wang conclusion of combining party leadership in rural affairs with official toleration (if not yet endorsement) of household contracting. A recent Chinese publication suggests, however, that Mao even intended to endorse household contracting openly. While at Beidaihe, in a private meeting with Tao Zhu, Wang Renzhong, and Zhang Pinghua, Mao asked them to draft a decision on behalf of the Central Committee authorizing contracting agricultural output to the household. Mao specifically added: "Not dividing up the land among peasants for individual farming. Contracting output to the household is still an operational mode of the collective economy."[123]

Wang started his version of the draft decision with these words: "The dangers of 'the communization wind' are past us. The main tendency of the moment is the division of land for individual farming. A good method to counteract individual farming is to contract field management and output to the household."[124]

The Suppression of Household Contracting

Thus, as the Central Work conference opened on August 6 at Beidaihe, Mao's subordinates had actually prepared two different drafts of a decision to be issued in the name of the Central Committee. One, drafted by Wang Renzhong, would permit household contracting in order to counteract the spread of individual farming; the other, drafted by Chen Boda, would ban both and seek to consolidate the collective economy.

On the eve of the conference, Mao still sought a middle road. Commenting on the gloom and doom some senior leaders had expressed, Mao said:

I traveled across the country, from central south to southwest, and talked with comrades from the big regions. Every provincial leader told me that last year was better than the year before last and that this year is better than last year. So the situation is not entirely gloomy. Some comrades have an excessively gloomy assessment of the situation. I am a middle-of-the-roader. The situation is basically bright, but there are many problems urgently awaiting solutions. It will take a few years before these problems are solved.[125]

Once the Central Work conference opened, however, Mao's patience with the various gloomy assessments of the situation began to wear thin. On August 9, a speaker commented that cadres were only allowed to talk about weaknesses, mistakes, and difficulties and were not permitted to speak of achievements and prospects. This struck a strong chord in Mao, who pushed the argument further and suggested that those who portrayed the situation as all gloomy and pushed for individual farming had doubts about socialism. By this time, Mao appears to have abandoned his earlier distinction between household contracting and individual farming. In making this shift, Mao was influenced by the first party secretary of a big region, probably the radical Ke Qingshi of East China, who commented to Mao: "[We] must not adopt contracting output to the household. Contracting household *is* individual farming, which leads to income polarization. In our region, [areas that] adopted individual farming saw acute income inequality."[126]

In short, the exchanges at the conference led Mao quickly to shift his attitude toward household contracting. To the surprise of conference participants, rather than persisting with his somewhat moderate stance, Mao decided to narrow the boundaries of discourse on rural policy, draw the line for the party, and, most important, shut off those who were probably using references to the rural disaster to undermine his prestige and power; all through his life, Mao tended to overreact to what he perceived as political challenges. In a series of talks at the conference and at the Tenth Plenum (September 24–27, 1962) of the Eighth Central Committee, he launched a sustained attack on what have become known as the three winds: the wind of gloom (*hei'an feng*), the wind of individual farming (*dan'gan feng*), and the wind of reversing verdicts (*fan'an feng*).[127] The crux of his talks was: "Never forget class struggle."

Mao believed that the adjustment measures of the past few years had hurt the collective economy and benefited individual farming. Prefectural and provincial leaders such as Zeng Xisheng, who advocated household contracting, had become representatives of rich peasants and other bad elements.[128] For Mao, household-based farming was the nemesis of the collective economy, just as capitalism was to socialism. In contradistinction to what was actually occurring in the countryside, Mao prophesied that the adoption of household responsibility in China would inevitably lead to the polarization of society (*liangji fenhua*), speculation and profiteering, concubinage, and usury, and the families of soldiers, revolutionary martyrs, workers, and cadres as well as those who enjoyed the five guarantees (childless and infirm old persons who were guaranteed food, clothing, medical care, housing, and burial expenses by the people's commune) would be plunged into poverty.[129] Thus he called for a fundamental solution to this problem (the spread of household-based farming) through class struggle. The party from now on must rely on poor and lower-middle peasants and seek the support of middle peasants in rural affairs.[130] Peasants must be educated to embrace class struggle continually.[131] If the proletariat did not take charge now, he cautioned, the collective economy could not be consolidated and China might turn capitalist.[132] In other words, production team accounting was all right; anything going beyond that fell under the rubric of unhealthy tendencies and ought to be combated. Thus Mao put class struggle at the top of the agenda.

As China's most powerful dialectician, Mao joined his colleagues in emphasizing the need to continue economic adjustment. It was he who pointed out that the slogan "Take agriculture as the foundation" had not really been put into practice since its adoption in 1959.[133] Besides ratifying a second revised draft of the Sixty Articles, which now included provisions for production team accounting and other changes,[134] the plenum also approved one document on grain work and one on the consolidation of the collective economy.[135]

Yet the plenum's message was loud and clear: Economic adjustment had to take place within certain limits, and the political prerogative of defining these limits lay with Mao.[136] Household-based agriculture and other "unhealthy tendencies" were politically unacceptable.[137] Senior leaders who had favored household contracting just a few months earlier now quickly shifted their position to Mao's side and were in fact harsher than Mao was toward household contracting. Liu Shaoqi, for example, chastised Deng Zihui for having abandoned the socialist road and advocated the adoption of household contracting of outputs. Calling individual farming a poisonous weed, he argued that it had no hope. "Only socialist big agriculture can prevent peasants from falling into poverty and bankruptcy," Liu asserted.[138] Tao Zhu also came under heavy pressure at Beidaihe for allegedly promoting individual farming, but he was saved by Zhou Enlai, who explained that Tao advocated contracting management and output to the household and not dividing up the land.

Once the political tide turned at the Tenth Plenum, the characteristics of the bandwagon polity accelerated efforts to suppress household contracting and individual farming. By October 21, the Hunan provincial leadership had submitted to Mao and the Central Committee a detailed program to bring back into collective production teams that had gone into individual farming. The Hunan program termed the struggle over the adoption of household farming "a struggle between socialist and capitalist roads." It provided for discriminatory measures to be applied to those who still adopted household farming.[139] As in October, the new Anhui leadership launched severe attacks on the *zeren tian* as individual farming. By early December, 23 percent of the production teams (about 60,100) that had adopted the *zeren tian* in Anhui had been brought back to collective agriculture.[140]

In the meantime, a socialist education movement emerged and lasted till the end of 1966.[141] At first mainly concerned with matters of cadre style and corruption, the movement later became a campaign to clean up politics, ideology, organization, and economics.[142] Work teams made up of cadres and office workers were sent to villages to mobilize poor and lower-middle peasants in a broad-based investigation of brigade and team cadres in order to strengthen the peasants' faith in the collective economy. Basic-level cadres were urged to emulate their counterparts in Shanxi's Xiyang county, home to the soon-to-be-famous Dazhai brigade, and to labor alongside peasants to prevent revisionist tendencies. In 1964, however, in tandem with the escalation of the Sino-Soviet conflict, what was originally billed as an educational effort turned into a broad attack on basic-level cadres for various misdeeds.[143] Almost two million party officials and administrative cadres in the countryside were subjected to denunciatory struggle sessions and humiliated by fellow peasants.[144] Their morale and authority declined further.

The socialist education movement reinforced the efforts to suppress household-based agriculture by raising the political costs for cadres who continued to support household responsibility. We have relatively little information about how the crackdown on household-based agriculture was carried out. Nevertheless, although by 1964 the majority of the production teams that had practiced household contracting were forced to revive collective labor, throughout the country there were still instances in the summer of 1965 in which basic-level cadres, in order to demonstrate their political rectitude, took over peasants' retained plots (*ziliudi*) and reclaimed land.[145] Needless to say, these excesses caused much dissatisfaction among basic-level cadres and peasants, who feared that the Sixty Articles were being changed. The center had to issue a directive to warn against "blind commandism."[146] While only about one-third of all counties and communes had gone through the motions of the socialist education movement by spring 1966, the center clearly had again prevailed over rural society. Beneath the veneer of conformity, however, powerful impulses for liberalization continued to lurk.

Conclusion

When Mao Zedong and his colleagues launched the Great Leap Forward in the fall of 1957, they, especially Mao, commanded enormous power and prestige among the people for their successful leadership in war and in peace.[147] They drew freely on that social power during the millennial leap. Indeed, many lower-level cadres and activists went further and faster than the center in pursuing various leap policies. For a moment, it appeared that state and society were working in unison.

The famine shattered that harmony. The central leadership, headed by Mao, had to retreat. Latent cleavages became manifest, and party unity was eroded. More fundamentally, the famine disabused the peasants of any illusions they might have harbored about the communes. Instead of staging only a limited retreat from commune-based production, as the Chinese leadership would have liked, peasants and basic-level cadres took advantage of the political relaxation and widely adopted household-based farming. While the data and sources currently available do not warrant statistically rigorous tests and firm conclusions, they (especially the survey in Guangxi) indicate that the more severely an area suffered from the Great Leap Famine, the more likely were peasants and cadres in that area to adopt liberal practices such as household-based farming in the early 1960's. The most outstanding example was the province of Anhui, which suffered the most among all provinces and became prominent for pursuing agricultural liberalization.

Just as the Great Leap Famine very much hinged on the outcome of the Lushan conference, the fate of household contracting was eventually sealed by Mao's interaction with his senior colleagues. One might wonder what the long-term consequences for China's political economy would have been had Mao officially sanctioned contracting output to the household in agriculture in 1962. Certainly the household responsibility system adopted as a major component of the post-Mao reforms would have been unnecessary, since that system was essentially household contracting. Moreover, more of the rural collective structure might have been retained than was the case in the 1980's. Furthermore, one might even speculate whether the political events of the early 1960's and even the Cultural Revolution might have turned out differently.

Yet Mao did turn against household contracting, which the majority of his colleagues had come to favor by the fall of 1962. By attacking a measure that he himself had earlier considered tolerable, Mao again underscored that he was the ultimate political leader in the system, as he had done at Lushan. The irony was that Mao did so in reaction to what his colleagues had done. By going against the crowd and asserting his leadership, Mao allowed himself to be defined by his political environment, albeit negatively.

Moreover, even though Mao could for now mobilize enough political resources to suppress household contracting, he was incapable of erasing the horror of the famine. The Great Leap Famine not only proved a catalyst for struggles within the Chinese elite, as Roderick MacFarquhar so eloquently argues, but also fundamentally reshaped the motivations and beliefs of the people it affected and removed the political base that Mao (and his colleagues) had tapped to launch the Great Leap Forward.[148] As will be argued in the next three chapters, the legacy of the Great Leap Famine was not limited to the early 1960's but endured through the Cultural Revolution decade and provided the underlying incentives for the reform of the late 1970's and early 1980's.

4

The Cultural Revolution Interlude

Rural policy during the Cultural Revolution is commonly referred to as agrarian radicalism, or Maoism. In his comprehensive study entitled *Agrarian Radicalism in China, 1968–1981*, David Zweig sums up the period:

During the Cultural Revolution decade (1966–1976) and continuing in part through the reign of Hua Guofeng (1976–1978), radical leaders in the Chinese Communist Party (CCP) tried not only to mobilize rural society for socioeconomic and political changes that would prevent private interests and inequalities from undermining the collectivization of the 1950's, but to move rural China to even higher stages of collectivism.[1]

Without denying the harmful effect of agrarian radicalism on rural life, however, a number of major rural policy patterns were the legacy of the Great Leap Famine rather than the result of Cultural Revolution radicalism.[2] Not only did the Chinese leaders around Mao keep the team-based rural institutional setup throughout this politically turbulent era, but in response to the famine the state also showed remarkable restraint with regard to grain extraction from rural areas. Ironically, the lower levels of grain extraction also reduced interprovincial grain trade, undermining agricultural diversification and causing provinces with grain deficits to focus on grain production even when their strengths lay in growing cash crops such as cotton and sugarcane. In other words, the emphasis on grain self-sufficiency, which is commonly considered a key component of Maoist radicalism, can be traced back to the impact of the Great Leap Famine.

Meanwhile, as in other oppressive agrarian regimes, including Stalin's Soviet Union, peasants resorted to a repertoire of everyday forms of resistance.[3] Some communities even took advantage of the political paralysis and turmoil to adopt household-based farming and other responsibility arrangements secretly. Moreover, as agriculture became less and less profitable over time, richer collectives increasingly turned to rural industry to improve their economic fortunes.[4]

The Famine, Cognitive Change, and Rural Policy During the Cultural Revolution

In light of the intensification of agrarian radicalism, especially in the last few years of Mao's life and immediately after, it is remarkable that throughout this period rural institutions in China remained largely as they had been in 1962. Specifically, the commune system remained based on the production team despite efforts by radicals to upgrade it to production brigade accounting. Similarly, grain procurement remained relatively stable. Both features can be traced to the cognitive changes wrought by the famine on the Chinese top leadership.

Cognitive Changes Among Top Leaders

I suggested in Chapter 3 that the Great Leap Famine caused both Chinese leaders and the rural population to modify their attitudes toward rural institutions. In particular, it appears that local cadres and peasants made alliances in the aftermath of the famine to liberalize agricultural organizational arrangements. In this section I examine the long-term attitude changes among China's top elites with regard to agriculture, since there should be little doubt about the preferences of peasants in rural organization.

Although systematic data are at present unavailable, it appears that the effect of the Great Leap Famine on the attitudes of the top elite varied according to how closely a leader was involved in agricultural policy-making. While there were exceptions, in general those who were on the front line of agricultural policy-making, including Deng Zihui, Tan Zhenlin, Zhou Enlai, and Mao Zedong, were most likely to change their attitudes toward collectivization significantly and promote more liberal practices. In contrast, urban-oriented leaders, such as Kang Sheng, Ke Qingshi, and the Gang of Four of the Cultural Revolution period, were more likely to call for radical agrarian policies. In this section, I focus on the attitudes of Mao, Tan Zhenlin, and Tao Zhu. (The views of Zhou Enlai will be indicated in passing in the next subsection.)[5]

Mao Zedong. As was pointed out in Chapter 3, Mao was among the very first to pinpoint problems with the Great Leap in the spring of 1959.[6] In the meantime, he began to draw lessons—however inadequate—from the disaster that befell the leap. Around June 1959, Mao mentioned in a private conversation with Wu Lengxi that people like them were probably incapable of governing the economy well and admitted that he had "suffered a defeat" (*da le yici baizhang*) in 1958.[7] Unfortunately, such a realistic assessment was sidetracked at the Lushan conference in July 1959. Over the next year and a half, he sensed that peasants did not have enough to eat, but like the gambler who suddenly loses huge sums of money, he was unwilling to confront the harsh realities and appeared to hope wishfully that things might somehow turn around. Only gradually did Mao regain his senses and begin to reassess the situation. On the first day (August 23, 1961) of the second Lushan conference, Mao summed up what was probably on the mind of most participants: "In building socialism, we do not have a sure program [*meiyou yitao*] and cannot be certain of success."[8] He repeated the same message at the enlarged Central Work conference in early 1962 (the 7,000-cadre conference): "We still largely act blindly [*you henda de mangmuxing*] in socialist construction."

All these comments contrast sharply with the unbridled optimism that seized Mao and most of his colleagues in late 1957 and 1958. Also at the 7,000-cadre conference, Mao offered a sober self-assessment. "Take myself," Mao said, "[I] still do not understand many issues of economic construction. I do not know much about industry and commerce. I know a little more about agriculture, but only relative [to industry and commerce], and it's hardly enough." He mentioned soil science, agricultural chemistry, and other subjects in agriculture as examples of what he did not know, and he urged more study. Mao's overall assessment of himself was very much to the point: "I have paid more attention to questions concerning the system and relations of production, but I know little about productive forces."[9] In other words, institutional changes such as the swift transition to communes would not work when the economic conditions were not ripe, as had occurred during the Great Leap Forward.

In the aftermath of the Great Leap Famine, the production team, not the commune or brigade, became the most appropriate basic unit of rural organization for Mao. The production team provided better balance between efficiency and equity than did production brigades or people's communes, without suffering from the polarizing effects of household contracting and individual farming. While Mao viewed individual farming as "capitalist" and refused to let peasants "go it alone," he also came to realize that China was not yet ready for higher levels of rural organization. Indeed, in the fall of 1962 Mao was close to authorizing the adoption of household contracting formally and appears to have changed his mind because of political considerations. Yet, even though Mao launched the socialist education movement in 1962,[10] championed Dazhai as a model of self-reliance beginning in 1964,[11] and unleashed the Cultural Revolution in 1966, he would never again push for the transition to brigade or commune ownership. Instead of social mobilization, Mao turned to agricultural mechanization and other technical steps for improving agricultural output.[12]

After meeting his Waterloo in the Great Leap Forward, Mao took care to temper his grandiose visions for socialist agriculture and stuck to a cautious approach to agriculture until the end of his life. In late July 1975, Vice-Premier Chen Yonggui, the former head of Dazhai, suggested to Mao that rural China make a rapid transition from team to brigade accounting. Drawing on the experience of Xiyang county in Shanxi, Chen argued that rural organization with the production team as the basic accounting unit served to accentuate inequalities and constrained the collective's ability to undertake water conservation projects and promote agricultural mechanization and asserted that those localities that did well had all adopted production brigade accounting. Claiming support from local cadres, Chen forcefully concluded that "production brigade accounting is inevitable" in order to develop agriculture fully.[13] Instead of giving his assent, Mao was undecided and instructed the Central Committee to discuss the Chen proposal. A forum on rural work, chaired by Deng Xiaoping and attended by Politburo members as well as twelve provincial party secretaries, was convened from September 23 to October 21, 1975. Because of strenuous opposition from a number of provincial leaders, such as Zhao Ziyang and Tan Qilong, the meeting ended in a deadlock.[14] Mao refrained from throwing his political weight behind the transition, even though he could have done so. In consequence, Chen Yonggui's suggestion was laid aside. Ironically, more than a year after Mao's death, a new leadership headed by Hua Guofeng formally endorsed the transition to production brigade accounting by invoking the very authority of Mao Zedong.[15]

Tan Zhenlin and Tao Zhu. As is clear from the last chapter, among the top leaders Tan Zhenlin led in fanning the flames of the Great Leap Forward. Partly owing to his forthright personality, partly because he got to know the rural disaster so closely from his extended trips to Henan, he was also perhaps the most contrite.[16] In spring 1959, he freely admitted that he was misguided in calling for allowing people to eat grain for free. During the Lushan conference of 1959, he again indicated his responsibility for the communization wind and was in favor of dismantling commune mess halls.[17] In 1961, he repeated that the lessons of the Great Leap should be remembered forever and promoted policies that brought peasant initiatives into play. The next year, at the 7,000-cadre conference of February 1962, he intended to present an extended self-criticism on his Great Leap errors and discuss the lessons he had learned. Although Deng Xiaoping asked him not to circulate his speech, he nevertheless made it available to cadres from the agricultural departments.

In 1962, Tan took over virtually all important posts concerning agriculture. He promoted the signing of output contracts between higher levels and communes. Like the risk-averse peasant in disaster-prone societies, he emphasized that the first priority in agricultural planning was the stability of output rather than the maximum growth that the Great Leap Forward was to achieve.[18] The lessons of the Great Leap Forward were so indelibly impressed on Tan's mind that in an article written shortly before his death in 1983, Tan again emphasized that Mao had failed in agriculture because he could not tolerate dissenting voices. Tan admitted that he should also share in the blame, because he had overall responsibility for agriculture during the Great Leap. He wanted others to remember this profound historical lesson.[19]

The attitudes of Tao Zhu, the Guangdong leader, paralleled those of Tan Zhenlin. Joining in the Great Leap fervor in 1958, he concluded that "we have so much grain that we have no place to put it" and called on peasants to eat as much as they liked for free in commune mess halls.[20] Overconsumption and a 35.6 percent decline in Guangdong's grain output in 1958 soon led to crisis and prompted Tao to change his views. In early 1959 he and Hubei's Wang Renzhong were the first two provincial leaders to write to Mao and admit their errors. During the Lushan conference of 1959, he suggested that peasants be allowed to abandon the mess halls, because they preferred to eat at home.[21] This led Mao to point out that Tao Zhu and Hunan's Zhou Xiaozhou were sympathetic to the position of Peng Dehuai.[22]

The brush with rightism at Lushan did not stop Tao from being pragmatic in agriculture. In speeches to numerous meetings, he continued to emphasize the lessons of the Great Leap and his own gullibility.[23] Upon assuming the post of first secretary of the central-south region at the end of 1960, he made his first priority the disastrous situation in Henan, and he supported a proposal from the Henan leadership to loan collective land to peasants for one season. Moreover, as discussed in Chapter 3, Tao also championed the adoption of household contracting. Later I will also note that Tao Zhu fought to keep the Cultural Revolution from disrupting economic production.

The Chinese leadership and agriculture. The efforts by the Chinese leadership to protect agriculture were most visible during the violent phase of the Cultural Revolution (1966–69). Both Zhou Enlai and Tan Zhenlin feared that the Cultural Revolution might cause even greater damage to the rural economy than the Great Leap Forward, and they secured Mao's support in limiting the scope of the Cultural Revolution in rural areas through a series of documents (including "The Stipulations Regarding Cultural Revolution Below the County Level," drafted by Tan Zhenlin and Tao Zhu in fall 1966).[24] "The Rural Five Articles" of September in particular called for giving priority to the autumn harvest and not launching cultural revolution below the county level. In December 1966 Lin Biao and Jiang Qing were able to issue documents calling for cultural revolution in industrial and transport sectors as well as rural areas. Because the radicals' call for class struggle in rural areas led to disruptions in agricultural production, Tan Zhenlin wrote a memo to Mao arguing for putting equal emphasis on production. Mao circulated Tan's memo with approval. And rural areas were called upon to desist from seizing power during spring planting in 1967. In May 1967, Zhou Enlai stated that it was justified to use incentives to stimulate agricultural production and called for providing chemical fertilizers and grain to cotton-growing areas so that these areas might recover more quickly from the ravages of the Great Leap Famine.[25]

When some rural localities did experience grabs for power, the center on November 7, 1967, issued a letter by Chen Yonggui that argued against Red Guards coming to rural areas and emphasized that "the spear of political struggle should absolutely not be pointed at the vast number of rural grass-roots cadres who are on our side."[26] This letter and the formal directive issued by the Central Committee in December 1967 served to protect rural cadres from attacks and stabilize the rural situation. Besides calling for the separation of rural from urban areas during the Cultural Revolution, the Central Committee directive also went out of its way to reaffirm existing rural institutions.[27] It stated that there should not be changes in the system of rural people's communes centered on the production team; private plots (as sanctioned by the Sixty Articles) should also be preserved.

The most conspicuous effort to stabilize the rural situation occurred at what had become known as the northern conference on agriculture. Chaired by Zhou Enlai, the fall 1970 conference of fourteen northern provincial units was convened amid political turmoil. Whereas the conference called for learning from the Dazhai experience, it nevertheless cautioned that local governments should not "indiscriminately copy [the Dazhai experience] without paying attention to local conditions." Most important, the conference sought to counteract the leftist trends in rural politics and emphasized that the Sixty Articles remained appropriate for contemporary rural China and must be implemented. While the collective economy should be strengthened, commune members should be allowed to till a small amount of private land and engage in family sidelines. Similarly, production teams should be given room for operational flexibility so as to avoid a repeat of the Great Leap errors of *yiping erdiao,* that is, the equalization of income and distribution within the commune and the transfer of property and labor from production brigades, teams, and households with little or no compensation.[28] At the end of 1971 and in the first half of 1972, the center again emphasized the need to preserve the existing rural organizational structure based on the production team and prevent "ultra-Left" policies from dampening the enthusiasm of the masses.[29] This refrain—on taking into account the interests not only of the state and the collectives but also of the peasants—would be repeated by Zhou Enlai and others in coming years, though it increasingly came into conflict with the policies sent out by the radicals toward the latter part of the 1970's.[30]

The stabilizing efforts by the central leadership were complemented by the structure of incentives prodding rural residents. As Deng Liqun pointed out, unlike workers and students, who were given salaries or stipends even when they roamed the country, joining up with others in Cultural Revolution activities, rural residents would go hungry if they stopped working. They were not entitled to the various amenities available to urban residents. In consequence, relatively few peasants (and workers in collective enterprises) took part in violence during the Cultural Revolution.[31]

Largely for these two reasons, the violence of the Cultural Revolution generally spared rural China. Richard Baum has found in an early study that only a relatively small percentage of China's villages were directly affected by revolutionary struggles of any kind, and most of those villages were close to urban centers.[32] As William Hinton puts it: "Starting in the universities of Peking, spreading to colleges and middle schools in urban centers, then leaping to factories everywhere, [the Cultural Revolution] tended to lose momentum and dissipate its forces when it hit the countryside."[33] Indeed, some Chinese scholars of the Cultural Revolution have concluded that "one major reason that the turmoil of 1967–76 was sustained was because agriculture suffered relatively little damage and even experienced growth."[34] The continued availability of food permitted the continuing political struggle.

While the violence of the Cultural Revolution was largely confined to cities and suburban areas, its disruptions did affect the rural economy. The transfer of some twelve million youths to the villages between 1969 and 1975 alone disturbed life in the countryside.[35] Yet, unlike the depression of 1959–62, when the downturn in the agricultural growth rate preceded that of industry, it was (urban) industry that was the first to plunge into a recession during the Cultural Revolution, leading to dramatic declines in the production of chemical fertilizers, pesticides, and other agricultural inputs, thereby dragging agriculture into a mild downturn the following year (Fig. 4).[36]

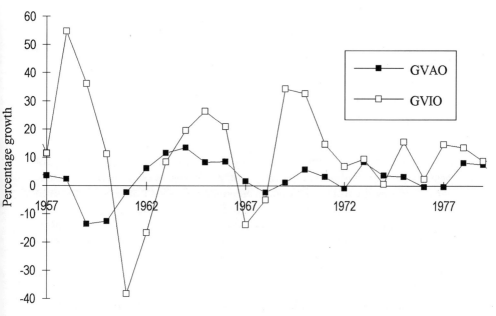

Fig. 4. Gross value of agricultural output (GVAO) and gross value of industrial output (GVIO) growth patterns, 1957–79

The Great Leap Famine's
Long-Term Effect on Rural Grain Extraction

As in any predominantly agrarian economy, the struggle over the division of the rural harvest epitomizes the relationship between state and rural society, which is usually mediated by a Janus-faced elite such as the gentry in Imperial China or rural cadres under the CCP. Among scholars of China, the consensus is that over the late Maoist period the state predominated over rural society. Yet, as the late Kenneth Walker pointed out, from the late 1950's to the late 1970's, growth in state grain extraction lagged far behind increases in production. Even when taking rapid population growth into account, per-capita grain procurement declined while per-capita grain output increased. Given the state's voracious appetite for grain, Walker concluded that there was a government "failure to extract enough grain from the agricultural sector in the late 1970's."[37]

In her *State and Peasant in Contemporary China,* Jean Oi seeks to resolve the apparent anomaly between recognized state capacity and actual extraction by hypothesizing that the state had a hidden agenda: It realistically and flexibly promoted local grain reserves, which gave it "greater control over the disposition of the surplus."[38] In consequence, Oi concludes, the state's interests predominated through a combination of administrative fiat and political pressure, and thus the decreased grain procurement did not reflect state weakness.[39]

Yet, as Victor Nee points out in a review, Oi's hypothesis is ad hoc and not entirely persuasive. In particular, Oi writes as if the state acted as a conscious body, but she does not provide documentation to substantiate the claim that the state (or its leaders) intended to pursue a realistic and flexible strategy of grain control.[40] It is suggested here that the apparent anomaly between state capacity and actual grain appropriation disappears if we take into account the cognitive impact of the Great Leap Famine on the Chinese leadership. Within this framework, one might appropriately interpret the establishment of grain reserves, which the center earnestly urged rural governments as well as peasant households to build up beginning in fall 1962, as one of the knee-jerk reactions to the Great Leap Famine rather than as an act of state cunning.[41] In fact, the 1965 state regulations on the management and use of reserve grain explicitly prohibited the expropriation of grain reserves, forbade increasing the procurement quotas for those localities that had more grain reserves, and stipulated that the reserves be used mainly in case of agricultural disasters.[42] This message was essentially reiterated by Zhou Enlai on May 3, 1967, when he invoked Mao to argue that grain procurement from peasants should be minimal and that it was better to store wealth among the people, especially in the context of war preparedness.[43] In light of the exhaustion of local grain supplies and the state's remarkable helplessness during the Great Leap Famine, what better strategy to avoid a repeat of that sort of disaster than for those who were most vulnerable to become self-insured?

Thus, I argue here that not only did the Great Leap Famine blunt the leadership's desire for higher forms of collective institutions in rural China, but it also produced a lasting effect on the level of state extraction from rural areas. Put concretely, the catastrophic famine led the leadership to reduce the unsustainable levels of grain procurement they had imposed on peasants during the Great Leap Forward. Indeed, the debacle of the leap, coupled with rapid population growth, served to hold down grain taxes and procurement as a percentage of total output through the late 1970's (Fig. 5).[44] These two components of the grain burden are discussed separately below.

Stabilization of the agricultural tax. As Figure 5 indicates, grain procurement—including the agricultural tax and unified grain purchases—reached extraordinary proportions during the Great Leap. It accounted for just under 40 percent of the total output in 1959. As the famine deepened, the center began to retrench. On June 23, 1961, the center approved a report from the Finance Ministry that called for adjusting the agricultural tax burden. The total agricultural tax of 1961 was reduced to

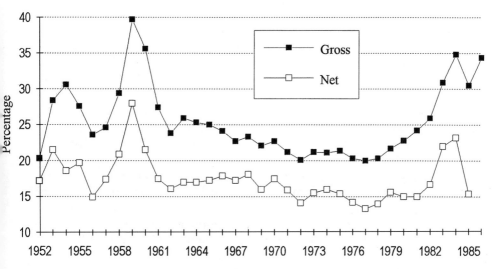

Fig. 5. Gross and net grain procurement as a percentage of output, 1952–86

11.1 million tons of fine grain (flour and rice), a reduction of 42 percent from the actual tax of 1960.[45] In 1962, the agricultural tax was further reduced to 10.75 million tons of fine grain.

In the context of widespread famine, these efforts were clearly too late and woefully inadequate. Nevertheless, the tax reductions contributed to the economic recovery of the early 1960's, when the total amount of agricultural tax and surtax stabilized and stayed at roughly the same amount. Because the rural economy gradually recovered, the total tax as a percentage of output declined from 13.8 percent in 1960 to 7.7 percent in 1964.

As the rural economy recovered, voices for increasing the agricultural tax came to the attention of Zhou Enlai. While Zhou had championed grain export increases in 1959, few central leaders had to confront the Great Leap calamity as directly as he did. As premier of the State Council, he made 115 recorded remarks on the subject of grain between June 1960 and September 1962 and was intimately involved in planning grain production, procurement, transport, and sales.[46] These brutal, bleak years left Zhou with an instinctive distaste for doing anything drastic with agriculture. Brushing aside attempts to increase the agricultural tax, he was reported to say emphatically: "Let it be put on record today that, as long as I am alive, you will not increase the agricultural tax burden. After my death, you should not think of exploiting the peasants at will either."[47] Like Mao, the premier had apparently learned a painful lesson from the Great Leap Famine. Forged during the traumatic famine, the stabilized tax burden became a central feature of state policy toward peasants in China through the late 1970's.

Stabilization of grain procurement. Just as the state reduced the agricultural tax burden, it also put a lid on the amount of grain purchased at state-fixed prices. The latter had been especially excessive during the Great Leap. In 1960, for example, the state procured 42.8 million tons of grain above and beyond the agricultural tax amount. This was reduced to just under 34 million tons in 1961 and to 32 million tons in 1962. Per capita, each rural resident in 1962 sold 20 kilograms (about 44 pounds) less than in 1960.[48]

As with the agricultural tax, the harrowing experience of the Great Leap Famine led the center to conclude that excessive procurement hurt peasant-state relations as well as rural production. In consequence, the center instituted a procurement stabilization program beginning in 1965. The national procurement target was set at 37.75 million tons per year for the 1965–68 period. This was further extended for another three years in 1968. In 1971, the target was set at 38.25 million tons per year for a five-year period (reduced to 37.75 in 1972), a system that lasted till 1978.[49]

The self-imposed restraint on grain extraction led the state to adopt a number of measures to balance its grain ledger during the Cultural Revolution. First, it sought to reduce urban demand. During the famine, this was partly accomplished by simply reducing the amount of grain rations each urban resident was entitled to. In fall 1960, at the height of emergency, the state reduced the monthly allotment for each urban resident by an average of one kilogram per month (1.5 in Beijing) and stopped state grain resales to grain-producing areas.[50] Meanwhile, the state decided to reduce the urban population by sending workers back to the countryside.[51] Some twenty million people had been sent back by 1962. Thereafter, the state imposed a tough caste-like residency registration system in order to limit urban population growth from rural migration. During the Cultural Revolution, a similar strategy was adopted by Zhou Enlai under the new guise of sending urban youths, especially secondary school graduates, to rural areas to be schooled in revolutionary spirit. Between 1969 and 1975, some twelve million urban youths were sent "up to the mountains and down to the villages,"[52] thus somewhat relieving the pressure on urban employment as well as grain distribution.[53]

Second, the state imported a fair amount of grain, although the net amount was far from sufficient. From 1967 to 1976, net import averaged 2.11 million tons per year, in contrast to 4.18 million tons per year from 1961 to 1966 or 10.45 million tons per year from 1977 to 1984 (net imports). Third, the state limited the amount of grain resold to the rural population. Despite rapid population growth in rural areas, the absolute amount of grain resales to rural areas during the 1966–74 period was less than that of 1963–65. When those sales are measured as a percentage of total grain output, the same pattern shows. From 1967 to 1975, it was less than 6 percent, some two percentage points less than that attained in 1964–65 and far less than in the 1980's. Since the rural population experienced rapid growth during this period, the amount of grain resales to rural areas actually declined on a per-capita basis.[54] Finally, when grain procurement appeared particularly difficult amid the political paralysis of the mid-1970's, the state sought to bolster its position as monopsony purchaser of grain. Thus on November 15, 1974, the State Council and the Central Military Commission issued a circular that strictly prohibited administrative institutions, enterprises, and army units from purchasing agricultural and sideline products in rural areas on their own, banned the exchange of state machinery and raw materials for agricultural products, and stipulated that rural units sell to state commercial departments only.[55] The issuance of such a circular suggests that shortages in urban areas had prompted urban units to secure grain and other agricultural products directly from rural areas and bypass the state commercial (rationing) establishment.

Patterns of Rural Extraction and Backward Specialization

The consensus view, shared by post-Mao Chinese officials as well as by both Chinese and foreign scholars, holds that, overall, the Chinese economy stagnated during the Cultural Revolution period (1966–76).[56] In spite of the increased application of modern inputs such as chemical fertilizers and new varieties of seeds, the rural economy saw sluggish growth at best. Using estimates made by Wen on the basis of official data, Justin Lin concludes that in the aftermath of the steep collapse caused by the Great Leap, agricultural total factor productivity did not recover its 1952 level until 1983. From 1959 to the late 1970's, it stayed substantially below the productivity levels reached either before 1959 or after 1982.[57]

This is not the place for a comprehensive assessment of the different explanations of rural economic stagnation during the Cultural Revolution.[58] Instead, I suggest that the conventional view, which attributes agricultural stagnation to the "grain first policy," is not supported by the data. In one of the ironies of history, by stabilizing rural extraction in the aftermath of the Great Leap Famine, the Chinese state inadvertently undermined interprovincial trade in agricultural products, causing backward specialization and reduced agricultural growth.

The myth of the "grain first" thesis. Chinese writings on the rural economy during the Cultural Revolution have taken what I shall term the "grain first" thesis for granted. According to this thesis, agricultural stagnation during the Cultural Revolution was significantly caused by a radical policy that put priority on grain at the expense of economic crops and was embodied in the slogan "Take grain as the key link." As one major Chinese text sums it up:

Within agriculture itself, owing to lopsided emphasis on grain production, which was taken as the key link, cultivation of cash crops, forestry, animal husbandry, sideline production, and fishery were all pushed aside [during the Cultural Revolution]. Things had gone to such extremes as destroying forests for reclamation and building dykes to reclaim land from lakes to boost grain production.[59]

Leading Western scholars of rural China have also tended to accept this thesis, not bothering to note where the argument originated. Jean C. Oi states matter of factly that "during the Cultural Revolution, . . . the policy of 'taking grain as the key link' forced an increasingly large percentage of a team's income to depend on the increasingly unprofitable sale of grain to the state." She refers to this period as one during which "profitable sidelines and cash cropping were criticized, cut drastically, or in some cases completely halted."[60] Similarly, Kenneth R. Walker, one of the most diligent students of Chinese agricultural development, begins his study of post-Mao agricultural changes by characterizing the pre-reform era as "a long period during which . . . grain was expanded at the expense of industrial crops." For him, the "emphasis on maximizing grain production in all provinces of China" was the leading cause of rural stagnation during the years between the early 1960's and 1979. "To meet production and procurement targets," he continues, "regional governments increased the grain sown area by plowing up pasture-land, by reducing the area of industrial crops, and by raising the multiple cropping index."[61]

In discussing the wide acceptance of the grain first thesis, I have deliberately chosen works that refer to China as a whole. There is little doubt that some localities, such as the model village of Magaoqiao in Sichuan, took seriously the slogan of "taking grain as the key link in achieving an all-round development" and planted their fields overwhelmingly in grain rather than cash crops.[62] But such cases should not be taken to represent the whole of China. Moreover, I do not deny that the Chinese state emphasized the priority of grain production in its rhetoric.[63] Abundant contemporary documents attest to the widespread currency of the slogan "taking grain as the key link." It is also likely that the official rhetoric reduced the speed of rural economic diversification more than if the rhetoric had not existed.

Empirical support for the grain first thesis is weak, however. As Perkins and Yusuf note in their review of rural development in China, in 1965–75, "despite the government slogan about taking grain as the key link, Chinese farmers also put greater emphasis on cash crops."[64] As can be seen from Table 12, the need for survival following the famine led to a rise in the share of land planted in grain to 86.7 percent in 1962. With recovery from the famine, that share declined to 83.5 percent by 1965. During the Cultural Revolution, it declined further, to 80.6 percent in 1976–77. Meanwhile, the share of land planted in economic crops rose proportionally, to a little over 9 percent of the total in 1976–77. Thus, rather than expanding at the expense of economic crops, the land planted in grain actually de-

TABLE 12

Share of Crops in Sown Acreage

	Grain	Economic Crops	Other
1952	87.8%	8.8%	3.4%
1957	85.0	9.2	5.8
1962	86.7	6.3	7.0
1965	83.5	8.5	8.0
1970	83.1	8.2	8.7
1975	80.9	9.0	10.1
1978	80.4	9.6	10.1
1979	80.3	10.0	9.7

SOURCE: *ZGNYNJ 1980*, p. 349.

TABLE 13

Crop Output per Mu, 1965–76

(*kilos per* mu)

	Average for 1964–66	Average for 1975–77	Percentage increase
Grain crops	110.7	157.3	42.1%
Rice	197.3	236.0	19.6
Wheat	64.7	108.3	67.4
Corn	100.0[a]	168.3	68.3
Soybeans	55.7	68.7	23.3
Economic crops			
Cotton	27.6	29.3	6.2
Peanuts	72.0	75.7	5.1
Sesame	27.0	27.3	1.1
Jute	159.0	153.0	−3.8
Sugarcane	2,466.0	2,168.7	−12.1
Sugar beets	792.0	520.3	−34.3
Tobacco	85.0	102.3	20.4

SOURCE: Calculated from *Zhongguo nongcun jingji tongji daquan (1949–1986)*.
[a] Average of 1964 and 1965.

clined relative to that planted in economic crops over the course of the Cultural Revolution.

Yet, despite the reduction in the share of land planted in grain, unit output of grain showed impressive growth during this period, growing a little over 42 percent from 1965 to 1976 (Table 13). Of all the grains, rice and wheat account for about 40 percent of all sown areas. The gain in the output of wheat per unit land was a robust 67.4 percent, indicating more productive land use and perhaps also the concentration of grain production on the most fertile land available (the question of total factor productivity is another matter). In comparison, the corresponding figure for rice is just under 20 percent, most likely owing to the deleterious effect of forced double planting. In contrast to the grains, per-unit land output of economic crops in general was stagnant. The two major economic crops, cotton and peanuts, had only 5 or 6 percent output per-unit land increases over this decade. Jute, sugarcane, and sugar beets declined in land productivity. The only bright spot was tobacco (20 percent increase), which accounted for less than half a percent of the total sown area.

The legacy of the Great Leap Famine and backward specialization. In place of the grain first thesis, the view advanced here takes into account the impact of the Great Leap Famine on interprovincial trade patterns. As has been discussed earlier, the Great Leap Famine caused the Chinese leadership to keep rural extraction lower through the 1970's than had the Great Leap Famine not occurred. The reduced extraction led to lower interprovincial trade in agricultural products, especially grain. Following the recovery from the famine, the lower level of interprovincial trade forced grain-producing provinces to put more effort into economic crops and provinces that were especially suited to economic crops to turn to the production of grain.[65] In other words, even though at the aggregate level the percentage of land planted in economic crops could increase, provincial efforts to achieve self-sufficiency would still work against comparative advantage, contributing to the persistence of poverty. That an increase in the percentage of land planted in economic crops nationally may be compatible with individual provinces going against their natural comparative advantage may be illustrated using the following hypothetical case.

Suppose there is an isolated country of two provinces, *A* and *B*, each with ten units of land. All other things being equal, assume that *A* is especially suited to growing grain and would plant nine units of its land in grain and the rest in economic crops if it could fully exploit its comparative advantage through trade; *B* is especially suited to growing economic crops and would plant six units of its land in grain and four units in economic crops under conditions of full interprovincial trade. Now suppose a famine or similar shock occurs and the central government in reaction decides to get less grain from *A* and encourages *B* to grow grain, and it stays with this arrangement. With reduced interprovincial trade, let us say that *A* now devotes seven units of land to grain and three units of land to economic crops; for *B* the ratio also becomes seven to three. Both now seek self-sufficiency in agricultural production. Before the famine five units of land (25 percent) were planted in economic crops in the country, compared with six units (30 percent) after the famine. Thus even though the country devotes more land to economic crops in the aftermath of the famine, it actually is not exploiting the comparative advantages of the individual provinces.

The lack of detailed provincial planting statistics makes it difficult to corroborate directly the hypothesis advanced here. But studies by leading economists on China's rural economy, especially the work of Thomas

Lyons, have produced conclusions that support the hypothesis. First of all, using a variety of statistical indicators, Lyons finds that the range of provincial per-capita grain output narrowed significantly between 1955–57 and 1970–81, with the coefficient of variation in provincial output per capita declining from 0.22 to 0.17.[66] Second, interprovincial grain flows (i.e., internal grain trade) show a decline from the late 1950's to the late 1970's. In the early 1950's, over 6 percent of the total grain output flowed out of the provinces. On the eve of the Great Leap Forward in 1957, 4.7 percent of the total grain output was transferred among the provinces. By 1965, the corresponding figure had declined to just 2.9 percent. By 1978, that figure had become a mere 0.8 percent, and over one-half of this grain was destined for foreign markets.[67] Thus the reduction in government effort to extract grain from the agricultural sector in the aftermath of the Great Leap Famine was related to the decline in the volume of interprovincial grain transfers. According to a careful study by Kenneth Walker, between 1953–57 and 1978 the number of grain-exporting provinces declined from nineteen to eight, and the volume of provincial grain exports fell by 75 percent, from 10 million tons per year to 2.5 million tons. At the same time the number of importing provinces rose from seven to eighteen, increasing the annual volume of grain imports from 7.7 million tons to 11.6 millon tons. The provincial grain trade surplus of 2.3 million tons per year achieved in the 1950's became a deficit of 2.3 million tons in 1965 and rose further to 9.1 million tons in 1978, thus necessitating net foreign imports.[68] In short, the reduction in the amount of internally traded grain, even in the absence of slogans such as "Take grain as the key link," forced grain-deficit areas to concentrate on grain production. In fact, the slogan "Take grain as the key link" came into vogue in fall 1960 in response to the decline in national grain production.[69]

I also suggest here that the changes in agricultural procurement and marketing practices had a deep effect on regional cropping patterns. Rather than specialization according to comparative advantage, provinces sought to be self-sufficient in major agricultural products.[70] Peanut-producing communes expanded the acreage planted in grain and perhaps also oils, while grain-producing areas expanded the acreage planted in economic crops and had less grain to export. The case of cotton exemplified this trend. In the 1950's, 18 percent of the cotton-producing counties accounted for two-thirds of China's total cotton output, with Hebei, Henan, and Shandong producing just under half of the total. By the late 1970's, however, cotton production was dispersed to over 1,200 counties, with most of them planting less than 9,000 acres and the three major cotton-producing provinces accounting for less than one-quarter of China's total cotton output.[71] This dispersal of production from areas especially suited to cotton production is generally believed to have contributed to the stagnation in cotton production. Meanwhile, many of the previous cotton-producing counties had to plant grain even though their land was ill-suited, leading to endemic poverty and begging.

The same pattern of dispersion was evident for a number of other industrial crops.[72] In Fujian, whose comparative advantage was in cash crops such as sugarcane, the province had to devote more of its resources to grain production and yet still had trouble maintaining an adequate grain supply.[73] In contrast, Guangdong's Dongguan county converted high-yield rice paddies to forests in order to become self-sufficient in timber.[74]

Backward specialization and post-Mao grain import policy. Owing to the problem of collective action, the tendency toward fragmentation "is likely to have become self-perpetuating in the absence of forceful and concerted efforts to counter it."[75] As the Chinese leadership debated in 1978 how to improve agricultural performance, a number of key economic officials, including Chen Yun, Li Xiannian, and Yao Yilin, drew on their experiences with economic adjustment during the famine and decided that China should import a significant amount of grain from abroad in order to readjust the structure of agriculture.[76] During his talk at the Central Work conference of late 1978, for example, Chen Yun put top priority on stabilizing the rural situation and stated that China might import twenty million tons of grain per year for three to five years. For Chen, "Once peasants have grain, [the problem of shortages of] cotton, non-staple foods, oils, sugar, and other economic crops may be easily solved."[77] In other words, the center would assume the role of coordinator and shift some of the foreign exchange used for importing cotton and sugar to grain so that those localities that could most profitably cultivate cotton and other economic crops, but had to grow grain for self-sufficiency, might now shift back to economic crops once they were assured of their food supply.[78]

As a result of this decision, China's net grain imports rose steadily from about 7 million metric tons in 1978 to 10.7 million tons in 1979, 11.8 millions tons in 1980, and 13.5 million tons in 1981. The net imports reached a peak in 1982 (15.3 million tons) and then rapidly declined over the next three years as the rural reforms unleashed the productive potential of the rural population. Owing to increased grain imports and higher grain-procurement prices, the state was able to lower grain-procurement quotas and still increase grain resales to rural areas, as is indicated by the increasing gap between gross and net grain procurement in the early 1980's.[79] By 1983, the pattern of fragmentation in cotton production had been largely reversed; the acreage planted in cotton by the three major cotton-producing provinces of Hebei, Henan, and Shandong had risen to more than 51 percent of the national total and their output accounted for more than 56 percent of the national total.[80]

Peasant Initiatives amid Agrarian Radicalism

Not only did rural institutions and state behavior remain relatively stable during the Cultural Revolution; peasants and local cadres also engaged in a variety of local initiatives that advanced their own material interests even as they were bombarded with a rhetoric of radicalism.

The Competition Between Rural Industry and Agriculture

State policies, whether intentionally or not, served to produce an open and dynamic shift from agriculture to industry in rural areas. The reason was simple. On the one hand, agricultural production became more and more unprofitable. In addition to the effect of lower interprovincial trade on agricultural growth, government prices for agricultural products stagnated throughout the Cultural Revolution (Fig. 6). Meanwhile, this period also saw the growing use of modern inputs such as machinery, fertilizers, and pesticides in the countryside, which substantially increased production costs per unit of output. Between 1957 and 1975, while the gross income from agricultural production increased by only 80 percent, produc-

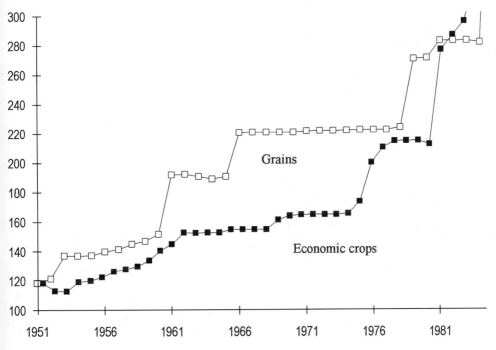

Fig. 6. Index of procurement prices, 1951–83

tion costs jumped 130 percent.[81] Increasing production costs and stagnant prices thus caused agricultural production to become less and less profitable. This undoubtedly contributed to the virtually stagnant standard of living in rural China from the late 1950's to the late 1970's and widespread abject poverty.

On the other hand, profit rates for the production of light industrial goods were set at relatively high levels by the state. Moreover, at the National Planning conference on the Fourth Five-Year Plan (held in February–March 1970), the leadership called for the vigorous construction of local "small industries" such as coal mines, iron and steel factories, chemical fertilizer plants, and machinery shops. In addition to tax relief for new factories, the state also authorized state banks to support them with easy credit.[82] Thus, in addition to providing some relief for growing underemployment in rural areas and producing much-needed goods, rural industries promised better returns than agriculture.

Not surprisingly, local leaders in rural China, especially at the commune and production-brigade levels in more developed areas, took advantage of the changing terms of trade between industry and agriculture and began to channel local resources into rural factories, most of which had been closed down during the famine. Making use of the collective structures erected under Communist leadership and aided by preferential tax and credit policies, local governments embarked on the road to rural industrialization at double-digit growth rates.[83] As a result, the growth trends for agriculture and rural industries were mirror images after 1972

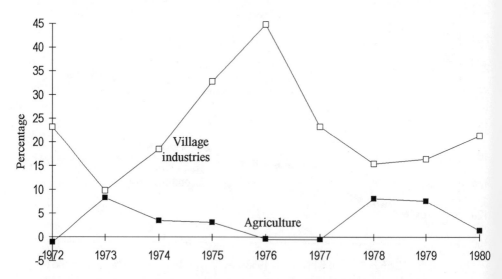

Fig. 7. Agriculture and village industries: contrasting growth patterns, 1972–80

(when data first became available). When rural industrial growth accelerated, agricultural growth decelerated, and vice versa (Fig. 7).

Covert Liberal Practices

As mentioned in the last chapter, practices such as household farming
were mostly (but not completely) eliminated during the socialist education movement that preceded the Cultural Revolution. In Anhui alone,
hundreds of thousands of people, both peasants and cadres, had to pay a
heavy political price through the late 1970's for encouraging or engaging
in household farming in the early 1960's. Many families split up as a result
of the political fallout.[84]

Throughout the Cultural Revolution, the national model for agrarian
radicalism was Dazhai, an isolated Shanxi locale originally extolled for its
spirit of self-reliance by Zhou Enlai, Mao Zedong, and others in 1963–64.
During the Cultural Revolution, Dazhai became known for its egalitarian work point system (remuneration based on both labor and political
evaluations) and its restrictions on sidelines and other so-called bourgeois
rights. From the 1960's to the 1980's, 7.1 million people, including more
than 25,000 foreign visitors, made a pilgrimage to learn from Dazhai.[85]

Yet, the winds of agrarian radicalism notwithstanding, rural residents
appeared to have used the liberal practices of the Great Leap Famine years
as reference points when difficulties arose in agricultural production.[86] In
meetings to recall past sufferings, when participants were supposed to
discuss how bad things had been before the Communists came to power
and how good things had become since then, peasants in areas that had
been hit hard by the Great Leap Famine recalled the famine instead.[87]

In spite of the oppressive political atmosphere, the idea of household
contracting continued to find adherents. Most prominently, amid the intense condemnation of Liu Shaoqi and Deng Xiaoping for advocating contracting in agriculture, Zhang Musheng, a Beijing youth who was laboring
in Inner Mongolia, produced a treatise in 1968 that argued that contracting
output to the household had been proven successful. Zhang's treatise,
which eventually landed him in jail in 1972, was reported in internal publications and fairly widely read. Hu Yaobang, who became CCP general
secretary in the 1980's, was one of the approving readers.[88]

Taking advantage of the political chaos and paralysis that disrupted
planning and increased local power, some localities even adopted some
form of such liberal practices in secret in spite of repeated attempts to snuff
them out.[89] In Sichuan's Luxian county, the Yusi and Fuji districts had
adopted household contracting in 1957, as well as during the Great Leap
Famine. Each time brought a crackdown, but at least some production
teams continued to contract surreptitiously once the work teams from
higher levels left. During the Cultural Revolution, the practice again

spread, and in 1970 181 production teams in Yusi district and 83 teams in Fuji district (10–20 percent of the total) were believed to be using limited household contracting. In some communes such as Yusi commune, the percentage was about 50 percent. Though the county authorities repeatedly sought to eradicate household contracting, the practice continued as localities camouflaged their activities.[90] Another interesting case was Jinqiao village in Jinzhai county. Because of its isolation, the village only learned of and adopted the *zeren tian* in 1962, when the practice was being suppressed in Anhui. But the village persisted with the practice throughout the Cultural Revolution. When a team of cadres from the outside came to suppress the practice in 1974, they were deceived into thinking that the village residents had recanted. As soon as the work team left, the village returned to contracting to the household.[91]

Because of the secrecy and the political complications surrounding such practices, we are unlikely to know fully and accurately the extent of these practices, though Chinese researchers have suggested that the relative resiliency of agriculture during the Cultural Revolution was partly made possible by cadre and peasant resistance to agrarian radicalism.[92] The following examples, which could easily be multiplied, thus serve more as pointers than as firm conclusions. In 1967, when the Cultural Revolution was in its most violent phase, Xinping production team in Guangdong's Gaozhou county took advantage of the political vacuum and delegated production tasks to work groups. Work groups were compensated on the basis of output. The practice was a success. Rice output in the team increased steadily, and per-capita distribution on the team increased from 57 yuan in 1967 to 122 yuan in 1978.[93]

As if the political turmoil in the cities were not disturbing enough, the alleged betrayal of Mao's designated successor, Lin Biao, in 1971 created more skepticism among party loyalists and thus affected the party's command over rural China.[94] More localities were emboldened by the paralysis among elites to jettison major elements of radical policies and adopt measures that linked effort with remuneration.[95] The case of Liwu brigade of Yuanzhou commune in Boluo county (Guangdong) was instructive. In the early 1960's, Liwu brigade had practiced the "three contracts and one reward" system (*sanbao yijiang*), which contributed to doubling output over 1962–65. In 1966, however, the brigade bowed to political pressure and began using the Dazhai work-point system. The egalitarianism entailed in this system undermined peasant incentives for collective production, and gross income in the brigade increased by only 0.45 percent per year from 1965 to 1971. The contrasting performances led cadres and ordinary peasants to conclude that the contract-reward system was superior. In 1971, the brigade secretly began to allocate work points on the basis of outputs. Peasants worked harder and more effectively, a major reason for the 8.5 percent annual growth rate of gross income from 1971 to 1978. Per-capita distribution also rose from 158 yuan to 211 yuan over the same period.[96] Similarly, Jiacun brigade in Jiacun commune of Yinxian county (Zhejiang) began to practice a group responsibility system in the second half of 1973. The fourteen production teams of the brigade were divided into 48 work groups; each group was allocated certain plots of land and responsible for producing a set output.[97]

The political paralysis surrounding the succession struggle after Mao's death in 1976 provided more room for local maneuvers and a new wave of rebelliousness.[98] In addition to the Tiananmen incident of April 1976, urban China witnessed a proliferation of everyday forms of resistance such as absenteeism, sabotage, even labor unrest. In rural areas peasants increased the size of their private plots and concentrated their efforts on those. On the basis of extensive provincial broadcasts from China, Jürgen Domes concluded that

peasants in the communes—in particular in Zhejiang, Jiangsu, Jiangxi, Gansu, and Liaoning—had begun to engage in the "restoration of capitalism." They "speculated," "started small production," and "corrupted the cadres and Party members." They "left agriculture to engage in commerce," and in this way, "the individuals made money while the collective fields were neglected."[99]

Conclusion

There is no doubt that agrarian radicalism, through its onesided emphasis on egalitarianism and on the restriction of sidelines and rural markets, adversely affected the lives of rural residents, especially from the mid-1970's to the reign of Hua Guofeng. There should also be no doubt that the Chinese state was coercive throughout the Cultural Revolution, as numerous authors have pointed out.[100] Over the same years constraints on private marketing and reductions (and in some places elimination) of private plots curtailed peasants' income.[101]

This chapter suggests, however, that major strands of rural policy during the Cultural Revolution were the legacy of the Great Leap Famine rather than the outcome of agrarian radicalism. No matter how radical or utopian Mao might have been at bottom, he refrained from tampering with the team-based organizational framework. As one Chinese writer puts it, "Comrade Mao Zedong was able to absorb the lessons of the 'Great Leap Forward,'" and, despite his leftist errors during the Cultural Revolution, "he was still comparatively careful in economic work."[102]

This chapter also argues counterintuitively that an important cause of backward specialization and agricultural stagnation during this period was the changing pattern of state grain extraction and redistribution. After the Great Leap Famine, the leadership decided to retreat from the excessive grain extractions of the Great Leap Forward and imposed limits on extraction. This restraint, however, also led to severe limits on the ability of the state to use grain redistribution to encourage agricultural production based on comparative advantage, thus causing provinces to pursue self-sufficiency, with or without ideological exhortation. In a sense, the state did too little, rather than too much, during this period (this does not necessarily mean that the various state policies toward the rural population were lenient). The reduced role of the state in assisting regional cooperation led to regional autarchy in agricultural production. Thus in a roundabout manner the Great Leap Famine constrained the policy options open to Chinese leaders when they sought to deal with the perceived agricultural crisis and alleviate the problems of regional self-reliance at the end of 1978.

The rural population, along with other strata of Chinese society, fared poorly during the Cultural Revolution.[103] But a coercive state did not halt the pursuit of interests by rural communities. To be sure, local preferences for more liberal rural policies were severely constrained by the radical policies emanating from the center. Yet various localities still found room, however little it might be, to adopt liberal practices without saying so in public. Furthermore, faced with stagnant agricultural prices, rural communities devoted their resources to more profitable rural industries. Policy stagnation in agriculture thus begot stagnation, but that very stagnation helped fuel the dynamic drive toward rural industrialization. Rural China did not resort to involution. Stagnation and dynamism went hand in hand.

The various central policies, from the socialist education movement to the winds of agrarian radicalism, no doubt severely limited liberal practices such as household farming. Even when a small number of localities adopted such practices during the Cultural Revolution, they had to do it surreptitiously. Nevertheless, by the end of the Cultural Revolution, rural China had had firsthand experiences with virtually the entire spectrum of agrarian organizational forms, from individual household farming to people's communes. The contrast between the rapid recovery in the 1960's following the famine and stagnant agricultural growth during the Cultural Revolution could not fail to persuade the ordinary rural resident which practice was superior in producing the food they needed. In this sense, the state acted as the dam that prevented the waters of reform—which had been deposited by the traumas of the Great Leap Famine—from flowing, but the reach of the state was not unlimited.[104] Once cracks appeared in the dam, as in the mid-1970's, the pent-up desires of peasants and local cadres in some areas were bursting to get out. In so doing, they would be making the waves of reform.

··· 5 ···

Structural Incentives for Rural Reform

The last two chapters dwelled on the effect of the Great Leap Famine on rural policy and practice both in the immediate aftermath of the famine and during the Cultural Revolution. After the famine, the interaction between the state and a rural society in the throes of profound crisis led to widespread liberalization of rural institutions. By early 1962, about one-third of the rural areas had adopted household-based farming under various guises. Although the state then suppressed these liberal rural practices by launching the socialist education movement, the crackdown took two full years and served to further demoralize the rural cadre force. In spite of the oppressive political atmosphere under the socialist education movement and the Cultural Revolution, the legacy of the Great Leap Famine continued. Even during the Cultural Revolution decade, the actions of the Chinese leadership reflected lessons learned from the Great Leap debacle. In this and the next chapters, I extend the argument about the legacy of the Great Leap Famine into the era of post-Mao reforms. Put simply, the Great Leap Famine furnished the structural incentives for peasants and their allies to take advantage of the political opportunity opened up by Mao's death and the succession struggle and to pursue liberalization in rural China.

It is important to point out at this juncture that the word "structure" is used here not to denote something static or causally deterministic.[1] Instead, it is inherently dynamic. By the historical structure of reform, I mean the pattern of incentives or desires and preferences that were forged in the trauma of the Great Leap Famine. As such, this structure was itself the product of interactions between elites and peasants in a revolutionary state. The depth of the trauma ensured that the structural incentives became deeply embedded in China, with its depth (or degree of embeddedness) varying with the severity of the famine.

For almost two decades the state took a high-handed approach and imposed a set of collective institutions on rural society. Yet much of Chinese rural society retained an alternative agenda derived from the lessons of the Great Leap Famine. As will be discussed in this and the next chapter, this alternative agenda was put into action when the Chinese leadership became embroiled in succession struggles after Mao's death. Thus the structural incentives produced by the Great Leap Famine prompted peasants and their allies to take actions not officially sanctioned.

In the rest of the chapter, I first discuss the perceived agricultural crisis that confronted China and then document the elite fissures over how to deal with that challenge following the death of Mao. Discord at the top created the political space for acting out unofficial practices. I then follow with a statistical evaluation of the propensity for reform across the provinces. Statistical tests from a number of angles suggest that there were fundamental links between the severity of the Great Leap Famine and rural institutional patterns in the early years of the reforms.

Elite Cleavages and the Expansion of Political Space

The Agricultural Challenge

Several years before Mao's death, the Chinese leadership came to realize that the country faced serious challenges in agriculture. In early 1973, Premier Zhou Enlai became deeply concerned that the amount of state grain sales, the total wage bill, and the number of state employees all exceeded planned figures in 1972. In knee-jerk reaction, Zhou ordered a hiring freeze in the state sector so as to restrain the growth of wages and of rationed grain sales. On the supply side, the state stepped up financial investment in agriculture to boost grain production and drew on its meager foreign exchange reserves to import grain for urban consumption. In 1974, the State Council and the Central Military Commission prohibited army units from selling or exchanging army-produced grain for other goods.[2] The leadership hoped that these measures would allow it to balance grain revenue and expenditure in 1973. It also hoped that grain reserves in 1974–75 could be replenished to the level of 40 million tons or above.[3]

Yet this patchwork of measures did not provide a long-term solution to grain shortages. Over the 1971–76 period, the state grain ledger balanced in only one year (1974, with a 2.1 million ton surplus). Overall, the grain deficit over the six years amounted to more than ten million tons.[4] At the time of Mao's death, even though total grain output had increased during the Cultural Revolution, per-capita grain consumption in China scarcely improved over the prefamine level of twenty years earlier. The production of cotton, the chief raw material for the textile industry, was in even worse straits. As can be seen from Table 14, while grain output stagnated, cotton output actually declined by 16.7 percent over the 1974–77 period.

A variety of factors contributed to the stagnant per-capita grain availability in China. A major one was the rapid population growth that followed the Great Leap Famine. Without accurate census figures, Chinese leaders at the time of Mao's death did not know what China's total population was. But they sensed a grim situation. Whereas the Chinese media usually referred to the ballpark figure of 800 million, Vice-Premier Chen Yonggui revealed in a 1976 meeting that the central leaders had an internal estimate of more than 900 million.[5] The challenge of feeding a rapidly expanding population became especially acute shortly after Mao's death. According to Zhang Pinghua, then minister of propaganda, the government in spring 1977 had only ten months' supply of grain left. Many warehouses were empty, and the foreign exchange reserve was almost exhausted. "At that point," said Zhang, "we, in a gamble, still appropriated reserve grain and used up all our foreign exchange to buy sugar, to import edible oils and flour."[6]

TABLE 14

Planned and Actual Outputs of Grain and Cotton, 1974–81

Year	Grain (million tons)		Cotton (million tons)	
	Planned	Actual	Planned	Actual
1974	270.0	275.3	2.55–2.65	2.46
1975	280.0	284.52	2.60	2.38
1976	290.0	286.31	2.60	2.06
1977	297.5–300.0	282.73	2.50–2.60	2.05
1978		304.8		2.17
1979	319.8 (1978)	332.1	2.42 (1978)	2.21
	312.5 (1979)		2.40 (1979)	
1980	350.0 (1977)	320.6	3.00–3.375 (1977)	2.71
	347.1 (1978)		2.46 (1978)	
1981	342.5	325.0	2.55	2.97

SOURCE: *ZGZSN*, pp. 371, 378, 380, 391, 394, 417; *JDJ*, pp. 379, 387, 410, 429; *ZGTJNJ 1983*, pp. 393–94.
NOTE: For some years, planned outputs were adjusted; and the years in parentheses indicate the planned target announced during that year.

Elite Disagreements over Rural Policy

Post-Mao leaders could easily agree that agriculture was a problem, but they had difficulty finding solutions. With Mao's death in September 1976, there were two divergent policy positions within the Chinese leadership for dealing with the agricultural crisis. One, a soft strain of agrarian radicalism, was associated with Hua Guofeng, Mao's chosen successor, and his associates Chen Yonggui and Ji Dengkui.[7] The other, a moderate stance, was associated with Deng Xiaoping (who was purged again in spring 1976 but returned to power in July 1977), Chen Yun, and their followers. For the sake of convenience, I focus on the positions of Hua and Deng in this section, though it should be kept in mind that others, especially Chen Yun, exerted important and more direct influence on rural policy in the late 1970's.

Over the 1973–75 period, Deng Xiaoping and Hua Guofeng had been allies against the radicals in the factional struggle for succession to Mao.[8] Yet Deng and Hua already had differences on rural policy before Mao's death, which were partly revealed during the First National Conference on Learning from Dazhai in Agriculture (September–October, 1975).[9] During the conference, Deng and Mao's wife, Jiang Qing, made diametrically opposed remarks, so much so that neither speech was officially published at the time. Deng pointed out that "grain output in some counties and prefectures is lower than in the 1950's" and the per-capita agricultural output value for 22 provincial units was merely 124 yuan. For Deng, agriculture, like other sectors, required rectification. Learning from Dazhai called for honest work. Jiang Qing, however, disagreed with Deng's gloomy assessment of the rural situation. She advocated anticapitalist mobilization and class struggle and regarded Deng and Hua's speeches as revisionist.[10]

Hua Guofeng took a position between Jiang's radicalism and Deng's moderate stance. "For most parts of China," Hua conceded in his summary report, "the rural people's communes' present system of 'three-level ownership,' with the production team as the basic accounting unit' is in the main still in harmony with the growth of productive forces in the countryside." Yet, the basic thrust of Hua's speech clearly diverged from Deng's. Hua called for building Dazhai-type counties all over the country and expanding the collective economy in order to realize "a step-by-step transition to the system of ownership that takes the production brigade or even the commune as the basic accounting unit when conditions are ripe."[11]

A year or so later, after both Deng and the Gang of Four had been purged, Hua apparently recognized that China faced major difficulties in agriculture. Yet, as Mao's anointed successor, he continued to espouse a radical rural development policy. The first national meeting convened under Hua's leadership was the Second National Conference on Learning from Dazhai in Agriculture (December 1976). In his speech to the meeting, Hua called for "a new upsurge . . . in the great revolutionary mass movement to further expose and criticize the 'Gang of Four' and learn from Dazhai in agriculture and build Dazhai-type counties all over the country." [12] Specifically, as embodied in Chen Yonggui's report on the "new upsurge," the program called for suppressing capitalist tendencies such as expanded private plots, rural trade fairs and household sidelines, and the division of land to individual households, stepping up land capital construction and agricultural mechanization, and consolidating and developing the system of people's communes. [13] By August 1977, over 1.7 million cadres from 29 provinces had reportedly been dispatched to the countryside to help implement this radical program. [14]

In short, the Hua regime stuck to Mao's legacy in agricultural development by continuing to emphasize mobilization in lieu of economic incentives. After all, the motto of Hua was expressed in the two "whatevers" contained in a *People's Daily* editorial: "Whatever policies Chairman Mao formulated we shall all resolutely defend; whatever instructions Chairman Mao gave we shall all steadfastly abide by!" [15] However, in contrast to 1975, when the presence of Deng partly deflected the implementation of policies advocated by the radicals, the Hua program dominated rural policy from the end of 1976 to the spring of 1977, though that dominance was threatened when Deng Xiaoping was returned to power in July 1977.

Besides the Second Learning from Dazhai conference, a few other policy milestones of the Hua regime serve to illustrate its approach to rural policy. On January 19, 1977, the Central Committee issued the "Report on Basically Achieving the Mechanization of Agriculture by 1980." The report, reaffirmed in January 1978, stipulated the impossible task that 70 percent of agricultural work be done by machinery by 1980, thereby necessitating a 66 percent increase in the number of tractors in just four years. [16] In agricultural capital construction, a similarly monumental goal was proclaimed at a national conference held in July–August 1977. [17]

Hua reiterated his radical rural program in his speech to the Eleventh Party Congress held in August 1977, calling for transforming one-third of all counties into Dazhai-style counties during the Fifth Five-Year Plan (1976–80) and for further strengthening and developing the collective economy centered on the commune. [18] In December 1977, the Central Committee (Document no. 49) urged all levels of party organizations to enthusiastically create the conditions for advances from team to brigade accounting as part of the effort to popularize Dazhai-style counties. [19] During the winter of 1977 and spring of 1978, about 10 percent of the brigades were urged to adopt brigade accounting, up from about 7.7 percent in late 1977. Chen Yonggui's 1975 suggestion to Mao, thwarted then by provincial opposition and Mao's own prudence, was now enacted into policy under Hua. The call for institutional change was combined with a provision for demolishing capitalist forces and weakening the capitalist tendencies among the people.[20] Indeed, as late as March 1978, Hua Guofeng and his supporters were able to put into the newly proclaimed Chinese Constitution, the third in as many decades, the stipulation that "a production brigade may become the basic accounting unit when its conditions are ripe." While it was conceded in the same article that "commune members may farm small plots of land for personal needs, engage in limited household side-line production, and they may also keep a limited number of livestock in pastoral areas for personal needs," these were permitted on condition that "the absolute predominance of the collective economy of the people's commune is ensured."[21]

In short, the agrarian policy of the Hua interregnum centered on the nationwide emulation of Dazhai in agriculture and rural affairs and the promotion of brigade accounting. "The use of a single national model," as Tsou and others put it, "was a concrete expression of the centralizing impulse" of politics under Hua.[22] With drums and gongs in huge mobilization rallies, there was during this period a spate of transitions to brigade accounting, often accompanied by the transfer of resources to higher levels without adequate compensation. Restrictions on the private sector were intensified, including tightened controls on cash crops in private plots and limits on the number of small household animals, such as chickens, ducks, and pigs, each household could raise.[23] The most striking evidence of agrarian radicalism during 1974–78 is indicated by the data in Table 15. While the commune and brigade levels' share of rural income grew, the team share steadily declined from over 85 percent in 1974 to just under 68 percent in 1978. The most drastic decline, 7.1 percentage points, occurred in 1977, when Hua's influence was at its zenith.

TABLE 15

Income Distribution Among Different Levels of the Commune System, 1974–79
(100 million yuan)

Year	Commune		Brigade		Team		Total amount
	Amount	Percentage of total	Amount	Percentage of total	Amount	Percentage of total	
1974	61.4	7.6%	57.5	7.1%	686.6	85.3%	805.5
1975	105.0	9.6	114.1	10.5	871.4	79.9	1,090.5
1976	141.6	12.1	149.2	12.8	876.7	75.1	1,167.5
1977	205.2	15.9	206.9	16.1	876.3	68.0	1,288.4
1978	228.1	15.7	238.2	16.4	986.3	67.9	1,452.6
1979	269.2	16.4	249.1	15.1	1,128.0	68.5	1,646.3

SOURCE: *ZGNYNJ 1980*, p. 383.

Deng's Political Revival and the Rise of Moderate Rural Policies

It was against a background of continuing agrarian radicalism that Deng was returned to power in July 1977.[24] Yet, as the preceding discussion indicates, until the spring of 1978, Deng's return, though strengthening the moderates, had no immediate effect on Hua's fervent championship of the Dazhai model. China's rural policy at the national level remained oriented toward agrarian radicalism, as shown in Hua's call for more transitions to brigade accounting at the end of 1977. (Local variations in rural policy implementation will be discussed in chapter 6.)

Behind closed doors, even as the media extolled the policies of learning from Dazhai and agricultural mechanization, the moderates had begun to seek change in the radical rural policy. The major advocates for moderation were from provinces such as Anhui. For the moment, however, they lacked sponsorship at the very top of the political hierarchy, and their ideas barely went beyond the meeting rooms. For example, at a meeting on agriculture in November 1977, provincial party secretaries in charge of agriculture called for rectifying the tendency toward egalitarianism in income distribution and reinstating payment according to labor. These suggestions were not immediately adopted, however, because the chairman of the meeting was unwilling to stick his neck out during Hua's push for Dazhai-style counties.[25] Similarly, in December 1977, at a centrally sponsored meeting of agriculture and forestry departments, cadres from the provinces complained of the uncompensated commandeering of property from peasants and teams, saying that peasants were harshly exploited during the Cultural Revolution. They called for the implementation of the 1962 Sixty Articles and drafted eight suggestions for rectifying commune and brigade management and improving agricultural performance. The suggestions, along with a draft *People's Daily* editorial supporting them, were submitted to the central leader overseeing agriculture, Ji Dengkui. But Ji shelved the suggestions and the editorial with the comment that currently "there is a lot of talk on policy issues and one should not hastily make one's opinions known."[26] Advocates for moderation had to bide their time.

That time came with the debate on the criterion of truth, which was formally launched with the publication of a special commentator's article, titled "Practice Is the Sole Criterion of Truth," in *Illumination Daily (Guangming ribao)* on May 11, 1978.[27] Masterminded by Hu Yaobang, then vice-president of the Central Party School, the article was planned for publication without Deng's knowledge.[28] Yet Deng made its theme the centerpiece of his speech at the Army Political Work conference in June and lent his prestige to those challenging Hua Guofeng's "whateverism."[29] For if there were objective measures of truth, then it would be difficult to sustain

Hua's propositions that whatever Mao had said or decided must be up-
held. By reshaping the epistemological landscape in which policy debates
occurred, the truth criterion thus undermined the legitimacy of Hua Guofeng, who claimed the scriptural authority of Mao's words.

As the truth-criterion debate progressed throughout the latter half of
1978, the political situation became more fluid. As one goes over the yel-
lowed pages of the *People's Daily*, one can easily sense the tensions in the
articles on rural policy. On the very same page in which "Practice Is the
Sole Criterion of Truth" was reprinted, for example, the paper also carried
a shorter article on rural labor management headlined "Criticizing the
Tendency of Egalitarianism," praising the county party committee of Pi-
xian in Sichuan for reintroducing task rates and quotas into rural work.[30]
(For publishing the "Practice" article, Hu Jiwei, chief editor of the *People's
Daily*, came under tremendous pressure from a number of orthodox party
leaders in charge of ideology and culture.)[31] The very next day, on May 13,
however, the *People's Daily* was forced to reprint, on the front page, a long
report—originally published in the *Shanxi Daily* on April 21—lauding the
experiences of Xiyang county, where Dazhai is located, in mobilizing the
socialist enthusiasm of peasants.[32] Yet, as if to counterbalance the report
on Xiyang, the May 13 edition also printed on page 2 a report on Guangdong's 16 measures aimed at reducing the burdens on production teams
and strengthening agricultural production.[33] In short, during much of
1978, moderate as well as radical policies jostled for position in the nation's
most important newspaper, thereby projecting an image of instability in
China's rural policy.

As the truth-criterion debate chipped away at the legitimacy of the Hua
Guofeng group, there was a detectable tilt toward moderation in a number
of key rural policy developments. The catch phrase "Learning from Dazhai in agriculture" was mentioned less and less, and attention was increasingly devoted to righting past wrongs (including giving production
teams more decision-making power), reviving rural trade fairs, and reducing peasant burdens—measures harking back to the early 1960s.
Xiangxiang county of Hunan, Hua Guofeng's home base, was praised in a
Central Committee document of June 23, 1978, for leading the way in easing the burdens imposed on peasants. The burdens included a poor remuneration structure, low income, egalitarianism, and indiscriminate requisition of team property. And a campaign was launched to study the
Xiangxiang experience nationwide.[34]

If Xiangxiang county perhaps represented an attempt on the part of
Hua Guofeng to move closer to the moderates, even though in so doing he
had to modify his own stance publicly, the case of Anxiang county, also in
Hunan, undoubtedly undermined his authority on rural policy and put
his personal prestige on the line. That county was a model Dazhai-style

county, the pillar of Hua Guofeng's agrarian program. Yet it was found that the county had falsified grain output figures over 1975–77. In order to meet state procurement amounts calculated on the basis of the falsified figures, even peasant reserve grain was requisitioned. As a result, peasant enthusiasm declined, as did grain output.[35] The county, now a fallen idol, was prominently featured on the front page of the *People's Daily* for having recanted. Indeed, a year later, Dazhai itself was similarly exposed.

Soon after the truth-criterion debate was launched, opponents started to repeat a general attack on the rural policies of Hua Guofeng, Ji Dengkui, and Chen Yonggui. "The problem of feeding hundreds of millions of people has by no means been solved," declared the *Illumination Daily* on May 22, 1978.[36] This was exactly the opposite of what Ji Dengkui had told his American visitors a year earlier, saying "We now have solved [the] problem of feeding [our] country."[37] Indeed, under the circumstances, perhaps the most damaging evidence and the most pressing challenge to the Chinese leadership were the continued agricultural stagnation, even decline. In 1977, China's grain output of 282.75 million tons was 3.55 million tons less than in 1976. Cotton output was also disappointing, reaching 40.8 million *dan*, 130,000 *dan* less than the already low output of 1976. The procurement of hogs was down, and market supply of agricultural-based items was uncertain.[38] To cover the 1977 shortfall and to ensure supplies to an urban society recovering from the political trauma of the Cultural Revolution, the state, in addition to limiting grain (award) sales to rural dwellers,[39] had to import 6.955 million tons of grain, 19.01 million *dan* of cotton, 0.29 million tons of oil, and 1.238 million tons of sugar in 1978. The import of these products cost $2.1 billion, fully one-fifth of China's foreign currency reserve at the time.[40]

The agrarian radicalism of Hua and Chen was evidently not living up to its promise in economic results. In October 1978, two prominent Chinese economists, Yu Guangyuan and Xue Muqiao, went on record to criticize the system of Dazhai work points.[41] Hua's fortunes in rural policy, as elsewhere, were clearly going downhill. Instead, "new" policies were to be introduced in accordance with the principle of "to each according to his work." Domestic sidelines and village trade fairs were also relegitimated. These policies did not constitute a political "reversal," explained a *People's Daily* commentator, but represented the true spirit of Mao.[42]

These different threads were pulled together in a *People's Daily* front-page article on October 6, 1978, by Hu Qiaomu. A former secretary to Mao and participant in the 1962 rural investigations, Hu now served as the president of the Chinese Academy of Social Sciences. His article, titled "Observe Economic Laws, Speed up the Four Modernizations," marked a turning point in the offensive against Hua's orthodoxy.[43] In the section on agriculture, Hu called for narrowing the price scissors between industrial and agricultural products and, apparently alluding to the adjustment policies of the early 1960's, for protecting and expanding the decision-making power of production teams. According to Hu, that power ought to be secured through the use of contracts with entities such as the commune. Only in so doing, Hu argued, could China leave twenty years' sluggish agricultural development behind. Otherwise, "a modern, prosperous and powerful socialist China cannot be built on the basis of a poor and backward countryside."[44]

Internally, the rural situation was analyzed in even starker terms. For example, the October 25, 1978, issue of the Central Party School's bulletin, which was under the control of Hu Yaobang, published an article entitled "[We Should] Absolutely Not Expropriate [the Labor of] Peasants." The article pointed out that peasants carried unreasonably heavy burdens, which were in essence outright expropriations made in the name of building socialism. Thus irrigation projects were launched using corvée labor, with production teams having to furnish the money and grain needed. Community enterprises were established by getting labor and levies from production teams. According to the article, such actions "seriously damaged the worker-peasant alliance and hurt the vitality of agriculture."[45] Vice-Premier Li Xiannian and a number of other leaders did not mince words when pointing to the political implications of rural stagnation. Upon hearing a report at the National Grain conference on October 20, 1978, Li commented: "Without reassuring [the interests] of the eight hundred million peasants and making it possible for their life to gradually improve, we *cannot consolidate our political power.*"[46] Twenty-two years earlier, at the Eighth CCP National Congress in 1956, Deng Zihui had made almost exactly the same point.[47]

In short, in contrast to the bandwagon polity of the 1950's, which served to exacerbate the effect of central policies during the Great Leap Forward, the Chinese political system as of late 1977 was characterized by cleavages at the top. Central leaders took two divergent, but relatively well-defined, positions on rural policy. Such cleavages meant the deconcentration of power and sanctions in the system, which in turn provided political space for some local elites to pursue their own policy agendas. As will be discussed in Chapter 6, cadres and peasants in some localities took advantage of the politically ambiguous situation to resurrect and pursue practices such as household contracting. But why did some localities aggressively pursue liberal or reformist practices such as contracting while other localities persevered with collective arrangements? In the rest of this chapter, I examine the structural factors causing such variations among China's provinces.

Structural Incentives for Rural Institutional Change

Measurement of Reform Propensity

What makes a province more likely to adopt reformist practices? To answer the question, one may start with a temporal measure of the progress of reforms in the provinces, focusing on the adoption of the household responsibility system, which was the centerpiece of the rural reforms. Unfortunately this is easier said than done. So far, detailed time-series data on the adoption of the household responsibility system are available beginning with 1981 only.[48] By then, the political fate of the household responsibility system had been sealed. More important, certain pent-up structural incentives that were present at the start of the rural reform might have been released and can no longer be captured in analyses using post-1981 data.

Nevertheless, the Chinese authorities have published data on the percentage of production brigades that adopted brigade-level accounting for the 1979–81 period. Both the radicals and the Hua Guofeng regime promoted the transition from production-team accounting to production-brigade accounting, with the latter being regarded as more socialist than the former. In contrast, the reforms involved the virtual dismantlement of brigade and team-accounting practices in favor of assigning responsibility to the peasant household. Therefore, the percentage of brigades with brigade accounting, or the brigade-accounting rate, in a province is a good indicator of the extent to which that province followed radical agrarian policies or reforms. A higher brigade-accounting rate indicates a province more inclined toward agrarian radicalism; conversely, a lower percentage implies a comparative aversion to agrarian radicalism and a greater propensity for reform (see Table 16, cols. 3 and 4). By this measure, Beijing, Tianjin, Hebei, Shanxi, Inner Mongolia, Heilongjiang, Shandong, and Xinjiang were evidently more inclined toward agrarian radicalism, while Anhui, Jiangxi, Henan, Hunan, Guangxi, Guizhou, Yunnan, Gansu, and Ningxia stayed away from it.

The Cultural Revolution and the Propensity for Rural Reform

Because of the oft-mentioned causal relationship between the dismal economic performance during the Cultural Revolution and the launching of the reforms, I begin by testing this relationship as a hypothesis rather than taking it for granted.

I collected data on the percentage change in the indexes of provincial gross agricultural output (with rural industries excluded) from 1965 to 1977 and from 1974 to 1977 and the percentage change in provincial grain outputs from 1965 to 1977.[49] According to the hypothesis, one or more of

TABLE 16
Data Used in Analyses of Reform Propensity

Province	Death[a] (%)	Brigade[b] (%) 1979	Brigade[b] (%) 1981	Brigade change[c] (%)	Distance[d] (km)	Party[e] (%)	Income[f] (yuan) 1978	Income[f] (yuan) 1979	Income[f] (yuan) 1981	Rice[g] (%)
Tianjin	14.87%	21.91%	15.32%	30.06%	137	—	1049	1158	1275	6.51%
Shanxi	18.33	35.03	22.55	35.62	514	2.92%	282	351	378	0.27
Shaanxi	22.12	9.36	5.53	40.91	1206	1.15	256	292	295	3.96
Shanghai	23.53	7.95	2.13	73.15	1462	—	2247	2354	2520	61.31
Inner Mongolia	25.48	14.67	13.31	9.29	686	1.78	257	273	320	0.40
Zhejiang	27.50	8.77	5.81	33.81	1651	0.78	290	370	465	74.08
Heilongjiang	28.86	16.52	15.32	7.28	1388	1.38	488	506	586	3.08
Ningxia	29.16	2.51	0.87	65.43	1507	—	282	302	332	6.86
Beijing	35.00	37.76	34.83	7.77	0	—	1037	1115	1246	9.30
Xinjiang	35.25	11.11	10.84	2.44	3774	1.27	273	313	389	4.27
Jiangxi	36.83	0.28	0.18	33.97	2005	1.39	243	290	326	89.48
Hebei	44.07	10.66	7.90	25.94	283	3.14	315	345	364	1.80
Yunnan	48.59	0.28	0.12	55.86	3554	0.98	203	222	261	30.45
Jilin	56.42	4.35	1.69	61.26	1146	1.62	330	359	418	7.23
Guangdong	57.84	3.87	2.59	33.17	2324	0.93	321	354	473	80.19
Jiangsu	68.81	2.04	1.46	28.43	1157	1.37	359	440	500	40.62

Province										
Shandong	91.35	12.74	8.92	30.01	494	2.14	273	304	404	1.70
Fujian	92.86	7.09	4.68	33.97	2623	1.06	236	255	354	77.23
Hubei	111.30	10.64	5.09	52.14	1229	0.77	297	370	418	50.07
Liaoning	111.69	4.52	3.23	28.54	841	1.75	610	642	710	12.66
Guangxi	141.80	0.42	0.25	39.89	2465	0.85	189	210	266	70.98
Hunan	162.50	0.92	0.25	72.31	1628	0.80	248	303	342	81.48
Gansu	186.81	0.89	0.51	43.01	1882	1.54	292	297	296	0.13
Henan	208.57	0.98	0.57	41.62	695	1.08	205	236	291	4.38
Sichuan	239.62	2.79	1.46	47.78	2048	0.71	212	252	288	30.34
Qinghai	272.26	3.52	1.76	49.99	2098	1.04	330	337	328	0.00
Guizhou	285.50	0.95	0.04	95.86	2917	0.86	156	174	203	33.34
Anhui	474.86	1.34	0.61	54.61	1092	0.83	222	244	305	35.31
Mean	105.43	8.35	6.01	40.50	1529	1.34	425	452	513	29.20
Std. Deviation	108.56	9.72	8.08	21.47	967	0.65	422	439	469	31.20

SOURCE: See Appendix.

[a] Percentage increase in mortality rate = (highest mortality rate during 1959–62 – average mortality rate for 1956–58) ÷ average mortality rate for 1956–58.

[b] Percentage of brigades still practicing brigade accounting.

[c] Percentage change in brigade accounting rate from 1979–81.

[d] Distance between the provincial capital and Beijing.

[e] Percentage of population who were CCP members as of mid-1956. Ningxia was included in Gansu. Dash = data unavailable.

[f] Per-capita national income.

[g] Percentage of grain crops planted in rice, 1981.

these indexes are expected to have statistically significant relationships with the measure of provincial reform propensity. In other words, one expects to see a higher propensity for reform in a province with poorer rural economic performance during the Cultural Revolution.

In fact, I found no statistically significant relationships between these variables and the percentage of brigades with brigade accounting in 1979 or 1981 or the changes in brigade accounting rates over 1979–81. These results were expected in light of the discussion in Chapter 4 that the Cultural Revolution was mainly urban. They lead us to the conclusion that the provincial patterns of rural economic performance during the Cultural Revolution had no systematic influence on the propensity for rural reform in China's provinces.

Determinants of the Propensity for Rural Reform

Famine effect. Two alternative hypotheses are formulated in place of the Cultural Revolution thesis. The first hypothesis refers to the causal link between famine-induced cognitive change and institutional innovation. As Nisbett and Ross point out in their discussion of psychological research: "The more vivid the information is, the greater its impact can be on inferences that occur at some temporal remove from the initial exposure to the information."[50] Therefore, I expect that people in those provinces that suffered more from the Great Leap Famine would be more likely to adopt reformist practices than people in provinces that were less affected.

> *Hypothesis 1*: The more a province suffered during the Great Leap Famine, the more painful the lesson was for the province as a collective and the less likely the province to favor measures of agrarian radicalism, such as brigade accounting.[51] In other words, the severity of the Great Leap Famine in a province is a good indicator of the cognitive changes the famine wrought on the population and hence of the incentives for reform in the province.[52]

Spatial effect. The second hypothesis pertains to the perennial difficulties of maintaining central authority in a large country beset by inadequate transportation. In *Economy and Society*, Max Weber explicitly considered this issue with regard to decentralized patrimonial domination: "Even under purely bureaucratic patrimonialism no administrative technique could prevent that, as a rule, the individual parts of the realm evaded the ruler's influence the more, the father away they were from his residence."[53] In general, since the size of a country and the conditions of transportation remained relatively stable, especially in premodern times, central authorities sought to counteract the centrifugal forces by making local elites dependent on the center and by reducing elite ties to local populations. In

Imperial China, the center did so by instituting examinations in Confucianism for aspiring elites and by prohibiting imperial officials from serving in their hometown areas. Nevertheless, the diminishing reach of the center is captured by a common Chinese saying: "Heaven is high and the emperor is far away" (*tian gao huangdi yuan*).

In the 1950's, the party had great revolutionary charisma, along with enormous power of sanctions. Provincial officials eagerly followed the center, often too much so. The Great Leap Famine, however, took much of the luster off the party and dampened the political enthusiasm of local officials. By the late 1970's, in spite of centrally engineered changes in provincial leaders and military commanders, most local officials had served in one province for extended periods. Moreover, their power in formulating and implementing economic policy had been enhanced by the progressive decentralization of economic authority since the early 1970's.[54] In the context of the elite contention at the top, local officials had both the wherewithal and the political space to maneuver in the late 1970's. It is therefore expected that certain spatial patterns would appear on the politically salient issue of agrarian policy. Indeed, under the reforms, the popular saying quoted above has gained wide popularity.

> *Hypothesis 2*: The farther away a province was from Beijing, the political center, the more freedom of maneuver it had and the less likely was the province to favor radical agrarian policies. Conversely, proximity to Beijing increases the likelihood that a province would adopt more radical policies.

Income effect. Chinese commentaries on the emergence of rural reform in post-Mao China have frequently mentioned that household contracting first took hold in less-developed areas.[55] It is thus expected that those provinces that had higher per-capita incomes would likely have, or could afford to have, a higher brigade-accounting rate. I therefore introduce the level of income as the control variable.

In operationalizing and testing the two hypotheses, I already have data on the severity of the Great Leap Famine (Chap. 2) and on the percentage of brigades with brigade accounting in each province (Tibet excluded).[56] In Hypothesis 2, each province's physical distance from Beijing is used as a proxy measure for political distance and central control, and, as will be discussed shortly, this measure is significantly related to the density of CCP membership in the provinces. For provincial level of income, figures on the per-capita national level for 1978, 1979, and 1981 are used.[57] All data employed in this chapter and their summary statistics are shown in Table 16.

Using ordinary least squares regression, I estimate the following equations for the determinants of the brigade-accounting rate in 1979 and 1981 (eq. [1]) and for the percentage change in the brigade-accounting rate over

1979–81 (eq. [2]). *BAR* is the abbreviation for brigade-accounting rate, "log" represents the logarithm of a given variable, and "e" is the prediction error or residual.

(1) $BAR = a + a_1 \log (\textit{famine severity}) + a_2 \log(\textit{distance}) + \text{e}.$

(2) % change in $BAR = a + a_1(\textit{famine severity}) + a_2 \textit{distance} + \text{e}.$

When adjustment for level of per-capita income is made, the equations are:

(1a) $BAR = a + a_1 \log (\textit{famine severity}) + a_2 \log(\textit{distance})$
$\qquad + a_3(\textit{income level}) + \text{e}.$

(2a) % change in $BAR = a + a_1(\textit{famine severity}) + a_2 \textit{distance}$
$\qquad + a_3(\textit{income level}) + \text{e}.$

Tables 17–22, showing the determinants of the brigade accounting rate and of changes in that rate from 1979 to 1981, present the regression results. For both 1979 and 1981, both independent variables have statistically significant and inverse relationships with the dependent variable. Moreover, the variable on level of per-capita national income is not statistically significant when it is included in the equations, and its inclusion does not significantly affect the results of the regression analyses.

TABLE 17

Brigade Accounting Rate, 1979

Brigade accounting rate, 1979	Coefficient	Standard error	t	$p > \lvert t \rvert$
log(*famine severity*)	−9.119009	2.756008	−3.309	0.003
log(*distance*)	−10.21981	3.494877	−2.924	0.007
Constant	55.75713	10.44671	5.337	0.000

NOTE: Number of observations = 27
$\quad$ F(2, 24) = 14.36
$\quad$ p > F = 0.0001
$\quad$ Adj. R^2 = 0.5068

TABLE 18

Brigade Accounting Rate, 1979, with Level of Per-Capita National Income

Brigade accounting rate, 1979	Coefficient	Standard error	t	$p > \lvert t \rvert$
log(*famine severity*)	−9.689625	2.955774	−3.278	0.003
log(*distance*)	−10.50755	3.576374	−2.938	0.007
Per-capita national income	−0.0016784	0.0028361	−0.592	0.560
Constant	58.41775	11.50574	5.077	0.000

NOTE: Number of observations = 27
$\quad$ F(3, 23) = 9.43
$\quad$ p > F = 0.0003
$\quad$ Adj. R^2 = 0.4930

TABLE 19
Brigade Accounting Rate, 1981

Brigade accounting rate, 1981	Coefficient	Standard error	t	$p > |t|$
log(*famine severity*)	−6.901918	2.117788	−3.259	0.003
log(*distance*)	−6.796491	2.685554	−2.531	0.018
Constant	38.71525	8.027517	4.823	0.000

NOTE: Number of observations = 27
F(2, 24) = 12.46
$p > F$ = 0.0002
Adj. R^2 = 0.4686

TABLE 20
Brigade Accounting Rate, 1981, with Level of Per-Capita National Income

Brigade accounting rate, 1981	Coefficient	Standard error	t	$p > |t|$
log(*famine severity*)	−7.847409	2.216541	−3.540	0.002
log(*distance*)	−7.24244	2.67315	−2.709	0.013
Per-capita national income	−0.0025611	0.0019992	−1.281	0.213
Constant	43.08136	8.624394	4.995	0.000

NOTE: Number of observations = 27
F(3, 23) = 9.08
$p > F$ = 0.0004
Adj. R^2 = 0.4824

TABLE 21
Changes in Brigade Accounting Rate, 1979–81

Change in brigade accounting rate	Coefficient	Standard error	t	$p > |t|$
Famine severity	0.0812782	0.0351628	2.311	0.029
Distance	0.0041541	0.0039478	1.052	0.303
Constant	25.58454	7.567488	3.381	0.002

NOTE: Number of observations = 28
F(2, 25) = 3.67
$p > F$ = 0.0401
Adj. R^2 = 0.1650

TABLE 22
Changes in Brigade Accounting Rate, Adjusted for Level of Per-Capita National Income, 1978

Change in brigade accounting rate	Coefficient	Standard error	t	$p > |t|$
Famine severity	0.0938134	0.0357978	2.621	0.015
Distance	0.0055106	0.0040096	1.374	0.182
Per-capita national income	0.0129201	0.0095209	1.357	0.187
Constant	16.88168	9.825023	1.718	0.099

NOTE: Number of observations = 28
F(3, 24) = 3.14
$p > F$ = 0.0439
Adj. R^2 = 0.1922

The two alternative hypotheses are thus confirmed. The adjusted R^2 figure for 1979 (0.5068) in Table 17 indicates that the two independent variables explain about 50 percent of the variation in the brigade-accounting rate in China's provinces in 1979 (just under 47 percent in 1981). The data analyses thus suggest that, generally speaking, the degree to which a province still practiced brigade accounting in 1979 or 1981 was inversely related to the severity of the 1959–61 famine in the province and to the provincial capital's distance from Beijing. In other words, the more a province suffered during the Great Leap Famine, the more the province was likely to adopt rural reform measures rather than follow leftist practices such as brigade accounting. The farther away a province was from Beijing, the more likely was the province to adopt rural reforms early. In separate statistical tests, *famine severity* explains more of the variation than does *distance* and invariably emerges statistically significant when adjusted for a host of other variables. This suggests that the explanation of brigade-accounting rate in terms of famine severity is a robust one.

The relationship between brigade accounting and the Great Leap Famine can be explored further with the aid of Figure 8. On the horizontal axis is the percentage increase in death rate during the Great Leap Famine; on the vertical axis is the brigade accounting rate in 1981. Clearly, all eight provinces experiencing extremely high increases in the death rate of more than 140 percent (Anhui, Guizhou, Sichuan, Qinghai, Henan, Gansu, Hunan, Guangxi) had very low rates of brigade accounting.[58] As is well known (and to be discussed in Chap. 6), Anhui, Sichuan, and Guizhou were the pioneers in rural reforms. In these provinces, the population's response to extreme famine was to engage in more individualistic practices.

Tables 21–22 examine the impact of famine severity and distance on changes in the brigade-accounting rate over the 1979–81 period. The adjusted R^2 (0.1650) is relatively weak. This is partly to be expected, because the starting date for the brigade-accounting rate was the end of 1979, and, as will be discussed in the next chapter, by that time much had already occurred in the politics of rural reform. More interesting, while both independent variables have positive relationships with the dependent variable, only *famine severity* is found to be statistically significant. This suggests that even though spatial factors contributed to variations in the degree of agrarian radicalism in China's provinces, changes over time were traced back to a highly political variable, that of the Great Leap Famine. In other words, the dynamics of rural institutional change were politically determined.

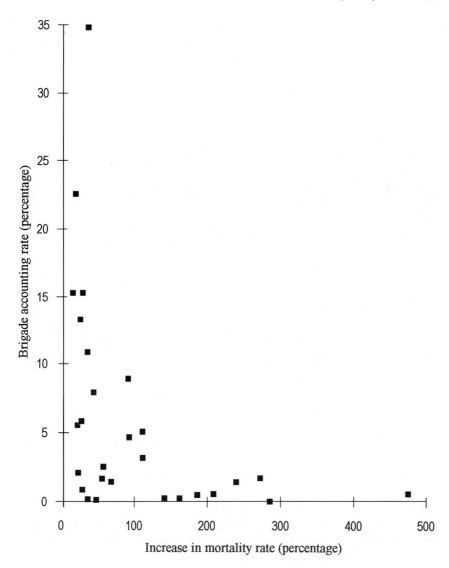

Fig. 8. The Great Leap Famine and brigade accounting rate, 1981

Additional Considerations

There is more than meets the eye with regard to the variable *distance.* Specifically, it is strongly related to the density of party membership discussed in Chapter 2 and to the percentage of crops that is planted in rice. Table 23 presents the correlation matrix of the three variables *distance, density of party membership,* and *rice planting rate* (all logged) as well as the

TABLE 23

Indicators of Multicollinearity

(logged variables)

	Distance	Density of party membership	Rice planting rate (1981)	Unadjusted R^2
Distance	1.0000			0.4942
Density of party membership	−0.7051	1.0000		0.6703
Rice planting rate, 1981	0.4562	−0.7284	1.0000	0.5311

NOTE: Table displays correlation matrix and unadjusted R^2 for regressions of one variable on the other two.

unadjusted R^2's derived by regressing each variable on the two others. The relatively high values indicate a significant degree of multicollinearity among the three variables.

Concerns about multicollinearity, which refers to too-strong interrelationships among the independent variables in a regression, precluded me from including these two new variables in the multivariate regressions presented above. Substituting *density of party membership* and *rice planting rate,* alternately, for *distance* in the regressions, I obtain broadly similar results. For the sake of space, only the results for the determinants of brigade accounting rate in 1979 are presented in Tables 24 and 25.[59]

Density of party membership. For *density of party membership,* or the percentage of population who were CCP members, I have again used the data for mid-1956, which were originally collected by Michel Oksenberg and Frederick Teiwes.[60] Because of the availability of data for 1956 only rather than for the late 1970's, the results presented here rest on the relatively strong assumption that patterns of party membership density did not significantly change over time. Moreover, the Oksenberg-Teiwes data do not show data for Beijing, Shanghai, and Tianjin, where party representation is relatively high; the inclusion of these three cities would have strengthened the statistical relationships presented here. On balance, it appears that the use of such data for indicative purposes is serviceable, but the regression results should be taken with a grain of salt.

As can be seen from Table 23, the density of party membership in China's provinces has a strong negative relationship to the provinces' physical distance from Beijing. In other words, if the density of party membership is positively related to the density of party networks, then the density of party networks gets weaker in provinces that are further away from Beijing. Since the CCP is commonly regarded as the bastion of conservatism and orthodoxy, then policy innovation would be more likely in areas that are further away from Beijing, the political center, at times when the center's power was weaker. Thus it appears that the

TABLE 24
Substituting Density of Party Membership for Distance

Brigade accounting rate, 1979	Coefficient	Standard error	t	p>|t|
log(*famine severity*)	−8.641082	3.461853	−2.496	0.021
log(*party*)	16.17947	7.754434	2.086	0.049
Constant	21.82025	7.041223	3.099	0.005

NOTE: Number of observations = 24
F(2, 21) = 10.18
p>F = 0.0008
R² = 0.4922
Adj. R² = 0.4439

TABLE 25
Substituting Rice Planting Rate for Distance

Brigade accounting rate, 1979	Coefficient	Standard error	t	p>|t|
log(*famine severity*)	−9.600233	4.298079	−2.234	0.036
log(*rice planting rate*)	−1.892397	0.8621784	−2.195	0.039
Per-capita national income, 1979	0.0047565	0.0038164	1.246	0.225
Constant	28.22592	8.350702	3.380	0.003

NOTE: Number of observations = 27
F(3, 23) = 6.37
p>F = 0.0027
R² = 0.4537
Adj. R² = 0.3825

spatial distribution of party membership has enhanced the apparent effect of space in determining the patterns of reform propensity in China's provinces.

Incidentally, the spatial distribution of party membership was constituted through a historical process centered on the spatial patterns of Communist takeover in the 1940's. In statistical terms, using the dates of "liberation" of provincial capitals to indicate the spatial patterns of takeover from North to South China, it was found that "liberation" is positively and significantly related to *distance*. Indeed, substituting *liberation* time for *distance* in equations (1) and (2), I obtain similar results.[61] I am tempted to refer to the causal sequence that runs from the geographical patterns of Communist takeover to the post-Mao reforms in the deep structure of revolution and reform in China.

Ecology. The location of Beijing in northern China suggests an ecological aspect to *distance*. Proximity to Beijing usually means a northern, and thus wheat-oriented, ecology (or pasture in the case of Mongolia); in contrast, southern China depends heavily upon rice cultivation.

In her book *The Rice Economies,* Francesca Bray has argued persuasively that efficiency in "skill-oriented" wet-rice cultivation depends less upon the range of equipment (capital investment) than on the quality of labor. As a result, wet-rice cultivation is not, like the wheat-oriented farming system of Northwest Europe, subject to economies of scale, nor does it respond well to managerial centralization.[62] In the context of collective agriculture in China, we would therefore expect to find a higher brigade-accounting rate in northern provinces than in the South. Bray's observations appear to be supported by the regional patterns of brigade-accounting rates. In 1981 eleven provinces—Beijing, Tianjin, Hebei, Shanxi, Inner Mongolia, Heilongjiang, Zhejiang, Shandong, Hubei, Shaanxi, and Xinjiang—still boasted a high brigade-accounting rate of more than 5 percent. Of the eleven provinces, all but Zhejiang and Hubei were located in North or Northwest China. Substituting the variable *rice* (percentage of acreage planted in rice) in equation (1), I can derive the familiar statistical relationship.

Land population ratio. In an insightful essay on the reforms in Fengyang, Anhui, Elizabeth Perry suggests that whether an area adopted reforms early or not depended partly on the land/population ratio. Because of the decimation of the Great Leap Famine, Fengyang had more land per person, in contrast to other areas of China, and especially south of the Yangtze River (Jiangnan). According to Perry, "To abandon a functioning collective for the risks of family farming must not have seemed a terribly attractive alternative when only a minuscule land base was available. Moreover, many affluent teams and brigades in Jiangnan—unlike their Fengyang counterparts—could boast substantial accumulation and welfare funds. Under these circumstances, peasants probably preferred the status quo to a profit-oriented system that threatened to undermine the 'moral economy' of the collective."[63]

Using the (provincial) ratio of planted acreage to the number of rural population in 1979, I tested the hypothesis suggested by Perry, but found no statistically significant relationship between the land/population ratio and the ratio of brigades with brigade accounting.[64] The addition of this item to equation (1) did not improve the goodness-of-fit. Indeed, as will be discussed in Chapter 6, Heilongjiang province, which had the second highest arable land/population ratio in China, was the last province to embrace the household responsibility system.

Conclusion

This chapter has investigated the structural context within which the struggle for rural reform took place. On the one hand, the political cleavages among the top elite over rural policy opened up the space for political innovation from below. On the other hand, statistical analyses suggest that the Great Leap Famine furnished the fundamental historical incentives for peasants and their allies in some localities to adopt practices that were not officially sanctioned. It was the traumas of the famine, more than anything else, that turned the vanguards of Great Leap radicalism, such as Henan, Anhui, and Sichuan, into the trailblazers of liberal reforms in the early 1960's and again in the late 1970's. While the liberal interregnum of the early 1960's was suppressed in the socialist education movement and the radicalism of the Cultural Revolution, it resumed, with greater resilience, after Mao's death.

The latter finding has important implications for our understanding of China's state-society relations prior to the 1980's. It suggests that the conventional literature places too much emphasis on the role of central leadership in launching rural reforms. In contrast, localities, rather than following the dictates of agrarian radicalism, responded not only to elite dictates but also to historical and environmental incentives to pursue their own interests, sometimes acting against elite policies. The finding thus gives more weight to the role of the past in constraining rural policy than the conventional emphasis on the centrality of the state in Chinese politics. The impact of the Great Leap Famine underscores the fact that what we did in the past influences our present and what we do now will affect our future.[65] In this sense, history is path dependent.[66] For political science, this means that policy outcomes are not merely dependent variables to be explained but are also independent variables constraining the future.

A secondary, but also interesting, variable determining the patterns of reform propensity is the role of geography, a much-neglected factor in mainstream economics and political science.[67] What is especially fascinating intellectually about the geographical dimension of China's reforms is not that space mattered; this is easy to comprehend, since Chinese officialdom remains dependent on rail travel to this day and internal communications are subject to various types of obstruction. Instead, I also found that embedded in my measure of space was the spatial distribution of party membership and by extension variegated local party networks, which in turn were related to the spatial patterns of the Communist takeover going from north to south as well as China's north/south ecological contrast. As the density of CCP membership grows weaker in proportion to the physical distance from Beijing, unofficial policy innovation is thus more likely to occur in the periphery, even though such innovation might later be taken up on its own by the establishment in the center. Needless to say, being in the periphery does not guarantee innovation, but the need to emphasize the study of the provinces (vis-à-vis Beijing) is evident if we seek to understand the dynamics of change in China.

· · · 6 · · ·

The Political Struggle over Reform

Having examined and established the structural incentives and political context for rural institutional change in Chapter 5, I follow up the story of reform and argue that the rise of rural reform in post-Mao China may best be viewed as the result of an interaction between state and peasant. That process—or, more appropriately, political struggle—was mediated by local and regional leaders and fundamentally conditioned by the incentive structures shaped by the catastrophic Great Leap Famine and the opening up of political space that followed Mao's death.

The importance of the famine in shaping post-Mao rural reforms is shown by the behavior of both elites and peasants. At the top, leaders such as Chen Yun and Deng Xiaoping promoted a sequence of policies that harked back to the adjustment policies of the early 1960's for reviving China's stagnant rural economy. Chapter 4 already mentioned that in late 1978 Chen Yun and others called for increasing grain imports—a measure that was similar to what had been done in the early 1960's and that was constrained by the famine's long-term effect on the agricultural structure. This chapter starts with the historic Third Plenum of 1978. This plenum produced an important decision on rural policy that the Chinese have referred to as the New Sixty Articles, and it was indeed fashioned after the earlier ones that were drawn up during the famine under Mao's supervision.

Peasants and cadres in those provinces that had suffered most from the famine had deep memories of it and were more likely to pursue liberal practices than those in areas that had fared relatively better. Even if leaders of the hard-hit provinces assumed their posts long after the famine, they still very likely learned about the famine and its impact. This was especially true in provinces such as Anhui, Guizhou, and Sichuan, which had not yet fully recovered from the famine in the late 1970's. Without denying the importance of elite initiatives, it is important to underscore that local leaders made choices in which their motivations and preferences were significantly affected by the environment and history. It was thus no coincidence that China's post-Mao rural reform originated in these provinces.

The variations in the severity of the famine as well as geographical location meant that people in different areas were differentially motivated to pursue rural institutional change. These differences are expected to translate into political cleavages and struggles both within the state and between state and society. By detailing the political struggles involved in putting rural reforms on the agenda, this chapter highlights the role of local elites and peasants in rural reforms and the mechanisms by which reformist practices spread from one locality to another and, eventually, to the entire country.

The multiplicity of actors and interactions in a period of rapid political change makes the story complicated. In order not to clutter the narrative, I begin with the Third Plenum decisions and discuss how they departed from existing policies and yet were still limited in their reformist orientation. In fact, months before the Third Plenum was convened, some localities had already adopted and even exceeded what the Third Plenum later authorized. The policy moderation of the Third Plenum nevertheless emboldened some local leaders to acquiesce to even more pragmatic practices being pursued by rural communities. The successes of these localities were in turn used as evidence in support of further rural reforms in the center, which were again taken as evidence by peasants and local cadres that they could engage in even more liberal practices. The reform was thus a process of cumulative causation: Positive feedback from individual cases helped reformers consolidate their political power and served to persuade more and more to jump on the reform bandwagon.

The Third Plenum, the New Sixty Articles, and the Limits of Policy Change

Already weakened by the debate on the criterion of truth, agrarian radicalism took a further beating at the Central Work conference held from November 10 to December 15, 1978, in preparation for the historic Third Plenum of the Eleventh Central Committee (December 18–22, 1978). (The conference decided that the focus of party work was to shift from class struggle to socialist modernization.) All three champions of agrarian radicalism, Hua Guofeng, Ji Dengkui, and Chen Yonggui, were forced to make self-criticisms at the conference for committing leftist errors.[1]

Agriculture topped the economic agenda at the conference. Chen Yun, just restored to his positions as member of the Politburo Standing Committee and vice-chairman of the Chinese Communist Party, made the most influential speech on that topic on December 10, 1978.[2] According to Chen,

We should not have tensions everywhere and should first placate peasants [*xian ba nongmin zheyitou anwen xialai*]. . . . To placate this side is to placate the majority. When over 700 million people [the rural population] are quiescent, there is stability under heaven.

It is nearly thirty years since the establishment of the PRC, yet there are still beggars, how can this continue? [We] should relax one side and let peasants have a breathing spell. If this problem [of having enough to eat] is not solved, peasants might rebel and party branch secretaries may lead [villagers] to come to beg in cities.[3]

Because of the attack on the sponsors of agrarian radicalism and the shift of the political balance, the "Decision of the Central Committee of the CCP on Some Questions Concerning the Acceleration of Agricultural Development (Draft)" drawn up under the supervision of Ji Dengkui, became unacceptable to conference participants. For moderates, the Ji version of the draft "Decision," to be submitted for approval at the Third Plenum, was written in the spirit of learning from Dazhai and thus failed to correct the leftist tendencies of the past. Instead, Hu Yaobang, who had masterminded the truth criterion debate and was awarded the post of party general secretary, was entrusted with the task of organizing a group of writers to craft a new version of the "Decision."[4] The Hu version of the plenum decision and the "Regulations on the Work in Rural People's Communes (Draft for Trial Use)" (hereafter, the New Sixty Articles) were approved for trial implementation at the Central Work conference and subsequently at the Third Plenum.[5]

Before I discuss the contents of the "Decision" and the New Sixty Articles, it may be appropriate to digress here and touch on the different roles played by members of the Chinese leadership in remaking China's rural policy. It is evident that Hu Yaobang played a key role by supervising the drafting of the "Decision." The available evidence indicates that Deng Xiaoping did not play a role in setting agricultural policy at this stage, though, together with other senior leaders, he did set the tone for future work and alluded to rural work by delivering what amounted to the keynote address at the Third Plenum, entitled "Emancipate the Mind, Seek Truth from Facts and Unite as One in Looking to the Future."[6] At this time, as one of the vice-premiers and a vice-chairman of the Central Military Commission, Deng's areas of responsibility were education, science and technology, army affairs, and foreign policy (especially China's policy toward the United States).[7] In contrast, Chen Yun and his associates, especially Li Xiannian and Yao Yilin, were more prominent in putting rural policy back on track. It was Yao Yilin who was the chief advocate for importing grain in order to help diversify agriculture into such products as cotton and peanuts. Li Xiannian, in addition to seconding Yao's argument for more imports, argued that it was imperative to raise agricultural procurement prices by 30 percent. Chen Yun, as the chief architect of economic readjustment in the early 1960's and again in the late 1970's, supported both Yao Yilin and Li Xiannian, saying that China "may import 20 million tons of grain each year" in the next three to five years.[8]

These two documents are commonly regarded as having guided rural policy in the early stage of the rural reforms. In the context of continued agrarian radicalism as of spring 1978, they clearly broke new ground by explicitly prohibiting transitions from team to brigade accounting; yet, as will be argued later, they also lagged behind local initiatives and were symptomatic of the limits of top-down reform in China. For the moment, let us first look at how they departed from the immediate past of agrarian radicalism, beginning with the New Sixty Articles. They began with a reaffirmation of the 1962 articles, saying that they were "formulated under Comrade Mao Zedong's personal direction and deliberated upon and approved by the Tenth Plenum of the Eighth Central Committee in 1962." While the implementation of the Sixty Articles aided in consolidating the people's communes system and developing agriculture, the disruptions during the Cultural Revolution caused serious damage to agriculture. Therefore, the Central Committee decided to reiterate the various rural policies stipulated in the original Sixty Articles.[9] In spite of various emendations and additions, the number of articles remained at sixty. Both in content and in form, what has been hailed as a bold act of reform was thus really a movement for restoration. The so-called reformers actually fought for returning to the policies of a past era (i.e., the early 1960's), which were believed to have been more effective than those the reformers tried to repudiate.

The "Decision" similarly bore striking resemblance to the readjustment policies of the early 1960's: emphasis on the production team, peasant interests, increases in procurement prices, reduction of peasant burdens.[10] It started with a frank admission that China's "agricultural development was sluggish in the last two decades." In 1977, "the per capita grain in the nation was even slightly less than it was in 1957; and there are more than 100 million rural dwellers who do not have enough to eat." As a result, the "Decision" suggested, "there exist extremely sharp contradictions between [sluggish agricultural growth] and the needs of the people and of the four modernizations." In short, the "Decision" painted a dismal picture of the rural situation; this was in sharp contrast to the obligatory reference to glorious achievements by the champions of agrarian radicalism.[11] The "Decision" drew a number of lessons from China's recent agricultural policy failure: "Policies that have proved effective in practice must not be changed lightly, so as to not lose the confidence of the people and hurt peasant enthusiasm. Meanwhile, those wrong policies that are not conducive to eliciting peasant enthusiasm and the development of productive forces must be revised and corrected."[12]

On that basis, the "Decision" listed twenty-five policy recommendations and measures designed to elicit peasant enthusiasm and to increase state support of agriculture. Most important, as during the adjustment of the early 1960's, the "Decision" called for respecting the interests of peasants.[13] It reaffirmed the rights and decision-making powers of the commune subunits, especially the production team: "It is absolutely forbidden to commandeer the manpower, funds, land, livestock, machinery, products and materials of any production teams." The principle of "to each according to his work" was adjudged a socialist principle; egalitarianism, such as that embodied in the Dazhai work-point system, was to be combated. On the condition of unified accounting and distribution by the production team, work could be contracted to small groups, with payment in accordance with the output produced. Moreover, it was concluded that private plots, family sideline production, and rural market fairs were all supplementary to the socialist economy and were not to be criticized and abolished as being capitalist. There should not be hasty transitions to brigade accounting; the emphasis was now on production rather than institutional change.

There were to be major changes in state investment and extraction policies with regard to agriculture. Agricultural investment as a percentage of state capital construction investment was to reach 18 percent, though in reality this would soon decline as reform progressed. Agricultural loans were to double. Grain procurement and tax would be stabilized at the 1971–75 level "for a fairly long period of time to come" and "grain procurement must never be excessive." Most important, the state decided to reduce the disparity in prices between industrial and agricultural products. Beginning in 1979, grain-quota purchase prices were to be increased by 20 percent, with an additional 50 percent premium for above-quota sales. The purchase prices for cotton, oil-bearing and sugar crops, animal by-products, aquatic and forestry products, and other farm and sideline products were also adjusted upward. In the meantime, the prices of farm machinery, chemical fertilizer, insecticides, plastics, and other manufactured goods for farm use would be cut by 10–15 percent in 1979 and 1980.[14]

Whereas the Third Plenum departed from the radical policies of Hua Guofeng, its restorative orientation also meant that it inherited the limitations that Mao had imposed in 1962. For example, the New Sixty Articles of 1978 categorically stated that "contracting output to the household [*bao-chan daohu*] must not be permitted; dividing the land to the household must not be permitted."[15] In short, the "household responsibility system" (including both *baogan* and *baochan daohu*), now generally recognized as the hallmark of the post-Mao rural reforms, was explicitly prohibited at the Third Plenum. As late as April 1979, the Central Committee, in authorizing a State Agriculture Commission report for redistribution, still termed "contracting everything to the household [*baogan daohu*] . . . a kind of retreat" and stipulated that "areas that have implemented the *baogan daohu* should actively reorganize peasants [into collectives]."[16] Later attempts either to explain these away as aberrations or to suggest that the Third Plenum did more than actually was the case were both contrary to the facts.[17]

The Trailblazers: Carrying Out Third Plenum–Style Practices Before the Plenum

Yet peasants and local cadres, especially in areas that had suffered more from the Great Leap Famine, were ready to take advantage of any policy opening, and, like leaders at the center, they also looked back to the experiences of the early 1960's for remedies. Indeed, even as the Third Plenum prohibited the household responsibility system, peasants in some areas, with the support or connivance of local cadres, were actively adopting it, just as had happened in the aftermath of the Great Leap Famine and, in some cases, continuing through the Cultural Revolution decade. Peasants and local elites did not just sit waiting for policy benefits to flow from Beijing. They took part in making that policy.

An examination of the reform experiences of these trailblazers thus promises to help us appreciate the role of local society and elites in launching the rural reforms. In this section, I shall mainly concentrate on Anhui and Sichuan, two well-known leaders of the reforms, though information on other areas is also provided.[18] Later sections will discuss the contrasting experiences of provinces such as Heilongjiang and Hebei, which held off the household responsibility system for as long as they could. The contrast is designed to highlight the political struggle surrounding the adoption of rural reform.

Anhui

Of all provinces, Anhui suffered the most during the Great Leap Famine of 1959–61; its mortality rate jumped a whopping 475 percent from the prefamine average. Because of the famine, Anhui widely adopted the *zeren tian* (responsibility land), carving up collective land among individual households. Though the *zeren tian* system was soon under political criticism for deviating from the "general direction" of politics, it left fond memories among peasants. By the late 1970's, peasants continued to use that experience as the reference point of their lives. Those who survived the famine credited the *zeren tian* for saving their lives. In at least one Anhui locality, the system was secretly retained for some two decades.[19] The searing experience of the famine thus predisposed a significant number of local cadres and peasants to try more pragmatic measures.

As was mentioned in the previous chapter, Hua Guofeng and Vice-Premier Chen Yonggui, at the end of 1977, strenuously promoted the building of Dazhai-style counties and transitions to brigade accounting. They were able to launch a wave of such transitions in that winter, causing substantial disruption to rural life. Yet all was not politically settled at the top. By then a number of political heavyweights who had favored household contracting in the aftermath of the Great Leap Famine, including Chen Yun and Deng Xiaoping, had reclaimed their political posts. Encouraged by the changing distribution of power, leaders from a number of provinces called in various meetings for reinstating the moderate policies of the past, including the Sixty Articles. While these demands were kept away from the public for the moment, the awareness on the part of regional leaders of the push for policy change probably encouraged them to be more flexible than the official rhetoric that was still dominated by Hua Guofeng's people warranted.

It was within this context that Wan Li was transferred from the post of first vice-minister of light industry to become first secretary of the CCP Anhui Provincial Committee in June 1977.[20] His appointment was part of a wave of leadership shifts the center launched to replace provincial leaders who were close to the radical Gang of Four and stabilize the situation in the provinces. Wan Li was probably chosen for this task because he was known for maintaining order as the minister of railways in 1975–76. The credentials of his lieutenants similarly indicate an orientation toward stabilizing the economy. Provincial Party Secretary Gu Zhuoxin was a vice-chairman of the State Planning Commission from 1954 to 1963 and had extensive experience in the Northeast. Provincial Secretary Wang Guangyu, whose role in the unfolding political drama appears to have been neglected by historians, was a native of Anhui. Wang had served continuously in Anhui, as party secretary of Fuyang Prefecture (1949–52), head of the rural work department of the CCP Anhui Provincial Committee (1953–56), and vice-governor (1956–66), before the Cultural Revolution brought his career to a halt.[21] In other words, he had seen it all: the rise of the collectives, the devastating famine, the struggle for survival, and the suppression of the *zeren tian*.

Unbeknownst to Wan Li, he came to Anhui at a critical historical juncture. For, in spite of repeated political attacks on those who favored liberal agricultural practices such as household contracting, many peasants and local leaders continued to believe that such practices were desirable for the invigoration of Anhui. By being flexible and supportive, Wan Li allowed these political demands to grow, thereby helping unleash a political mandate for rural reform. This is not to belittle the leadership roles played by Wan Li and other members of the elite in China's reforms. But it is important to recognize that Wan (as well as his colleagues) was an effective leader precisely because he recognized and followed the impulses from below and offered his helping hand on various occasions. Following extensive travels across the province, Wan Li concluded that "Anhui has been famous over the years for exaggeration, for making false reports, and for the egalitarian and indiscriminate transfer of resources, and the lessons this has brought are tragic ones. The cruel requisition purchases of grain from the peasants have caused hunger."[22] The same Wan Li, if he had been appointed party secretary of Heilongjiang or Jiangsu province, would probably not have become the prominent reformist leader he was later known as, and certainly not for discovering and promoting the household responsibility system.

Once the new provincial leadership had made headway in purging the radicals, they turned to the economy. Here the problem was obvious: This overwhelmingly agrarian province had much difficulty feeding its more than 40 million rural residents. Large numbers of peasants subsisted by seasonal begging in other places. While the problem was clear, the solution to it was much less so, however, especially because Wan Li had had an urban career and had not dealt with rural policy since the Communist takeover. Wan turned to Zhou Yueli, who was Zeng Xisheng's secretary in 1961 and now headed the Provincial Agricultural Committee Policy Research Office. Zhou had no illusions about the Dazhai model and reported on the grim realities in rural areas caused by ultraleftist policies.[23] Wan and his colleagues also received a report from Chuxian prefecture, which was headed by Wang Yuzhao.[24] Contrary to the prevailing political wisdom, Wang also argued that agrarian radical policies, including the suppression of private plots and agricultural sidelines, had promoted politics at the expense of economic growth and undermined peasants' enthusiasm for production.[25]

The Chuxian report prompted Wan Li and his colleagues to find out more about the countryside. They sent rural investigation teams on fact-finding missions and heard briefings from local leaders; some provincial leaders also visited basic-level cadres and peasants. After several revisions, the provincial leadership on November 15, 1977, issued a document entitled "Regulations on Several Issues in Current Rural Economic Policy."[26] Also known as the Six Articles, the Anhui regulations were in essence a watered-down version of the Sixty Articles, which was reaffirmed in 1970 by Zhou Enlai but had been eclipsed by Hua Guofeng and Chen Yonggui's push for the Dazhai model in recent years. While paying lip service to the need for developing socialist agriculture and strengthening commune management, the Anhui regulations called for respecting the autonomy of the production team, reducing the burdens on the team and the peasants, and encouraging peasants to pursue sidelines. Against the prevailing political current, the regulations also stipulated that the private plots that had been confiscated from commune members should be returned, though household contracting of output or production tasks was not permitted.[27]

The Anhui regulations foreshadowed the Third Plenum "Decision" and predated it by one full year and "were widely supported and welcomed by cadres and peasants."[28] Predictably central leaders such as Chen Yonggui disliked the Anhui document for failing to give prominence to learning from Dazhai.[29] Yet it was politically difficult to assail the Anhui document because it had not gone beyond the Sixty Articles Mao had authorized. In fact, in the process of drawing up the Six Articles, the Anhui leadership made it clear that they were not seeking bold departures but were merely implementing (*luoshi*) the party's policies.[30] As in the forthcoming Third Plenum, reform began with restoration.

On February 3, 1978, the *People's Daily,* which was dominated by pragmatists, prominently carried a report on the birth of the Anhui Six Articles and hailed the document as a return to the genuine spirit of Mao, who stressed grass-roots investigations and the mass line.[31] Later commentaries and articles emphasized that the key for motivating peasants lay in implementing policies on respecting the rights of production teams and on private plots, incentives, and payment according to work, all taboo items just a few months earlier.[32] As the title of one article on Dingyuan county in Anhui put it, "Agricultural output will increase once the production teams are given their autonomy."[33] By April 1978, the *People's Daily* was already reporting on the effectiveness of the Anhui regulations in Chu county and Lu'an prefecture. It was claimed that with the universal adoption of group work and task rates (*ding'e guanli*, literally quota management), labor productivity increased dramatically during spring plowing and seeding.[34]

Other Provinces

Put simply, Anhui had implemented Third Plenum–type policies one year before the plenum was held. Yet Anhui was not unique. While provinces such as Shanxi (Chen Yonggui's home base) obstinately resisted such changes, other provinces, most of which suffered more than average during the famine or were far away from Beijing, as the statistical analyses in the last chapter would predict, also adopted similar policies before the Third Plenum was held. In Gansu, the provincial leadership, led by Song Ping, put out a document entitled "Suggestions on Several Questions in Current Rural Work," which called for restoring various rural policies, including payment according to labor, task rates, sideline production, and respecting the rights of the production team.[35] Similar "suggestions" or "regulations" were also adopted by the spring or summer of 1978 in Sichuan (twelve items), Guangdong (sixteen articles), Xinjiang (eight articles), Fujian (twelve articles), Jiangxi (eighteen articles), and Tibet.[36] Task rates were also adopted in Henan's Xinxiang Prefecture and in areas of Jiangsu.[37]

The different number of articles or items in the provincial documents on rural policies indicates that these policies were not coordinated by the center. Adoption of these policies in or before the spring of 1978 was also against Hua Guofeng's advocacy of rural institutional transformation. Moreover, only a select number of provinces had adopted such policies by the summer of 1978. Of these, Jiangxi's "Suggestions on Several Questions in Present-Day Rural Policy" (eighteen articles), adopted somewhat later than the others, came closer to the Third Plenum "Decision" in content. Besides emphasizing the need for policy stability, the "Suggestions" stipulated that state grain procurement be set for five years and prohibited the various bureaucratic levels from increasing the production team's burdens. Above-quota grain output could either be sold to the state at premium prices or distributed to peasants.[38]

Yet it is also evident that Wan Li and other provincial leaders who advocated rural adjustment were careful not to challenge the official canon on collective agriculture. In an article published in March 1978, for example, Wan Li, then still the top leader in Anhui, called for giving teams more rights and the allocation of work tasks to work groups. Yet he specifically pointed out that "contracting output to the household" [*baochan daohu*] is *not* permitted."[39] It is well known that Wan Li did not like the dogmatic manner in which the learning from Dazhai campaigns were carried out. Yet, even though by early 1979 Hua Guofeng and Chen Yonggui had lost control over the rural policy agenda, Wan Li still insisted at a provincial work conference that the Dazhai spirit of self-reliance was worthy of emulation.[40]

The Reemergence of Output Contracting

In reality, just as Wan Li was disclaiming *baochan daohu* in spring 1978, that practice began to spread in Anhui. When the provincial authorities gave an inch, local authorities took a mile.

In 1978, Anhui suffered from a severe drought, which affected more than 60 million *mu* of cultivated land, nearly 90 percent of the total.[41] Lack of water spelled agricultural ruin. Caught in such a crisis, the provincial party committee decided to "lend" those plots that the collectives could not sow to commune members rather than let the land go to waste. In accordance with a time-honored tradition in China, harvests from these otherwise cropless plots were exempted from taxation.[42] Moreover, the provincial directive explicitly instructed that each peasant be lent 0.0165 acres of land for private cultivation. These measures directly linked effort with survival and elicited the enthusiasm of peasant households. Not only was autumn sowing sped up, but the acreage under cultivation was also expanded by more than two million *mu*.

The implementation of the Six Articles and the "land-lend" policy emboldened residents in some localities to try even more freewheeling practices such as "contracting everything to the group" (*da baogan daozu*), "contracting output to the household" (*baochan daohu*), and "contracting everything to the household" (*da baogan daohu*).[43] These measures were to be explicitly prohibited in the forthcoming Third Plenum "Decision." By the time the Third Plenum was held at the end of 1978, an estimated 1,200 production teams had contracted output to peasant households in Anhui, though this figure was still less than 1 percent of the total.[44] In Anhui and elsewhere, every one of these pioneering cases stirred controversy and entailed political risks for the practitioners. An examination of these cases provides us with a number of insights into the roles of local leaders and into the adoption and spread of liberal practices.

Contracting Output to the Group

Weiying production team in Anhui's Lai'an county started with fixing production tasks for small groups in spring 1978 but found that the practice encouraged groups to go for quantity at the expense of quality.[45] Drawing on past experiences, the team switched to contracting agricultural output to small groups. Similar practices were also adopted in 32 of the 42 production teams in Mahu commune in Fengyang county as of May 1978.[46] This practice further evolved from contracting agricultural output to the group to contracting everything (*da baogan*) to the group in 1979.

Opinions on group contracting were divided in Weiying and among leaders at the brigade, commune, and county levels. One county leader explicitly asked that the practice be stopped for contravening central directives. Some brigade and commune cadres believed that the Weiying practice was "individual farming in disguise" and "going capitalist." In spite of the political pressure, the majority of commune cadres believed that they should allow Weiying to continue for a year. One commune cadre declared that cadres would support Weiying to the end even if they lost their jobs. By fall, Weiying's superior record brought vindication as an investigative team from the Chuxian prefectural Party Committee and the Lai'an county Party Committee declared that the Weiying practice actually served to keep peasants close to the collective. The investigative team concluded that the Weiying method was more suited to the backward conditions in the countryside and should be further refined and gradually popularized through pilot projects in each county.

Contracting Output to the Household

Far more controversial than group contracting was contracting output to the household. This may take a variety of forms, ranging from contracting only for certain crops such as cotton to contracting everything to the household.

Xinjie commune in Anhui's Tianchang county adopted the limited version of household contracting in 1978 by fixing responsibility for cotton output to individuals (in reality households). The linking of output with remuneration greatly stimulated peasant effort, and, in spite of the extreme drought, the 1978 cotton output per unit of land in Xinjie was double the 1977 figure. However, cadres at various levels in the county feared that this measure could be seen as "individual farming" and were afraid to extend it to other crops and other areas.[47]

If limited household contracting already carried considerable political risks, then, in light of the severe attacks of the early 1960's and the atmosphere of agrarian radicalism in China, contracting everything to the household was politically taboo as of 1978. The legendary case of Fengyang's Xiaogang production team provides us with a cogent example of the perceived risks involved. This village of twenty households had suffered terribly during the Great Leap Famine and had never recovered from it and the subsequent political crackdown on *zeren tian*. In January 1979, team leader Yan Hongchang and other household heads of the tension-riven village got together and swore an oath to adopt household contracting (*da baogan*).[48] They put their fingerprints on a piece of paper that specified the terms of the vow, including "If someone is imprisoned for *da baogan*, the rest of the village will take care of his family."[49]

On a larger scale, Tang Maolin, party secretary of Shannan District in Feixi county in Anhui, supported basic-level cadres to "do what was done in 1961," that is, contract production to individual households in September 1978 in order to fight the severe drought.[50] Tang secured the tacit approval of county Party Secretary Chang Zhenying and then promoted household contracting in the district. Within days, however, critics of Tang reported on what he was doing to the provincial party committee, accusing Tang of seeking to restore the *zeren tian* and triggering an investigation from the provincial agricultural committee. Fortunately for Tang, provincial leaders agreed with him. When Wan Li visited Shannan in May 1979, he endorsed the locality as a pilot project for contracting.[51]

The Role of Local Elites

Given the political risks involved in pioneering liberal practices, the support of local elites was especially significant. In Weiying, Xiaogang, and Shannan, basic-level cadres led their local populations to adopt liberal practices in the beginning and then secured political support from higher levels. Yet such support was not readily forthcoming. When a peasant from Lujiang county visited Shannan district of Feixi county and learned of the adoption of contracting production to individual households, he returned to his village and made an agreement with five families to do the same and reaped a bumper summer harvest. But the county authorities soon suppressed their practice.[52]

The case of Xiaogang team in Anhui's Fengyang county also illustrates the importance as well as the limitations of support from upper-level cadres. When the commune leadership reported to county Party Secretary Chen Tingyuan that Xiaogang had adopted household contracting, Chen could have immediately stopped it before its influence was felt elsewhere. Instead, he decided to leave Xiaogang alone, thinking that one in more than 3,000 teams would not affect the overall situation. But he explicitly ordered that the Xiaogang practice not be promoted.[53]

By 1979, Fengyang had become known nationally for pioneering the adoption of group contracting (*da baogan daozu*), beginning in Mahu commune. Ironically, even though by this time both provincial and prefectural leaders had indicated that peasants be allowed to try all forms of rural organization except egalitarianism and individual farming, the Fengyang leadership under Chen Tingyuan decided to stick by and promote group contracting in the county. In a series of meetings from late 1979 to March 1980, Chen and other members of the county party committee referred to household contracting as individual farming (*dan'gan*) and admitted that household contracting was superior to group contracting in economic performance.[54] Chen realized that if they followed provincial policies and allowed some areas in the county to practice household contracting, the entire county would erupt into household contracting.[55] To save the cause of group contracting, the county leadership adopted the rhetoric that household contracting was not permitted and sought to turn around localities that had adopted household contracting. The Xiaogang team, for example, was pressured into group contracting in late 1979. But the effort to maintain group contracting was hopelessly lost by spring 1980. As Chen Tingyuan recalled in May 1981: "Starting from spring planting in 1980, many places in the county switched to household contracting while concealing the practice from us. . . . Household contracting was like an irresistible wave, spontaneously topping the limits [we had placed], and could not be suppressed or turned around."⁵⁶ In other words, rural communities won over the county leadership.

The experience of Guanghan in Sichuan was similar to that of Feng-yang, with the county party secretary playing a crucial role in fostering the group responsibility system from the start; unlike in Fengyang, how-ever, the Guanghan leadership embraced household contracting over time. Despite its location in the fertile Sichuan basin, Guanghan epito-mized the stagnation in China in the 1970s. At the time of the formation of advanced cooperatives in 1957, the rural per-capita grain ration was 508 *jin* and per-capita income was 68 yuan. Twenty years later in 1976, the grain ration and per-capita income had barely increased, to 535 *jin* and 74 yuan.⁵⁷ In 1977, Chang Guangnan, party secretary of Guanghan county, was traveling through Jinyu (Goldfish) commune. He was surprised to find crops of one production team growing uniformly well, without the stark contrast between collective and private plots. His curiosity piqued, Chang queried the team leader about the team's success but was met with equivocations. Only after repeated urging did the team leader confess that the team for three years had secretly contracted the land to three groups. Each group was responsible for supplying a specified amount to the col-lective and received the remainder. In this way, the enthusiasm of peasant households was raised.⁵⁸ With support from the Sichuan Provincial Party Committee headed by Zhao Ziyang, Chang Guangnan made the entire Jinyu commune (population over 20,000) an experimental area in 1978. In that year, the commune's grain output increased by 2,515 tons. While cad-res and peasants welcomed the changes, they were also deeply uneasy about their political implications. In the end, Zhao Ziyang supported these changes by saying that "the measure has no problem in terms of [political] direction and line."⁵⁹ Ten days after the conclusion of the Third Plenum in 1978, *Sichuan Daily* put the Jinyu experience on contracting output to the group on the front page. The responsibility system soon spread across the province. By September 1979, half of all production teams in Sichuan had adopted it. Neighboring provinces Yunnan, Guizhou, and some areas in Hubei also learned from the "Sichuan experience."⁶⁰ In 1980, when a pro-duction team in Sanshui commune began to adopt the household respon-sibility system, Chang Guangnan supported the team's decision in spite of the central injunction that "advanced" areas should not adopt that system. By 1980, the per-capita income in Guanghan had risen to 194 yuan.⁶¹

In short, while the rural reform initiatives, as embodied in the house-hold responsibility system, originated from below, in the beginning sup-port from local and regional leaders often proved crucial to their spread. As can be expected, not all local cadres were willing to stick their necks out; many of them had been criticized in the past for pursuing liberal policies and were afraid of committing new political errors. Others, however, were willing to try anything that helped feed the people. In the jargon of Chinese politics, these were the "comrades who stood for letting the facts speak for themselves and for using practice as the criterion for showing what is right and what is wrong."[62]

Yet the case of Fengyang county also suggests that once the rural reform had gained momentum, it was difficult for elites to block it completely. Developments in Guizhou province were particularly instructive. On November 11, 1978, the *Guizhou Daily* reported with approval that Ding-yun commune in Guanling county had practiced fixing output to the group and pointed out that the practice was not "capitalist." Soon, so many production teams began to emulate Dingyun that the provincial authorities became nervous and instructed lower-level authorities to "correct the tendency toward group contracting."[63] Yet, by then it was too late, because localities were not afraid anymore once the number of contracting teams had vastly expanded. With the promulgation of the Third Plenum decision and the fluid political environment, household contracting also began to emerge in the province. By the end of 1979, 58.5 percent of the production teams had adopted group contracting and another 10 percent had adopted the household responsibility system.[64]

The Politics of Emulation

The adoption of liberal practices by one team or village usually led some neighboring rural unit to emulate it, leading to a chain reaction, or snowball effect. This occurred for at least two reasons. First, information in rural China travels fairly quickly and usually cannot be hidden for long because of multiple networks ranging from marriage ties to market fairs. Second, once one locality has adopted a politically suspect practice, the perceived political risks for the emulator go down significantly. On the one hand, the adoption of the practice indicates the political possibility of doing so; on the other, should a political crackdown occur, the emulator can always claim that it has followed in someone else's footsteps and expect to escape punishment. Once peasants in other localities learned that Xiaogang had adopted household contracting, they demanded to be treated like Xiaogang: "[We are] led by the same government. If Xiaogang can do it, why can't we?"[65] Thus, as the rest of this chapter shows, the adoption of the household responsibility system snowballed.

Results of emulation were already in evidence in 1978. Once Weiying stuck with group contracting, two neighboring production teams secretly adopted the practice.[66] A neighboring village got wind of the Xiaogang development and also adopted the practice in secret.[67] The official vindication of the Weiying method in fall 1978 prompted many other localities in the area to emulate the practice. Similarly, the official approval of group contracting in Mahu commune encouraged other production teams in Fengyang county to copy it. By the end of 1979, 83.5 percent of all the production teams in the county had done so.[68] Feixi had a similar story. In the spring of 1979, only 23 percent of all production teams in Feixi county practiced contracting production to individual households, but during the summer fight against drought, the percentage shot up to 37 percent, and by fall it had increased to more than 50 percent.[69]

In short, well before the center permitted the practice of group and, later, household responsibility in agriculture, various localities had already adopted them secretly.[70] In describing these local reform experiences as they occurred in Anhui and Sichuan, Chinese and Western publications usually refer to them as reform experiments (*shiyan*).[71] The use of the word "experiment" is in this case misleading, because it suggests, contrary to the facts, that there was a prior policy design that these provinces were carrying out.[72] There is no evidence to indicate that Deng Xiaoping or someone like him in the center deliberately authorized such practices as experiments. Had Deng done so in 1978, a time when he was still consolidating his power vis-à-vis the "whatever" group, he would have made himself vulnerable ideologically. In fact, the process was a fluid one, and there was a lot of give and take between peasants and cadres at various levels in the provinces. Lower-level cadres, such as the county party secretaries in Fengyang and Guanghan and the provincial and prefectural leadership in Anhui, played key roles in nurturing these practices, but the practices grew out of the actions of peasants and basic-level cadres at the team or brigade level.

Because of the lack of systematic data, it is difficult to generalize about the role of local elites, but the evidence from Anhui and Sichuan allows us to make some tentative generalizations. It appears that if a locality engaged in the responsibility system without authorization, cooperation (or collusion) between basic-level cadres and peasants was essential. Such cooperation might simply have been the lack of cadre objections to peasant demands, though active cadre involvement was likely. If the practice were to spread beyond one locality and into nearby areas, then protection from (some) cadres at higher levels, such as the commune or county, was needed. Split leadership at higher levels may have encouraged localities to adopt measures not officially sanctioned.

The adoption and spread of the output-linked responsibility system from spring 1978 to spring 1979 first occurred in brigades and teams located in provinces that had suffered more from the famine or were far away from the political center. According to one official account, the pioneers included Anhui, Sichuan, Guizhou, Gansu, Henan, Inner Mongolia, and Guangdong.[73] The people in Anhui's Xiaogang were not the only ones willing to risk imprisonment in order to adopt the household responsibility system. Tang Junying in Qingjiang commune of Huining county

(Gansu) did the same in 1979. With the adoption of the responsibility system, the gross output of grain in Qingjiang more than doubled in one year, rising from 2.2 million *jin* in 1979 to 4.65 million *jin* in 1980.[74]

While there doubtless were other cases, it was the nature of the game that peasants and local cadres had to hide what they were doing from superiors. One Chinese phrase commonly used in describing the pioneers in rural reform is *manshang bu manxian*, which literally means concealing (the practice) from superiors but not subordinates. Hence it would never be possible for us to count directly the number of teams or brigades secretly adopting more liberal policies without central authorization, though the results from the earlier regression analysis indicate that variables other than central policy explain about half of the variations in provincial reform propensity. As a result, just as we were pleasantly surprised by the swiftness of the democratic revolutions in East Europe and the former Soviet Union, students of China were surprised by the rapidity with which the commune system was dismantled, in less than five years.[75] As of the beginning of 1979, however, the political struggle over the adoption of the household responsibility system was still to come. The rest of the chapter again concentrates on the struggle at the top, but with a view to its linkages to local developments—thus the interests of peasants—through a devoted group of opinion makers and local officials.

1979: A Window of Opportunity for the Household Responsibility System

On January 11, 1979, the CCP Central Committee issued the draft "Decision" and the New Sixty Articles. Even though the two documents did not authorize the household responsibility system, their emphasis on team rights, on distribution according to labor, and on protection of private plots, family sidelines, and rural market fairs clearly signaled a departure from agrarian radicalism. There was also talk of "letting some commune members become prosperous first."[76] These were a timely tonic for areas that had adopted some form of the responsibility system. As discussed earlier, in Anhui, Sichuan, Guizhou, and other areas, *lianchan daozu* (linking output to the group) and even *lianchan daohu* (linking output to the household) were already spreading, even though the latter was explicitly prohibited by Third Plenum documents. The promulgation of the two documents also resulted in demands for dividing rural organizations, election of rural cadres, and tension between lower-level cadres and their superiors.[77]

These developments introduced elements of instability in rural areas, undermining support for the "team as the foundation" and disrupting agricultural work (especially preparations for spring plowing and planting).

Not surprisingly, they aroused controversy within the Chinese leadership. From March 12 to March 24, 1979, the newly established State Agriculture Commission, headed by Vice-Premier Wang Renzhong, convened a meeting of agricultural leaders in seven provinces (Guangdong, Hunan, Sichuan, Jiangsu, Anhui, Hebei, and Jilin) to discuss the responsibility system. At the meeting, it was agreed that it would be unreasonable to request peasants living in isolated valleys to walk several *li* of mountainous paths to go to the production team every day. Therefore, the meeting suggested that these peasants be permitted to practice contracting output to the household. Nevertheless, the minutes of the meeting, which were approved for general issue by the Central Committee in April, concluded that contracting output to the household was by nature "little different from dividing the land to households (i.e., individual farming)" and therefore should not be permitted. Indeed, the Central Committee's commentary in the minutes called on "areas that have implemented the *baogan daohu* to actively reorganize peasants [into collectives]."[78] Wang was willing to tolerate limited diversity as long as the collective economy remained dominant in rural China.[79]

To stem the rising tide of dividing up collective property, Wang Renzhong and his supporters allegedly orchestrated the publication of the "Letter by Zhang Hao" while the State Agriculture Commission meeting was in session.[80] On March 15, 1979, the *People's Daily* printed on half of the front page a letter from a certain Zhang Hao of the Gansu Bureau of Archives as well as the editor's comments and an accompanying report.[81] The letter, which had previously appeared in internal reference publications, reported that in Henan's Luoyang prefecture, production teams were being or would soon be divided into groups. The groups were each given a share of collective property and assigned output responsibility; they were replacing the team as the accounting unit. According to the letter, not only did contracting to groups undermine the team, the pillar of the collective economy, but it was also against the wishes of cadres and peasants and therefore incorrect. In the editorial comments, the "editor" affirmed that "Comrade Zhang Hao's opinion is correct."[82] For added effect, the paper printed on the same page the story of Nanweizi commune in Jilin, which cracked down on the practice of making the small group the accounting unit.

The publication of the Zhang Hao letter and the editorial comments on the front page of the *People's Daily* were a political bombshell for rural cadres accustomed to reading between the lines, and they suspected that powerful political forces in Beijing were seeking to put a stop to liberalization in rural areas. In the various localities in Anhui that had already adopted the group and household responsibility systems, cadres and peasants especially felt the threat behind the publication. They feared that "they are once again to suffer from [political] criticism. Those who feared that the party's policies might change are becoming even more suspicious." Still others apparently liked what they read and condemned the output-linked responsibility system as totally without merit.[83] The sense of policy instability at the local level threatened spring planting. In Huoqui county (Anhui), which had adopted a responsibility system, the county leaders read the *People's Daily* and became afraid. They telephoned the provincial authorities for a decision.[84]

The day after the Zhang Hao letter was published, Wan Li happened to be visiting in Chuxian prefecture. The letter caught him flat-footed. Yet, faced with jittery cadres who eagerly awaited him, Wan Li, in what came to be regarded a bold act of leadership, asked the cadres not to waver and contended that not only was contracting to groups acceptable, but even when localities had adopted household contracting, as in Feixi, they should also be permitted to continue.[85] On the same day, Wang Renzhong, the head of the State Agriculture Commission, telephoned Wan Li on behalf of Hua Guofeng to find out what was going on in Anhui. Wan Li stated that he had authorized experiments with various forms of contracting and struck an accord with Wang that small-group contracting be permitted in order to protect peasant initiatives and that, although the experiments with contracting might continue, they would not receive any publicity. Even Hua agreed that Anhui might experiment with household contracting on the condition that the collective road must not be changed and must be insisted upon.[86] In the meantime, the Anhui Agriculture Commission was instructed to write a letter to the *People's Daily* to explain and defend the province's policies. The letter argued that contracting to the group produced superior results and that people avoided the word "*bao*" because of the lingering influence of the Gang of Four.[87] In light of the spring planting season, the letter suggested, those areas that had adopted contracting to the group should be stabilized so as to avoid unnecessary disruptions, and they would "sum up experiences later." The *People's Daily* printed the Anhui letter on March 30 in the name of airing different opinions—a concession in itself. However, as a reflection of the divergent views within the Chinese leadership, the paper simultaneously printed another letter from a Henan commune party secretary affirming the need to stop the practice of dividing up teams.[88] A *People's Daily* commentary published on April 6, 1979, further emphasized that dividing up the team (or making the accounting unit smaller than the team), individual farming (*fentian dan'gan*), and contracting output to the household "were not in conformity with the Party's policies" and ought to be rectified.[89]

As results of the summer harvest began to come in, those who supported the Zhang Hao letter were put on the defensive, especially in light of the Chinese leadership's urgent quest for more grain production to cover the state grain deficit.[90] In the aftermath of the 1978 drought, Anhui's summer wheat output in 1979 increased by 32 percent over 1978.[91] Indeed,

despite a severe drought, Chuxian, Lu'an, and Chaohu prefectures in Anhui saw their summer wheat output increase by 20–30 percent over 1978,
far outpacing the national growth rate. Anhui's Jiashan county and Sichuan's Leshan prefecture were similarly praised. The bumper harvest in
these areas was attributed to their higher percentages of teams having
adopted an output-linked responsibility system.[92] One read headlines like
these: "Policies Win Popular Support, Miracle amid Severe Drought,"
"Convincing Facts Prove Group Responsibility System Promotes the Development of Production."[93] As an unnamed, but clearly well-placed, reporter for the Xinhua News Agency wrote in an overview of the summer
harvest: "The more completely an area eradicated 'egalitarianism' and
adopted a production responsibility system . . . , the larger the increase in
output that area enjoyed." Arguing that the system "was conducive to
speeding up collective production and was a popular policy," the reporter
apparently deemed it politically safe to take a jab at the Zhang Hao letter
affair by rhetorically asking why such a good policy was "criticized as
'rightist retrogression' by certain people" in the spring and even the summer of 1979.[94]

In the meantime, the leadership in Feixi county in Anhui was having
second thoughts about continuing with practices that Beijing had not authorized. In late July, it wanted to take back the land that had been assigned to households and instructed local cadres to do so. But peasants
and local cadres were unenthusiastic about the reversal. Wang Xuezhou,
party secretary of Ruidian commune, where the 1979 summer harvest
more than quadrupled from 1978, actively lobbied county and provincial
officials. In the name of the masses, he argued that household responsibility was conducive to the consolidation of the collective economy and
stimulated peasant initiatives. In early August, the Feixi county decision
was reversed.[95]

In Sichuan, the situation also began to brighten for those desiring
household contracting. On September 20, 1979, *Sichuan Daily* reported that
one production team in Luxian county, by contracting small fields to
households for soybean cultivation, saw a big increase in production.
This immediately encouraged numerous other localities to adopt similar
practices.[96]

When the Eleventh Central Committee of the Chinese Communist
Party convened its Fourth Plenum on September 25–28, 1979, formally to
approve the "Decision on Some Questions Concerning the Acceleration
of Agricultural Development," the evidence from the summer harvest
pointed to the potential benefit of further policy moderation. At the plenum, a senior cadre, who had taken part in the rural investigations, again
suggested the phrase "with the exception of" to modify the two "do not
permit" phrases contained in the draft "Decision."[97] This time, the modification was adopted. The final version of the "Decision" reads: "Dividing

land to the household must not be permitted. With the exception of certain sideline productions with special needs and of isolated households living in inaccessible mountainous areas, contracting output to the household should also not be adopted."[98]

Reaching a Verdict: 1980–81

Not only did the reformist experiences of Anhui, Gansu, Guizhou, Sichuan, and other areas help soften the Chinese leadership's resistance to moderate policies, but they also helped the careers of provincial leaders who rode the reform tide. Zhao Ziyang, known for his experiments with industrial reform as well as for his support of more liberal agricultural practices, became a member of the Politburo in September 1979 and, together with Hu Yaobang, a member of its standing committee in February 1980; Wan Li became a full member of the newly formed secretariat of the Central Committee (Hu Yaobang was general secretary and Wan Li was ranked ahead of Wang Renzhong) in February 1980.[99] In early 1980, both Zhao Ziyang and Wan Li were appointed vice-premiers, while Ji Dengkui, Hua Guofeng's agriculture policy point man, was stripped of his post. Zhao Ziyang assumed overall responsibility for the economy, Wan Li for agriculture. In August 1980, Wan Li formally took over Wang Renzhong's portfolio as chairman of the State Agriculture Commission (Wang had in the meantime become head of the powerful Central Propaganda Department of the Central Committee). The initial success of the rural reforms up to 1979 apparently facilitated the rise of the reformers to more prominent positions, which in turn made it easier for them to push for more reformist measures. The posthumous rehabilitation of Liu Shaoqi, the man whose name was inexorably linked with and vilified for promoting household contracting during the Cultural Revolution, also served to loosen up the political environment for discourse about the household responsibility system.

As of spring 1980, central policy still lagged behind local initiatives pushing for the household responsibility system. The addition of the qualifying clause to the "Decision" at the Fourth Plenum was a small and seemingly innocuous concession to peasant interests on the part of the state. For rural communities scouting for political signals, however, the clause became a rare window of opportunity. By late 1979, contracting output to the household was spreading like a plague, as some reformers later put it. Poor as well as wealthy localities were adopting the measure. By spring 1980, the percentage of households engaged in contracting output already accounted for 25 percent of the total, and increased to 30 percent by July–August, 1980. In Guizhou, the percentage increased from about 17 percent in the spring to more than 50 percent in August. Such households also appeared in Gansu and Inner Mongolia.[100] In Anhui, household contracting was adopted by less than 1 percent of the production teams in 1978, but expanded to 16 percent of all teams in 1979 and to 90 percent in 1980.[101] Even though some provinces such as Hebei, Heilongjiang, and Jiangsu continued to resist the introduction of the responsibility system, local initiatives generally overstepped the bounds set by the center.[102]

As the number of areas adopting the household responsibility system increased, so did the intensity of debate about the direction for Chinese agriculture. The debate occurred at all levels of the Chinese political system, from the Central Committee down to the production team. Wan Li fired the first salvo in January 1980, shortly before he left for Beijing. With explicit reference to the deaths of several million people in Anhui during the Great Leap Famine, he stated that "everyone should accept the lessons of history on this matter. It has very greatly harmed the people and very greatly injured the cadres."[103] Talking at a provincial agricultural conference, Wan stated that contracting output to the household was not only economically beneficial but also politically acceptable. It was not individual farming but simply one form of the responsibility system. In arguments that bore striking resemblance to those that had been used by Deng Zihui and others nearly two decades earlier, Wan pointed out that household contracting was socialist because the land still belonged to the collective.[104] For Wan Li,

Contracting production to individual households is not something we [cadres] came up with. The problems already existed, and the child was already born. Its mother was extremely happy. Ah! This will solve a lot of problems. Better apply for a residence permit. This child is wonderful! Many people went to see it and felt very warm, but after returning, they cooled off. And why? Illegal; will be criticized! There is nothing frightening about contracting production to individual households! Our basic attitude is to do nothing that will attack the masses' initiative. The masses have already approved, and are imploring: "Let us do it for two years, will you!" Comrades, approve it! Why not? Why so much blame![105]

In the same month, the first published defense of the household responsibility system (*baochan daohu, baochan daoren*) was made in a short essay of the *People's Daily*. According to the author, the individual who signed grain contracts with the collective was just like the worker fulfilling a certain quota at the factory. If the latter was already widely accepted in practice, why should the former be termed revisionist? Therefore, household, even individual, contracting in agriculture was nothing to be afraid of.[106] This may seem reasonable enough, but the essay was immediately criticized by a number of high-placed officials in the leadership.[107] Among those officials was Wang Renzhong, who praised Dazhai and criticized household contracting in his first speech as head of the Central Propaganda Department.[108] For more than two months thereafter, the *People's Daily* was noticeably reticent on the rural reforms, including the household responsibility system.

The editors of the *People's Daily,* then under the leadership of the liberal-minded Hu Jiwei, had reason to be cautious at the time. According to one participant in the policy-making process, less than one-third of China's top provincial leaders were supporters of the household responsibility system as of spring 1980.[109] Even fewer provincial leaders were willing to champion it openly, as Wan Li did in Anhui. Take the case of Zhao Ziyang, the renowned reformer. On February 9, 1980, two months before he left to assume leadership of the State Council, Zhao emphasized at a provincial forum that contracting output to the work group was to be the outer limit of liberalization.[110] Zhao may have made the remark to make himself more acceptable to those who opposed the wholesale decollectivization of agriculture. Alternatively, it might be that he had not foreseen the shape of the rural changes to come. No matter what the reasons behind Zhao's remark, he was evidently not openly supporting household responsibility at this time. A year later (February 3, 1981), while touring Sichuan, Zhao conceded that his 1980 remark had constrained the progress of rural reforms in Sichuan during that year.[111]

Cadres at the prefectural and county levels were also divided. Most continued to be wary of liberal policies for fear of being criticized in future political campaigns, as had happened several times before. In a number of provinces such as Heilongjiang, the leadership strongly believed collectivism was the only road to success in Chinese agriculture and vehemently denounced the household responsibility system as undermining the collective and, by implication, socialism.

As the leading supporter of household responsibility, Wan Li struggled with pressures from above, obstructions from below, and severe infighting among provincial leaders. Should the political fortunes of household responsibility falter, these political forces would have gladly contributed to his downfall. Thus, even though he put on a brave face to support localities pursuing contracting, he was in fact extremely worried about whether contracting was desirable economically and politically. It was not until the end of 1979 that he was assured that contracting was both economically superior to other forms of agricultural organization and politically supportable.[112] To gain greater political leverage for contracting, Wan Li, who had just been appointed a vice-premier, took the case to Deng Xiaoping in spring 1980. He reported to Deng on the success of Feixi and Fengyang in implementing the household responsibility system and increasing agricultural production but also on the resistance to liberal policies by middle-level cadres. Deng, who had refrained from commenting on the fate of household contracting during the Huangshan conference of July 1979, made the following statement in May 1980:[113]

Now that more flexible policies have been introduced in the rural areas, the practice of fixing farm output quotas on a household basis has been adopted in some localities where it is suitable. It has proved quite effective and changed things rapidly for the better. Fixing output quotas on a household basis has been adopted in most of the production teams in Feixi County, Anhui Province, and there have been big increases in production. Nearly all the production teams in the same province's Fengyang County . . . have been practicing an all-round contract system [contracting everything to the household], which inside of a year has resulted in an upswing in production that has transformed the county's prospects. Some comrades are worried that this practice may have an adverse effect on the collective economy. I think their fears are unwarranted.[114]

Thus Deng indicated his approval of the practices, though not in strong terms. As it spread, Deng's talk gave a boost to advocates of the household responsibility system. In Anhui's Chuxian prefecture, one of the pioneers in rural reform, the prefectural leaders immediately informed county leaders of Deng's message and took it as unambiguous support for household contracting. In consequence, the spread of contracting in eastern Anhui sped up.[115] In Guizhou, the provincial leadership invoked Deng to counter the opposition and obstruction by bureaucrats at the provincial, prefectural, and county levels. Given Deng's great weight in politics, his talk may also have led uncommitted provincial leaders to reconsider. Most provincial leaders, however, remained unconvinced.[116]

Yet the rapid spread of the household responsibility system in the summer of 1980 compelled the Chinese leadership to come to a decision on its political nature. Consequently the already heated debate on the nature of the household responsibility system intensified at the center, mirroring debates in the provinces.[117] The debate was on two interrelated questions, one economic, the other normative. Was the household responsibility system really effective in improving rural production and peasant welfare? By contracting output and even land to peasant households, was not the household responsibility system heralding a return to individual farming and the abandonment of collective agriculture and therefore socialism? In other words, whether the household responsibility system was to be permitted or not depended on whether it was socialist or not; China's political commitment to socialism demanded that any reform must remain socialist.[118]

There were high stakes for the politicians participating in the debate. To be on the losing side of the debate would reduce one's future influence on policy-making, even though one's formal position might not be demoted. Conversely, at least for some of the participants, to be on the winning side of the debate promised increased influence and career advancement. Power and policy are inseparable in politics.

In this context, both halves of the debate marshaled their troops to support their sides of the story. Early in 1980, Li Youjiu, vice-minister of agriculture, and his entourage undertook an investigation in Anhui, including Feixi. His conclusion: Contracting output to the household was inferior to contracting output to the work group; contracting output to the work group was inferior to collective production.[119]

Advocates of the household responsibility system proved that they had become entrenched enough to field even larger armies of investigators. In April 1980, Premier Zhao Ziyang suggested that the State Agriculture Commission and the relevant departments organize people to undertake rural investigations. In all, ten groups of scholars and practitioners went to the countryside, including researchers from the Rural Policy Research Office of the Central Committee Secretariat (the major advocates were Du Runsheng and Wu Xiang), the Institute of Agricultural Economics of the Chinese Academy of Social Sciences, and the Rural Development Research Group (the major advocates were director and skeptic turned supporter Zhan Wu, and Wang Guichen, Wei Daonan, Chen Yizi, and Wang Xiao-qiang).[120] Most of the researchers had been sent to do manual labor in the countryside during the Cultural Revolution and had come to sympathize with the peasants' plight.

It is both impossible and unnecessary to go over the numerous writings in favor of the household responsibility system here.[121] Their main argument, however, is remarkably simple. Citing figures from provinces such as Anhui, Sichuan, Jiangsu, Guangxi, Zhejiang, and other areas, they suggested that "all areas that adopted output-linked responsibility systems saw their output increase more than their neighbors that had not adopted the system" in 1978–79.[122]

Perhaps the most sustained and convincing defense of the household responsibility system was a report written by Chen Yizi, who did fieldwork in Anhui from April 15 to July 15, 1980. In the report, Chen offered an abundance of data from the village to the province to show systematically that the more household-oriented the responsibility system, the more growth; and vice-versa (see Table 26). Citing the authority of Lenin, Chen dismissed those who came to the opposite conclusion as having used isolated instances to obscure the overall picture.[123]

But Chen went a step further. Using disaggregated data on how differ-

TABLE 26

Output Increases Under Different Responsibility Systems

(percentage change, 1978–79)

Form of Responsibility System	Quanshu county	Chuxian county	Lai'an county	Jiashan county
Whole County	12.4%	12.5%	0.7%	0.3%
Not output-linked	6.0	4.3	−6.7	−6.3
Output-linked	12.8	16.5	5.0	6.0
Contracting output to the group	12.7	16.3	3.4	4.0
Contracting everything to the group	—	—	15.9	12.5
Contracting output to the household	35.7	68.9	37.1	31.0

SOURCE: Political Research Office, Chuxian prefecture, Anhui province; Chen Yizi, "Nongcun de shuguang," p. 37.

ent types of households fared, he showed that the average peasant household, as well as the politically privileged *sishu* families (urban cadres and
urban workers with rural dependents, families with soldiers or martyrs),
enjoyed impressive gains in income, though in relative terms the former
benefited more from the more liberal policies. Because the income of the
absolute majority of households was increasing rapidly, however, there
was no need to worry about income polarization, a major concern of critics
of the household responsibility system. Finally, in regard to some of the
problems in liberalizing the rural economy, including the collapse of some
production teams, the misuse of land, the division of collective property,
and the predatory use of agricultural land for short-term gains, Chen believed, in the universal style of reformers, that they could all be relatively
easily corrected.[124]

After he returned from Anhui in July, Chen Yizi spent most of his time
through November 1980 presenting his findings to various departments
and also at the Beijing Agricultural Economics Association. More important, Chen, partly because of his earlier association with the son of Deng
Liqun, had access to Deng Liqun as well as Hu Yaobang, talking with each
for four to five hours about his rural investigation. According to Chen's
own account, both Deng Liqun and Hu Yaobang remarked that Chen's
report was an important piece of evidence in the months leading to the
meeting of provincial secretaries held in September.[125] This policy success
would help catapult Chen to a number of influential positions, including
the directorship of the now defunct Economic System Reform Institute.

The debate about the status of the household responsibility system
went on amid a general liberalizing trend in summer 1980. Dazhai and the
county it was in (Xiyang) were exposed for falsifying production figures
during the Cultural Revolution.[126] In mid-August, Deng Xiaoping called
for the reform of the system of party and state leadership.[127] In this context,
the Secretariat of the Central Committee entrusted the party group of the
State Agriculture Commission with drafting a document titled "Several
Questions Concerning the Further Strengthening and Improvement of the
Responsibility System in Agricultural Production." The document was
submitted for approval at the meeting of first provincial secretaries convened by the Secretariat of the Central Committee from September 14 to
September 22, 1980.

It appears in retrospect that sponsors of the draft document, led by Wan
Li, sought to issue a final verdict on the household responsibility system.
They were unable to do so. At the meeting, it was clear to all that the
household responsibility system resulted in superior economic performance. This much was "generally acknowledged."[128] Yet heated debate
continued on the political nature of the household responsibility system.
On the first day of the meeting, Du Runsheng, then a deputy commis-
sioner of the State Agriculture Commission and China's top agricultural

policy adviser in the 1980's, argued in his explanation of the draft document that both contracting output to the household and contracting everything to the household remained tied to the collective through contracting.[129] They were the component parts of the collective economy and were different from the *dan'gan* (individual farming) of the past. They should therefore be regarded as a *socialist* operational form, thus fully resurrecting Deng Zihui's argument of 1961–62.[130] The first secretaries from Anhui, Guizhou, Inner Mongolia, Gansu, and Sichuan agreed with Du and favored contracting output to the household. But they were adamantly opposed by leaders from Heilongjiang, Jiangsu, Zhejiang, and a number of other provinces.[131] For them, in the view of one of the leading advocates of household responsibility, that system was transforming collective operations into individual ones and thus represented a retreat from socialism. Politically, it was going in the wrong direction. The commune remained the road leading to socialism.[132]

As a result of the confrontation at the meeting, the final version of the document, issued as Document no. 75, was—like most CCP documents—understandably a product of compromise and appeared schizophrenic.[133] It began with fulsome praise for the collective economy: "The collective economy is the rock-solid foundation on which the advance of our country's agriculture toward modernization rests. The history of agricultural development of the past twenty years has proved that it is incomparably superior to the individual economy." Nevertheless, for remote and mountainous areas as well as ones chronically dependent on state aid, where peasants had lost faith in the collectives, the document stipulated that both contracting output to the household and contracting everything to the household could be adopted and should be stabilized for a relatively long time in order to "solve the problem of bare subsistence." Even though an average area might continue with the household responsibility system if it had already adopted it, the document stipulated that the average area should generally not adopt the system but rather concentrate on the consolidation and development of the collective economy. As to the nature of the household responsibility system, the document argued that, with the absolute dominance of socialist (i.e., state-owned) industry, commerce, and collective agriculture, the household responsibility system "will not leave the socialist orbit, runs no danger of restoring capitalism, and is therefore nothing to be afraid of." But it fell short of saying that the developments were socialist and thus skirted the fundamental political question on just about everybody's mind.

Yet by saying that even relatively prosperous areas could continue with the household responsibility system if they had already adopted it, Document no. 75 recognized de facto developments, a provision localities could exploit to their advantage. At the time of the September meeting, an estimated 20 percent of all production teams had already adopted the system,

Du Runsheng reported.[134] As soon as the document was issued, the trend accelerated. By July 1981, almost half of the basic accounting units in rural China had adopted the household responsibility system (either contracting output to the household or contracting everything to the household, or *shuangbao*) even though the document stipulated that "average areas should not adopt" this system. Even the Shanghai suburban counties, the richest of all rural areas in China, sent a study group to Henan and Sichuan to learn about their experiences in implementing the responsibility system and decided to promote the adoption of all forms of responsibility arrangements, including household contracting.[135]

It was now essential for the center to decide on the nature of *shuangbao* if the party did not intend on making a mockery of its own document and its own authority. Moreover, whereas the center had permitted different areas to adopt different forms of rural organization, peasants took this and the different attitudes of elites to mean that the CCP was not yet wholly committed to the household responsibility system. The lack of explicit party approval undermined peasant confidence in the durability of the contracts and prompted peasants to adopt short-term economic behavior.[136]

Final, official assessment began in July 1981, when the Rural Policy Research Office of the Central Committee and the State Council Rural Development Research Center began to prepare the document for the Rural Work Conference to be held in October 1981. As it was a year before, sharply divergent opinions could be found in every province, every county, even every unit. When those preparing the document invited provincial representatives for a discussion, confrontation ensued. The representative from Heilongjiang was filled with doubt about *shuangbao*, while the Guizhou representative praised it. The Anhui representative was the most ardent advocate for contracting everything to the household (*dabaogan*). For him, both contracting output to the household and contracting everything to the household were socialist and should be supported. Nevertheless, most of the participants favored referring to contracting output to the household as a responsibility system, but not contracting *everything* to the household. The army also joined in the debate, with its representatives arguing that the household responsibility system (*shuangbao*) was leading the army toward collapse.[137]

These arguments were brought into the National Rural Work conference held in a secluded air force hostel (*zhaodaisuo*) from October 5 to October 21, 1981.[138] By then, the majority of production teams had already adopted the household responsibility system and divided up team property. As the Chinese saying goes, the rice is cooked already. At the top, all the major leaders, including Deng Xiaoping, Chen Yun, Hu Yaobang, Zhao Ziyang, and Wan Li were in favor of the household responsibility system, as were most participants at the Rural Work conference. It threatened rural stability to delay the decision or to decide to clamp down on the practice.

Thus, after much argument and numerous drafts, the conference finally produced a document with 25 items, ranging from advice on the use of fertilizers to an injunction on consolidating rural party organizations. Most important, the document termed all forms of responsibility systems, from group contracting to contracting everything to the household, "production responsibility systems of the socialist collective economy." The key was to respect the wishes of peasants. It was time for consolidation and improvement.[139] Central policy finally caught up with local behavior.

If there were lingering grievances about the wholesale introduction of the household responsibility system, they were effectively smoothed by the bumper harvests that followed. In 1982, grain output increased by 9.1 percent; in 1983, by 9.3 percent; in 1984, by 5.2 percent. Other agricultural products, such as cotton, also saw impressive gains. Cotton output, for example, expanded by 66 percent over 1978–82. Agricultural value added increased at even greater speed. All these were trumpeted as indications of the success of the responsibility system and of party policies, even though perhaps equally important were the effects of rising procurement prices, increased supplies of farm inputs such as chemical fertilizers, and the revival of markets.[140] Euphoria was the mood of the day. As one influential Chinese publication put it proudly, "All these developments, though they may seem more like fairy tales than an account of social progress, are actually what has been achieved in China's rural areas in the last five years."[141] Thus when preparations were made for drafting Document no. 1 of 1983 in the summer of 1982, the attention of the drafters turned from the household responsibility system to issues concerning private commerce, labor hiring, long-distance hauling for profit, and private purchases of tractors. The resulting document had only praise for the household responsibility system (*shuangbao*). By November 1982, the percentage of such units had risen to 78.8 percent.

While by late 1982 the household responsibility system had been adopted by more than two-thirds of the rural units, the November 1982 figure also indicates that adoption of household responsibility after the central document was issued was less than clear-cut. Just as some localities were ahead of the center in adopting the system, others evidently lagged behind. The divergence between policy and implementation serves to highlight the role of localities in making and implementing rural policy.

Spreading the Household Responsibility System

Once the Chinese leadership accepted the household responsibility system (*shuangbao*), it made it its own and in the process fully resurrected and adopted the arguments made by Zeng Xisheng and others during the Great Leap Famine that all forms of production responsibility arrangements were elements of the socialist collective economy.[142] Moreover, whereas Central Committee policy statements called for a selective policy, recommending household contracts only where the collective had failed, implementation of the household responsibility system soon became the litmus test in many areas of a cadre's support for reforms. Most cadres, skilled at following political changes, quickly jumped on the bandwagon of reforms (see Table 27). Those who did not were subjected to political pressure by 1982.[143] It was time to close ranks. China's ruling class now took it upon itself to promote and spread a practice it had opposed earlier.[144]

The pressure to conform was particularly acute in areas known for their support for agrarian radicalism. In Shanxi, home to Dazhai, the paragon of agrarian radicalism, Hinton reported in 1983 that "the pressure on all collectives, good or bad, had been relentless." Even though then Vice-Premier Wan Li denied that this was central policy, provincial "leaders were demanding break-up regardless of the circumstances, an all-or-nothing thrust that people called 'one stroke of the knife [*yidaoqie*].' " To Hinton's regret, Long Bow village, the subject of two of his books, "finally bowed to extreme pressure and broke up what had developed into one of the most advanced joint farming efforts in China" in 1983.[145] Needless to say, Dazhai was also subjected to immense political pressure and adopted household contracting (*da baogan*) at the end of 1982.[146]

Shanxi was hardly alone. Nearly all provinces had a few localities that

TABLE 27

Adoption of the Responsibility System in Agriculture

	Jan. 1980	Dec. 1980	June 1981	Oct. 1981	June 1982	Dec. 1983
Contracting fixed quotas for jobs	55.7%	39.0%	24.2%	16.5%	5.1%	
Contracting of specialized tasks	—	4.7	7.8	5.9	4.9	
Contracting output quotas to groups	24.9	23.6	13.8	10.8	2.1	
Contracting output quotas to laborers	3.1	8.6	14.4	15.8	12.6	
Partial contracting of output quotas to households	0.03	0.5	—	3.7	2.2	
Contracting output quotas to households	1.0	9.4	16.9	7.1	4.9	
Contracting jobs to households	0.02	5.0	11.3	38.9	67.9	97.9%
Other					0.3	

SOURCE: Zhongguo Shehui Zhuyi Jianshe Bianxie Zu, p. 157.

held out against household contracting in 1982–83, and the provincial leadership applied pressure to them.[147] Where the provincial leadership itself was deemed the problem, the center paid special attention. The case of Hebei, in which the city of Beijing is situated, is illuminating. The province was under the sway of Liu Zihou and his followers at the beginning of the 1980's. A close associate of Li Xiannian's, Liu had served in Hebei since 1958 and was provincial party secretary from 1966 to 1979.[148] During this time, Hebei was in the forefront of leftist practice, having gone through the Great Leap Famine with only relatively minor upsets. Even after Liu was removed through a "promotion" engineered by Hu Yaobang in early 1980, his supporters remained entrenched in the province.[149] In 1981, 8 percent of the province's production brigades continued to practice brigade accounting.

All this, plus the fact that Beijing was situated right within Hebei, made Hebei a thorn in the reformers' sides. In June 1982, Hu Yaobang was able to convene a special meeting of the Central Committee Secretariat to deal with the "Hebei problem." The meeting decided to send a nine-member work team to Hebei to rectify the situation there. The team, headed by Gao Yang, the new Hebei party secretary, made implementation of Document no. 75 a test of cadre loyalty. Within a short period, the household responsibility system spread.[150] Indeed, because of the need to demonstrate their political allegiance to reform, cadres appeared to have carried a more extreme version of the responsibility system whereby all collective property that could be divided up was distributed among peasant households. By spring 1983, Hebei was spearheading new rural reforms. Daming county, for example, began in spring 1983 to extend household contracts to fifteen or twenty years in order to give peasants incentives to invest in the land. This measure was later incorporated into Central Document no. 1 of 1984.[151]

Like Hebei, Heilongjiang escaped the famine relatively unscathed, with the mortality rate in Heilongjiang increasing by just under 29 percent, versus a whopping 475 percent for Anhui. Moreover, almost unique in China, Heilongjiang is renowned for its favorable arable land/population ratio. Both factors appear to have contributed to the delayed adoption of rural reform in Heilongjiang. For the period discussed here, Heilongjiang's first Party Secretary Yang Yichen, who in 1978 was one of the first provincial leaders to support the argument for making practice the criterion of truth, was more interested in spreading agricultural mechanization than in adopting household contracting.[152] For Yang, Heilongjiang's favorable land/population ratio meant that the province should engage in "socialist big agriculture" (*da nongye*). In this pursuit, Yang was supported and "guided" by senior leaders in the State Agriculture Commission. As mentioned earlier, he or his representative argued fervently for the commune and other collective structures at various central forums. In the province, even though a number of localities risked political disapproval by adopting the household responsibility system before the end of 1982, Yang was able to limit its spread severely. While other provinces took Document no. 75 as the signal for liberalization and the adoption of household contracts, Yang interpreted the document to mean that Heilongjiang would be different by going ahead with more mechanization in the commune. Several reports on the superiority of the household responsibility system were kept from becoming policy before 1982.[153]

As mentioned a little earlier, the household responsibility system was already a foregone conclusion nationally by the summer of 1982. Under the leadership of Yang Yichen, Heilongjiang was alone in still resisting the spread of the household responsibility system. The most the provincial leadership was willing to countenance was contracting output to labor. Under this scheme the local cadres had far greater power over production and distribution than if land were allocated to individual households.

Yet the pressure for change was building up. Within the province, peasants and an increasing number of cadres wanted to emulate what people in Anhui and other areas were already doing. They were well aware that provincial policy diverged from national policy and were therefore not afraid of the political repercussions of asking for change. Policymakers at the center also made their preferences known. In November 1982, when a meeting of provincial secretaries in charge of agriculture was held, Du Runsheng, head of the Central Committee's Rural Policy Research Office, and other policy leaders pointed out that contracting output to labor was not particularly effective in stimulating peasant initiatives.[154] The center evidently wanted to see more liberalization of Heilongjiang's rural policies.

Almost immediately after the November central meeting, the Heilongjiang provincial leadership sprang into action. By the end of 1982, a provincial group led by second provincial Party Secretary Chen Junsheng had completed an investigation of five counties in Nenjiang prefecture, covering brigades at different levels of economic development. In his summary report to the provincial party committee, Chen Junsheng argued that peasants especially liked household contracts because they made the link between labor and reward direct and solved problems of egalitarianism and cadre abuse. Following Document no. 1 of 1982, the report clarified that contracting everything to the household should not be regarded as politically suspect. It suggested that in Heilongjiang, contracting everything to the household would grow to become the main form of the responsibility system in agricultural production.[155]

While Chen Junsheng investigated the situation within Heilongjiang, Wang Yusheng, a member of the standing committee of the CCP Heilongjiang Provincial Committee and director of the province's Rural Work Department, led a provincial delegation on a trip to learn from other provinces beginning in early December 1982. In 44 days, the delegation visited

15 counties in Henan, Anhui, Jiangsu, Shandong, Liaoning, and Jilin and came back to report that by the end of 1982 contracting everything to the household already accounted for some 90 percent of all the teams in the six provinces, leading to rapid agricultural growth and improvement in peasant welfare. In particular, contracting everything to the household was far superior to contracting output to labor. The delegation concluded that, even though central documents permitted various forms of the responsibility system, most areas had chosen to adopt contracting everything to the household (*baogan daohu*). More important, members of the delegation came to understand that it was politically safe to do this. Contracting everything to the household was "the trend of the times." [156]

The two reports proved the turning point in the thinking of Yang Yichen, who was in any case already under pressure to follow the national trend. In January 1983, at a provincial meeting of party secretaries of prefectures, cities, and counties, Yang admitted frankly that the central conference of November and the two reports "inspired him, brightened his thinking, and raised his level of consciousness." [157] As a result of the provincial meeting, Chen Junsheng's report was approved by the provincial committee and distributed as a policy guide to lower levels in January 1983. The next month, Yang Yichen lost his job as Heilongjiang provincial party secretary and was "promoted" in June 1983 to the post of procurator-general of the Supreme People's Procuratorate. [158] For his advocacy for the household responsibility system, Chen Junsheng was also called to Beijing. He became secretary-general of the State Council in 1985 and was made a state councillor in 1988.

With the departure of Yang Yichen, the Heilongjiang provincial leadership began to spearhead the introduction of the household responsibility system: "Following the unified plan of the provincial committee, leaders of localities personally launched localized tests, trained cadres at various levels, and formulated relevant regulations and laws; [they] grasped this the whole year around and ensured the healthy development of this transformation." [159] By the beginning of 1984, of the 66,000 basic accounting units in Heilongjiang, 87.1 percent had adopted the household responsibility system. [160] The last bastion of collective agriculture in China gave in.

Conclusion

In July 1978, four months before the Third Plenum came up with the "Decision on Some Questions Concerning the Acceleration of Agricultural Development (Draft)," the CCP Central Committee issued its "Decision on Some Questions Concerning the Acceleration of Industrial Development (Draft)." Now rarely remembered, the latter "Decision" delegated leadership over industrial enterprises in an attempt to increase enterprise autonomy and reduce losses in industry.[161] Trial implementation of the industrial reform measures was first practiced in six enterprises in Sichuan beginning in October 1978.[162] These industrial reform measures were much praised at the time. Partly for being the first to try them in Sichuan, Zhao Ziyang was promoted to the premiership of the State Council in early 1980. Yet, despite the implementation of these and many additional reform measures, much of China's state industry remains in a sea of red ink. While started earlier than the rural reforms, the urban reforms have yet to succeed. In contrast, Chinese reforms made their initial breakthrough in the vast countryside with the adoption of the household responsibility system. What made the rural reforms work?

In seeking to answer this question, it is impossible to separate the how (the procedures) and the why (the causes) of reforms. In contrast to the one-sided emphasis on the role of the central leadership, this study has emphasized the multicausal nature of the reforms. No single variable is adequate by itself for an explanation. Four key variables have been identified: the impact of the Great Leap Famine, the spatial distribution of party networks, society (peasants and local cadres), and state. While the first two structural variables are independent, the latter two are both dependent (acted upon by the two structural variables) and independent.

The two structural variables have already been discussed in Chapter 5. Here I shall focus on the role of state and society. But first I wish to point out that peasants have often referred to the institution of the household responsibility system as the "second land reform." This brings us to a rarely stated, but nevertheless crucial, insight, for the institution of the household responsibility system was a special kind of land reform—a land reform *without landlords*. The back of the landlord class had already been broken, often literally, in the land reform of the 1940's and 1950's. Thus, as the household responsibility system was adopted, there was no landlord class stubbornly defending its property rights. At most there were some cadres who feared that they might lose power.[163] Quite often, it was the local cadres who led in the division of land and collective property among peasant households, allocating the cream of what was available to themselves and their relatives. The lack of genuine class struggle helps explain why the rural institutional reforms were effected in a few years without spilling blood.

The fact that the rural economy was never regarded as a stronghold of the *planned* economy was also important. Justifiably or not, urban dwellers (whether the bureaucrats or the democratic activists) have tended to regard—and dismiss—peasants as unenlightened and the rural economy as backward.[164] For them, Chinese agriculture was important, but it was more suited to the "small peasant economy," and the dissolution of rural collectives did not affect the commanding heights of the planned economy as long as enough grain and other agricultural outputs were produced. In this case, "backwardness" became an advantage. Witness the sorry state of the far more mechanized agricultural sector in the former Soviet Union.

We now come to the role of state and society in the making of rural reforms. Both were conditioned by the structural variables. Peasants and cadres alike have more room to maneuver in a remote place such as Guizhou, where the party presence was weaker. They also have more incentives to adopt more liberal policies if the province had experienced more suffering during the famine. Yet society and state are also independent variables. Cleavages within the state opened up the political space for local initiatives to break through. The interaction between state and society helped these initiatives gain legitimacy. For, otherwise, we will be hard pressed to explain why the big wave of rural reforms came in the late 1970's rather than earlier, even though the two structural variables were in existence throughout the 1960's and 1970's.

As I argued at the beginning of this chapter, the conventional literature errs in its overemphasis on the role of the state, especially that of the central leadership.[165] Throughout this chapter, I have argued that local initiatives preceded state policies on the adoption of liberal rural policies, leading to the adoption of contracting everything to the household (*dabaogan daohu*). In contrast, even the most "daring" of the reformist leaders, including Zhao Ziyang and Wan Li, toned down rural liberalization in its early days. One contribution of this chapter is to establish that localities responded to factors other than the state and played a key role in forging the path of reform.

Yet it would be misguided to exchange one sort of imbalance for another. After all, various localities had already adopted liberal practices secretly even when Mao was alive. It would be inconceivable to think that these liberal practices would make up an open reform movement under Chairman Mao or Chairman Hua. Therefore, the death of Mao and the struggle against Hua provided the window of opportunity that local cadres and peasants exploited to their advantage.

After the reforms were started in 1978 (without being called reforms then), state leadership or, more appropriately, "followership," was also significant. Even when central policies lagged behind local initiatives, each time the center relaxed its policies, localities felt safer to move further. It is therefore apposite to think that state and society were engaged in a dynamic interaction. In this process, the central leadership at first dragged its feet, then grudgingly accepted some forms of the responsibility system, and, when the household responsibility system was spreading like a prairie fire with or without central approval, the leadership accepted it and promoted it as its own idea, thereby proclaiming the prescience of "party leadership." Many cadres were concerned about adherence to the correct ideology, but the state leaders were also concerned about having enough grain and other produce to feed the expanding population. The latter concern triumphed over the former. Local cadres experienced a similar learning process, though it is important to recognize that, in the early stages of the process, the audacity of some local cadres, sometimes risking imprisonment, made the difference between continuing on the collective road or adopting the household responsibility system.

A final factor to take into consideration is the nature of the household responsibility system. In studying the spread of Keynesianism across nations, Peter Hall suggests that "a new set of economic ideas must be seen to have a minimum level of viability on all three of these dimensions—economic, administrative, and political—in order to be incorporated into policy."[166] These same criteria appear appropriate to understanding why the liberal rural reforms were quickly adopted as central policy. First, the stark contrast between the liberal policies adopted in the aftermath of the Great Leap Famine and beyond and the radical policies advocated during the Cultural Revolution had already revealed the economic superiority of the former over the latter, a point further underlined by the contrasting practices and outcomes in different provinces. Second, the rural reforms, centered on the responsibility system, were largely self-executing, since peasants and local cadres knew what they were doing. Third, the economic viability of the measure proved a potent political weapon with which the reformers battled their opponents and silenced skeptics. In the event, the political victory of the Deng-Chen alliance over Hua Guofeng meant the promotion of reformist leaders such as Hu Yaobang, Zhao Ziyang, and Wan Li, who in turn made sure that the reforms were adopted nationwide.

• • • PART III • • •

State and Rural Society Under Reform

··· 7 ···

Reform Euphoria, Policy Myopia, and Rising Rural Discontent

In earlier chapters, I concluded that the Great Leap Famine profoundly ruptured and then reshaped the relationship between state and rural society, generating the impetus for rural reform in China. I also found that in the ensuing dynamic process of reform, rural society, in response to the incentive structure created by the Great Leap Famine as well as contingent political opportunities, played a role that was independent of the political center.

By the mid-1980's, the pent-up momentum for rural change arising out of the Great Leap Famine had largely been released.[1] Yet if rural society already displayed much initiative for change at a time when the Chinese state was commonly regarded as ranging between being extremely authoritarian and outright totalitarian, then we expect to see even more vigorous local action as post-Mao reforms progressively liberalized the economy, society, and, to a more limited extent, politics.[2] It is therefore necessary for us to bring the story up to date in order to better appreciate the dynamics of change in China over the *longue durée*. As Vivienne Shue warned at the height of optimism about China's reforms, rather than passing quick judgment on the reforms, we should instead ask questions about "how the forms and ethos of the state were altered; how the structure and ideals of society evolved; and how, in consequence, state-society conflicts, interpenetrations, and alliances were remolded."[3]

In the spirit of Shue's perceptive comments, this and the following chapters seek to delineate the evolution of state–rural society relations un-

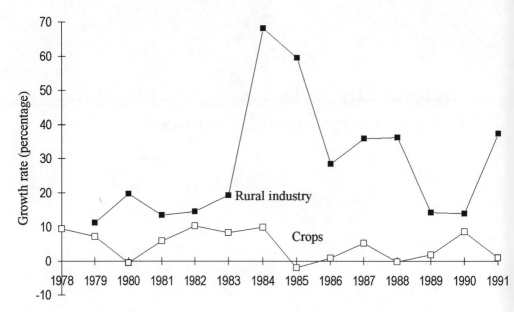

Fig. 9. Contrasting growth patterns for rural industry and crop production, 1978–91

der the reforms. In light of the increasing diversification of rural China, I focus in this chapter on the agricultural sector, which accounts for 60 percent of China's working population, and in the next one on the rural nonagricultural sector.[4] In the real world, there are numerous linkages and interconnections between the two sectors. As in the 1970's, the growth patterns for agriculture and rural industries continued to resemble a mirror image (Fig. 9) through the 1980's.[5] The sectoral division between these two chapters is made for the sake of analytical convenience. As will be pointed out in the next chapter, the blurring of boundaries in contemporary China compels us to go beyond overly simplified categories and recognize the important variations within rural society and between different regions.

Broadly speaking, as we look back at the interaction between the state and the agricultural sector over the past decade or so, we can see multiple ironies, instead of the infectious optimism of the early 1980's. Indeed, many of the difficulties confronting rural China today may be traced to the euphoric manner with which China's policymakers greeted the unexpected good harvests of the early 1980's, from which they inferred that policy pronouncements and science could work wonders.[6] Each year from 1982 to 1986 the Central Committee issued a Document no. 1 outlining rural policy. In the meantime, investment in rural infrastructure, such as

waterworks, on which the Maoist era had put much emphasis, was neglected.[7] The reformist General Secretary Hu Yaobang reportedly showed
little interest in irrigation projects and frequently became ill-tempered
when the minister of waterworks reported to him.[8] Having fought against
the Dazhai model, which put a premium on building waterworks, Hu appeared to throw the baby out along with the bathwater. Thus it was
scarcely surprising that the rural share of state capital construction
expenditure steadily declined from about 12 percent in 1978–79 to only
7 percent by the mid-1980's, even though the Third Plenum "Decision" of
1978 had promised that that share would rise to about 18 percent in three
to five years, that is, by 1981–83 (Fig. 10).[9]

The Third Plenum also set the reduction of peasant burdens as a major
policy objective.[10] Yet, as the rest of this chapter will document, the issue
of excessive levies and charges became more prominent by the late 1980's
and early 1990's. In particular, I present evidence that the rationalizing
reforms led instead to bureaucratic expansion, increasing the burdens on
peasants. Instead of meekly submitting, however, peasants took advantage of the more liberal environment to fight, often literally, for their own
interests. Meanwhile, peasants were also turning away from officialdom
in favor of alternative forms of authority such as lineages and religious
organizations. Rural China by the end of the 1980's had become the land
of discontent.

In the aftermath of the crisis of 1989, rural stability took on paramount
urgency for the Chinese leadership. The rest of the chapter examines the

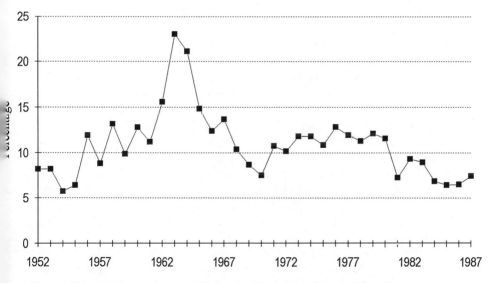

Fig. 10. Rural share of state capital construction expenditure, 1952–87

evolution of state-peasant relations over the 1989–94 period, with particular emphasis on the rural socialist ideological education campaign and the renewed attempts to reduce the peasants' burdens.

Expansion of the Township Bureaucracy

In October 1983, after conducting small-scale experiments in various localities, the CCP Central Committee and the State Council issued the "Directive on Implementing the Separation of Party and Government and on Building Township Government" and thus kicked off a series of political structural reforms that, if successfully carried out, would lead to the withdrawal of the party from daily management and administration at the county and township levels. To that end, each township, the lowest level of formal state power, was to have a township party committee, a township government, as well as an economic management committee or corporation; all three were to have equal bureaucratic rank.[11] Moreover, the organizational rationalization would also streamline personnel.

Yet, as Jacobs, White, and others have shown, the reforms failed miserably in the separation of party, government administration, and economic management in townships.[12] Party secretaries, for example, were told not to interfere in daily economic management but were nevertheless held accountable for local economic performance. Caught in this dilemma, they could hardly be expected to stay away from economic management. Indeed, in certain areas the power of party secretaries was expanded to provide leadership over all three arenas.[13]

Not only were the local level reforms less than successful in bureaucratic rationalization, but in many aspects the reforms backfired. Most striking, the size of the township bureaucracy, defined to include members of the party committee, the government, and the economic committee, was not streamlined but expanded rapidly as a result of the reforms. As can be seen from Table 28, when decollectivization was proceeding apace, the number of management personnel declined from 1981 to 1982. In 1982, the number of people engaged in management in township government totaled 339,000, 29,000 fewer than in 1978, when the rural reforms started. As a result, the ratio of township management to labor (M/L), my measure of the level of bureaucratization, declined from 1.2 in 1978 and 1980 to a low of 1.0 (per 1,000 labor-force population). The reduction of collective functions and the uncertainty surrounding decollectivization resulted in the demoralization of basic-level cadres, weakening the party's presence in rural areas.[14]

In 1983, with the issuance of the Central Committee–State Council directive on party-government separation, the number of management personnel grew explosively by 63.4 percent, far outstripping the growth rate

TABLE 28
Expansion of the Township Bureaucracy, 1978–89

| Year | Rural Labor Force[a] (10,000) | Township Management | | Management/labor ratio (per 1,000) |
		Number of employees (10,000)	Growth rate (%)	
1978	30,637.8	36.8		1.2
1979	—	—		—
1980	31,835.9	37.0		1.2
1981	32,672.3	35.9	−3.0	1.1
1982	33,866.5	33.9	−5.6	1.0
1983	34,689.8	55.4	63.4	1.6
1984	35,967.6	73.9	33.4	2.1
1985	37,065.1	80.9	9.5	2.2
1986	37,989.8	103.4	27.8	2.7
1987	39,000.4	119.6	15.7	3.1
1988	40,066.7	128.6	7.5	3.2
1989	40,938.8	137.3	6.8	3.4

SOURCE: *ZGTJNJ 1985*, p. 224; *1988*, p. 220; *1990*, p. 224.
[a]Here "rural labor force" is a translation of *xiangcun laodongli*, which differs from *nongcun laodongli*. The latter equals *xiangcun laodongli* plus the number of people employed in state-owned enterprises as temporary workers or in other capacities.

of the rural labor force. This occurred despite increased discussion in Chinese publications of the need to "lighten the peasants' burden" through a reduction in the number of rural cadres and thus the costs of administration.[15] Rationalization, as intended from above, was instead transformed into duplication at the local level.

As the rush to separate party and government at the township level was completed, the expansion of township personnel slowed to under 10 percent in 1985. By then, the township management had more than doubled its 1982 size, to more than 809,000. In 1986, the center called for counties to delegate more power to the townships, which were in turn urged to regularize staff size in rural local governments and strengthen financial management.[16] In consequence, the size of township management grew by another whopping 27.8 percent in 1986, followed by a 15.7 percent gain the following year. It is thus the supreme irony of Chinese political reforms that the more reforms were introduced to rationalize and streamline, the faster the bureaucracy expanded. As a result of the two waves of expansion in 1983–84 and 1986–87, rural China was perhaps more bureaucratized than at any time since 1949. By 1989, the M/L ratio had jumped from a low of 1.0 in 1982 to 3.4. Though the trend toward expansion has moderated since 1988, the township bureaucracy continues to expand at around 7 percent a year. By the beginning of 1989, China had 69,842 townships, led by 350,000 township party secretaries and township heads. They were in turn in charge of 845,025 village councils, led by

TABLE 29

Peasant Income Level and Management/Labor Ratio, 1989

Province	Rural income per capita (yuan)	Management/ labor ratio (per 1,000)	Province	Rural income per capita (yuan)	Management/ labor ratio (per 1,000)
Shanghai	1,380	8.8	Xinjiang	546	4.6
Beijing	1,230	4.8	Heilongjiang	535	4.5
Tianjin	1,020	5.9	Ningxia	522	2.2
Zhejiang	1,010	4.6	Anhui	516	1.3
Guangdong	955	3.9	Shanxi	514	13.1
Jiangsu	876	2.6	Sichuan	494	1.8
Liaoning	740	9.4	Guangxi	483	3.0
Fujian	697	2.5	Yunnan	478	3.6
Hainan	674	4.3	Inner Mongolia	478	2.3
Shandong	630	2.3	Qinghai	458	1.5
Jilin	623	5.9	Henan	457	1.7
Hebei	589	3.6	Shaanxi	444	9.4
Hubei	572	4.0	Guizhou	430	1.0
Jiangxi	559	6.2	Tibet[a]	397	2.2
Hunan	558	1.5	Gansu	367	1.6

SOURCE: *ZGNCTJNJ 1990*, pp. 225, 229, 327.
   [a]The figures for Tibet are for 1988.

2,530,000 village party branch secretaries and council chairmen (few women serve in these positions).[17]

   Some of this bureaucratic expansion can be attributed to the functional demands placed on the bureaucracy by increased commercialization and rural industrialization. In other words, more developed areas are expected to have higher levels of rural bureaucratization. Using 1989 data on rural income level and M/L ratio (Table 29), I find that the two variables are positively related statistically.[18] Nevertheless, it is also evident that waves of bureaucratic expansion occurred in response to the issuance of the two directives mentioned above. Moreover, as I detail below, the burden of bureaucracy is disproportionately heavy on peasants who still rely on crop production and have relatively little monetary income.

Bureaucratic Expansion and the Peasant

Besides its discretionary power over taxation and levies, the township bureaucracy is also the most important supplier of inputs and buyer of agricultural outputs. The township-level bureaucracy, or different parts of it, affects the lives of peasants at three stages of the agricultural production and extraction cycle. By manipulating the prices of inputs such as seeds, fertilizers, and pesticides, it lowers or increases the expenses of agricultural production. By adjusting the level of procurement prices, it affects the level of gross income a peasant earns. Finally, the bureaucracy can impose levies that reduce the peasants' net income after the harvest.

Since the mid-1980's, all three aspects of the extraction process hurt the peasant. Operating in an inflationary environment and dependent upon operating profits for bonuses, the supply and purchasing agencies manipulated prices for their own benefit (and bonuses). As a result, the price of fertilizers, pesticides, and seeds rose. Agricultural production expenses skyrocketed (Table 30). In 1984, production expenses accounted for 36.6 percent of gross receipts. By 1989, the figure had risen to more than 55 percent (Table 31). In consequence, income as a share of gross receipts declined sharply. This situation is summed up in a popular peasant jingle: "The price of grain increases one cent at a time, that of fertilizer one dime at a time, that of pesticides one dollar at a time."

TABLE 30

Rural Gross Receipts and Their Distribution

(100 million yuan, current prices)

| Year | Gross receipts | Expenses | Income | Distribution of income | | |
				State taxes	Collective levies	Peasant share
1978	1,881.3	748.0	1,133.3	60.3	188.8	884.2
1980	2,464.5	963.7	1,500.8	66.3	221.7	1,212.8
1983	3,987.0	1,428.3	2,558.7	110.1	201.4	2,247.2
1984	4,891.0	1,790.0	3,101.0	139.2	222.8	2,739.0
1985	5,990.1	2,533.3	3,456.8	188.3	279.2	2,989.3
1986	6,881.9	3,090.7	3,791.2	225.5	297.2	3,268.5
1987	8,408.0	4,035.8	4,372.2	272.2	393.1	3,706.9
1988	11,005.0	5,814.6	5,190.4	303.5	530.0	4,357.0
1989	12,637.6	6,977.2	5,660.4	352.6	596.7	4,711.1

SOURCE: *ZGNCTJNJ 1985*, p. 189; *1988*, p. 175; *1990*, p. 189.
NOTE: Income = gross receipts − expenses.

TABLE 31

Distribution of Rural Gross Receipts

(percentage)

| Year | Expenses | Income | Distribution of income | | |
			State taxes	Collective levies	Peasant share
1978	39.8%	60.2%	3.2%	10.0%	47.0%
1980	39.1	60.9	2.7	9.0	49.2
1983	35.8	64.2	2.8	5.0	56.4
1984	36.6	63.4	2.8	4.6	56.0
1985	42.3	57.7	3.1	4.7	49.9
1986	44.9	55.1	3.3	4.3	47.5
1987	48.0	52.0	3.2	4.7	44.1
1988	52.8	47.2	2.8	4.8	39.6
1989	55.2	44.8	2.8	4.7	37.3

SOURCE: *ZGNCTJNJ 1985*, p. 189; *1988*, p. 175; *1990*, p. 189.
NOTE: Income = gross receipts − expenses.

While expenses rose, levies and state taxes grew too, squeezing the peasant at both ends, as can be seen from Tables 30–32. From 1984 to 1989, the period for which we have data on annual growth rates, the average growth in both state taxes and collective levies exceeded the growth of peasant income and far outstripped the official inflation rate (Table 32). Recognizing the growing burdens on the peasants, the Central Committee and the State Council issued the "Circular on Curbing Arbitrary Levies and Charges on Peasants" on October 31, 1985.[19] In reality, the circular appeared to have had little effect. Meanwhile, the share of collective levies in rural income, even without making allowance for underreporting by township and village cadres, increased by 3.2 percentage points from 1984 to 1989, while the peasant share of the rural income declined from 88.3 percent in 1984 to 83.3 percent in 1989 (Table 33).

Township governments and their agencies collected levies for four major reasons.[20] First, the budget of many of the agencies had been set in the

TABLE 32

Annual Growth Rate of Rural Gross Receipts

(*percentage*)

Year	Gross receipts	Expenses	Income	Distribution of income			Official inflation rate[a]
				State taxes	Collective levies	Peasant share	
1984	22.67%	25.32%	21.19%	26.43%	10.63%	21.89%	2.8%
1985	22.47	41.53	11.47	35.27	25.31	9.14	8.8
1986	14.89	22.00	9.67	19.76	6.45	9.32	6.0
1987	22.18	30.58	15.32	20.71	32.27	13.41	7.3
1988	30.89	44.08	18.71	11.50	34.83	17.54	18.5
1989	14.84	19.99	9.06	16.18	12.58	8.13	17.8

SOURCE: ZGNCTJNJ 1985, p. 189; 1988, p. 175; 1990, p. 189; ZGTJNJ 1990, p. 249.
NOTE: Income = gross receipts − expenses.
[a]Index of retail prices in China.

TABLE 33

Distribution of Rural Economic Income

(*percentage*)

Year	State taxes	Collective levies	Peasant share
1983	4.4%	7.8%	87.9%
1984	4.4	7.3	88.3
1985	5.4	8.1	86.5
1986	6.0	7.8	86.2
1987	6.2	9.0	84.8
1988	5.9	10.2	83.9
1989	6.3	10.5	83.3

SOURCE: ZGNCTJNJ 1985, p. 189; 1988, p. 175; 1990, p. 189.

early 1980's and was eroded by inflation. In Putian municipality of Fujian, a relatively prosperous area, the budget for agricultural technical stations was mostly set in 1980, when financial responsibility contracts were signed. Levies had therefore to be collected to maintain operation.[21] In many areas, because of a limited budget, the technical guidance assistant was so strapped for funds that he was frequently directed to help with family planning, grain procurement, and other chores.[22]

Second was the effect of bureaucratic expansion. Madian township in Shandong, for example, saw the addition of sixteen employees (a 200 percent increase) to its payroll in just four years (1984–88). A number of these positions had to be financed with levies and fines. In addition, the director of the family-planning office and the assistant in mass relations each enjoyed a fifteen yuan per month job-related allowance, which also needed to be financed.[23] In order to have revenue for bonuses of all types, the fees charged by various offices increased year after year, causing damage to self-sustaining development. In Yiyang county (Hunan), the owner of each hand-operated tractor had to obtain at least ten licenses and was responsible for at least 1,500 yuan of fees for road maintenance, management, taxes, and fines. This, coupled with the difficulty of obtaining fuel and the increasing costs for repair, made it hard for many owners to continue operation. In early 1991, 64 percent of all such tractors in Yiyang were reported to have stopped operation or been sold. Indeed, the growing operating expenses led to retrogression in rural transport in many areas, to the extent that peasants substituted human labor for tractors during the summer harvest of 1990.[24]

Third and most important was the increased number of project-related levies and collections. While the central government urged the development of rural education, health care, water irrigation, and public security, it made only meager provisions for funding these projects. Instead rural communities were urged to develop the so-called *minban* (literally, people-sponsored) projects. In their competition to win the approval of superiors, however, heads of local governments at the county and township levels frequently made these *minban* projects mandatory. As localities vied with each other to build spacious classrooms, grand hospitals, and other public projects, the burden on peasants rose. In Wanjiacun township of Pingdu county, Shandong, for example, the township established a *minban* local police station and hired four *minban* policemen. The costs for salaries, administration, medical expenses, police uniforms, and a motorcycle came to 13,200 yuan, which was divided among all households. A *minban* court hired two *minban* judges and cost 2,000 yuan. The *minban* post office cost 4,500. *Minban* education cost 8.5 yuan per head. The *minban* militia cost one yuan per person. In addition, there was a costly sports center, and each peasant was required to contribute one yuan toward a *minban* film project. Peasants reportedly comment with sarcasm and anger: "What sort of *minban* [is this?]. The ideas simply come from above and the peasants pay the bill."[25] The number of levies in Wanjiacun was probably above average, but the spread of *minban* projects was nationwide.

Fourth were the levies imposed for local (industrial) development purposes. In order to develop industries in processing, which, besides generating local employment, were high in profits and an important source of local revenue, local governments found it expedient to get hold of more local agricultural products such as grain, pigs, cotton, and wool for these industries, often at below-market prices.[26] As a result, besides state contract procurement, each level of government, from province to prefecture to county, usually added its own procurement targets, which were referred to as the "second contract procurement" by peasants. Thus, despite central directives calling for open markets beyond state (central) procurement, much of what remained after state procurement was purchased by local governments at lower than market prices. In some areas, the imposition of multiple procurement targets meant the de facto return of the unified procurement and sales of the prereform years.[27]

Like other types of levies, examples of this sort of local domination abound in the Chinese press. Although hogs were to be bought and sold on the market, areas in Hubei and Anhui allocated quotas on hog sales to state agencies and required those without pigs to sell to pay a fee.[28] The cases of Leqing county in Zhejiang and Chuxian county in Anhui illustrate grain procurement. In 1988, Leqing leaders decided that 5,000 tons of rice, the equivalent of 16 percent of state contract procurement, were needed (above the state contract procurement amount) for local processing industries and allocated the extra quota to each village. Even after we take into account fertilizer incentives, the price the county paid for the rice was only 0.44 yuan per *jin*, well below the market price of 0.54 yuan per *jin*. Similarly, Chuxian county in Anhui paid only 0.36 yuan per *jin* of rice in late 1988, compared with 0.42–0.45 yuan per *jin* in neighboring Jiangsu and the even-higher prices paid by buyers from Guangdong and Fujian.[29]

Coping with Change: Peasant Behavior in a Time of Stress

The increase in both state taxes and collective levies, coupled with an inflationary spiral that pushed up production expenses, gradually cut into the benefits peasants dependent on agriculture could derive from the reforms and contributed to dissatisfaction. Since the collection of both state taxes and collective levies and the enforcement of state regulations on family planning and cremation fell on the shoulders of village cadres, these cadres bore the brunt of peasant dissatisfaction.

How have Chinese peasants reacted to the increasing burden of levies and taxes? Available evidence indicates that, in line with the historical patterns of popular resistance to taxes, peasants in post-Mao China have taken advantage of the more liberal political atmosphere and increased their resistance as the burdens increased.[30] Peasants complained the loudest around 1988–89, when growth of their income fell below the rate of inflation. In what follows, I provide a broad description and sampling of the forms of resistance put up by Chinese peasants. In most cases, they fall into what James C. Scott terms "everyday resistance," or "nearly continuous, informal, undeclared, disguised forms of autonomous resistance by lower classes."[31] These include foot-dragging in paying levies and delivering grain to the state as well as acts normally considered criminal, such as theft, arson, sabotage, and other forms of reprisals against cadres. In others, resistance takes official form, such as making appeals to upper levels of government (*shangfang*) and casting votes of protest.

Resistance to Levy Collection

Peasants dislike just about all levies (*tanpai*), whether a contribution to a local project or the grain tax. Most commonly contested are the grain tax and the negotiated grain purchases by the state and localities. Peasants sought to avoid payment of the grain tax and the sale of grain to the state for three major reasons. First was the price differential. With rare exceptions such as the bumper harvest year of 1984, state procurement prices consistently remained below market prices, often by a wide margin. In many areas, peasants had to provide grain (which was low priced) and could not substitute cash for grain. Second was the widespread use of IOUs, or white slips (*bai tiaozi*), in lieu of cash payment, because local governments and their agencies often found it more profitable to apply the grain procurement fund to industrial and commercial uses. For 1988, one authoritative estimate put the percentage of agricultural procurement paid in IOUs at 20–40 percent nationwide and, in one province, 60 percent. Despite much criticism and a number of central directives, IOUs worth tens of millions of yuan remained uncashed in many areas such as Hubei and Inner Mongolia by late March 1989, months after the 1988 harvest.[32] Since most peasant households relied on grain sales as the main source of cash income and usually waited till the harvest season to make planned purchases or to repay debt, the issuance of IOUs in a highly inflationary environment seriously weakened peasant confidence in government policies. Third, peasants who were awarded fertilizer or diesel oil coupons for sales to the state often found either that they could not redeem them or that the indicated type of fertilizer was not available. Supply and marketing stores sometimes deliberately announced an earlier deadline than indicated on the coupon so that they could declare some of them void and thus market the fertilizer at market (and higher) prices.[33]

Given the quirky environment of IOUs, low prices, and undependable "awards," the reluctance of peasants to sell grain and other agricultural products to the state was hardly a surprise. In order to get peasants to sell grain to the state, local governments, with the connivance of superiors, including provincial governments, frequently closed local grain markets during procurement season in order to force grain producers to sell to them at below-market prices. Many discontented grain producers refused to oblige, however, preferring to wait till procurement prices were increased by the government, as occurred every year in the late 1980's.[34] Sometimes, they collected the grain from many households and sold it to the state in the name of one household only. In this way that household's quota was easily fulfilled, and the rest was counted as above-quota sales. Bonuses and awards were thus collected for the above-quota sales and distributed among the families.[35]

It was commonplace and indeed a must for village cadres to make house visits during procurement season so that the local quota could be fulfilled. On such visits, the cadre was often treated far more rudely than an IRS employee making a tax audit. In at least one case, cadres collecting levies in one village were shut up in a storeroom for twelve hours, without a drop of water to drink.[36] More common however, were curses by discontented peasants venting their rage. Here are two of the more polite remarks: "The goods at state-fixed prices are not coming to us, yet you demand things from us the whole year around. I want to keep the grain for higher market prices."[37] "You can't help when we need fertilizer; now you come to get the grain; what sort of cadre are you? You are really like a bandit."[38]

By pleading poor harvest or lack of money, or by using strong language, even brute force, a small percentage of the households managed to evade the payment of at least some of the dues each year. Since the salaries of cadres depended on collecting the levies, however, it was not unusual for house visits to degenerate into quarrels. In some areas, grain-procurement quotas were not fulfilled. In Shangyunqiao township of You county in Hunan, the procurement goal amounted to 8.9 million *jin*, or 400 *jin* per capita in 1987. Because of the difference between the negotiated price (30 yuan per 100 *jin*) and the state-fixed price (17.09 yuan per 100 *jin*), peasants were unwilling to sell. Thus, despite strenuous effort on the part of the township bureaucracy, only 7.7 million *jin*, 1.2 million less than the goal, was supplied.[39]

Thus, in contrast to the euphoric years of 1983-84, when peasants rushed to sell grain to state granaries, the mood of peasants had turned sullen toward the end of the 1980's. In a survey conducted in early 1989 of household attitudes toward contract grain procurement in Hebei, it was found that only 28.2 percent of the total sample, mostly party members, cadres, and demobilized soldiers, were willing to sell grain to the state on time; 55 percent would only sell reluctantly and after being repeatedly urged to do so by cadres in house calls. This group felt strongly that selling to the state did not pay and had complaints about the supply of agricultural inputs. Finally, 16.8 percent tried to sell less (12.8 percent) or none at all (5 percent).[40] Other surveys turned up similar results.[41] Indeed, not only were a majority of peasants unwilling to sell grain to the state, but they also admired those who refused to pay their agricultural tax and other levies and even cast votes for them in elections.[42]

Violent Reprisals

Tense cadre-peasant relations sometimes escalated into violence, with peasants taking reprisals for what they considered injustices. Such reprisals have always occurred in rural China, but the situation appeared to have become worse nationwide since the mid-1980's and remains a major problem as of the early 1990's.[43] A *Peasant Daily* commentary in 1989 suggested that the reprisals against basic-level cadres, together with other forms of social malaise, were depriving cadres of their sense of security.[44]

The situation in Suining, Jiangsu province, and in Chongyi, Hebei, is indicative of the national trend. In Chongyi township, Wu'an county, Hebei, there were seven explosions at cadres' homes from 1984 to 1987 and four already in the first seven months of 1988. Peasants bombed the homes of cadres because the rural cadres enriched themselves at the expense of the community.[45] The case of Suining was little different. From 1987 to May 1988, a survey of twelve towns and townships there uncovered 381 cases of peasant reprisals against cadres: 32 percent of the cases were due to enforcement of the family-planning policy and 30 percent were due to procurement and levies. Another 13 percent were disputes over housing sites and 12 percent over the enforcement of cremation practices. In September 1989 alone, fifteen of the twenty village party branch secretaries in Longji township in Suining suffered reprisals (Table 34).[46]

TABLE 34

Peasant Reprisals Against Local Cadres

(*twelve towns and townships, Suining county,
Jiangsu province, January 1987–May 1988*)

Proximate cause	No. of cases	Percentage of total
Family planning	122	32.0%
Cremation rather than burial	45	11.8
Disputes over housing sites	51	13.4
Procurement and levies	115	30.2
Other	48[a]	12.6
TOTAL	381	100.0%

SOURCE: Su Suining, p. 1.

[a]Adjusted from the total number of cases. The original figure was 47.

Most cases of peasant reprisals, as in Suining and Chongyi, were by peasants acting either individually or in small groups. Because of the heavy penalties against organizers by a state bent on social control, collective action has always been rare for peasants, as for other social groups. Nevertheless, there have been more major confrontations between cadres and peasants in China. Because of press censorship, most of these remain unreported. Two cases from Liangshan county of Shandong do indicate, however, that peasants are willing to take matters into their hands when they perceive serious injustice. In one case, a village in west Liangshan received some 10,000 yuan in payment for contracts on experimental land and other plots. When the villagers suggested that some of the money be used for irrigation projects or the purchase of machines, they were told by cadres that there was "no money." The angry peasants asked: "Where have the collective's funds gone?" Village cadres responded that they were used to entertain cadres from upper levels. The peasants appealed to the township repeatedly in order to look into the accounts. Finally, the township sent some twenty cadres to support the village cadres. One leading cadre said at the meeting that "there is no need to look into the accounts. There are no problems and it's normal to spend money on food and drinks. Whoever wrangles with village cadres will be put into custody." Infuriated, the peasants threw bricks at the cadres. In another village, the party secretary used his power to contract an orchard to himself on very favorable terms. Angry peasants ruined the orchard before the fruits were ready to be picked.[47]

Petitions and Votes of Protest

So far this section has focused on the informal types of peasant protest. This should not lead one to think that Chinese peasants do not resort to legal channels; peasants have also used appeals and their voting power to express their concerns. For example, as cadre-peasant tensions increased in the 1980's, the number of people going to the county administration to appeal (*shangfang*) rose to 40 people a day in Xiajin county of Shandong.[48] In recent years, peasants have also increasingly made use of the court system, especially in matters of economic relations such as contract disputes.[49]

Sometimes local elections become avenues of protest when peasants dislike the incumbents and yet are instructed to vote for someone not of their own choice. As one country youth wrote: "As I daily carry primitive agricultural implements and labor in the fields, tired; as I see the number of children going to school dwindling day by day; as I repeatedly hear the curses of my fellow countrymen and the words of youths who have no desire for progress; and, more important, as I see my hometown moving at a snail's pace in this age of reform, I cry with a pained heart: The leaders ought to be changed."[50] Thus when they have had the chance to vote, villagers have frequently cast votes of protest. In early 1989, for example, in elections held in a number of villages in Jingmen municipality of Hubei, the elected were the dumb, the blind, and the mentally ill (the election was voided in this case). The villagers simply refused to elect those who had been village cadres.[51] In Sichuan and southern China, there were cases where villagers deliberately chose illiterate cadres so that a "secretary" had to be provided to read documents. Such cadres were said to be both obedient to superiors and less capricious toward fellow villagers (thus fewer levies).[52]

In short, China's peasants, like other social strata such as the intelligentsia, appear to have become more assertive in pursuing their interests during the post-Mao period. Village cadres have clearly perceived the more independent and even rebellious mood of peasants. The following quotation from a village cadre's letter to the editor of the *Peasant Daily* captures that mood: "Nowadays, as we village cadres deal with peasants, we have a sense that peasants have changed. They are less willing to obey orders and, in fulfilling cropping tasks, grain and pig sales [to the state], peasants seek not to carry out the tasks to the letter; these things are no longer as easy as they used to be. One peasant posted this couplet on his door frames: 'As oils and fertilizers become dearer, I do not buy; as [state] grain prices plunge, I do not plant, as long as I have enough to eat.' "[53]

Implications of Cadre-Peasant Tensions

Amid the daily confrontations between cadres and peasants, we can identify at least two major trends in state-peasant relations that bear profoundly on China's future. One points to the declining legitimacy of the Communist Party among peasants; the other concerns the search by peasants for alternatives to state organizations. In essence, these two trends are but the two sides of the same transformative process in China's state-peasant relations.

The Decline of the Party

At the end of 1989, China had some 1.3 million rural basic-level party organizations, including over 700,000 village party branches. Those organizations, which were already dealt a heavy blow by the dissolution of communes in the early 1980's, have continued to deteriorate since then. According to a national survey of 1,358 village party branches conducted in 1989, a majority of village party branches were plagued by problems of unqualified leaders, infighting and abuse of power and failed to meet the party's standards. Of the sample, only 443 (32.6 percent) played their proper role as defined by the party, 107 (7.9 percent) were paralyzed and basically played no role, and the remaining 808 (59.5 percent) were some-where in the middle, below party standards.[54]

A separate survey of 42 villages in fourteen Hunan counties showed the same basic trend, with more alarming detail: Party members were poorly qualified and getting older, and, most important, few young people were willing to join the party. Of the 1,496 party members (2.4 percent of popu-lation) in these villages, 41.2 percent (616) were above 50 years old and only 10.9 percent (164) were below 30; 75.2 percent had had a primary school education. While 46.1 percent (689) of them joined the party during the Cultural Revolution, only 11.4 percent (170) were recruited in the 1980's. Three villages did not recruit new party members at all over the 1986–88 period. When 90 party members from Longshan county in Hunan were asked to fill out a questionnaire, only five of them (5.6 percent) knew who the current CCP general secretary was, and 84.4 percent of them were unclear about the contents of the several no. 1 documents issued by the CCP central committee.[55]

With members such as these representing the party-cum-state among peasants, it was hard to inspire peasant confidence in the party. While in the past intense political campaigns frequently required party branches to bring peasants together to hear party documents read, toward the late 1980's villagers' meetings were rarely held without the cadre requesting levies or stumping for grain procurement or birth control. Local cadres were busier turning profits than making connections with the residents. As a result, the party's image became severely tarnished among peas-ants. Peasants commented: "We fear the indiscriminate fines, the arbitrary orders to refuse our children in school, and wantonly putting us into cus-tody." Yet "we have not heard the party's voice, seen the party's cadres, nor received the party's care. . . . I have been wondering, where has the party gone in these years? What is it busy about?"[56]

The party's own history of policy gyrations did not inspire confidence either. As a ditty popular among peasants says, "The party's policies are like the moon, changing shape from the first to the fifteenth day [of each lunar month]" (dang de zhengce ru yueliang, chuyi shiwu bu yiyang).[57] This attitude was confirmed in a January 1988 survey of rural households. While an overwhelming majority of the sample (87.4 percent) were satis-fied with the progress of reforms up to 1988, only 42.2 percent of the sample believed that the party's rural policies would remain stable.[58] Lack of confidence has led peasants as well as rural entrepreneurs to focus on short-term profit rather than long-term growth.

The Party's Competitors

While rural party organizations have languished following the demise of the commune and the drastic weakening of collective institutions, other groups have thrived and filled the party's place both organizationally and ideologically. In the dialectic of sociopolitical change, the processes of disintegration and integration appear to go together and are complementary to each other.

The revived, as well as new, groups include secret societies, technical associations, and credit associations (different from rural credit cooperatives), which provide much-needed loans to rural households and enterprises.[59] While the credit associations are mainly economic and the secret societies are little known outside, two other forms of associations, lineages and religious groups, are of far greater social and political import.[60]

Lineages. Times of rapid sociopolitical change and crisis have frequently led to the resurgence of primary groups based on the family, namely lineages. In France, the crisis of the tenth century as well as those of the fourteenth and fifteenth centuries were each accompanied by the revival and reconstitution of lineage institutions.[61] In Imperial China, the militarization of Chinese society in the middle of the nineteenth century tapped into lineage and local organizations for local defense.[62]

In China's imperial political order, the state legitimated agnatic organizations, which, up to a point, mediated the relations between central power and individual subject. Lineages regulated their own affairs and collected the tax that their members were each individually obligated to pay the state. Nevertheless, the state's tolerance of lineage organization and power had its limits, as evidenced by "the screams against fraudulent genealogies and the sporadic attempts to put down interlineage fighting."[63]

After the communist takeover, the traditional lineage structure came under systematic attack as a feudal relic and was stripped of its political and legal functions.[64] The ancestral estates were confiscated, and the rituals that were the symbolic expression of lineages were proscribed. Collectives were to replace the lineage. Yet, as Sulamith H. Potter and Jack M. Potter convincingly argue, while the cultural articulation of lineages was suppressed, its core structure—a group of co-resident, property-owning kinsmen, related through the male line—survived the radical revolutionary changes of land reform and collectivization for about three decades, partly because of the "feudal" household registration system and other administrative practices.[65]

Despite disapprobation from official circles, many Chinese lineages have been reconstituted amid a craze for genealogical records that parallels the stupendous efforts at writing annals for townships, counties, and provinces.[66] Reconstitution typically centers on the reconstruction of genealogy, whereby local lineages are grouped into higher-order lineages by genealogical manipulation and the setting up of tombs and shrines. In East Jiangxi, genealogical interest renewed around 1984 and built up a lot of steam by 1987, with 300,000 people participating actively, according to the most conservative estimate.[67]

The revival of lineage groups is inevitably bound up with issues of power and authority. Lineage rivalries are rife, and there have been reports of interlineage violence. In Yueyang municipality of Hunan, there were over 600 incidents of interlineage feuds and fighting in 1988 alone, accounting for 58 percent of the rural violence in the area, resulting in over 500 dead or injured.[68] In some areas, the patriarchs of the clan now take precedence over the village head, enforcing clan rules on marriage and inheritance and administering "justice" through the clan rather than through party and government organizations.[69] In the countryside of Yueyang, one-third of the villages had established lineage organizations by early 1989. In Linxiang county, 230 of the 273 villages had such organizations, with many of the lineage heads being also party members and village cadres. In elections held in late 1988 in the eight villages where the "village law" (*cunmin fa*—the Organic Law Governing Village Committees of the People's Republic of China) was set up as an experiment, four of the eight village heads were replaced by lineage heads.[70]

Unofficial religious activities. Unlike lineages, religion has officially been accorded a place under Chinese Communism. The freedom of religious belief, for example, was enshrined in the 1954 Constitution and other important documents. In reality, however, the freedom to oppose religion became a widely accepted practice, particularly during the Maoist era.[71] When they are not openly persecuted, religious groups are under the watchful eyes of the Religious Affairs Bureaus, and they must be patriotic before they are religious.

The end of the Maoist era has ushered in a new period of interest in various religions. That interest cuts across social groups, with many members of the intelligentsia joining churches and sects because of their disenchantment with corruption both in the CCP and outside it. In rural areas, religion, like lineages, has helped fill the spiritual and organizational vacuum left by commune dissolution, the virtual demise of youth league activities, and the decline of other party-sponsored activities. The case of a Henan woman is instructive. When her husband died, she first sought the help of village and township cadres to arrange the funeral, but to no avail. In contrast, a group of Christian sisters came with donations and a helping hand. Soon the woman was a Christian convert.[72]

Officially, the number of Christians under the umbrella of "patriotic churches" grew from some three million in 1982 to over four million in 1987 and an estimated seven to eight million in 1994. Unofficially, underground religious activities appear to be far more widespread, and one estimate puts the total number of Christians in China at 50 million in 1994.[73] There is, according to one reporter, "an untrammelled groundswell of religiosity among young and rural Chinese."[74] Geographically, the spread of religion reaches all areas of China. While Buddhists are found all over China, Muslims are located primarily in Ningxia, Xinjiang, and Shaanxi, and Christians are found chiefly in the coastal region, central China, and along the Yangtze River, areas in which earlier Christian activities were concentrated prior to the Communist takeover.[75] In one county in Shaanxi, not a single peasant applied to become a member of the party during 1988. In contrast, the number of Buddhists and Christians was growing rapidly. In 1987–88, the number of recorded Christians increased from 400 to over 800, and their places of congregation increased to 27, up from only 4 two years earlier.[76] In Henan province, an official estimate put the number of underground meeting places for Christians at a minimum of 2,000 in 1988.[77] In Cangnan county of Zhejiang, it was reported in early 1989 that there were already 837 newly built religious temples and 498 newly built lineage temples.[78] In villages of many areas, 80 percent or more of the villagers became believers (thus exerting tremendous pressure on those who still held out).[79] According to a report by Chinese Central Television in early 1989, the incense money spent by pilgrims going to Mt. Hengshan alone amounted to 100 million yuan in 1988, which was equal to the budget of China's Natural Science Foundation.[80] As one county party leader commented wryly, in his county, the number of religious believers not only had grown rapidly to outnumber the total of party members but they had also become well organized. By comparison, the party members had difficulty in convening a meeting.[81]

The Party-State's Responses

From the Third Plenum of 1978 until 1985, China's reformist leaders relied on the relaxation or liberalization of government policies to boost rural development.[82] In 1985, however, Chinese agriculture suffered a downturn after four years of sustained growth. On the basis of comparable prices, the value of crop production in 1985 declined by 2 percent from 1984, but grain output dropped by nearly 7 percent, leading the conservative patriarch Chen Yun to reiterate the cardinal importance of stable grain production to social stability at the party conference of September 1985.[83] Whereas in years of strong growth the increasing amount of taxes, levies, and surcharges discussed earlier could be absorbed by peasants relatively easily, these burdens and their continual proliferation now appeared far more onerous to peasants. In consequence, peasant complaints and cadre-peasant skirmishes increased substantially and were particularly noticeable in 1985.

In response to stagnant production, rising cadre-peasant tensions, and conservative criticism, the central leadership shifted its focus from liberalizing policy to bringing the rural situation under control. In addition to tightening grain procurement to ensure urban supply, the center launched a two-pronged program to soothe cadre-peasant relations. First, the Central Committee and the State Council issued the "Circular on Curbing Arbitrary Levies and Charges on Peasants" on October 31, 1985.[84] The circular called for regularizing and strictly controlling the types and amount of levies imposed by various levels of local government and for reducing the number of staff in township governments and villages. Strong on exhortation, the circular was short on the mechanics of implementation, and, as the data presented earlier indicate, it failed overall to stem the rapid increase in peasant burdens.

Nevertheless, in a limited number of localities, the rising cadre-peasant conflicts and peasant resistance to levies prompted local authorities to adopt tension-reducing reforms by specifying the amount of levies in advance (Wadian in Nanyang county, Henan, and Xiajin county, Shandong),[85] by linking the payment of levies with cadre performance (Beijie village in Neihuang county, Henan, and Sanxing village in Binhai county, Jiangsu),[86] or, where they could afford it, by stipulating that cadres get their salaries only from village enterprises rather than from levies on peasant households (Dayuqiao town, Hubei).[87] In all these cases, cadre-peasant relations reportedly relaxed following the introduction of the changes. Yet there were limits to such attempts. First of all, their success depended on local rather than central initiative. So far it appears only a limited number of areas adopted such measures. A village or township with more energetic leadership would more likely adopt measures conducive to good cadre-peasant relations. Second, they were related to local economic conditions. An area more developed in rural enterprises could apparently afford to reduce local levies and might even provide subsidies to those who remained in agriculture as well as a variety of public services such as better health and education facilities. In contrast, areas still relying on less-profitable crop production found it harder to give up any of the collections.

The second plank of the central program for gaining greater control of the countryside was a rural party rectification program launched in November 1985, two years after a similar campaign had been started in urban areas. The center explicitly pointed out that some rural party organizations lacked discipline and even ceased to function. Moreover, a substantial number (*bu shao*) of party members failed to perform; some had abused their power for personal gains and even committed crimes.[88] Though the party dispatched more than half a million cadres from upper levels to help villages and townships conduct the rectification, it proceeded superficially and eventually lost momentum as the central leadership grappled with urban unrest and its political consequences in winter 1986 and spring 1987. According to a study by Hsi-Sheng Ch'i, by the conclusion of the rural party rectification campaign in spring 1987, the offenses by party members had worsened, and mass discontent had in fact increased: "Overall, the rural rectification campaign represented wasted energy and accomplished little insofar as [party] discipline was concerned."[89] As Wei Qichang, party secretary of Liangshan county in Shandong, put it none too subtly in 1988, "Rural cadre-mass relations have reached a critical point, which, if not resolved, will lead to trouble."[90]

Thus when the more cautiously inclined Li Peng formally assumed the State Council premiership in spring 1988, the rural problems—stagnant grain production and peasant income, tense cadre-peasant relations, and declining party influence—had been simmering for some time. These problems became even worse when the abortive price-reform program pushed by Deng Xiaoping in the summer of 1988 unleashed galloping inflation, sharply increasing input prices for agricultural production. Compared with 1987, both the output value of crop production (in real terms) and grain output declined in 1988.

As the central leadership scrambled to stabilize the economy in fall 1988, it made a determined effort to promote agriculture so that an increased supply of agricultural products would help bring down inflation. In September, the State Council decided to make state agencies the sole purchasers and sellers of fertilizers, pesticides, and plastic film for greenhouses for agricultural use in order to cut private speculators out and hold down the prices of these key agricultural inputs.[91] In November, the Central Committee and the State Council issued a joint decision calling for measures to achieve bumper grain harvests in 1989–90.[92] The following month, the State Council directed that a special agricultural development fund be established on the basis of a number of revenue sources to boost the amount of agricultural investment.[93]

State-Peasant Relations After Tiananmen

Though they were only partially implemented at the time, the above-mentioned measures, together with diminishing opportunities in nonagricultural activities induced by the economic austerity program, appeared to have indeed contributed to the record-setting grain harvests in 1989-90.[94] Most fundamentally, the absence of an agricultural crisis in 1989 allowed the regime to concentrate on its crackdown in urban areas, which in turn testified to the political importance of boosting agriculture and maintaining rural stability. A year after the Tiananmen crackdown, General Secretary Jiang Zemin underscored this point: "When the rural areas are stable and peasants live and work in peace and contentment, the overall stability of our country and society will be fundamentally guaranteed."[95]

The post-Tiananmen leadership adopted a carrot-and-stick approach to ensuring stability in the rural areas. On the one hand, it sought to impose political domination over the countryside through a rural socialist ideological education campaign. On the other hand, it placated peasants by offering to increase agricultural investment and reduce their burdens. Since the failure of the ideological education campaign and the resurgence of reformism, the carrot approach has become dominant. Capping this trend, the central authorities in early 1994 decided to extend existing agricultural land contracts for 30 more years, thus assuring peasants that existing agricultural policies introduced during the post-Mao reforms would not be reversed.

The Politics of Control

In the immediate aftermath of the Tiananmen crisis, the central leadership nervously preoccupied itself with social control and political stability. Pointing out that social stability crucially depended on rural social stability, then Minister of Civil Affairs Cui Naifu in July 1989 called for "rectifying the situation of paralysis and semiparalysis of village residents' committees in certain areas."[96] In August, the party Propaganda Department concluded that "rural ideological and political work was still weak," for which Zhao Ziyang, the deposed party general secretary, became the scapegoat.[97] According to Dai Zhou, a deputy director of the Propaganda Department, Zhao had allegedly made the "mistake of trivializing the party's leadership and weakening ideological and political work." In consequence, "many people weakened their faith in communism, their party consciousness, and their socialist ideology. This is an important source of the many rampant unhealthy tendencies in rural society."[98]

Among the tendencies Dai referred to were the revival of lineages and the spread of religion, as well as the rise of various crimes. One writer referred to the reconstruction of genealogies as a type of "anarchistic behavior" (wu zhengfu xingwei) that defied state power and argued that such behavior should be "resolutely stopped."[99] In the context of China's political crisis, combatting these tendencies acquired urgency for the leadership. In a letter to General Secretary Jiang Zemin dated April 4, 1990, patriarch Chen Yun wrote that he was "deeply disturbed" by "the increasingly rampant counterrevolutionary activities [being committed] under religious guises." He pointed out that religious encroachment, especially the use of religion to attract youths, was one of the main reasons that Communist parties in certain countries had fallen from power.[100] In response, Jiang Zemin called for "adopting strong measures in order to avert serious consequences."[101]

The most prominent of the measures was a rural socialist ideological education program for the 1990–93 period, which the Central Committee launched in late 1990. That the name of the 1990 program reminds us of the socialist education movement of the 1960's is no coincidence, for both were efforts by central elites, following periods of liberalization, to "educate" the masses so that they could be better controlled. The goals of the 1990 program were to "carry out the party's basic line, strengthen and improve the leadership of the party over rural work, enhance the building of rural party organizations and political power, uphold social stability, solidify the rural socialist front, and promote rural economic development and social progress." [102] By mid-February 1991, 607,000 cadres from offices at the county level and above in 25 provinces had been dispatched in work teams to reside in some 410,000 villages, or 54.9 percent of the national total.

Yet, in comparison with the 1960's, the 1990's finds a vastly transformed Chinese countryside. Indeed, two years before the 1990 socialist education program was launched nationally, an epitaph for it was in a sense already written. In a 1988 special editorial commemorating the tenth anniversary of the official start of the reforms, the *Peasant Daily* declared: "The peasants of today are different from the peasants of the past. They have become independent commodity producers." Therefore, said the editorial, "it will not do solely relying on [ideological] education." [103]

We have already encountered that transformed peasant earlier in the chapter. Full of complaints about cadres and state policies and somewhat rebellious, he or she is a master at distinguishing between genuine benefits and empty words. Like other segments of society, the peasant is also under the influence of "reverse mentality" (*nifan xinli*).[104] Efforts to educate peasants without concomitant changes in the structure of incentives may have a boomerang effect by making them even more distrustful.

The cadres sent to educate the peasants have undergone profound changes as well. Unlike in the 1960's, when the party could count on the support of a corps of dedicated party members and activists from urban areas, cadres are now very unwilling to go down to the countryside. A survey of 170 cadres sent to the countryside in Dandong, Liaoning, showed that only 20 percent of them got involved in the rural situation. Most shunned involvement in the complexities of rural work and simply took the three-month stay as another of the many onerous and futile tasks to be endured.[105] A separate fall 1989 survey of 100 county cadres indicated the same attitudes. Indeed, most cadres had to be given additional benefits for going to the countryside.[106]

In the final analysis , the rural socialist ideological education program largely failed to achieve its intended goals and was eclipsed by the reform euphoria that swept China following Deng Xiaoping's southern tour in early 1992.

The Politics of Conciliation

At the same time that the Chinese leadership sought greater political control over the countryside, it also offered a carrot approach to placating rural sentiments. I shall first briefly discuss the evolution of the central leadership's emphasis on policy stability in agricultural organization and then analyze the problem of excessive burdens on peasants and assess the center's renewed efforts to reduce peasants' burdens.

Policy stability. One major concern around 1990 was whether the leadership's turn to orthodoxy in the aftermath of the Tiananmen crisis would signal changes in policies toward agricultural organization. This question arose because, with the slowdown in agricultural growth since the mid-1980's, some scholars and policymakers came to believe that an agriculture based on individual households working on tiny plots was no longer efficient. Instead they called for enlarging the size of farms and for strengthening collective management and services in the name of consolidating the two-tier rural operational system.[107] One major rural survey undertaken in early 1991 skewed the questions as well as interpretation of the data collected in order to show that even peasants favored more collective organizations.[108] General Secretary Jiang Zemin's rhetoric attacking income polarization was in some sense a reflection of these sentiments.[109]

The emphasis on collective economy was taken as a cue by some local cadres. In the name of strengthening the collective economy, some arbitrarily changed the terms of contracts with peasants and increased the fees and levies peasants had to pay. Still others allegedly took back some or all of the land that had been contracted.[110] While these actions undoubtedly also occurred before 1989 (though it is unclear how frequently they occurred), they nevertheless served to undermine the peasants' confidence in central policies and were not conducive to rural stability.

To counter these developments, senior officials in charge of agriculture made strenuous efforts to underscore the importance of policy stability. At the National Rural Work conference held in January 1991, Agriculture Minister Liu Zhongyi stated:

On agriculture and rural economy, [we] must especially emphasize basic policy stability. Only by consistently implementing the policies set by the Party Central Committee and the State Council over the long run can the overall situation be stabilized and popular feelings assured. The household responsibility system is the Party's main and fundamental policy in the countryside.[111]

In early 1994, central authorities decided to extend existing agricultural land contracts for 30 more years and "permit the compensated transfer of the right to land use according to law." This constituted a de facto recognition of peasants' rights to land use.[112]

Agricultural production and peasant income. In the aftermath of the Tiananmen crisis, the Chinese leadership also renewed its emphasis on boosting agricultural production. The State Council, for example, picked up the tasks it had started a year earlier. It issued a decision on promoting the construction of water conservation works in October 1989. This was followed in November by a decision on strengthening the dissemination of agricultural technology. In December, the State Council issued an updated circular on the supply and sale of key agricultural inputs.[113]

The above list of decisions was evidently intended to boost agricultural production through an improvement in investment and the supply of agricultural inputs. The problem, however, was that good harvests did not equal good income for peasants because of stagnant grain prices, rising production costs, taxes and levies, and slow rural industrial growth. As discussed earlier, the rise in financial burdens on peasants had been at the center of the troubling cadre-peasant relations. According to an estimate from the Ministry of Agriculture, over 1986–90 the rise in peasant burdens was more than twice the growth in peasant per-capita income. Without taking inflation into account, peasant burdens increased by 22.2 percent per year while per-capita net income increased by only 9.6 percent.[114]

As a result of the factors discussed here, while grain outputs set records in 1989 and 1990, peasant per-capita net income declined by 1.6 percent in 1989 and increased by only 1.8 percent in 1990, making for a two-year increase of merely one yuan per person.[115] Most ominously, the relative consumption difference between urban and rural areas steadily increased (Fig. 11). By 1991, the urban/rural consumption ratio had reached 3.0, surpassing the prereform ratio of 2.9 (in 1977).[116] Rural real income growth

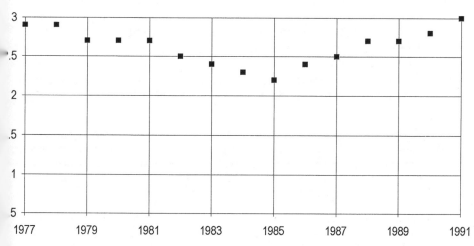

Fig. 11. Urban/rural consumption ratio, 1977–91

has consistently lagged behind urban income growth for nearly a decade. In the rest of this section, I provide a descriptive analysis of the state-peasant negotiations over the problem of peasants' burdens and then suggest that market pricing for grain has emerged as a partial solution to the challenge of increasing peasants' income.

The problem of levies. Concerned about growing peasant complaints and rural stability, the center decided to tackle first the growing burdens on peasants imposed by rising taxes and levies.[117] In February 1990, in a virtual admission that the 1985 circular on curbing arbitrary levies on peasants had failed to work, the State Council issued a strongly worded circular calling on local officials conscientiously to reduce burdens on peasants. The new circular pointed out that the increase in peasant burdens had outpaced the rise in peasant income and stated that these burdens "have exceeded peasants' ability to bear [them], seriously dampened peasants' enthusiasm for production, and harmed party-mass, cadre-mass relations." In addition to specifying what levies and charges were permitted, the circular stipulated that in each township the total amount of levies and charges for each person should not exceed 5 percent of the previous year's per-capita net income. Moreover, the State Council authorized the Ministry of Agriculture to examine all local government regulations and cancel those that contravened the circular.[118]

The circular had no apparent effect. In fact, village and township levies and charges rose from 7.67 percent of rural per-capita net income in 1989 to 7.88 percent in 1990, clearly exceeding the 5 percent limit the State Council had stipulated.[119] In some areas, levies as a percentage of net income easily exceeded 10 percent.[120] Given the absence of effective measures for monitoring local officials, this increase in levies was not surprising. To add insult to injury, as the economic atmosphere grew more speculative in 1992–93, grain procurement funds were increasingly diverted to speculation, and peasants were given IOUs in an inflationary environment. Even post offices withheld remittances sent by migrant workers to peasant families and issued IOUs instead. Premier Li Peng summed up the situation succinctly on December 24, 1992:

Because a lot of the funds earmarked for the procurement of agricultural products are squeezed or diverted, there was a lack of funds for the procurement of autumn grains and cotton [in 1992], leading to widespread use of IOUs. In some places, the tendency to neglect agricultural production has gained ground, as evidenced by the transfer of rural funds into nonagricultural sectors and urban areas. All sorts of levies and project funds have increased peasants' burdens.[121]

What Li Peng failed to mention in this official speech was the growing incidence of peasant protests and riots. Internal Chinese government documents cited more than 200 rural incidents in 1992, and the official Chinese press reported peasant protests in a dozen provinces. In one widely reported case that occurred in early June 1993, some 10,000 peasants in Sichuan's Renshou county delayed grain payments, stormed government offices, held officials captive, and set fire to the house of a deputy party secretary. While the spark that touched off the protest was a levy for road building, the protest was clearly directed at the exorbitant burdens. At the same time, peasants in eleven provinces and cities reportedly stormed post offices over the nonpayment of remittances.[122] Peasant uprisings occurred in twenty of China's thirty provinces.[123]

The chorus of rural protest alarmed the central leadership. Patriarch Deng Xiaoping reportedly stated in spring 1993 that the peasants' burdens already surpassed the limits of their endurance. He warned cryptically that if trouble were to erupt in the 1990's, it would probably occur in the countryside.[124] The state bureaucracy apparently shared Deng's deep concern. On March 19, 1993, the offices of the Central Committee and the State Council issued an emergency circular reiterating the need to reduce the peasants' burdens. Unlike similar documents of the past, however, the emergency circular now emphasized that the roots of excessive burdens on peasants "lie with various superior departments." Many of the documents stipulating levies, charges, and fines were issued by central and provincial bureaucratic departments. These departments were asked to review the documents they had issued. These documents were in turn examined by a State Council interagency small group on peasants' burdens.[125]

Following the examination and verification, the offices of the Central Committee and the State Council in late July 1993 issued, with great fanfare, a circular on what levies and charges should be abolished and what should be continued.[126] The circular pointed out in blunt terms that "reducing peasants' burdens is not simply an economic issue, but is also a political issue. It is important not only for national economic development, but also for political stability in the countryside and even the entire country." The circular proceeded to list a mind-boggling array of fees, charges, and contributions required of peasants. It retracted 37 types of fees stipulated in documents issued by central ministries, delayed 2 others, amended 17 more, and delimited 14 others, leaving 29 types of fees that should still be collected. Another 43 varieties of contributions for reaching targets specified from above were also to be abolished. In addition, the circular called for efforts to reexamine levies imposed by provincial governments and abolished all levies imposed by subprovincial governments.

The July 1993 circular demonstrates the central leadership's determination to deal with the problem of excessive burdens on peasants. By holding ministries and provincial bureaucracies responsible, this new round of burden reduction appears to have had some effect. According to data from the Ministry of Agriculture, the amount of peasant burdens was slashed by 10.3 billion yuan, or 11.6 yuan per capita, in 1993. Not counting labor contributions (which amounted to 18.8 working days per person), village and township levies now accounted for 4.68 percent of the rural net income.[127] In Liaoning province, which has a rural population of 20 million, each peasant on average reportedly paid 40 yuan less in levies and charges in 1993, making for a total reduction of 800 million yuan.[128]

Even if this round of reductions is relatively successfully implemented, the question remains of whether the success can be maintained over time.[129] The trajectory of reduction over the past decade and the relative autonomy of middle- and lower-level officials make it difficult for one to make a sanguine forecast. Indeed, the *People's Daily* has reported that some places and departments have revived levies that had been canceled by the central government and have continued to add to the burdens. Sometimes, the burdens were simply shifted from individuals to rural enterprises or transformed into corvée labor. "The phenomenon of wantonly overcharging peasants has not been checked," the paper concluded.[130] There are also intimations that some local officials deliberately exaggerated the amount of local income in order to justify more levies. Surveys of selected localities in Anhui and Sichuan also revealed much higher levies than the 5 percent authorized by the center.[131]

Concerned that the burden reduction of 1993 will not have a lasting effect, the Ministry of Agriculture has reportedly proposed a unitary tax tied to household income to replace an array of levies and charges. Peasants surveyed have expressed strong support for the certainty and simplicity of a single tax rather than the vagaries of multiple levies and charges.[132] Before a unitary tax becomes official policy, however, the multiple levies and charges will remain a fact of life in rural China, causing friction between cadres and peasants and undermining the legitimacy of the state. China's leaders in turn must continue to keep a watchful eye on the rural scene. As Sichuan Governor Xiao Yang pointed out in March 1994: "This year there will be small-scale protests but not major chaos." "We must pay attention to what peasants want."[133]

Conclusion

Despite their initial successes, China's rural reforms have unleashed sociopolitical change with unanticipated, yet far-reaching, political consequences. While the administrative reform was intended to streamline and rationalize the rural bureaucracy, it has instead fueled an extraordinary administrative expansion and a concomitant imperative for more revenue. While the price reform was supposed to help the peasant, its incompleteness has until recently given rent-seeking bureaucracies a golden opportunity to squeeze the peasant on both input and output prices. And in the name of promoting development, a plethora of central and provincial bureaucracies have mandated local projects for which peasants have had to bear the costs. As a result of these trends, just as the peasant has found it harder to make a living under worsening economic conditions, levies have increased dramatically despite central injunctions against the imposition of severe burdens on peasants.

It is no exaggeration to say that the fundamentals of state power and authority are constituted and decided in the quotidian interaction between village cadres and peasants. To a large extent, the legitimacy of the state among peasants has rested or been lost on the humdrum collection of taxes and levies and the merciless enforcement of regulations on family planning and mandatory cremation. In a process that bears striking resemblance to what occurred in the first half of this century in China, cadre-peasant relations have severely deteriorated, and the legitimacy of the party-state among the peasant population has declined.[134]

In contrast to the commune period, when the life of the peasant was under the cadre's tight control, economic liberalization in the reform period has enabled the peasant to pursue his or her interests with greater assertiveness, and the increasing demand on the peasant has been met with stronger resistance.[135] Indeed, the collective impact and wider political implications of individual peasant resistance, as well as collective protests, have caused the center to introduce policy and institutional changes aimed at curbing the increase in levies and improving cadre-peasant relations.[136]

As rural party organizations and public order have decayed, peasants increasingly have turned to alternatives such as lineages and religious organizations.[137] These lineage and religious organizations obviously cater to more than just the economic or social needs of the community. Like the crises of earlier eras, the sudden weakening and even dissolution of collective institutions introduced uncertainties and anxieties into the lives of peasants who had been living a humdrum, yet stable, life under the commune. Neither the derelict collective nor the state, with its attendant crisis of legitimacy, is capable of providing the individual with the moral and material anchoring he or she needs.

The Chinese leadership has recognized the perils these developments present to its power and authority and has sought to remedy the situation by seeking greater political control, especially following the political crisis of 1989. But the socialist ideological education program launched by the urban elite in late 1990 simply fizzled out. Indeed, in contrast to imperial times, there is no unifying ideological orthodoxy to which the party could appeal, since socialism has lost its relevance and appeal for the average rural dweller. The Organic Law of Villagers' Committee, through which the Chinese leadership hopes to combine grass-roots democracy with state control, holds greater promise to rebuild rural political institutions. But as of early 1994 it was under experiment in 58 demonstration counties only.[138]

Moreover, the trial implementation has revealed tremendous difficulties in combining village autonomy with party control, and it is as yet unclear how widely and how fast the Organic Law will be adopted in the country.[139]

In fact, my study of the Chinese leadership's efforts to reduce excessive financial burdens on peasants suggests that the real problem with state-peasant relations in China lies in the Chinese state's inability to speak with a single voice. Instead, the center must contend with a multiplicity of interests. In consequence, repeated exhortations by the central leadership to reduce the peasants' burdens were thwarted as central and local bureaucracies issued a plethora of documents resulting in the collection of more than 100 different kinds of fees and charges. Even if each bureaucratic agency had shown restraint, the multiplication of these demands still amounted to huge burdens on the rural population, whether or not local cadres were rapacious. From this perspective, by starting with an attempt to sort out the documents issued by central ministries, the 1993 effort to reduce peasants' burdens made sense. But as bureaucracies are likely to continue to expand their programs and power, the problem of excessive burdens on farmers is unlikely to disappear.

Nevertheless, the perception of a crisis in agriculture among the elites has important implications for the life of peasants, who made their aspirations known by complaints and protests and by abandoning agriculture. As China continues to industrialize rapidly, more farmland will be lost to nonagricultural uses, especially in the southeastern coastal provinces. In the meantime, demand for grain and other agricultural products will continue to increase. Since grain production is likely to stagnate unless peasants can make some profits, the government, in fulfilling its stated objective of increasing peasant income, will have to provide incentives for peasants to produce. In the last few years, the Chinese leadership has already freed up grain prices.[140] Moreover, it appears that there has emerged, especially in the more developed provinces, a nascent, tentative turn away from the bias against agriculture commonly found in developing countries and toward agricultural support through programs such as agricultural zoning, price protection, subsidies, and marketing programs. This trend did not originate in rational planning but emerged out of the interaction between state and peasants in a given resource environment. If this trend continues, it will not be because the leadership is generous but because it is fearful. As long as China's rapid industrialization continues, these measures will not stop the relative shrinkage of the agricultural sector, but they will help moderate the pains of adjustment.

··· 8 ···

Rural Industrialization, Political Empowerment, and State Policy

Whereas the going has become tough for the agricultural sector since the mid-1980's, the rural enterprise sector, commonly regarded as the most economically dynamic part of the Chinese economy, has enjoyed an unprecedented boom, save for a temporary interruption around the crisis of 1989.[1] Crises focus people's attention, intensify leaders' search for new information and alternatives, and may provide windows of opportunity for policy change.[2] For the social scientist studying authoritarian regimes characterized by an opaque policy-making process, crises may also reveal relationships that are normally hidden or blurred, thus turning crisis points into moments of truth. China's complex crisis around 1989 was such an occasion for both policy shifts and scholarly inquiries.[3] In addition to the bloody military crackdown captured on worldwide television, the crisis also elicited a wide range of policy changes, including a dramatic reversal of central policy toward the rural enterprise sector. Whereas that sector enjoyed extremely rapid expansion through 1988, the implementation in autumn 1988 of a needed austerity program under a new economic leadership team headed by Premier Li Peng discriminated in favor of state-owned enterprises. Yet, by late 1989 and early 1990, the Li Peng administration itself had reversed the discriminatory stance in both rhetoric and policy.

In this and the second part of my discussion of the evolving relationship between state and rural society, the focus will be on the policy reversal experienced by the rural enterprise sector. It is suggested that this reversal highlighted the growing bargaining position of the rural enterprise sector vis-à-vis the state. Just as the fear of rural instability led the Chinese leadership to modify its positions on agriculture, similar concerns, as well as the growing importance of rural enterprises in China's economy, led the leadership to modify its position on rural enterprises. We thus again confront the myopic and haphazard nature of elite policymaking. I also suggest that even in the absence of democratic mechanisms Chinese society can exert significant influence not only on policy implementation but also on policy formulation.

The rest of the chapter is organized as follows. After a brief discussion of the changed position of the rural enterprise sector in the national economy, I examine the transformation of central policies toward rural enterprises under the Li Peng administration in 1988–90. This is followed by a discussion of how the rural enterprise sector fared under the austerity policy regime and the reasons for that sector's relative resilience. Next I explain the adoption of the discriminatory policy toward the rural enterprises as well as the later policy change.

The Changed Role of Rural Enterprises in the Chinese Economy

The rise of rural enterprises in China has been of great significance since at least the 1970's. The rural enterprise sector produced a mere 3 percent of the national gross value of industrial output (GVIO) in 1971 and 9 percent in 1978. By the end of 1989, the corresponding figure had risen to more than 26 percent of the national total.[4] To most Chinese leaders and the majority of China observers, the extraordinary expansion and dynamism of China's TVP (township, village, and private enterprise) sector in the post-Mao period, especially since 1984, were a genuine surprise.[5]

Table 35 presents a number of aggregate indicators of the growth of

TABLE 35
Growth of Rural Enterprises

	1978	1988
No. of enterprises (millions)	1.524	18.882
No. of employees (millions)	28.266	95.455
As percentage of total rural labor force	9.5	23.8
Gross output value (billion yuan)	49.31	649.57
As percent of gross rural social product	21.20	58.10
Total enterprise income (billion yuan)	43.15	661.97
State taxes (billion yuan)	2.20	31.03
As percent of total state revenue	1.96	11.81
Profits (billion yuan)	8.81	55.00
Total wage bill (billion yuan)	8.67	96.35

SOURCE: *Zhongguo xiangzhen qiye nianjian* 1989, p. 71; *ZGTJNJ* 1990, p. 229.

rural enterprises in China for 1978 and 1988. I have used data for 1988 instead of later years in order to isolate the effect of the austerity program on the rural economy, which will be discussed in detail later.

As can be seen from the table, rural enterprises employed roughly 28 million people (9.5 percent of the rural labor force) in 1978, in contrast to more than 95 million, or nearly 24 percent of the rural labor force, in 1988.[6] In 1978, rural enterprises produced a total of just under 50 billion yuan in output (21 percent of the gross rural social product); by 1988, the comparable figure had ballooned to nearly 650 billion yuan (58 percent of the gross rural social product).[7] Over the same period, the rural enterprise sector's contribution to state revenue increased nearly sixfold, rising from a little over 2 percent to just under 12 percent. Similarly, the amount of exports generated by rural enterprises also rose dramatically, accounting for nearly 17 percent of China's total exports in 1988.[8]

Even allowing for possible overestimation in the data, these figures suggest that China's rural enterprises had by the late 1980's outgrown their marginal status to become a major source of rural nonfarm employment and income, local and central government revenue, and export earnings.[9] Furthermore, rural nonfarm employment and agricultural commercialization have contributed to the swift expansion of consumer society beyond urban China. By 1989, 75 percent of rural income and expenditure was in the form of money rather than goods, up from 52 percent in 1980. On the income side, the cash component increased from 52.3 percent in 1980 to 75.2 percent in 1989; on the expenditure side, from 54.7 percent to 76.7 percent.[10] This monetization of rural incomes has contributed to the articulation of rural demand and therefore to further commercialization and industrial growth.

In short, before the onset of the austerity program in fall 1988, China's rural enterprises were already a substantial economic powerhouse in the economy. That they expanded at great speed in the mid-1980's and became a major cause of China's overheated economy, however, also ensured that they would become a prime target of the central government's austerity policy and of the jealousies of state industrial enterprises. This tug-of-war between the rural enterprise sector and the central government, mediated by numerous self-interested government bureaucracies both in the center and at local levels, provides us with a major opportunity for studying policy change in an important arena.

Shifts in Rural Enterprise Policy, 1988–90

By summer 1988, China was in the grip of an economic crisis, characterized by galloping inflation and severe economic imbalances. While inflationary pressures had been building in China throughout the 1980's, they began to accelerate in the spring of 1988, fueled by panic buying in anticipation of further reforms in the price system (i.e., price increases), and become a major source of social discontent.[11] This conjuncture of economic and social pressures compelled the Chinese leadership to adopt remedial measures. At the Third Plenum of the Thirteenth CCP Central Committee in September 1988, the leadership hastily abandoned its plans for extensive price reform and adopted a series of austerity policies designed "to bring the economic environment under control, and reestablish economic order." The restrictive monetary and fiscal policies were chiefly enforced administratively and included limits on new lending and controls over investment and prices.[12] For 1989, according to Vice-Premier Yao Yilin, the government's goals were to reduce economic overheating, control price inflation, and strive for a bumper agricultural harvest.[13]

Politically, the adoption of new policies heralded a real change to a new management team for China's economy. After he succeeded Hu Yaobang as CCP general secretary in early 1987, Zhao Ziyang entered into competition with Li Peng, who succeeded Zhao as premier, in the area of economic management. Though the younger and more technocratic Li Peng was supposed to assume leadership of China's economy, until fall 1988 Zhao Ziyang more than upstaged Premier Li Peng by launching the coastal development strategy in early 1988 and by supporting Deng's push for the ill-fated price reform.[14] While Deng Xiaoping had pushed for the price reform, Zhao's intervention in the economy meant that he was blamed for the chaotic economic situation by the conservatives and had to make a self-criticism.[15] Henceforth Premier Li Peng and Vice-Premier Yao Yilin would have primary responsibility for economic affairs. The austerity program that was implemented bore their imprimatur.

The Toughening of Policy

While he was CCP general secretary, Zhao Ziyang saw the dynamic growth of rural enterprises as one aspect of his reform strategy to let the economy outgrow the plan.[16] (The use of the leaders' names should not be construed to mean that they can act unilaterally. The forces that constrain and shape their policies and actions will be discussed later.) In his report at the Third Plenary Session of the Thirteenth CCP Central Committee in September 1988, which launched the austerity program, Zhao called for the laggard state-owned enterprises to "draw on and absorb the experiences of rural and foreign-funded enterprises in operations and management."[17] In a sense, Zhao's approach, like that of Mao Zedong during the revolutionary war years, was to use the rural areas to surround and conquer the cities (the citadels of planning). Rural enterprises and foreign-funded enterprises, both of which are outside the formal planning system, were to be the alternative to reforming China's centrally planned economy.[18]

In contrast to Zhao's program, China's official industrial policy under the Li Peng administration's austerity program put emphasis on industries involved in agriculture, energy and transport, export, and raw and semi-finished materials. Across-the-board support (including subsidized credit and low-priced inputs) was given for nearly all heavy industrial sectors, particularly for large and medium-sized state-run factories, the core of the planning system.[19] Because energy and transport had become the major bottlenecks in the Chinese economy, the renewed emphasis on these two sectors was understandable. The same was true of agriculture.[20] Because the major component of inflation had been increases in the prices of food and cognate agricultural products, ensuring an adequate harvest of these products was regarded by the authorities as vital to urban and rural stability.

In contrast to the favorable treatment for large and medium-sized state factories, the flourishing rural enterprises were to fend for themselves and would bear the brunt of economic rectification and readjustment. On the basis of an extensive reading of official reports, Premier Li Peng's implicit view of rural enterprises in 1988–89 may be summarized this way: Rural collective enterprises were second-class players and niche seekers; they were to be excluded from the privileges of planned allocations and were to play only subsidiary roles in the national economy.[21] In February 1989, for example, Li Peng commented that rural enterprises should pay attention to processing raw materials produced in their own village or county, especially in animal husbandry, and coarse grains and feed grains (rather than enter into competition with big state industries).[22] While Li Peng conceded the useful role of rural enterprises in the economy in his March 1989 government report to the National People's Congress (NPC), he called on them to

appropriately reduce their pace of development in accordance with state macro-economic demands and the market requirements, rectify and improve their operational work style, pay attention to readjusting their product mix, improve product quality, reduce input consumption, raise labor productivity, and prevent pollution. The township and town industries should concentrate on developing the processing of agricultural and sideline products, production of certain raw materials, and production that dovetails with urban industry. They should develop the production of export commodities that earn foreign exchange. The capital needed by the township and town enterprises should mainly come from their own accumulation.[23]

In short, rural enterprises had to undertake all those tasks with little expectation of state financial support. The contrast with the government's policy of supporting large enterprises could not be greater.

This line of thinking appears to have characterized Li Peng's views on rural enterprises both before and after June 1989. In a September 1989 talk that was billed as an important one, Li Peng made remarks on three sectors—grain production, rural enterprises, and large state enterprises. Again, he made clear his preferences by urging the development of grain production and large enterprises and by downplaying the growth of rural enterprises. All levels of government should increase their investment in agriculture and steadfastly embrace grain production by "fully mobilizing peasant initiative and using science." The state should create a relatively good external environment for large enterprises. In contrast, on rural enterprises, he said that their development should be premised on utilizing local resources and that they should not compete for raw materials and energy with large enterprises.[24]

In a speech to the National Production Conference (October 11, 1989), Li Peng made perhaps the most sustained exposition of his position and explicitly referred to his differences with Zhao Ziyang on rural enterprise development. "We do not agree with comrade Zhao Ziyang's inappropriately exaggerating the role of rural enterprises and seeking to introduce certain unhealthy elements of rural enterprises into state-owned large and medium enterprises," he said. While admitting to the importance of rural enterprises, Li further indicated that they should stay where they were and develop local raw materials rather than compete with large state enterprises. He elaborated: "The market for rural enterprises, with the exception of a portion in urban areas, should be mainly in the countryside, supplying the rural areas with commodities needed in agricultural production and peasant livelihood." While not ruling out that some rural enterprises might do well, Li Peng underlined his disregard for rural enterprises by saying that most of them owed their existence to "relatively preferential conditions and are supported by fairly cheap labor."[25] The premier was more interested in high-tech industries than in labor-intensive workshops, even though the latter probably better reflected China's comparative advantage. In articulating his position, Li appears to have agreed with a State Statistical Bureau policy report of July 1989, which argued that "the too rapid development of rural industries further intensified the tense contradictions already existing in energy, raw materials, and transportation in China's economy, and overall is not conducive to the balanced development of the national economy." The report argued that rural industrial development should be coordinated with that of the state-owned big industries and called for limiting the growth of rural industries.[26]

The Softening of Policy

For most of 1989, the Li Peng administration took a tough stand toward the rural enterprise sector. By the end of 1989 and early 1990, however, Li Peng had clearly shifted to a more supportive stance, effectively removing the restraints placed on rural enterprise development one year earlier. One sign of the shift was his speech at the National Planning Conference (December 11, 1989). "The role of rural enterprises ought to be affirmed," he said, because rural enterprises "are an important economic form for developing the rural economy, improving agricultural production conditions, and increasing rural employment." Moreover, in contrast to his March 1989 NPC report, where he stated that rural enterprises should rely on self-funding, he now declared that "banks at all levels should give appropriate support to rural enterprises in terms of operating funds" in 1990.[27]

To underscore his new attitude, the premier also made a high-visibility trip to Jiangsu province—a leader in rural enterprise development—in January 1990 and articulated his modified position on rural enterprise development in an address to provincial cadres. Moreover, in another indication of political posturing, only the part of the speech dealing with rural enterprises was subsequently published in the party journal *Qiushi* (Seek truth), under the title "Rural Enterprises Should Continue to Advance." Li's article contained what was virtually a self-criticism. He admitted that his administration had "not adequately . . . affirmed the role of rural enterprises in the national economy." As a result, "cadres and masses felt that the policy [toward rural enterprises] was unstable and feared changes in policy."[28] He now promised policy stability and continuity and called on rural enterprises to improve themselves further.

Premier Li's new attitude toward the rural enterprise sector was echoed by other leaders, suggesting the emergence of an elite consensus. During a visit to Guangdong in January 1990, Vice-Premier Tian Jiyun urged all concerned, but especially the banking and financial sector, to help rural enterprises. He emphasized that "rural enterprises occupy an important position in China's national economy. The development of rural enterprises also has an important role in stabilizing the overall situation. China's development cannot do without rural enterprises."[29] General Secretary Jiang Zemin reportedly felt the same way. For Jiang, rural communities could become prosperous only through the development of rural enterprises. Without them, there would be no "money bag," and the "vegetable baskets" and "rice bags" would be empty since agriculture depends on an infusion of funds from rural enterprises. Similarly, without rural enterprises, state revenue and export earnings would be hurt.[30]

In short, by early 1990, central policy toward the rural enterprise sector had decidedly turned supportive. Moreover, this official attitude has not wavered since. As a *People's Daily* commentary put it in May 1991, rural enterprises "are indispensable and irreplaceable." Criticizing those who "merely find fault with them or even satirize them," the commentary urged that "all economic improvement and rectification measures must be conducive to the continuous and healthy development of township and town enterprises."[31]

Economic data confirm the shift in rural enterprise policy. In the first nine months of 1990, the Agricultural Bank of China and credit unions issued 97.6 billion yuan in loans to rural enterprises, an increase of more than 15 billion over the same period in 1989, or 18 percent. Credit targeting was a central feature of the loan policy, with export-generating rural enterprises receiving 37 billion yuan. In the same period, rural enterprise output reached 343.5 billion yuan, an increase of 11.6 percent over 1989.[32]

To summarize, over 1988–90, China's rural enterprise policy went through a cycle of changes: from support to blame and back to support. Why did the policy cycle occur? What can these policy shifts tell us about the nature of policy-making and state–rural society relations in China? These are the two questions that the rest of this chapter will attempt to answer. Before I do so, I shall first take a look at how the rural enterprise sector fared under the austerity program.

The Rural Enterprise Sector Under the Austerity Program

The most important indication of the center's differential policies toward state-owned versus rural enterprises can be seen through an examination of official lending behavior. Total loans outstanding from state banks to state industrial enterprises expanded from 208.5 billion yuan in 1988 to 272.5 billion in 1989, an increase of 30.7 percent (year-end figures, which do not include loans to state materials and commercial departments).[33] In contrast, loans to rural enterprises from the Bank of Agriculture and Rural Credit Cooperatives outstanding at year-end grew from 84.8 billion yuan in 1988 to 96.1 billion in 1989.[34] This represents an increase of 13.3 percent, far below the average loan growth rate for the 1980–89 period (36.1 percent). Such year-end figures underestimate the degree of credit tightening on rural enterprises earlier in the year. In the first nine months of 1989, the amount of bank credit to key state enterprises and industries increased by more than 22 billion yuan over the same period of 1988. In contrast, loans to rural enterprises were reduced by 7.4 billion yuan.[35] Indeed, the cumulative total of loans from the Bank of Agriculture and Rural Credit Cooperatives to rural enterprises was reduced from 134.9 (1988) to 123.0 billion yuan in 1989. This is a net *decrease* of 8.8 percent. Moreover, loan collection from rural enterprises tightened, rising from 89.74 percent in 1988 to 90.89 percent in 1989.

The above figures suggest that rural enterprises became a major victim of the retrenchment measures in 1989 (all figures in this paragraph use 1988 as the base year). As loans from official channels were cut off, factories closed and rural workers were sent home. While only one or two state enterprises were declared bankrupt, with great reluctance, the number of rural enterprises dropped by 195,000 (1 percent). Several hundred thousand other enterprises, though not yet closed, stopped production or shifted to other product lines. The number of rural enterprise workers fell by nearly 1.8 million (1.9 percent); rural industrial employment was especially hit hard, declining by 4.6 percent. As a result of staff reductions, tens of thousands of rural nonfarm workers had to look for alternative employment. As a result, the rural labor force employed in agriculture increased by 3.1 percent in 1989, temporarily arresting the 1980's trend toward more nonfarm employment. In the meantime, there were an estimated 50 million itinerant rural dwellers searching for jobs in urban centers.[36]

Since the rural population derived a significant part of its cash income from the TVE sector, the retrenchment policies had an adverse effect on rural welfare, widening the rural-urban gap. In 1989, rural net cash income per person declined 3.3 percent, and the first half of 1990 saw a further 4.4 percent decline, while real urban wages rose 9.5 percent in the first three quarters of 1990.[37] In short, the pains of economic adjustment fell disproportionately on the rural population.

Growth Under Austerity

As can be expected, the growth rate of the rural enterprise sector slowed after the center tightened credit policy. However, in comparison with the state sector, which had to keep redundant workers, the rural enterprise sector responded more flexibly to the austerity program and retained its dynamic edge over the former. In terms of industrial output, while the state sector grew by an anemic 3.9 percent in 1989, the comparable figures for rural enterprises run by town governments was 10.2 percent and for village-based rural enterprises a high 17.9 percent.[38] The data for 1990 conform to the same trend (see Table 36). These data seem to indicate a continuation of the productivity growth rate patterns of 1978–88, with nonstate industries experiencing greater total productivity growth than state industries.[39]

TABLE 36

Industrial Growth Rate by Type of Ownership

(*percentage*)

Industries	1988–89	1989–90
All	8.5%	7.76%
State-owned	3.9	2.96
Collective	10.5	9.02
Private	23.8	21.11
Other (including foreign and joint ventures)	42.7	39.33

SOURCE: *ZGTJNJ 1990*, p. 415; *ZGTJNJ 1991*, p. 395.

Besides its faster growth rate, the rural enterprise sector also underwent important structural changes. While the number of industrial enterprises decreased, the number in commerce, catering, transport, and mining increased. Many smaller enterprises were consolidated into larger ones. By the end of 1989, 85 percent of China's rural enterprises had adopted national quality standards.[40]

A visible sign of rural enterprise dynamism was the phenomenal expansion of exports.[41] Rural enterprise exports already amounted to $8.02 billion in 1988, or just under 17 percent of China's total exports. Under the austerity program and thus prompted by weak domestic demand, rural enterprises, especially those in the coastal region, took advantage of preferential policies for exporting firms and stepped up their search for alternative markets overseas, often with the help of overseas partners.[42] In 1989, total rural enterprise exports increased nearly 25 percent, to just above $10 billion (or 19 percent of the total).[43] By the early 1990's, rural enterprises accounted for about one-quarter of China's exports. In short, the austerity program "forced [rural enterprises] into a new way out."[44] As one Chinese researcher put it, the strategy of rural enterprises in East China was "to use the foreign market to supplement the domestic market, and use the foreign market to spur the domestic one."[45] The result was not merely an increase in the amount of exports but also improvement in export structure, as exporting firms moved up the product cycle from handicrafts to light industrial products, textiles, and electrical appliances.

Forces for Resilience

In addition to managerial flexibility, two other factors also significantly contributed to the buoyancy of the rural enterprise sector in hard times. One was the involvement of local governments and the other the mobilization of nongovernmental resources.

Local government involvement. As numerous authors have pointed out, the rapid growth of local industry, especially at the township and village levels, owes much to the role of local governments responding to fiscal pressures and incentives introduced by fiscal decentralization.[46] To be more specific, with the progression of reforms, the fiscal capacity of local governments to cope with intense budgetary pressures has become highly dependent on the financial health of local enterprises, including rural enterprises. In 1988, for example, rural enterprises in Jiangsu province paid 3.5 billion yuan in taxes, and accounted for one-third of provincial revenue. In Shandong, rural industries accounted for 26.7 percent of provincial revenue in 1989. Zhejiang province derived 36 percent of its fiscal revenues from rural industries.[47] Lower levels of government, such as townships and villages, which have many rural enterprises under their auspices and often direct management, are even more dependent on rural enterprises for revenue and, in some areas, were found to engage in "fiscal predation."[48]

The revenue imperative, coupled with local governments' desire to generate jobs and income for the local population, appeared to forge an alliance between rural enterprises and local governments to cope with, if not defeat, the central government's drive to reduce the growth rate of rural enterprises, sometimes serving to thwart the aims of the center. This may be illustrated through a cursory analysis of how funds for agricultural procurement were used. For the sake of social stability, the center desired more grain and related products but was unwilling to stimulate agricultural production by significantly increasing the procurement prices for those products for fear of adding to inflationary pressures. The relatively low agricultural prices meant, however, that profit margins from agricultural production in general would stay low in comparison with industrial production. Hence rural residents favored working in rural enterprises for income, and local governments promoted the growth of rural enterprises for both revenue and employment. The interplay of these interests appeared to contribute to the bias in favor of the rural enterprise sector at the expense of agriculture (and the farmers). One development, widely reported in the Chinese press, was the diversion of funds earmarked for agricultural procurement to other uses, especially rural enterprises, leaving farmers holding IOUs. In China's sixteen grain and cotton production bases, over 70 percent of total agricultural procurement was adversely affected, accounting for 80 percent of the procurement credit shortage. In an official survey of 27 provincial units, over 20,000 grain enterprises used 2.06 billion yuan of bank credit, or 10 percent of the total, for other purposes.[49] As a result, as was discussed in Chapter 7, state procurement and supply policy was undermined, and, in peasants' eyes, the image of the state damaged.

Nongovernmental sources of capital. In addition to funds from official sources, rural enterprises were able to tap into alternative sources of funds made available by the diversification of the economy.[50] The accompanying table (Table 37) lists the sources of investment funds expended by township and village enterprises (TVEs) in 1989. Because data on private enterprises are not included, this source significantly understates the extent of alternative sources of capital for the rural enterprise sector. Nevertheless, the table shows that the TVEs obtained nearly 51 percent of all fixed investment capital from these alternative sources (categories 4–6): investments from overseas, internal funds (including funds contributed by workers), and other unspecified sources such as loans from private credit associations. On this basis, one may say with confidence that the rural en-

TABLE 37

Sources of Fixed Asset Investment Funds for TVEs, 1989

Source	Amount (10,000 yuan)	Percentage
Support fund	96,803	3.85%
Funds disbursed by supervisory departments	198,637	7.90
Bank loans	940,726	37.40
Overseas funds	305,566	12.15
Internal funds	709,126	28.19
Other	264,261	10.51
TOTAL	2,515,119	100.00%

SOURCE: *Zhongguo xiangzhen qiye nianjian* 1990, pp. 180–83.

terprise sector relies on nongovernmental sources for most of its investment funds, making it less dependent on state policy than the state sector
and more capable of defending itself in times of difficulty.[51]

Explaining Policy Shift: The Imposition of the Austerity Program

Having provided a descriptive account of changes in rural enterprise
policy and the interaction between central policy and the rural enterprise
sector, I now turn to the task of explaining why the policy shifts occurred.
The approach adopted here is influenced by the collective choice of political economy, represented by the work of Robert Bates, which has focused
on economic incentives to explain policy outcomes, especially on how the
interaction between politicians and pressure groups has tended toward
certain policy outcomes in the developing world.[52] In this section, I offer
an explanation of the differential policies toward state versus rural enterprises that were adopted during the austerity program. In the next section,
the same approach will be used to account for the policy change under
Premier Li Peng.

For a theoretical approach to account for the policy shift, it must first of
all be capable of explaining the imposition of discriminatory policy toward rural enterprises during the austerity program. For the political
economy literature, that policy outcome is due to the government's reaction to the differential strengths of divergent interests that exert pressure
on the policy-making process. Specifically, governments in developing
countries tend to opt for policies that favor urban residents at the expense
of rural dwellers because urban residents are politically more potent, owing to their geographical concentration and strategic location, while rural
residents are less easily organized. Concern about urban unrest thus com-

pels the government to shift the burdens of adjustment to rural residents. This policy outcome is generally known as urban bias.[53]

In the Chinese case, the leadership's fear of urban unrest was in hindsight justified: The demonstrations in 1989 were indeed largely concentrated in urban centers. Because rural enterprises had been competitors against the state industrial sector, discriminating against them while helping the state sector and continuing to provide benefits to urban workers in factories that were losing money placated urban interests.[54] Similarly, the official efforts to bolster agriculture may also be interpreted as aimed at ensuring urban stability through consumer price stability. In the meantime, there is evidence that the Chinese leadership that imposed the austerity program at first regarded rural dwellers, including workers in rural enterprises, as politically passive and tame, in contrast to the volatile urban students and workers. This was clearly the attitude of Yuan Mu (the State Council spokesman) at the start of 1989. Shortly after the austerity program was launched, Yuan pointed out that the (urban) unemployment rate would increase somewhat in 1989. When asked about the large number of workers from rural areas who were employed in urban construction companies, Yuan responded that the government departments would persuade them to return to the countryside. Moreover, he asserted that "the problem of unemployment does not exist for these people."[55] In consequence, as has happened again and again throughout the world in times of difficulty, the leadership shifted the burdens of adjustment onto the politically less powerful social group—here, the rural population.

The interplay of coalitional interests also put rural enterprises at a disadvantage. While the rural enterprise sector was allied with local governments at the provincial level or below, it lacked bureaucratic muscle at the center, where its main bureaucratic champion was the Rural Enterprise Bureau within the Ministry of Agriculture. In contrast, the state sector was favored by an alliance between the planning and financial coalitions, which included an array of industrial ministries and called for recentralization of the allocational process.[56]

Finally, such an approach also seems to shed light on the different positions taken by Zhao Ziyang versus Li Peng. As Zweig pointed out in an insightful article, General Secretary Zhao Ziyang, like Hu Yaobang before him, catered not only to urban interests but also to the hundreds of thousands of rural party branches. In contrast, the most important constituents for Li Peng (and Zhao Ziyang when Zhao was premier) were the state industries, which constituted the bedrock of urban employment and were the main source of central government revenue.[57] Therefore, the general secretary (Zhao Ziyang) tended to be more balanced toward both urban and rural enterprises, while the premier (Li Peng) sought to protect state enterprises from rural enterprise competition.

Interests, Perceptions, and Policy Change

Yet one might ask: The interests described above were still in existence in 1990, but why was central policy toward the rural enterprise sector changed by Premier Li Peng himself? In the following account, I argue that the imposition of the austerity program unleashed new pressures such as huge migrant flows and underscored old constraints on the central government, thereby forcing the Chinese leadership to reconsider its position. To be sure, such pressures do not preclude the possibility of state autonomy, but, assuming that China's leaders are as intent on retaining power as their counterparts in other parts of the world, the scope of activities for the leadership would nevertheless become constrained by the pressures.

"The Floating Population" as a New Source of (Potential) Social Unrest

The austerity program focused on clamping down on investment. Through the multiplier effect, the decline in investment diminished the overall level of employment. Not only did many rural enterprises (especially those in the construction industry) reduce the number of workers, but huge numbers of rural residents working in state enterprises as contract workers suddenly found themselves out of work. In Beijing alone some 110,000 rural construction workers belonging to more than 600 construction companies saw their contracts terminated by the municipal construction committee and had to leave in the spring of 1989.[58] While some of these rural residents working in urban areas returned to the countryside, the imposition of austerity policies forced millions of others who had become used to working in urban areas into a frenzied search for new employment opportunities in other urban areas.[59] The result was a massive human flow, which the Chinese leadership referred to as the "blind flow." After the Spring Festival (February 1989), reports spoke of enormous numbers, variously estimated at between 30 and 80 million, of rural laborers flooding into various Chinese cities in search of work. They came mainly from provinces such as Sichuan, Henan, Hubei, Shandong, Shaanxi, Jiangsu, Zhejiang, and Anhui, and their main destinations included Guangdong and Hainan, as well as areas in the northeast and northwest of the country, where high-wage jobs could be found.[60] They crowded into already packed railroad cars, slept at railway stations, and camped on the streets. Enormous strains were put on the transportation system and the host cities.

The suddenness and magnitude of the migrant flow demanded the immediate attention of local governments and the center. As 2.5 million itinerant job seekers swarmed into Guangdong (population ca. 62 million) in the spring of 1989, the provincial government of Guangdong sent urgent telegrams to the State Council and provincial authorities in Hunan, Hubei, Sichuan, Guangxi, and Henan, seeking their help in stemming the inflow. Within the province, it requested that cities and counties send the job seekers back and issued a new set of labor-management regulations under which local units and enterprises were prohibited from hiring new workers from other areas.[61] In Beijing City, the municipal government adopted draconian measures by simply driving out many groups engaged in unofficial business transactions and shutting down the various black markets formed by those groups. It also tightened tax collection and residency requirements on the migrant population in Beijing. Faced with declining revenues in the aftermath of the massacre (partly owing to the dwindling number of tourists), the ever-resourceful municipal government was reported to have learned from Shanghai and Tianjin and was planning to charge a fee (*rongna fei*) on outsiders who wanted to stay in that glorious city.[62]

Upon receiving the telegram from Guangdong, and perhaps additional ones from other areas, the State Council Office immediately issued an emergency directive, which called on central ministries and provincial governments to "do a good job of strictly controlling the blind outflow of laborers." Pointing to the burden on railways and problems of social instability associated with the flow, the Office ordered local governments to persuade laborers not to leave their hometowns without a contract in hand and directed that transportation to main railway stations be reduced in order to reduce the number of people getting on trains.[63]

At least one scholar has suggested that such a floating, or transient, population "pose[d] no serious challenge [to the state]."[64] For my purposes, however, what matters for policy-making is not whether it poses a threat to the state and social order but whether it is *perceived* by policy-making elites to have such a potential. Abundant evidence points to an elite perception that the floating population posed just such a threat. The State Council directive, for example, clearly linked the migrant population with social instability, albeit in restrained terms. There is evidence to suggest that behind closed doors, central elites interpreted the situation in far more apocalyptic terms. He Xin, an associate research fellow at the Chinese Academy of Social Sciences and ardent supporter of the official line after June 1989, warned the authorities of the dangers posed by the migrant population in an internal memorandum published in April 1989. He wrote: "The emergence of a rootless, mobile part of the rural population has created a huge unorganized force. (It is already a hotbed of crime.) Once they get organizations with an educated leadership and a political program, the floating peasant population could be molded into a political force, a mobile, armed and formidable antisocial coalition."[65] He Xin was not alone. Another Chinese author saw an "underground society" taking shape among the growing numbers of rural migrants. Referring to the migrants as lumpenproletarians, the author argued that "conditions are ripe for today's lumpenproletariat to become destructive because the years of political movements led by Mao Zedong after the founding of the People's Republic greatly undermined the country's traditional morality."[66]

In light of these comments, it appears that the measures taken by local governments and the center to deal with the floating population in early 1989 were mere stopgaps. The magnitude of the perceived problem demanded long-term and imaginative solutions.

The Pursuit of Rural Enterprise Interests

As can be expected, interests tied to rural enterprises would seek to cope with, deflect, and even reverse the centrally imposed austerity policy toward rural enterprises. While authoritarian rule made overt collective action for such purposes difficult, an implicit alliance—as I discussed earlier—between local governments and the rural enterprise sector softened the blows of the central policy, even though it must be understood that adoption of the countermeasures varied across localities and was more prominent in provinces such as Guangdong and Shandong. In the rest of this subsection, my focus will be on the role of the Ministry of Agriculture (MOA) in representing, organizing, and protecting rural enterprise interests, though other state organizations, including the State Science and Technology Commission, have also been supporters of rural enterprises. This focus is justified on the ground that the MOA's bureaucratic interest and potential influence were bound up with the fate of rural enterprises. Thus it can be expected that the MOA would be the most strenuous advocate for central policy relaxation.

In March 1989, shortly after the center decided to tighten control over rural migrant workers, the MOA convened a meeting of rural enterprise representatives and more than 40 NPC delegates from rural enterprises. The participants concurred that the sudden increase in the migrant population represented a threat to social stability. Yet, rather than advocating stricter control, they argued that the root of the problem was the central government policy on rural enterprises. Minister of Agriculture He Kang commented that rural stability depended not only on agriculture but also on rural industry. He urged that state loans to rural enterprises be maintained at a certain level. The NPC delegates agreed. For them, "Agriculture cannot be strengthened without rural enterprises." Because state agricultural investment was limited, agriculture had to rely on rural enterprises. Therefore, "the healthy development [of rural enterprises] should be protected during the austerity." They countered that criticisms of rural enterprises were misleading. Such criticisms alleged that rural enterprises "compete with large industries for markets and raw materials," "their products are inferior and higher priced," and "they are the main source of corruption." For the delegates, these criticisms were merely a pretext for "negating rural enterprises."[67]

Just as the debate on rural enterprise policy was heating up in April, demonstrations erupted in Beijing and soon spread across the country. In the context of a deepening sociopolitical crisis, the rural enterprise interests launched a series of articles and exploited the central leadership's preoccupation with stability to advocate a more favorable policy environment for rural enterprises.

One of the first salvos of the offensive was a tough-worded *Peasant Daily* commentator's article, which refuted the official policy on rural migrant labor.[68] The article began by saying that China's state-led industrial development strategy had entailed the exploitation of peasants through the price scissors. Such a strategy retarded rural development and resulted in the huge rural surplus labor pool. In contrast, rural industrialization promised to solve the labor problem and bring development to the countryside. As the author wrote: "With only a moderate amount of self-accumulated funds, China's peasants have in 10 years established 15 million rural enterprises which employ 80 million rural laborers." Praising this as a "wonderful achievement," the author asked, rhetorically, "Just imagine, can the state labor departments find employment for so many people and solve the problems? If we now rush to push these peasants back into the fields, *unthinkable problems may result*." Yet peasants going to cities now often discovered that the labor markets had been closed down by the authorities. Instead, the author argued, government should help build up a new labor-market order to facilitate the transfer of labor out of agriculture.

While the *Peasant Daily* commentary criticized the strict limits placed on rural migrant labor, a spirited article by Zhang Yi (a deputy director of the Bureau of Rural Enterprises in the Ministry of Agriculture), published on June 6, 1989, in *Economic Daily*, the State Council newspaper, argued that rural enterprises had been treated unfairly.[69] According to Zhang, while the PRC Constitution stated that both state and rural collective enterprises belonged in the socialist economy,

in reality, certain departments and comrades have often regarded rural collective enterprises as alien to the socialist economy. Rather than follow the stipulations of the Constitution to encourage, guide, and help them develop, [they] restrict and discriminate against the development of this socialist economic element and think that [rural enterprises] compete with large [state] enterprises for funds, raw materials, energy, market share, as well as pollute the environment.[70]

According to Zhang, symptoms of this attitude were easy to find. Labor services in other areas by migrant workers were derogatorily called "blind flow." Local mining was castigated for "causing damage to resources."

While the state bought up most agricultural and sideline products for processing at state-owned plants, local processing efforts were criticized for "competing for raw materials and restricted administratively."[71]

For Zhang, these criticisms were unfair, and he mounted a vigorous defense against the charge that rural enterprises competed for funds, raw materials, and energy with state enterprises and found the charge baseless. Unlike state enterprises, rural enterprises did not receive capital construction funds from the state treasury and accounted for a mere 3.9 percent of the total bank loans in 1987. Rural enterprises also produced more energy than they consumed, even though they did not receive state investment funds. In materials supply, rural enterprises were consistently discriminated against; they had to rely on higher-priced supplies from the market and, in times of electricity scarcity, were the first to be cut off by energy bureaus. When rural enterprises entered into cooperative arrangements with state-owned industries, it was the rural enterprises that felt the pains of adjustment. Having enumerated these points, Zhang urged that "it was imperative to strengthen the worker-peasant alliance" by supporting the development of rural enterprises in times of economic difficulties.[72] Misguided criticisms could only worsen the alliance, with potentially ominous social and political consequences.

In the aftermath of the June crackdown, the rural enterprise interests took further advantage of the political crisis to drive home their message that rural enterprise was crucial to social stability. And they were unusually vocal in identifying the rural enterprise sector with the communiqué of the Central Committee session in late June (the Fourth Plenum). The communiqué emphasized the continuity of reformist policies. These included the line, principles, and policies formulated since the Third Plenum of the Eleventh Central Committee as well as the basic line of "one focus and two basic points" ("one focus" referred to economic construction; "two basic points" were adherence to the four cardinal principles and to reform and opening up), set down at the Thirteenth Party Congress in 1987.[73] The communiqué set forth four major tasks: Further stabilize the national situation; continue the strategy of "improving the economic environment and rectifying the economic order, persist in reforms and opening to the outside world, and promote sustained, stable, and harmonious economic development"; strengthen ideological and political control; and strengthen party building. All four were thus concerned with stability and control.

As they had done before the crackdown, the rural enterprise interests latched on to the emphasis on stability. In late July 1989, at a meeting of (provincial) bureau directors of rural enterprises, it was announced that the rural enterprise sector should

conscientiously put into effect the spirit of the Fourth Plenum of the Thirteenth Central Committee of the Party and the important talk by comrade Deng Xiaoping, unify thinking, actively adjust, deepen reform, struggle against adversity, promote the sustained, balanced, and healthy development of rural enterprises, and make a greater contribution to maintaining the excellent political situation of stability and unity in our country and to the sustained and stable development of the national economy.[74]

In a remarkable keynote speech to the meeting on the same theme, Vice-Minister of Agriculture Chen Yaobang defended the rural enterprise sector by repeatedly invoking the authority of Deng Xiaoping, who had just set the tone for continuing reform and opening up following the June crackdown.[75] Quoting Deng as saying that all policies and lines since the Third Plenum of 1978 were to continue, Chen Yaobang documented the emphasis on rural enterprise development in various official policies and concluded that the development of rural enterprises was an important component of the guiding principle of reform and opening up and must therefore "be firm and unshakable, without the least wavering."[76]

Praising Deng Xiaoping as the chief architect of China's reform and opening up, Chen Yaobang produced a number of specific Deng quotations on rural enterprise development from remarks made between 1984 and 1987. Deng was quoted as saying on June 12, 1987, that "the greatest gain which we completely failed to expect was the development of rural enterprises." Yet, for Deng, "the development of rural enterprises, especially industry but also including other fields, has solved the problem of providing employment for half of the rural surplus labor force. . . . The center's contribution to this lies in the central policy of enlivening [the economy]." Therefore, Chen argued, developing rural enterprises was "an important part of [Deng's] grand blueprint of building socialism with Chinese characteristics." Moreover, since Deng had just called for stabilizing the economy after the crackdown and since rural enterprise development could play an important role in preventing an economic slide and stabilizing China's economic, political, and social situation, Chen called for "paying the utmost attention to the stable development of rural enterprises." Pointing to the tough situation facing rural enterprises, Chen said that "we fervently hope all levels of the party and government further strengthen leadership over rural enterprise work, [and] earnestly help [rural enterprises] solve problems."[77]

The publication of Chen's speech in September 1989 and other writings calling for more support for rural enterprises appeared to indicate that the tide of rural enterprise policy was turning. Four days after Chen Yaobang's speech was published, the Ministry of Labor announced that it favored continued encouragement of rural enterprises to employ rural surplus labor, so that these would not enter urban areas and exacerbate the urban employment problems under the austerity program.[78]

In addition to serving as a persistent policy advocate, the MOA also sponsored the establishment of the Chinese Association of Rural Enterprises (CARE) in 1989–90.[79] CARE was designated as a civil group, and its purpose was to "coordinate external relations and provide services" for rural enterprises and to serve as "the spokesman that represents the opinions and wishes of rural enterprises and pass these on to the government in a timely fashion."[80] He Kang, then the minister of agriculture, was elected its first president. More symbolically, Bo Yibo, vice-chairman of the Central Advisory Commission and one of China's most powerful elders, not only received participants at the meeting but also agreed to become the association's honorary president. In a short speech entitled "The Development of Rural Enterprises Is a Strategic Task," Bo strongly reaffirmed his support for rural enterprises. Saying that he was "extremely fond of this new-born thing," Bo pointedly mentioned that "it is necessary for many of our comrades to deepen their understanding of rural industrialization"—a clear indication of internal disagreement over the development of rural enterprises. According to Bo, China's developmental experience indicated that "industrialization cannot be achieved solely on the basis of building industries in cities with state investment. This is because industrialization . . . also means transferring most of the agricultural surplus labor into industry and services. Therefore, in our country, which has 1.1 billion people, of whom 80 percent are peasants, [industrialization] must rely on peasants developing rural enterprises through savings."[81] Thus, in sponsoring the establishment of CARE, the MOA not only contributed to the emergent trend toward corporatism in China but also joined the articulation of bureaucratic interests with the paternalistic side of Chinese authoritarianism.[82] Later, in indicating his shifting stance during his Jiangsu visit, Premier Li Peng appeared to go out of his way to echo Bo's emphasis that "the rural enterprises are a new-born thing."

Fiscal Constraints on the State

In the context of the crisis facing the Chinese state, the strong flows of migrant workers and the MOA's mobilization of support for rural enterprises both from the top (Deng Xiaoping, Bo Yibo) and from below (CARE) served to highlight the growing social and economic importance of rural enterprises and put pressure on the Chinese leadership. This political pressure on the center interacted with another element: the fiscal constraints on the central government.

As has been pointed out by Chinese and Western analysts, China has witnessed an era of relative fiscal decline during the reform period. The consolidated government budget as a percentage of national income decreased from 38–39 percent in the late 1970's to about 24 percent in 1988–89.[83] Since the government has not been able to curtail its obligations in line with the slower-growing revenue, the government budget deficit has increased significantly.

Part of the growing deficit may be regarded as the necessary cost of successful reforms. The most obvious item was consumer price subsidy. While the government raised agricultural procurement prices to stimulate agricultural production, it simultaneously paid out subsidies to urban residents when staple grain prices were increased. Since urban residents are already economically better off than their rural counterparts, the subsidies evidently raise questions of social equity. But such subsidies (and other benefits provided for workers in loss-making state enterprises) were clearly used to secure urban stability and therefore made political sense.

More important, however, the persistent budget deficits have deeper structural causes. As originally constructed for the command economy, China's fiscal system depended on the state industries for most of its budgetary revenues—over 80 percent in the 1970's. As reform allowed other types of enterprises to enter into economic competition, however, the rate of profitability for state industry overall has declined significantly, thereby eroding the government revenue base.[84] In the meantime, state enterprise losses covered through the budget as a percentage of adjusted budget revenues doubled from just over 9 percent in 1978 to more than 18 percent in 1989–90.[85] These developments later led Chen Yuan, a deputy director of the People's Bank of China and son of conservative patriarch Chen Yun, to warn that the decline of central financial revenue as a share of national income may lead to "the further loss of economic control and economic disintegration."[86]

The economic austerity program started in late 1988 highlighted and accentuated the fiscal dilemmas facing the center and the need to locate new sources of revenue. While the economic slowdown put brakes on revenue growth, it also increased the need for welfare. In order to avoid massive layoffs and the social consequences high unemployment entailed, the central government kept these state factories afloat through the infusion of central government funds. From 1986 to 1989, in addition to huge loans, state subsidies to state enterprises rose from 32.5 billion to 60 billion yuan a year.[87] Over the same period, consumer subsidies rose from 25.7 billion to 37 billion yuan per year.[88] Meanwhile, the shoddy output of state factories piled up in warehouses as overstock.[89]

The fiscal dilemma facing the Chinese state sets limits on leadership choice of public policy. In light of this fiscal dilemma, the importance of the rural enterprises is magnified: Rural enterprises and enterprises with foreign investment make up the most dynamic part of the economy. According to one estimate based on official statistics, in 1990 these two elements accounted for 70 percent of China's industrial growth.[90] Importantly, these enterprises contribute revenue but do not get state investment grants or subsidies; hence any revenue contributions they make are net.[91] By 1991, the rural enterprise sector accounted for 15 percent of all taxes and just under 30 percent of China's exports.[92] From this perspective, the central government would do well to support these enterprises, as well as foreign-funded enterprises, to generate growth, revenue, employment, and exports.

Conclusion

The argument so far may be summarized as follows. Public officials adopt policy in politically expedient ways, and economic rationality rarely attains priority in the policy-making process. Political calculations lead officials to respond to the (real or perceived) political clout of pressure groups. This explains why the austerity program launched by the Chinese leadership inflicted more of the pains of adjustment on rural residents than on urban workers.

Yet the austerity program soon led to migrant labor flows of unprecedented magnitude in the history of the PRC. These flows strained urban services and infrastructure and caused urban resentment. For the leadership, the labor flows conjured up visions of "unthinkable problems" and made the arguments from rural enterprise interests palpably persuasive. Thus, even though the laborers might not have intended it, their uncoordinated social impact was converted into political influence. Moreover, these developments also interacted with the fiscal constraints on the center, which were put into relief by the austerity program. The interplay of these factors amid the sociopolitical crisis of 1989 thus called into question the existing austerity policy toward rural enterprises.

To remedy the situation, we would expect that, if possible, the leadership would at least seek to guide and control, if not stem, the labor flows by issuing more regulations aimed at controlling them and by tackling the source of the flows. In the event, Premier Li Peng in late 1989–early 1990 eased credit policy for the rural enterprise sector in the hope that this would generate more rural nonfarm employment to absorb the labor flows, not to mention taxes for the state. This implied a more evenhanded approach toward rural and urban enterprises and, as a return to the *status quo ante*, it appears to have been the path of least political resistance.[93] In light of the political shocks that the regime had gone through in 1989, it was clearly much easier just to remove or modify a policy than to undertake something dramatic. In the meantime, the government continued to maintain careful supervision over labor flows in an apparent attempt to soothe urban sensibilities. Premier Li Peng, for example, emphasized in 1990 that rural-to-urban labor movement would be strictly controlled in order to reduce the pressures on urban employment.[94] As Labor Minister Ruan Chongwu later put it: "The government would maintain its strict control over migration into cities to prevent *urban* discontent, and would instead help surplus rural workers to set up their own industries."[95]

In short, this chapter has provided a plausible explanation of why the discriminatory policy toward the rural enterprise sector was imposed and why it was changed by the same leadership and suggests that explanations of public policy formation in China must take into account the growing importance of societal forces as well as the role of politicians and bureaucracies. Leaders are obviously important, but they function within a policy environment of multiple political constraints. Similarly, while bureaucracies must be taken into account, they are usually not the only actors. In effect, the shifts in rural enterprise over 1988–90 suggest that local governments and social forces (especially the highly visible migrant workers) contributed significantly to the revision of central policy, to the extent that one might be tempted to say that local governments and society could veto central initiatives.[96]

• • • • •

Conclusions and Reflections

Beliefs matter. As the authors of a leading text in cognitive psychology put it, "Much, if not most, everyday human behavior, especially social behavior, becomes explainable and predictable only when we know, or can accurately guess, the subjective interpretations and beliefs of the people involved."[1] Since beliefs about opportunities are crucial to human *choice*, a better understanding of belief formation and belief change is therefore vital to the social sciences.[2]

Most studies in the rational choice tradition tend to take beliefs and preferences as given and focus on the dynamics of choice in a strategic context with certain institutions or rules of the game.[3] The present study accepts that the rational choice method remains the best tool social science has acquired, but it departs from the strong assumptions of rationality generally required by rational choice and recognizes also that there are significant limits to human rationality and that cognitive biases are an inherent element of choice, having important implications for politics. As Herbert Simon argued almost four decades ago, "However adaptive the behavior of organisms in learning and choice situations, this adaptiveness falls far short of the ideal of 'maximizing' postulated in economic theory."[4] Instead of optimizing, humans adapt to satisfice. Incomplete rationality coupled with environmental constraints leads to inefficiencies in history, some of which we call tragedies.

In this concluding chapter, I first revisit the historical dramas that have been the subject of this book. Then I place the Chinese case in comparative perspective. I conclude with some reflections on the limits of elite social engineering.

Beliefs, Cognitive Biases, and the Path of Institutions

Change in rural institutions in China provides striking evidence of path dependence across time. In the 1950's, there was a forceful push toward higher levels of collectivization. But the Great Leap Famine brought about a reorientation of rural policy and the institutional path, followed by nearly two decades when rural institutional arrangements were virtually frozen. Finally, rural reforms introduced what one might call the institutional paradigm of contracting, which has persisted for more than a decade.

The Push for Collectivization

The developments in the 1950's and especially the people's communes movement of 1958 underscore the crucial role of political leaders' substantive beliefs and cognitive processes in shaping the path of institutional change. Throughout this period, the Chinese polity resembled North's simplified model of a polity made up of a ruler (in this case an oligarchical leadership headed by Mao) and his constituents.[5] Both the political system and the composition of the leadership experienced few changes. It thus appears that the beliefs as well as the cognitive biases of the key political leaders were crucial in accounting for the leadership's stubborn perseverance in building ever-higher levels of collective institutions in rural China. Specifically, the leadership appears to have truly believed that higher levels of collectivization would bring about ever-more bountiful harvests and improve income distribution.[6] When bouts of collectivization before the Great Leap did not to lead to an appreciable increase in agricultural production but instead caused disruptions in rural China, Mao and others attempted to "check impetuosity and rash advance" but nevertheless continued to believe in the eventual success of collectivization. They failed to entertain seriously the thought of failure.

Thus, at a time when the leaders of the party-state clearly possessed enormous political resources and controlled the pace and direction of rural institutional change, they chose to push ahead and launch the Great Leap Forward. And it was during 1958 that the cognitive biases of the Chinese leaders were most evident. Instead of verifying the various wild claims about agricultural production, leading officials such as Mao and Tan Zhenlin, the Politburo leader for agriculture, apparently took the claims as confirming their initial beliefs. Their encouragement of local enthusiasm in a tightly constrained political context only served to fuel even more exaggerations, leading to disaster.

An alternative argument would probably counter that the successive pushes for rural collective institutions meshed well with the other institutional transformations then going on in China, particularly the establishment of a planned economy. In other words, an institutional matrix tended to exhibit the characteristics of increasing returns, including lock-in and network externalities.[7] On this account, the imposition of state grain procurement and rationing arrangements in 1953 in response to rising urban demand called for tighter control over the rural population to facilitate rural extraction. Likewise, the push for people's communes was partly justified on the ground that larger rural organizations would make it easier to undertake rural infrastructure projects.

The problem with this alternative argument is that lock-in and network externalities are generally used to explain why institutions change slowly. In contrast, the push for collectivization in China resulted in extremely rapid institutional changes. Moreover, the purpose of each of these changes could potentially have been at least as well served by alternative arrangements that put less emphasis on collectivization and the suppression of markets. We are therefore led back to ask why the leaders chose to proceed with collectivization, and we must seek answers in the beliefs and cognitive biases of these leaders.

The Paradigm of Contracting

Whereas in the 1950's the leadership appeared to be cognitively locked on to the path of collectivization, the reformist leadership turned the other way and ultimately became firmly committed to the household responsibility system. Yet, as I pointed out at the start of Chapter 7, many of the difficulties confronting rural China today can be traced back to this: Policymakers who rose to power on the tide of rural reforms centered on institutional change continued to believe in the magic of policy pronouncements at the expense of long-term investment in agriculture.

Not only did the reformist leaders push for the nationwide adoption of the household responsibility system in agriculture, but they also promoted the paradigm of contracting outside agriculture once agricultural reforms had been deemed successful in the early 1980s. As Deng Xiaoping put it on June 18, 1983, while industry and agriculture differed, "the basic principle [of reform] should be based on the responsibility system; and this must be affirmed."[8]

To the chagrin of successive Chinese leaders, however, adoption of the contract responsibility system has failed to revitalize the state industrial sector.[9] As the economist Lin Zili pointed out in 1983, it would be difficult for large and medium-sized state enterprises to adopt profit contracting for long because of the difficulties in balancing the interests of state, enterprise, and workers. He predicted that in the long run all forms of contracting arrangements would have to be transformed into tax payments.[10]

The Great Leap Famine, Belief Adjustment, and Reform

Throughout human history, famines, pestilence, and war have been the scourges of human societies, yet few famines have caused such profound transformations as in China. In order to understand why it happened this way in twentieth-century China, we need to specify the causal mechanism that connected the Great Leap Famine with rural decollectivization.[11] The key lies in the drastic cognitive changes that the Great Leap Famine wrought among both elites and masses, many of whom had gone along with the commune movement reluctantly in the first place.[12] This was because the Great Leap Famine was fundamentally political and was irrevocably bound up with the people's communes movement of the Great Leap Forward. Once massive famine resulted, the people's communes were delegitimated in spite of official rhetoric to the contrary. In Hirschmanian terms, "the frenzy and the millenarian expectations" surrounding the people's communes movement during the Great Leap Forward guaranteed "failure and massive disappointment."[13] In precipitating the reform, the Great Leap Famine thus served a role for China that is similar to Japan and Germany's defeat in war.

We expect that people would learn, albeit imperfectly, from this traumatic experience and seek alternatives to the people's communes. Moreover, we also expect that the degree to which people's beliefs and motivations concerning rural institutional arrangements were affected would be positively related to the degree the famine had affected them. The more "vividly" one observed and was affected by the famine, the more likely one was to favor liberal practices. While data from nationwide surveys are not available to verify this hypothesis, abundant anecdotal evidence clearly indicates that the famine had a dramatic impact on people's attitudes and beliefs. Moreover, a partial survey of cadres in Guangxi conducted in early 1962 provides support for the hypothesis and bears repeating. The survey found that about 25 percent of the cadres at the commune level or below were inclined toward the division of land among peasant households, household contracting for output quotas, and the restoration of individual farming. The proportion of cadres who favored individual farming varied with local economic conditions and with cadre rank. In areas with relatively good economic conditions, 15 percent of the cadres believed in and promoted individual farming, in contrast to about 60 percent in areas that had been devastated by the famine. While 20 percent of the commune party secretaries favored individual farming, 48 percent of the members of commune party committees did so. The percentage was even higher among basic-level cadres in production brigades and teams.[14]

The changes in people's beliefs and motivations created the momentum for institutional innovation. My empirical investigation of this claim took three routes in this volume. First, I looked at the immediate reactions to the failure of the communes. Contemporary documents circulated internally indicate that, in the immediate aftermath of the Great Leap Forward, some 30 percent of all rural units adopted some form of household responsibility—the essence of the post-Mao rural reforms—without central authorization. Although such practices were eventually suppressed during the socialist education movement, an unknown number of rural units still resorted to them in secret during the Cultural Revolution, when the official rhetoric was filled with exhortations of agrarian radicalism. Moreover, over this period the patterns of economic change in the rural sector broadly followed the economic logic; rural communities diverted their scarce resources to rural industries, which were more profitable than crop production.[15]

Second, I looked at how the leadership reacted to the Great Leap Famine and modified official policy. In the aftermath of the Great Leap, the leadership took a series of actions that virtually returned the organization of agriculture to the pre-leap days, eventually making the production team the basic organizational unit. Official concessions fell short of the peasants' demand for household-based farming, to be sure, but they represented a dramatic retreat from the utopian people's communes. The leadership, especially Mao, retained the production team in an attempt to salvage what was left of the ideals of socialist collectivism and retain political control in rural areas.

While the Communist Party launched the socialist education movement to combat "revisionism" and advocated agrarian radicalism during the Cultural Revolution decade, what is interesting is that the rural organizational framework based on the production team was kept in place throughout this period. Even when Mao's cronies advocated that rural China shift from team accounting to brigade accounting, Mao, while sympathetic to their ideals, refrained from supporting them. He, like Zhou Enlai and others, had apparently drawn a lesson from the failure of the Great Leap Forward. As a result, in spite of the winds of agrarian radicalism and in contrast to the chaos in urban areas, rural policy during the Cultural Revolution was remarkably stable as far as rural organization and grain extraction were concerned (though I do not deny in other respects rural areas were affected).

Third, I examined the linkages between the magnitude of the Great Leap Famine and the propensity to adopt reformist practices as of the late 1970's. Given our knowledge about the patterns of cognitive change, I expected that those areas that had suffered more from the famine would remain more inclined toward reformist practices. My cross-provincial comparisons confirmed that the more a province suffered from the famine, the more likely it was to refrain from radical practices such as brigade accounting. In other words, the enthusiasm with which a province pursued reform in the late 1970's and early 1980's was in direct proportion to the pain it experienced during the Great Leap Famine. Owing to the methodological problem of ecological fallacy, these conclusions, derived on the basis of provinces rather than primary rural organizations (such as communes) as the units of measurement, should be interpreted with caution.[16] In light of their complementary nature and other information, including local studies, however, my conclusions appear robust. The long-run outcome of the utopian Great Leap Forward was thus exactly the opposite of what was intended by Mao.

If we look at it from a different angle, we need to answer the counterfactual question: What if the Great Leap Forward had not been launched, resulting in its diabolic effects? A partial answer is suggested by John W. Lewis: "There was a point in 1956 or 1957 when the Party leaders could have retained the basic apparatus established up to that time and expected that the newly introduced formal organizations would be accepted and utilized by the Chinese people." "At that time," Lewis continues, "the Party had not yet alienated the youth and had not experienced grave failures."[17] It is thus conceivable that the party-state could have maintained rural institutions at the advanced APC level, adjusting production incentives through mesoeconomic measures (such as price changes). By maintaining production expansion but avoiding catastrophe, collective agriculture might have been more long-lasting in China than was the case.[18]

In the final analysis, the politically caused catastrophe served to shake profoundly the cognitive foundations of the old paradigm—which emphasized control, planning, and mobilization in the economy—and became a powerful impetus for institutional change. Prior to the famine, everything appeared to be within reach for China's leaders, and consequently local cadres vied with each other to launch the most fantastic grain output "sputniks." The famine changed all that. Indeed, one might say that the famine sounded the death knell for the paradigm of collectivization and launched the new paradigm of reform. The famine made people see the world through a different set of lenses and alter their survival strategies. As they did so, the foundations of Chinese politics were transformed.

Peasants, the State, and the Politics of Institutional Change

Yet the movement from cognitive changes to institutional changes is not automatic. Major institutional changes, such as the transition from collective agriculture to household farming in China, do not occur in a political vacuum but frequently involve political struggle, sometimes of a life-and-death nature. They are intensely negotiated and contested among major coalitions in state and society. Two questions then arise: What were the political dynamics that led to the eventual adoption of the household responsibility system in rural China? What does the Chinese reform tell us about the role of local cadres and peasants in Chinese politics?

The Political Dynamics of Rural Institutional Change

In making the shift from collective to household farming, peasants and basic-level cadres made judgements about the costs and benefits of such a move. Their options were shaped primarily by three factors: the pressure of the Great Leap Famine, the historically constituted spatial pattern of party presence, and the constraints imposed by the state. In terms of both time and space, the extent to which rural China adopted household farming also appears to be a function of these factors.

The Great Leap Famine clearly demonstrated to peasants the high costs of the people's communes movement and provided powerful incentives for them to seek a return to household farming, which was familiar to them, was known to have worked reasonably well, and allowed them to reap the fruits of their labor directly. As my quantitative investigations showed, the magnitude of the Great Leap Famine in a province was a good predictor of the propensity for reformist policies in that province. Calamity generated the incentives for institutional innovation.

While the Great Leap Famine created the incentives for peasants to exit collective production, their action was constrained by the political costs of doing so. For much of the period covered in this volume, especially during the socialist education movement and the Cultural Revolution, household farming was viewed as opposed to the collective and was therefore antisocialist. Those caught engaging in household farming were given severe political penalties. For a local cadre, it usually meant the loss of his or her position and the power and privileges that came with it. Both cadres and peasants undertaking household farming were criticized and often "struggled against." Under these circumstances, the individual or unit that wanted to adopt household farming faced the dilemmas of an assurance game. If all peasant communities were to turn simultaneously from collective to household farming, then it would be inconceivable that the state would have had the will or the administrative capacity to crack down. In consequence, household farming could then be adopted. Yet few dared to move first for fear of being caught and left alone to be punished. Thus, during the Cultural Revolution, few rural units dared to engage openly in practices that linked effort with reward. However, some tightly knit communities were able to use evasive tactics to overcome the dilemma of collective action. They overtly sang paeans to radical ideals to please superiors but secretly practiced liberal measures.

The payoffs of the game were not constant but varied over time and space, thus opening up windows of opportunity for local initiatives. This was clearly the case during the depths of the Great Leap Famine and immediately after it. For peasants, their very survival was at stake, and thus they were willing to take great risks. In the meantime, the Chinese leadership was in shock, as indicated by Mao's depression, and unsure of what measures to take. This meant that the leadership was willing to tolerate measures that deviated from its own preferences, thus reducing the political risks faced by peasants and local cadres. The combination of greater incentives (or desperation) and lower risks made for widespread adoption of household farming around 1961–62.

During the latter part of the Cultural Revolution and especially after disillusionment set in following the alleged betrayal of Lin Biao, the center gave contradictory signals on rural policy, as evidenced by the confrontation between Jiang Qing and Deng Xiaoping in Dazhai in 1975. Following Mao's death, the clash between Hua Guofeng (whose rural policy was seen as ineffectual in increasing grain output) and the moderates also underlined the political opportunity for change. In this sense, the political struggle around the succession to Mao was therefore a proximate cause of reform inasmuch as it undermined the control of the state. Likewise, leaders such as Deng Xiaoping and Wan Li were important because they were more attuned to the potential for change from below than their opponents.[19]

While the cleavages at the center encouraged some local communities to take matters into their own hands, it should be emphasized that these communities still hedged their bets. Indeed, one of the most commonly used phrases during the early stage of the post-Mao reforms was *manshang bu manxia*, which literally means "concealing from superiors but not subordinates." In other words, peasants and local cadres refrained from revealing their true preferences. The conflicting demands of political sanctions, social norms, and personal autonomy led to the divergence between public and private preferences.[20] Once the cost of expressing one's true preferences went down, however, the rural population quickly adopted the practice that it preferred, leading to the rapid adoption of the household responsibility system.

The relationship between reform and political control was also evidenced through an examination of the spatial patterns of party formation, which appeared to arise partly from the spatial pattern of the Communist takeover, going from northern to southern China, and partly from the technological limits on the spatial reach of the state. I found that the density of party membership and, by extension, party networks weakened further away from Beijing. Moreover, the policy effect of the pattern of party formation depended on the context of political change. During the Great Leap Forward, areas that had a greater density of party membership were more likely to stick to the letter of the central directives and were thus more moderate, while outlying areas, in their eagerness to demonstrate their loyalty to the party, were more likely to overreact to central directives, thus more severely exacerbating the incidence of famine in these areas. In contrast, the political paralysis at the center in the late 1970's encouraged the outlying areas to have a greater proclivity for reformist practices than those close to the center of political orthodoxy.

To sum up, I have stressed the historical and contextual nature of reform in China: The rise of reform in China must be understood with reference to the horrible failures of the Great Leap Forward. The lessons drawn from the Great Leap Famine by both the leaders and the masses were crucial. In this equation of historical change, the leadership opened the windows of opportunity for reform; and peasants and basic-level cadres played their crucial part as carriers of historical lessons and agents of change. Just as a functioning railway needs both locomotives and railroads, the making of reform calls for a combination of the elements mentioned above. There was no *one* master strategy or plan for reform. Instead, reform—specifically the introduction and adoption of the household responsibility system—was the outcome of dynamic struggles and interactions between state and society under constraints imposed by the past.[21]

Between Passivity and Rebellion

Numerous studies from different methodological perspectives have studied the political impact of peasants in nondemocratic settings.[22] Despite their methodological differences, scholars have generally drawn attention to the powerlessness of peasants.

For Robert Bates, under conditions in which people and wealth are concentrated in agriculture, peasants are powerless because states bolster their power and resources by manipulating markets and other institutions to extract resources from agrarian societies. Thus, "it is the state that creates peasants."[23]

For Eric Wolf, peasants choose between revolution and rebellion, on the one hand, and passivity and weapons of the weak, on the other. There is no other alternative. Thus, "peasants are often merely passive spectators of political struggles or long for the sudden advent of a millennium, without specifying for themselves and their neighbors the many rungs on the staircase to heaven."[24] Even in the making of a peasant rebellion, however, peasants depend on outsiders for leadership and organization to be effective. Citing the cases of Russia, China, and Vietnam, Wolf concludes that "it was the political parties of middle-class revolutionaries who engineered the seizure of power and created the social and military instruments which conquered the state, and ensured transition to a new social order."[25]

The adoption of the household responsibility system in China suggests, however, that, short of rebellion and other forms of organized collective action, peasants are not condemned to passivity and political impotence.[26] Under certain circumstances, peasants allied with elites can play an important role in determining the fundamental direction of agrarian change and reshape the contours of the state.

First of all, because of the historical context (the Great Leap Famine), the goal of individual peasant actions was specific. Peasants disliked collective agriculture and desired greater control over their own labor and output. Their desire could be fulfilled by a turn from collective to group and then household responsibility; both had been tried before and were well liked. They thus couched their demands in terms of specific grievances that could be remedied through specific and proven measures. This stood a better chance of success than demands expressed in terms of political ideals that called into question the legitimacy of the regime.

Second, in the vanguard reform areas, the peasants had local cadres as allies. Moreover, the leadership transition following Mao's death provided a political opportunity. Some of the national leaders championed the peasants' cause in their fight for influence. As the rural reforms began to bear fruit, these leaders gained more influence and further spread the reforms. The conjuncture of political forces made it easier for local actions to be legitimated.

Third, the relatively low level of technical development in Chinese agriculture mattered. Peasants leaving collective agriculture generally faced little or no technical difficulty in managing production because the institutions for the provision of fertilizers, pesticides, and tractor power remained in place and were easily adapted to household farming. Similarly, because of the relatively high population/land ratio, peasant families usually had adequate labor power to take care of the strips of land they had been allocated. Hence, once peasants were compelled to leave collective agriculture, they were capable of taking up the responsibility for household contracting. In contrast, while the Soviet Union under Gorbachev adopted a leasing law on November 23, 1989, which permitted the individual or small group to lease land from the state or collective farm for up to 50 years, there were few takers among farmers.[27]

The Chinese case thus calls for us to study the shifts in the overall balance of power rather than take the configurations of power in a political system as fixed. Political power is not a static attribute of the groups or actors involved but must be examined with attention to the process of politics. Even groups that are generally considered weak may gain great strategic influence at certain crucial moments of history.

State and Rural Society Under the Reforms

The rural reforms, by substituting factor markets for administrative control, have not only spurred the diversification of rural society, but also brought about a realignment in the relations between state and rural society. Because of the Chinese definition of what is "rural," it makes little sense now to speak of a single rural society, let alone a peasantry, in China. There are many possible angles from which one might analyze the dynamic changes occurring in rural China. In Chapters 7 and 8, I chose to emphasize the bifurcation of rural China and divided my analysis into two broad, if somewhat amorphous, sectors—the agricultural and the nonagricultural. While the weight of the local state has increased on the agricultural population, the rural *non*agricultural population has enhanced its influence in the calculus of the central state. Overall, it appears that the relationship between state and rural society is changing from suppression (emphasizing extraction) to accommodation.[28]

The reforms, including the introduction of the household responsibility system, have proved no panacea to the challenges facing the agricultural sector, especially in light of the declining land/population ratio. This resource constraint has become an obsession of China's policymakers. In the words of Ma Zhongchen, a vice-minister of agriculture: "A large population, farmland shortages, a weak agricultural foundation, and relatively insufficient per-capita resources are the basic facts and the most fundamental agricultural situation of China." Between 1952 and 1990, China's population increased by over 568 million while the farmland area was reduced by more than 183 million *mu* (30.14 million acres).[29] Despite relatively rapid labor absorption in the rural enterprise sector during the last fifteen years, rural unemployment and underemployment remain endemic and are projected to become even worse by the end of the century.[30]

My empirical investigation revealed that after the high tide of rural reforms the Chinese peasant has been in an economic squeeze, caught on the one hand by the declining profitability of agricultural production (especially relative to the rural enterprise sector) and on the other by a fast-growing local bureaucracy. He or she has mounted resistance to such pressures in terms of both voice and exit. Whereas concerns about rural political stability and urban supply have prompted the government to reiterate the cardinal importance of agriculture vociferously, it appears unlikely that the economic squeeze will be reversed soon owing to the low income elasticity of the demand for agricultural products, the huge rural labor supply, and the poor fiscal health of the central government.[31] From a long-term perspective, it appears that China's peasants are destined to follow in the footsteps of their counterparts in more developed countries such as France and Japan.[32] Their share of the labor force will gradually stabilize and then dwindle.

While it appears to be a big headache for agriculture, the huge rural population has provided tens of millions of docile and hard-working first-generation workers that are perhaps the most powerful factor driving China's industrialization from below. Indeed, as the rural population derives more and more of its income from nonagricultural occupations, a dramatic shift has already occurred, especially among the younger generation, in rural attitudes toward occupations, with industry clearly taking priority over farming.[33] China is on its way to becoming an *industrial* nation.

The investigation in Chapter 8 suggests that the relative position of the rural enterprise sector vis-à-vis the state, as well as the state industrial sector, has strengthened. This argument may be illuminated using the framework developed by Rogowski in his *Commerce and Coalitions*.[34] Rogowski bases his analysis on the three-factor version of the Stolper-Samuelson theorem, originally published in 1941.[35] Simply put, the theorem predicts that liberalization of trade harms owners of factors in which, relative to the rest of the world, that society is *poorly* endowed, as well as producers who use the scarce factor intensively; and liberalization of trade benefits those factors that—again, relative to the rest of the world—the given society holds *abundantly*, and the producers who use those locally abundant factors intensively.[36] In China, since both land and capital are scarce and labor is abundant, the Rogowski thesis predicts that increased liberalization benefits rural enterprises and their workers relative to state industries, which tend to be more capital intensive. Since the central state (far more than the local one) has relied on the state industries for tax revenues, liberalization strengthens the local state more than the center.

The case study in Chapter 8 supports the deductions from Rogowski's framework. As the rural enterprise sector has increased its significance in generating growth, employment, exports, and taxes, it appears that the central state, for both fiscal and political reasons, is moving itself away from the inefficient state sector and becoming more evenhanded toward both rural enterprises and (urban) state enterprises. As both the state and the peasants turn to rural industrialization, this augurs well for the breakdown of state-imposed urban-rural segmentation.[37] It also indicates that China is turning away from the state-led, heavy-industry orientation of industrial development (the big push) and toward a more indigenously based industrialization pattern (with a diversified portfolio of ownerships), or industrialization from below combined with government involvement. This industrialization from below is more congruous with China's comparative advantage and will likely be more self-sustaining.

The shift in central policy toward the rural enterprise sector as well as foreign-funded enterprises is in a sense a de facto recognition of this transformation. Previously the state concentrated its resources on the development of state industries, especially large and medium-sized state enterprises, and then relied on the state sector for its revenue. As the importance of the state sector as a revenue base declines, however, it is natural for the central state to seek revenues elsewhere. Thus the turn to nonstate sectors is an attempt by the state to rationalize the burdens and obligations of government. If the Chinese state successfully makes this transition by harnessing economic forces outside the state sector, thus forcing it to reinvigorate itself, then China will have succeeded in reforming its economy without relying on shock therapy, which in my view is but another kind of central planning.[38]

Path Dependence, Path Rupture, and Historical Change

In contrast to Douglass North's "stubborn" emphasis on institutional incrementalism, the decollectivization of rural China represents a remarkable case of discontinuous institutional change.[39] Not only did rural China veer off the path of collectivization only after an unprecedented human catastrophe, but, even with the Great Leap Famine, adoption of household-based agriculture was neither smooth nor automatic. Instead, what occurred was an episodic historical process of institutional change.

It appears to me that there are two major types of institutional changes that correspond to the contrast between gradualism and discontinuous change in evolutionary biology.[40] Gradualism occurs after an institutional framework or system has been established and, as North argues, tends to be path dependent. The other, like the Chinese case studied here, involves a change of system or paradigm shift and is frequently associated with crisis. Thus, as Stinchcombe has long argued, organizations and institutions of a given type tend to be established in spurts, and their structures, once established, tend to persist over long periods of time.[41]

The very notion of path dependence calls for the opposite idea of path rupture. Moreover, a full understanding of a set of path-dependent institutions requires the investigator to go over the sequence of changes made along the way, including attention to the critical junctures of path rupture that set the present set of institutions onto its present course. As Paul David has stated: "It is sometimes not possible to uncover the logic (or illogic) of the world around us except by understanding how it got that way. A *path-dependent* sequence of economic changes is one in which important influences upon the eventual outcome can be exerted by temporally remote events, including happenings dominated by chance elements rather than systematic forces."[42] It is not enough to assert the presence of the past. The task of the social scientist is, when possible, to specify how and why the past matters by supplying the causal mechanisms leading from the past to the present.

In the literature on international relations and comparative politics, much attention has already been paid to the role of crises or critical junctures in reshaping institutions.[43] In the words of Stephan Haggard, "International shocks and pressures, and the domestic economic crises associated with them, have been the most powerful stimuli for changes of policy. These critical historical junctures shifted the balance of power among sectors in predictable ways and provided incentives to institutional innovation."[44] What is especially interesting about the Chinese case is that the reorientation of institutional development was caused not by exogenous shocks but by a catastrophe generated from within the system. It calls attention to the effect past policies exert on present policy and institutional options. The unintended consequences of the Great Leap rerouted the path of institutional change in rural China, with both ideas and interests coalescing. In the meantime, certain other policy ideas and options are blocked owing to the particular history of institutional change.[45] It is now scarcely imaginable to propose rural people's communes as a policy option in China.

The problem with path dependence (also known as hysteresis among economists) is that it is not amenable to general statements of a lawlike nature.[46] As Robert Bates points out in his study of Kenya, "The course of the path is shaped by the initial institutional endowment. In this way, each society generates its own history."[47] Theorists interested in the relationship between crises and path-dependent change have had to be content with frameworks of analysis.[48] The exact nature of the path-dependent changes effected by the shocks or crises will vary depending on the contexts in which the shocks occur. Whereas famines have tended to produce long-lasting socioeconomic readjustments,[49] the sequence of changes they lead to may exhibit striking contrasts, which may be illustrated through a comparison of the Great Leap Famine with the Great Irish Famine of 1845–49, the last major famine in Western European history.[50]

Before the Great Irish Famine, the Irish economy was heavily dependent on the potato and dominated by small peasant holdings; it was also characterized by subsistence wages that were linked to potato prices. Between 1700 and 1845, Ireland's population steadily rose to over eight million. Over 1845–48, however, blight caused a collapse in potato cultivation, which in turn led to the Great Irish Famine, with excess mortality of about one million people. Most important, the famine induced changes that set the small, but open, Irish economy onto a different path.

Three aspects of this fundamental shift in the Irish economy are especially worth mentioning. First and most obvious was the permanent restructuring of agriculture. The role of the potato was much diminished, decreasing from 55.5 percent of all crops before the famine, to 36.4 percent a decade later, to only 12.5 percent at the start of the twentieth century.[51] Meanwhile cattle raising increased significantly. The dramatic shift in agricultural structure caused by the Great Irish Famine is analogous to the shift to the pursuit of self-sufficiency that the Great Leap Famine brought about more than a century later.

Second, like the Great Leap Famine, the Great Irish Famine also produced momentous, though less drastic, changes in the land tenure system. The demographic decline during the Great Irish Famine made land relatively more plentiful and facilitated the switch to extensive farming (such as cattle grazing), to which Ireland's prefamine land tenure system of small peasant holdings (in contrast to the capitalist farmers of England) had served as an obstacle. O'Rourke reports that data from the 1850's support the hypothesis that, across counties in Ireland, increases in cattle numbers, declines in population, and increases in the percentage of farm holdings over 30 acres were correlated. He suggests: "From the perspectives of landlords and farmers, the Famine cleared large tracts of land and of the smallholdings which made large-scale grazing difficult. Viewed in this light, the Famine served as a sort of speeded-up enclosure movement."[52]

Finally, population growth usually increases after a famine or epidemic; the Great Leap Famine, for example, was followed by a baby boom. Following the Great Irish Famine, however, the Irish population declined for more than a century, during which large numbers of Irish people emigrated.[53] This distinctive pattern was due to a number of factors. To begin with, Ireland's openness facilitated the mass emigration of the poor that the Great Irish Famine initiated. Second, the Great Irish Famine caused its survivors to cling to their land as the best guarantee against starvation. The ensuing enlargement of farms and the conversion to cattle grazing favored landowners but diminished employment opportunities, serving as a push for emigration. Third, there was growing labor demand from Britain and the New World, the fastest growing industrial economies of the time.

Once mass emigration started, it developed its own momentum, as those who emigrated earlier sent earnings home and constituted the networks or connections through which others followed. Furthermore, the success of the emigrants appears to have also contributed to the delayed fertility decline in Ireland as compared with most Western European societies. In the words of Guinnane, "Irish emigrants continued to send large sums home to parents and to finance the emigration of siblings, leading couples in Ireland to think of a larger family not as a burden, but as so

many chances in a generous lottery."[54] Even though the absence of industrialization and the employment opportunities associated with it had been
a cause of the emigration in the first place, it is also possible that the mass
emigration in turn further undermined industrialization at home. After
all, not only was the mass emigration a brain drain, but the emigrants had
also found alternatives to Irish industrialization in the fastest-growing industrial economies of the nineteenth century.

The Great Leap Famine thus poses a striking contrast in that severe limits were placed on migration both domestically and internationally. Indeed, as the famine deepened, the center sent some twenty million people
to the countryside from urban areas. This unique policy and the prolonged
and severe restrictions on population movement closed off migration as
the major route for alleviating the pains of famine. This policy position
may have thus inadvertently contributed to preserving the lessons of the
Great Leap famine so that they could be unleashed for reform as well as
providing strong incentives for rural industrialization.[55]

Final Reflections

This study has so far focused on how the political dynamics of state–rural
society interaction in China resulted in consequences that were contrary
to what the revolutionary Mao and his supporters had intended, and on
the linkages between cognitive biases and the politics of institutional
change. In this dynamic process, agents committed to social revolution
first pushed for the collectivization of rural China but instead precipitated
the worst famine in human history. By differentially altering people's motivations and beliefs, the Great Leap Famine in turn provided the fundamental structural incentives for decollectivization, which became a reality
when the Chinese leadership jockeyed for power following Mao's death.
Though decollectivization provided an initial boost to agricultural production in the early 1980's, it proved no panacea. But the leadership that
rose to power on the wave of the rural reforms apparently failed to appreciate this, and their shortsighted policies contributed to the difficulties
faced by the agricultural sector in the latter half of the 1980's.

"The architect of social change can never have a reliable blueprint,"
declared Albert Hirschman in a different context.[56] Historical developments during more than four decades of Communist rule in China have
again and again shown us how the unanticipated consequences of elite
policies subverted their attempts at fundamental social engineering. By
embedding the dynamics of institutional change in China in a historical
process, I hope to have shown that this is by no means a process endowed
with perfect rationality. Instead, it is subject to contestation between elites
and masses, state and society. As a result, the rural China of the 1980's and

1990's is a far cry from the socialist paradise envisioned by Mao and his supporters.

Economists now routinely talk of the *emergent* nature of social phenomena, which may be very far from the motives of the individuals in interaction.[57] To be sure, given the political system which existed, leaders such as Mao Zedong were indeed able to cause much suffering as they sought to transform China and propel it into "the radiant future." Yet when the fury has calmed and historians issue their verdicts, it is not at all clear what Mao and his colleagues accomplished except for having unleashed massive destructive power and caused untold suffering. Anyone who can cause great suffering to others may be rightly said to possess great power, but for the philosophical Mao this would be scant consolation.

This study thus points to the crucial importance of guarding against those who claim to know some magic route to the radiant future, be they politicians like Mao or party intellectuals who supported Mao by invoking the mythology of "being swept into the future by irresistible forces" or the new technocrats who claim to have found a scientific way to make China rich and powerful and happily clamor for more power for themselves.[58] However wise the leaders may be, their ability to comprehend and deal with the real world is restricted by their cognitive limitations as well as leakages in the chain of command. This calls for mechanisms to correct misguided policies emanating from the center. Had there been a free press and other institutions of oversight that are commonly found in open political systems, the Great Leap Famine would certainly not have attained the magnitude it did.[59] Instead, my analysis in Chapter 2 indicates that the tightly controlled political system magnified the consequences of central policies.

Yet even in the absence of full democratization, much could still be done to mitigate the effects of the policies of excess by overzealous leaders who arrogantly think they can mastermind a complex, but fragile and evolving, adaptive system. To some extent the trend toward decentralization, market-based competition, and legal rule has spread decision-making power throughout the system and served this purpose (though not without creating additional problems).[60] From the bottom up, the proliferation of consumer groups, trade associations, and other groupings, not to mention the incidence of peasant protests, student demonstrations, and worker strikes, will continue to increase the demands on the government. Faced with the growing diffusion of power and rising social demands, fearful of the uncertainties of the succession to Deng Xiaoping and the specter of social instability, China's current leaders, unlike their cocksure predecessors of the 1950's, seem tentative, reactive, and at times schizophrenic. They are less driven by firm ideological convictions than by the sheer desire to remain in power and the fear of losing control. The balance between state and society thus appears precarious, but it is also less susceptible to elite manipulations and more likely to produce policies dealing with the concrete problems that crop up in a state that is undergoing rapid economic development and social change.

. . . . .

Reference Matter

Main Sources of Data for Analyses of the Great Leap Famine

Mortality Rates

Fujian: Fujian Province Bureau of Statistics and Bureau of Public Security, pp. 132–144.

Gansu: Gansu Province Statistical Bureau, p. 85.

Guangdong: Zhu Yuncheng, Chen Haoguang, and Lu Datong, p. 121.

Guangxi: Huang Xianlin and Mo Datong, p. 113.

Guizhou: Pan Zhifu, Zhang Zhengdong, Chen Yongxiao, and Lü Zuo, p. 134.

Hebei: Wang Mingyuan, p. 135.

Heilongjiang: Heilongjiang Province Statistical Bureau, p. 64.

Henan: Advisory Committee on Economic and Social Development Strategy and Planning of Henan Province and Office of Investigation and Study of the Henan People's Government, p. 32.

Hubei: Tan Zongtai, Cheng Du, and Liang Wenda, p. 106.

Hunan: Mao Kuangsheng, p. 138.

Inner Mongolia: Song Xigong, Zhang Zengzhi, Wang Mingzhong, and Mao Zhaohui, p. 131.

Jiangsu: Du Wenzhen and Gu Jirui, p. 113.

Jiangxi: Ma Juxian, Shiyuan, and Yi Yiqu, p. 108.

Ningxia: Chang Naiguang, Song Chuansheng, and Chen Xinhui, p. 111.

Shaanxi: Zhu Chuzhu, p. 124.

Shandong: Wu Yulin and Chen Longfei, p. 153.

Shanghai: Statistical Bureau of Shanghai, p. 100.

Tianjin: Li Jingneng, Wang Qiang, and He Ziqiang, p. 125.

Yunnan: Zou Qiyu and Miao Wenjun, p. 172.

Zhejiang: Wang Sijun and Wang Ruizi, p. 115.
For other provinces and for China as a whole: Center for Population Research of the Chinese Academy of Social Sciences and the Editorial Office of China Population Yearbook. Data for Tibet were not collected for the period.

Per-Capita National Income by Province (Various Years)

State Statistical Bureau, *Quanguo gesheng zizhiqu zhixiashi lishi tongji ziliao huibian 1949–1989* (Compendium of historical statistics for Chinese provincial-level units, 1949–1989).

Mess-Hall Participation Rate as of 1959

NJZWH, 2:297.

Distance Between Provincial Capitals and Beijing

Zhongguo lüyou (China tourism), no. 19 (January 1982), pp. 66–67; *Zhongguo dituce* (Atlas of China). The latter was used in estimations for Inner Mongolia, Anhui, and Ningxia.

Brigade Accounting Rate and Percentage of Grain Crops Planted in Rice

ZGNYNJ, various years.

Percentage of Population Who Were Members of the CCP as of Mid-1956

Teiwes, "Provincial Politics," p. 165, table 9.

Per-Capita Amount of Income Distributed by Collectives in 1979

World Bank, *China: Socialist Economic Development*, vol. 1, p. 376.

• • • • •

Abbreviations

The following abbreviations are used in the Notes and Bibliography:

BDZX   Zhongguo fazhan wenti yanjiu zu (Research group on Chinese development), *Baochan daohu ziliao xuan* (Selected materials on fixing farm output quotas for each household), 2 vols.

CCP   Chinese Communist Party

FBIS   U.S. Foreign Broadcast Information Service, Daily Report: China.

JDJ   *Zhonghua Renmin Gongheguo guomin jingji he shehui fazhan jihua dashi jiyao (1949–1985)* (A summary of major events in national economic and social development planning of the People's Republic of China, 1949–1985).

JGD   *Zhonghua Renmin Gongheguo jingji guanli dashiji* (A chronology of major events in economic management of the People's Republic of China).

JJYJ   *Jingji yanjiu* (Economic research).

JZD   Zhao Dexin, comp., *Zhonghua Renmin Gongheguo jingji zhuanti dashiji* (A chronology of major economic events in the People's Republic of China, arranged by subject), 2 vols.

NJZWH   Guojia Nongye Weiyuanhui Bangongting (General Office of the State Agriculture Commission), *Nongye jitihua zhongyao wenjian huibian* (Compendium of important documents on agricultural collectivization), 2 vols.

NMRB *Nongmin ribao* (Peasant daily).

NYJJWT *Nongye jingji wenti* (Problems of agricultural economy).

RMRB *Renmin ribao* (People's daily).

SNHS *Shandong sheng nongye hezuohua shiliaoji* (A compendium of historical materials on agricultural collectivization in Shandong province), 2 vols.

SZQH Zhonggong zhongyang wenxian yanjiushi, *Sanzhong quanhui yilai zhongyao wenxian xuanbian* (A selected compilation of important documents since the Third Plenum), 2 vols.

XNNWX *Xinshiqi nongye he nongcun gongzuo zhongyao wenxian xuanbian* (Compendium of important documents on agriculture and rural work in the new era).

XSN Wang Gengjin, Yang Xun, Wang Ziping, Liang Xiaodong, and Yang Guansan, eds., *Xiangcun sanshi nian: Fengyang nongcun shehui jingji fazhan shilu (1949–1983 nian)* (The countryside over three decades: A veritable record of rural socio-economic development in Fengyang, 1949–83), 2 pts.

XZNJJ Li Debin, Lin Shunbao, Jin Bihua, He Fengqin, and Jin Shiying, *Xin Zhongguo nongcun jingji jishi 10/1949–9/1984* (Major events of new China's rural economy, October 1949 to September 1984).

ZGFS Liao Gailong, Ding Xiaochun, and Li Zhongzhi, eds., *Zhongguo gongchandang fazhan shidian* (Chronicle of events of the Chinese Communist Party's development).

ZGNCTJNJ State Statistical Bureau, *Zhongguo nongcun tongji nianjian* (China rural statistics yearbook), various years.

ZGNMB *Zhongguo nongmin bao* (Chinese peasant bulletin).

ZGNYNJ *Zhongguo nongye nianjian* (China agriculture yearbook), various years.

ZGTJNJ State Statistical Bureau, *Zhongguo tongji nianjian* (Statistical yearbook of China), various years.

ZGZSN Ma Qibin, Chen Wenbin, Lin Yunhui, Cong Jin, Wang Nianyi, Zhang Tianrong, and Pu Weihua, *Zhongguo gongchandang zhizheng sishi nian (1949–1989)* (The Chinese Communist Party's forty years in power, 1949–89), rev. ed.

•   •   **•**   •   •

Notes

Preface

1. Braudel, p. 679. Compare the statement by Braudel with Marx's famous quote: "Men make their own history, but they do not make it just as they please; they do not make it under circumstances chosen by themselves, but under circumstances directly found, given and transmitted from the past" (Marx, p. 595).

Introduction

1. Nevertheless, mobilizational strategies have continued in other arenas. See T. White, "Postrevolutionary Mobilization," pp. 53–76; Peng, "China's Population Control," pp. 319–37.

2. D. G. Johnson, "Economic Reforms," p. S225.

3. For broad overviews of China's reforms, see D. G. Johnson, *People's Republic;* and Harding.

4. For econometric studies of the impact of reforms on agricultural growth, see McMillan, Whalley, and Zhu, "Impact," pp. 781–807; and J. Lin, "Rural Reforms," pp. 34–51. In an article published in *Red Flag*, then-premier Zhao Ziyang admitted that the Chinese leadership was pleasantly surprised by the larger-than-expected agricultural outputs, saying that they were more than what the state and society needed at the time. Zhao Ziyang, "Fangkai nongchanpin jiage," pp. 10–14, esp. p. 10.

5. For an overview of the Marxist theory of collectivization, see Pryor, *Red and the Green*, pp. 33–64.

6. The quote is from Berlin, p. 194.

7. See Feher, Heller, and Markus.

8. In the Communist system, the end of 1981 saw the imposition of martial law by General Jaruzelski in Poland, evidence that Communist power must be based on force and that the Communist parties were ready to defend their rule with force.

9. Shue, *Reach of the State*, p. 125.

10. Watson, "Family Farm," p. 26.

11. For a theoretical argument on the complementary nature of reforms, see Milgrom, Qian, and Roberts, pp. 84–88.

12. The rationale for the critical case is made in Eckstein, pp. 79–138.

13. For an indication of the popularity of these arguments among Chinese, see the script for the TV documentary program "Decade of Upsurge," trans. in FBIS-CHI-92-107, June 3, 1992, pp. 22–29.

14. This and two other quotations in this paragraph come from the leading Chinese text on the contemporary Chinese economy: Liu Suinian and Wu Qungan, p. 340.

15. Quoted in Solinger, *From Lathes*, p. 71. These words by Xue were hardly original at the time or afterward. They were but the hackneyed verdict on the Cultural Revolution that would find its way into numerous Chinese publications.

16. Liu Suinian and Wu, *China's Socialist Economy*, pp. 416, 434.

17. L. Pan, p. 23.

18. Vogel, "China," p. 10.

19. Pye, "Reassessing," p. 611.

20. Pye, "On Chinese Pragmatism," p. 224.

21. Field, "Performance," p. 639.

22. Perry and Wong, pp. 2, 6; see also the introduction in Joseph, Wong, and Zweig, p. 14, and the essays by Andrew Walder and Lowell Dittmer in the same volume.

23. Lupher, p. 666. Interestingly, in making the connection between the Cultural Revolution and the post-Mao reforms, Lupher argues against an overemphasis on the role of leadership.

24. Findlay and Jiang, p. 18.

25. For two recent examples, see Grindle and Thomas, pp. 213–48; Harberger, pp. 343–50.

26. See esp. Jin and Chen; Gao and Li; Zong. Numerous other titles of a similar nature can be cited. Commentators in Hong Kong and Taiwan have followed in the same track by focusing on the role played by reformists. See, e.g., Lu Fanzhi, esp. pp. 3–44.

27. At the 1993 annual meeting of the Association of Asian Studies, the panel on Deng Xiaoping included papers titled "The Politician," "The Social Reformer," "The Economist," and "The Soldier."

28. For a summary statement, see P. H. Chang, "Political Reform," pp. 119–40.

29. Schram, "China," p. 177.

30. Harding, p. 2.

31. Ibid., pp. 101–2. Emphasis added.

32. MacFarquhar, "Succession," p. 397. Similarly, Fewsmith writes: "Without the support of central leaders, China's rural reforms could not have developed" (p. 6).

33. Shue, "China," p. 158.

34. For one brief critique of this tendency, see Bachman, "Review," pp. 242–44.

35. Thurston, p. 12.

36. Imagine for the moment studying the democratization in the former Soviet Union by focusing solely on the conflicts between Gorbachev and the "conservatives" or between Gorbachev and Yeltsin while paying little attention to social forces.

37. For an interesting discussion of how peasants are perceived in the Chinese political system, see Kelliher, "Are Peasants?"

38. Hu Xiao.

39. *Webster's Ninth New Collegiate Dictionary.* A leading text has the following definition: "Peasants are farm households, with access to their means of livelihood in land, utilizing mainly family labor in farm production, always located in a larger economic system, but fundamentally characterized by partial engagement in markets which tend to function with a high degree of imperfection." Ellis, p. 12.

40. Potter and Potter, pp. 296–312; Zhang Qingwu, pp. 22–106; and Guo Shutian, Liu et al. On the different definitions of the rural population used in Chinese official publications, see M. F. Martin, pp. 392–401.

41. In the present study, crop production and rural industry will be placed within the same framework; special attention will be paid to their linkages.

42. Little, "Rational-Choice Models," p. 48. See also Perkins, *Market Control*, pp. 23–28. For an assessment of the various schools of thought on peasant behavior, see Little, *Understanding*; and P. C. C. Huang.

43. Schultz, *Transforming*, p. 5.

44. Whyte, p. 56. Parish and Whyte, chap. 15. See also Oi, "Chinese Village," pp. 67–87. For a theoretical statement, see Hansen, pp. 79–96.

45. See esp. R. H. Bates, *Markets*; Lipton; Olson, *Rise and Decline*, pp. 167–82; Nelson.

46. For statements to this effect by two leading reformers now in exile, though still unappreciative of each other's contributions, see Chen Yizi, *Zhongguo*; and Ruan, p. 76.

47. O'Leary and Watson, pp. 1–34; Watson, "Family Farm," pp. 22–26; J. Y. Lin, "Household," p. S201; and esp. Kelliher, *Peasant Power*. Contrast these with Unger, "Decollectivization," pp. 585–606. Fewsmith (p. 19) refers to those authors who argued that there was a "groundswell of peasant demand for reform" as having produced "romanticized renditions of this period."

48. See esp. North, "Economic Performance." For extensive bibliographies on this subject, see Eggertsson, *Economic Behavior*; and North, *Institutions*.

49. North, "Institutions" and *Institutions*.

50. Eggertsson, *Economic Behavior*.

51. Schultz, "Institutions," pp. 1113–22; Ruttan and Hayami, "Strategies," pp. 129–48, "Toward a Theory," pp. 203–23; North and Thomas.

52. See esp. Bromley, chap. 2; and Knight, pp. 28–37.

53. These writings include *Institutions, Institutional Change and Economic Performance*; "Economic Performance Through Time"; "Institutional Change: A Framework of Analysis"; and "Institutions."

54. North, *Institutions*, p. 84. North uses the word "framework" deliberately. In his 1990 book, North states that his revised framework constituted a set of hy-

potheses for further testing, but in his Nobel lecture he mentions that a theory of economic dynamics comparable to general equilibrium theory, but incorporating institutions and time, is unlikely to be developed.

55. Ibid., p. 17.

56. North, "Institutional Change," pp. 43, 48.

57. North, *Institutions*, p. 89.

58. Ibid., chap. 10; Stinchcombe, p. 153.

59. North, *Institutions*, p. 8.

60. Arthur, p. 359.

61. For North (*Institutions*, p. 23), ideology means "the subjective perceptions (models, theories) all people possess to explain the world around them. Whether at the microlevel of individual relationships or at the macrolevel of organized ideologies providing integrated explanations of the past and present, such as communism or religions, the *theories* individuals construct are *colored* by normative views of how the world should be organized."

62. Ibid., p. 86. See also North, "Economic Performance," p. 365.

63. For general discussions, see esp. Newell and Simon; Simon, *Models*; Simon et al., pp. 32–53; Hogarth.

64. This summary draws on Nisbett and Ross, esp. pp. 6–8.

65. In addition to the general term "schemas," psychologists have also used a variety of other terms, including "frames," "scripts," "nuclear scenes," and "prototypes." For further references, see Nisbett and Ross, p. 28; and Larson, *Origins*, pp. 50–57.

66. Tversky and Kahneman, pp. 207–32; Kahneman and Tversky, "Subjective Probability," pp. 430–54, and "Psychology of Prediction," pp. 237–51; Tversky, pp. 327–52. See also Kahneman, Slovic, and Tversky.

67. Nisbett and Ross, pp. 8, 44–62.

68. Most cognitive psychologists, including Kahneman and Tversky, have focused on inferential failures. For a more balanced approach, which emphasizes both successes and failures, see Fiske and Taylor.

69. Nisbett and Ross, p. 3. See also the excellent chapter by Suedfeld and Tetlock, "Psychological Advice," pp. 51–70.

70. Bacon, *New Organon*, p. 50. For general discussions of the relevant psychological literature, see Ross and Nisbett, chap. 3.

71. Anderson, Lepper, and Ross, pp. 1037–49.

72. For an overview, see Kahneman, Knetsch, and Thaler, pp. 193–206; Samuelson and Zeckhauser (pp. 7–59) discuss many manifestations of what they call status quo bias.

73. W. R. Scott, pp. 493–511; Sjöstrand (p. 9) defines an institution as "a human mental construct for a coherent system of shared (enforced) norms that regulate individual interactions in recurrent situations."

74. Samuelson and Zeckhauser, p. 47. A classic statement of the implications of the rational model for voting is Arrow, *Social Choice*.

75. North, *Institutions*, pp. 90–91, quote on p. 90.

76. Gould, p. 305.

77. Borgida and Nisbett, pp. 258–71.

78. Nisbett and Ross, pp. 44–59.

79. See Kuran, "Tenacious Past," pp. 168–69.
80. Kingdon (p. 123) refers to a policy primeval soup.
81. Stinchcombe, p. 153. On the episodic nature of institutional changes, see Krasner, "Sovereignty"; Ikenberry, pp. 219–43.
82. Hirschman, *Rhetoric*, chap. 6.
83. Baum, *Prelude*; MacFarquhar, *Origins*, vol. 2.
84. I use the term "province" to denote a provincial level unit, including provinces, the three municipalities of Beijing, Shanghai, and Tianjin, and autonomous regions. While the comparative studies cited below in this section must justify the choice of cases, I use quantitative data from all Chinese provinces (Tibet excluded, owing to the lack of data), though in discussion I draw on materials on some provinces rather than others owing to the availability of local accounts. Such a procedure minimizes the sampling problem that usually attends case studies.
85. Elster, *Nuts and Bolts*; Kiser and Hechter, pp. 1–30.
86. Elster, *Political Psychology*, p. 5.
87. For a quick overview of the limitations of cross-country regressions, see Levine and Zervos, pp. 426–27.
88. For an easily accessible discussion of selection bias, see King, Keohane, and Verba, pp. 128–39.
89. For a sophisticated discussion of methodological issues in comparative historical sociology, see Goldstone, pp. 39–62, esp. 53–60, on "robust processes" in history.
90. R. M. Solow, p. 329. In this essay, Solow lamented the ahistorical nature of mainstream economics. He wrote: "To my way of thinking, the true functions of analytical economics are best described informally: to organize our necessarily incomplete perceptions about the economy, to see connections that the untutored eye would miss, to tell plausible—sometimes even convincing—causal stories with the help of a few central principles, and to make rough quantitative judgments about the consequences of economic policy and other exogenous events. In this scheme of things, the end product of economic analysis is likely to be a collection of models contingent on society's circumstances—on the historical context, you might say—and not a single monolithic model for all seasons." In my view, Solow's vision for economics is equally applicable to political science.

1. Path to Disaster

1. This period has been the subject of much study, and I have not thought it necessary to cover the ground again in detail. Actually, the CCP's general line of socialist construction, the Great Leap Forward, and the people's communes were called the "three red banners" in CCP history. It is now customary to subsume the people's communes movement under the general rubric of the Great Leap Forward.
2. The emphasis on outputs is not meant to neglect the human toll that was involved. Rummel (p. 244) estimates that as many as 7,474,000 people, or 1 percent of the population, may have perished during the collectivization period as the direct or indirect victims of party policies.
3. *RMRB* editorial, October 2, 1949; repr. in Zhang, Liu, and Xiao, pp. 10–11.

4. Some of the reasons for the adoption of the Stalinist model are discussed in Teiwes, "Establishment," pp. 63–67. For a broad review of China's development strategy, see Dong Fureng, *Jingji*, chap. 2, and "Development Theory," pp. 228–53.

5. A. M. Tang, pp. 38–39. According to Walker, a self-sufficiency level required 275 kilograms per capita, providing 1,700–1,900 calories daily (*Food Grain*, p. 3).

6. Tang, p. 40; see also Yeh, pp. 327–63.

7. "Low cost" pertains to perception only, since Chinese leaders, like leaders the world over, believed or hoped that their decisions would be effective. Post facto cost-benefit tallies may well reveal the low-cost measures to be prohibitively costly, as in the Great Leap Forward.

8. Lardy, *Agriculture*, pp. 129–30.

9. Li Fuchun, "Report," p. 47.

10. See esp. the thorough analysis of land reform in Shue, *Peasant China*, chap. 2.

11. Rural cadres' sentiments after land reform are analyzed in Bernstein, "Keeping," pp. 239–67.

12. Figures cited here come from Domes, *Socialism*, p. 14.

13. On the struggle over the division of the harvest in the PRC, see Oi, *State and Peasant*.

14. For an overview of the Marxist theory on collectivization, see Pryor, *Red and the Green*, chap. 2.

15. The weather was apparently a factor. However, it would be misleading to use Chinese statistics for an area that was affected by natural disasters as an indicator of the severity of such disasters; this is because the statistics are derived from agricultural output figures, which may have been affected by factors other than nature. Chinese agricultural scientists have classified the weather conditions from 1950 to 1957 as follows: above-average years, 1950–52; average years, 1953, 1955–57; below average, 1954 (Liu Zhideng and Huang, *Zhongguo liangshi*, p. 211). Thus, with the exception of 1954, it might be said that the weather was not the determining factor for the rest of 1953–57, all of them being years of average weather. A separate Chinese study also suggests that the effect of nature on agricultural fluctuations for the 1950–86 period was not very significant (Liu Zhideng and Huang, *Zhongguo nongye*, p. 26).

16. One might similarly discuss changes in the growth rate for cotton, the major raw material for the textile industry. In this case, output was also significantly affected by the changing price ratios between cotton and grain. The Chinese government changed such ratios to manipulate the output of cotton. See Perkins, *Market Control*, pp. 33–38; and Zhao Dexin, ed., p. 393.

17. From 1949 to 1952, the average per-capita peasant income increased by 30 percent and consumption increased by 20 percent. Nevertheless, according to a survey of 15,432 households in 23 provinces, the average household had only 0.47 draught animals and could spend only 3.5 yuan per year on farming implements (Lin, Fan, and Zhang, pp. 270, 272).

18. The index of grain output in 1952 was 109.3 (with 1936 as the base year), draught animals 109.9 (with 1935 as the base year), and pigs 114.3 (with 1934 as the base year). State Statistical Bureau, *Guanghui*, p. 60. I am not in a position to ascertain how much of this growth was due to land redistribution and to the recovery effect that came with the end of prolonged war and the return to peace.

Chinese writings have generally asserted the favorable effect of land reform on agricultural production. See, e.g., Zhao Dexin, ed., 1:156. Victor Lippit views the land reform in terms of its beneficial effect on development financing in his *Land Reform and Economic Development in China*; Dwight Perkins considers certain disincentive effects of land redistribution in his *Agricultural Development in China, 1368–1969*, p. 108.

19. Kenneth R. Walker dates the campaign from December 15, 1951 ("Collectivization," p. 9). My focus is on the mutual aid–cooperativization craze that came on the heels of the two catalysts mentioned here. This craze is often referred to as the small "rash advance" by Chinese scholars, to distinguish it from the rash advance, or small leap forward, of December 1955–June 1966.

20. *XZNJJ*, p. 54.

21. Zhao Dexin, ed., pp. 150–53; Shue, *Peasant China*, p. 99.

22. *ZGZSN*, pp. 61–62.

23. For an overview of the various coercive pressures on peasants, with numerous examples from internal party documents, see Lin, Fan, and Zhang, pp. 336–44. The case of Wugong in Hebei is detailed in Friedman, Pickowicz, and Selden, pp. 139–51.

24. Mao Zedong, pp. 89–91.

25. *ZGZSN*, p. 60.

26. Mao Zedong, p. 91.

27. *ZGZSN*, p. 68 (entry for Oct. 4).

28. *XZNJJ*, p. 76.

29. Zhonggong zhongyang dangxiao dangshi jiaoyanshi, pp. 1–10, quote on p. 2.

30. Bo, *Ruogan*, 1, chap. 12, esp. p. 263. The grain situation and the rationale for the unified purchasing and marketing of grain are presented in Chen Yun's speech of October 10, 1953 (*Chen Yun wenxuan, 1949–1956*, pp. 202–16). Also see Bernstein, "Cadre," pp. 366–69. For assessment of the system in practice, see Walker, *Food Grain*, chap. 2.

31. Many Western scholars, needless to say, would not regard a peasant economy as a form of capitalism, however fuzzy the definition.

32. Mao Zedong, pp. 131–40.

33. Lin, Fan, and Zhang, p. 373. For a summary of the minutes of the meeting, including the initial and (upwardly) revised targets, see pp. 373–75, 380–81; see also the table in Teiwes, "Establishment," pp. 112–13.

34. "The Resolution on the Development of Agricultural Producers' Cooperatives" was officially approved by the CCP Central Committee on December 16, 1953. A full text of the resolution can be found in Zhonggong zhongyang dangxiao dangshi jiaoyanshi, pp. 11–27.

35. Zhao Fasheng, p. 82; Shanxi sishi nian bianji weiyuanhui, p. II-35.

36. In Gaoyao county of Guangdong alone, 111 people committed suicide after having been tortured during grain procurement. *NJZWH*, 1:291–93.

37. *ZGTJNJ 1983*, p. 393.

38. Teiwes, "Establishment," p. 118; Selden, pp. 32–97.

39. This point is most effectively argued in Teiwes, "Establishment," pp. 118–19; see also R. Martin.

40. *XZNJJ*, p. 97.

41. The number of draught animals (yichu) in China actually increased by 2,450,000 in 1954 over 1953 (year-end figures), indicating that the killing of animals was most likely less widespread than the sale of animals. As will be detailed later, significant reductions in the number of farm animals did occur in the 1956–61 period. *ZGTJNJ 1983*, p. 177.

42. Deng Zihui, pp. 2–9, esp. p. 3. The speech was originally delivered on April 21, 1955.

43. Quoted in Bian and Han, p. 698.

44. This section draws on Walker, "Collectivization," pp. 17–21; and Lin, Fan, and Zhang, pp. 537–39.

45. *NJZWH*, 1:227–84.

46. Mao Zedong, p. 290. On the publication of this Mao speech, see Schram, *Thought of Mao Tse-Tung*, p. 104 n. 18, and "Chairman Hua," pp. 126–35.

47. In addition, Deng also had the cooperation of Tan Zhenlin, who became deputy secretary-general of the CCP CC and director of the second office (overseeing local work) of the CC Secretariat in December 1954 (Tan Zhenlin Zhuan Bianji Weiyuanhui, pp. 301–3).

48. *NJZWH*, 1:295.

49. Deng Zihui, pp. 2–9.

50. The closed APCs were concentrated in Zhejiang (15,500), Hebei (7,000), and Shandong (4,000) provinces, with small increases in some provinces and little change in most others. Bian and Han, pp. 700–702.

51. In the meantime, the Chinese leadership also sought to reduce grain resales to rural areas, urging them to balance their own grain needs. See the discussion in Bernstein, "Cadre," pp. 365–99, esp. pp. 390–91.

52. Shue, *Peasant China*, p. 242. In reality, changes in the three-fix system were introduced in 1956 in conjunction with the "high tide" of collectivization. Shue also analyzes the effect of the changes in grain procurement policy on the attitudes of different peasant classes (pp. 242–45).

53. English translations of the speech may be found in *Mao Zedong*, pp. 184–207, and as "On the Cooperativization of Agriculture," in Kau and Leung, pp. 589–612.

54. Teiwes, "Mao," p. 13.

55. Bian and Han, p. 702.

56. Qiang and Lin, pp. 10–17.

57. Bian and Han, p. 702.

58. This speech is extensively quoted in Lin, Fan, and Zhang, pp. 555–56.

59. The clearest indication of this was Mao's comments of July 29, 1955, on a report from the Rural Work Department. The comments can be found in Lin, Fan, and Zhang, 557–59.

60. Li Fuchun, "Report," p. 55.

61. *ZGZSN*, pp. 96–97.

62. It appears that Mao took advantage of his position as party chairman to convene this conference, which was officially sponsored by the Central Committee. The quotations below are from Kau and Leung, 1:589–612.

63. Quoted in Tan Zhenlin Zhuan Bianji Weiyuanhui, p. 303.

64. *Communist China*, pp. 106–17.

65. A. Goldstein, pp. 98–103. It ought to be pointed out that not all provincial first secretaries supported Mao's full platform, or with equal enthusiasm (Goodman, "Provincial Party First Secretaries," pp. 68–82).

66. For excerpts from these provincial reports, see Lin, Fan, and Zhang, pp. 566–71.

67. For an analysis of the effect of changes in grain procurement policy on the attitudes of different peasant classes, see Shue, *Peasant China*, pp. 242–45.

68. MacFarquhar, *Origins*, 1:91.

69. Pang, p. 24. According to Pang, who served as Mao's librarian at this time, Mao believed before then that the transformation of 500 million individual peasants was going to be the most difficult task, requiring a long time and much work.

70. *XZNJJ*, p. 124.

71. *XZNJJ*, p. 143.

72. With the establishment of collectives, statistical reporting was done collectively, thus capturing what was previously left out. See *Dangdai Zhongguo de tongji shiye*, pp. 48–49.

73. *ZGTJNJ 1983*, p. 177.

74. Walker, *Planning*, pp. 61–63.

75. Official sources reveal that more than 550 people died of starvation and 14,700 people left the province. Needless to say, far more suffered from malnutrition and related illnesses (*ZGZSN*, pp. 126–27).

76. See Table 6.

77. Cong, pp. 68–70; *ZGZSN*, pp. 120, 128, 133. It is quite likely that these estimates understated the amount of social pressure, because the Rural Work Department's mission was to promote collectivization.

78. For brief overviews of household contracting in 1956–57, see Lu Xueyi, *Lianchan*, pp. 30–41; Yang Xun and Liu, pp. 56–57. For an interesting case in Sichuan, see Qu, pp. 453–55.

79. Lu Xueyi, pp. 30–31.

80. Mao wrote, in reference to the well-to-do peasants, that "a small number [of them] clamor to withdraw [from the collectives], eager to take the capitalist road" (*Selected Works*, p. 475).

81. Lardy, "Chinese Economy," pp. 360–361.

82. Lardy, "Economic Recovery," p. 169.

83. *Chen Yun wenxuan (1956–1985)*, pp. 69–77 (quote on pp. 69–70; emphasis added). As solutions, Chen called for the production of chemical fertilizers, chemical fibers, and irrigation projects, but, as Bachman points out, Chen's enthusiasm for the looming campaign for water conservation was at best lukewarm (*Bureaucracy*, pp. 199–200).

84. The historical details of the Great Leap Forward are covered in MacFarquhar, *Origins*, 2; and Schoenhals, *Saltationist Socialism*. The politics of the leap are discussed in Bachman, *Bureaucracy*; and Lieberthal.

85. Mao Zedong, 5:483–97.

86. For excerpts of these self-criticisms, see Cong, pp. 121–31. Cong argues that the self-criticisms were partly acts of self-protection, partly genuine expressions of remorse, in the belief that Mao, who led the CCP to victory in war, had truth on his side. See especially Zhou Enlai's remarks on pp. 127–28.

87. MacFarquhar, *Origins*, 2:17.

88. Cong, p. 105. The Moscow announcement was revealed in China by Liu Shaoqi and Li Fuchun in early December.

89. *Selected Works*, p. 281.

90. Xie Chuntao, p. 25.

91. These changes are detailed in MacFarquhar, *Origins*, 2.

92. Domes, *Socialism*, p. 22; see also Oksenberg.

93. This was revealed by one leader at the 1959 Lushan conference. Quoted in Su and Jia, p. 257. It is possible that the number of deaths was a misquote and could be 3,000 (7,000 + 3,000 = 10,000). I have opted to use the printed lower figure.

94. Xie Chuntao, p. 72.

95. Mainland forces began artillery shelling of the islands of Jinmen and Mazu in late August 1958.

96. *XZNJJ*, p. 199.

97. For a description of the situation in Guangdong, see Vogel, *Canton*, pp. 243–52.

98. Pennell, p. 3. While this describes the scene in Henan and other "vanguard" areas well, there were clearly places that were not as enthusiastic.

99. *ZGZSN*, p. 158.

100. In 1959, Zhang Wentian, a Central Committee member, estimated that perhaps only 5 of the 22 million new workers were genuinely needed (*Zhang*, p. 485).

101. Avery Goldstein suggests that such policy distortions were due to the administrative consequences of bandwagon politics (*Bandwagon*, chap. 7).

102. For a list of such claims, see Xie Chuntao, pp. 59–67; on the pressure on the statistical system, see Xue, "Zai Zhou Enlai," p. 37.

103. Quoted in Domes, *Socialism*, p. 27.

104. Tan Zhenlin, pp. 320–22.

105. On the relationship between increased procurement and the subsequent famine, see the pioneering article by Bernstein, "Stalinism," pp. 339–78.

106. The changing views on the impact of the Great Leap Forward are discussed in Mosher, *China*, pp. 110–18.

107. Demographers on China believe the official data are usable in representing the trend of population change. Needless to say, death registration during a severe famine was subject to underreporting, especially in severely affected areas. Nevertheless, the reader will quickly discover that the use of official data reveals a story on which the official media have understandably been reticent. For discussions on the reliability of Chinese population data, see Banister, chap. 2; P. Kane, *Famine*, pp. 2–5.

108. Coale, pp. 267–97; Aird, pp. 85–97; Peng, "Demographic Consequences," pp. 639–70; Ashton, Hill, Piazza, and Zeitz, pp. 613–45; Cong, pp. 272–73. Note that Cong's figure includes both excess deaths and postponed or lost births. Peng estimates the number of postponed or lost births at 25 million, making for a total of 48 million, compared with Cong's 40 million.

109. Banister, pp. 85, 118.

110. Livi-Bacci, esp. pp. 759–63. Also see Conquest, esp. p. 301. According to Nove (p. 408 n. 50), who cites Conquest with approval, V. Danilov questioned Conquest's figures in *Voprosy istorii*, no. 2 (1988).

111. Arnold, p. 20.

112. Lardy, "Chinese Economy," pp. 372–76. The somber atmosphere in urban areas was poignantly captured in Lindqvist; see also the short novel by Lu Wenfu, pp. 76–86; on the impact of the famine on soldiers, see the documents in Cheng.

113. Sen, *Poverty.*

114. In one Chinese dictionary of famines (Meng and Peng, *Zhongguo zaihuang,* pp. 1–154), the authors list famines that had occurred from 2598 B.C. to A.D. 1949.

115. As the information cited below indicates, this general statement is based on a small number of contemporary observations as well as internal documents.

116. Lindqvist, p. 103.

117. Cheng, p. 164.

118. Cheng, p. 14.

119. Wang Zhenmin, p. 35.

120. Ou, pp. 4, 52.

121. Cheng, p. 11.

122. Cheng, p. 138; see also "Report by Comrade Fu," Cheng, pp. 117–23. General Yang Chengwu said (Cheng, p. 138) that the problems were "found not only in Honan and Shantung, but in other places as well."

123. Quoted in Garside, pp. 275–76.

124. Quoted in Lindqvist, p. 94.

125. Quoted in Garside, p. 274.

126. The internationally noted missile expert Qian Xuesen, e.g., wrote that if plants could utilize just 30 percent of the light available, the output of rice and wheat per *mu* (1/6 of an acre) could reach 20,000 kilograms. *Zhongguo qingnianbao* (China youth daily), June 16, 1958. Mao Zedong was impressed by Qian's logic.

127. Cohn, p. 319.

128. In remarks to the son of his former teacher, Zhou Enlai, who as premier must share responsibility for causing the Great Leap Famine, made the following comment in 1961: "Mistakes were made out of good intentions, what could [we] do! [*you you shenmo banfa*]" We do not know whether Zhou was referring to the intentions of Mao or of the Chinese leadership collectively. Nor do we know whether Zhou reflected on who were responsible for the famine, though the remark appears to indicate that he looked upon the whole affair with moral equanimity (quote from Qiu, p. 7). For an interesting profile of the relationship between Zhou and Mao, see Quan, *Zouxia shentan,* pp. 345–94.

2. Political Economy

Epigraph from Jung Chang, p. 233.

1. See esp. Sen, *Poverty,* which adopts an entitlement approach to analyze factors of ownership and exchange that cause starvation and famine.

2. *ZGZSN,* p. 156.

3. *ZGTJNJ 1983,* p. 393.

4. MacFarquhar, *Origins,* 2:140–42; a Chinese biography of Zhao Ziyang was silent on this episode (see Zhao Wei).

5. Li Rui (1989), pp. 18, 29, 144.

6. Domes, *Socialism,* p. 38. The extent of such disturbances was clearly more widespread than indicated by the censored press. By January 22, 1959, the CCP Central Committee specifically requested the press generally not report on the

problems of 1958 relating to cadre style, people's livelihood, production arrangements, and market supply (*ZGZSN*, p. 159).

7. At the time he wrote, Domes did not have access to the population data I cite here.

8. These are only a few general titles. In 1959, the First Ministry of Machinery alone published 89 internal bulletins—an indication of the prevalence of such publications (*ZGZSN*, p. 183).

9. *Mao Zedong sixiang wansui* (n.d.), pp. 275–87.

10. Ibid., pp. 287–88.

11. Pang, pp. 28–72; Quan, *Zouxia shentan de Mao*, pp. 58–60.

12. In *Socialism* (pp. 39–40), Domes tends to mention Liu Shaoqi's name and omit Mao in referring to the adjustments of late 1958 and early 1959.

13. Zheng and Shu, p. 263.

14. *Mao Zedong sixiang wansui* (n.d.), p. 297.

15. *Mao Zedong sixiang wansui* (1967), p. 3.

16. Quoted in Zheng and Shu, p. 263.

17. Mao's Zhengzhou speeches are thoroughly discussed in MacFarquhar, *Origins*, 2:146–55; see also Bo, pt. 2, pp. 820–24.

18. *ZGFS*, p. 729. I have simply used the words "brigade" and "team" for the sake of consistency, even though their use here is somewhat anachronistic. For a discussion of the terminological confusion of the period, see MacFarquhar, "A Rectification of Names," in *Origins*, 2:181–86.

19. Bo, pt. 2, p. 827.

20. Cong, pp. 175–76.

21. A summary of this document is found in *ZGFS*, pp. 731–32. This document was drafted by Mao's secretary Tian Jiaying.

22. Quoted in *ZGFS*, p. 732.

23. *Mao Zedong sixiang wansui* (1967), p. 64.

24. At this time, Chen was a vice-premier and a member of the Politburo standing committee. He also headed the Central Finance and Economy Small Group, which was formed in June 1958 and was charged with overseeing China's finance and economy by the Politburo and the CC Secretariat. For an overall discussion of the role of Chen Yun, see Bachman, *Chen Yun*, pp. 70–72.

25. *ZGZSN*, p. 169. See also p. 164 on the situation in Hubei, Hebei, and Guangdong in early May. In Guangdong, incomplete figures show that at least 134 people died of starvation and 10,930 suffered from edema.

26. *NJZWH*, 2:186–88.

27. Cong, p. 181.

28. *Miscellany of Mao Tse-tung*, pp. 170–72. I have chosen to translate the original wording *xianshi kenengxing* more freely here.

29. *Chen Yun wenxuan (1956–1985)*, pp. 116–19.

30. The following list is derived from *JGD*, pp. 126–28; *ZGZSN*, pp. 164–66.

31. The stipulation that 90 percent of all commune members have increased incomes was clearly unrealistic, since many communes had much less to distribute owing to reduced acreage and output declines.

32. *ZGZSN*, p. 166.

33. Tan Zhenlin Zhuan, p. 325.

34. Contrast this with A. L. Chan, pp. 52–71. Chan (p. 71) argues that the pro-

vincial leadership enjoyed little or no independence in policy-making in 1958: "It was hamstrung by the direct central control and interference as well as the multiple and conflicting goals set for it by the center. All of these led to rather ritualistic implementation. The GLF [Great Leap Forward] had brought about more uniformity, not spontaneity and diversity."

35. Pang Xianzhi, pp. 32–33.
36. Sichuan Sheng Nongye, p. 10.
37. Bernstein, "Stalinism," pp. 366–67.
38. *NJZWH*, 2:250.
39. Gao Yi, pp. 39–44.
40. See Jiang Boying, pp. 328–38.
41. Cong, p. 233.
42. *NJZWH*, 2:254–57.
43. Ibid., p. 250.
44. Ibid., pp. 251–52.
45. Ibid.
46. Ibid., p. 221.
47. Ibid., p. 250.
48. Li Rui (1989), pp. 58–59.
49. Cong, p. 191.
50. The Lushan conference is composed of two meetings: an enlarged Politburo conference (July 2–August 1) and the Eighth Plenum of the Eighth CC (August 2–16). For a detailed account of the Lushan conference, see Li Rui. See also Peng Dehuai; Su, Luo, and Zhen; Tan Zhenqiu. For a Western account, see MacFarquhar, *Origins*, 2: chap. 10.
51. *Mao Zedong sixiang wansui* (1967), pp. 64–65.
52. The letter can be found in Peng Dehuai; and Yang Jianwen et al., pp. 186–89.
53. The Lushan confrontation between Mao and Peng Dehuai highlights the crucial role of historical contingency. First of all, while Peng was evidently concerned about the domestic situation, he originally had not planned to attend the Lushan conference, because he had just returned from an exhausting trip to the Soviet Union and East Europe, which lasted more than 50 days. He went at the urging of General Huang Kecheng. Second, Peng Dehuai's letter was copied out by a staff officer in the early morning of July 14. The staff officer reversed the order of four characters in an important sentence of the first part of the letter. While the original should read, "There have been successes and failures in the Leap," the copy became, "There have been failures and successes." In consequence, Peng was understood as emphasizing the losses arising from the Great Leap. Later this would be regarded as a crucial piece of evidence that Peng was savagely attacking the Great Leap. Li Rui (1993), p. 110; Yuan and Wang, p. 179.
54. On how Mao's senior colleagues behaved during the episode, see Li Rui; MacFarquhar, *Origins*, 2:228–33.
55. *Xuexi ziliao*, 2:384, 394–97.
56. *Xuexi ziliao*, 2:391–92; *ZGZSN*, p. 169; Li Rui (1989), pp. 270–71.
57. *NJZWH*, 2:231–32.
58. Bo, *Ruogan*, pt. 2, p. 871.
59. *NJZWH*, 2:251–52.

60. *BDZX*, 1:291–95, quote on p. 292; see also pp. 296–300.

61. *BDZX*, 1:295.

62. The stridency of the renewed campaign is indicated by the titles of *People's Daily* editorials—some of which had Mao's personal blessing—that appeared at the time: "Overcome Rightist-inclined Sentiments and Endeavor to Increase Production and Practice Economy" (August 6), "Make the People's Communes Manifest Their Superiority to Beat Droughts, Floods, and Insect Pests" (August 18), "Long Live People's Communes!" (August 29), "Let Us Put an End to the Theory That 'There Was More Loss than Gain [in the Great Leap Forward]'" (September 1), "Communal Mess Halls Have a Boundless Future" (September 22), "Long Live the Mass Movement" (October 26). The titles of editorials are taken from Oksenberg and Henderson; I have made some modifications in the translations. In a letter to Wang Jiaxiang, dated August 1, 1959, Mao wrote that he planned to write on the superiority of the people's communes (*Mao Zedong sixiang wansui* [1967]), p. 77.

63. *NJZWH*, 2:238.

64. Ibid., p. 271.

65. Cong, pp. 238–39.

66. The CC and State Council directive calling for campaigns of building large-scale water works and making manure can be found in *NJZWH*, 2:271–74.

67. *ZGTJNJ 1983*, p. 393.

68. On March 9, 1960, the CC issued a directive calling on urban areas also to build communes. By May 9, 1,039 urban communes, with over 39 million people, or 55.6 percent of the urban population, had been at least formally established in some 180 large and medium-sized cities (*ZGZSN*, p. 183).

69. *NJZWH*, 2:318; Cong, p. 247.

70. *NJZWH*, 2:249.

71. There were, to be sure, a number of pragmatic measures in the fall of 1959, including the limited opening of rural markets and Mao's call for raising pigs. But in the context outlined here, these pragmatic measures were dwarfed by the revived political fervor.

72. For a discussion of the other political consequences of the Lushan confrontation, see Lieberthal, esp. pp. 316–22.

73. J. Lin, "Collectivization." For Lin's defense against his critics, see his "Exit Rights."

74. J. Lin, "Collectivization," p. 1229.

75. See Dong and Dow; Kung; M. Liu; MacLeod; and Putterman and Skillman. All can be found in *Journal of Comparative Economics* 17, no. 2.

76. G. Hardin.

77. It is important that the size of the commons be limited. In a world of superabundance, however, the problem disappears. See R. Hardin, p. 17 n. 4.

78. M. Liu, p. 551.

79. Frequently, when commune mess halls were set up, peasants' private plots were also confiscated, and peasants thus had no alternatives.

80. Zhao Fasheng, p. 109.

81. Zhang Guangyou, quoted in Wu Si, p. 66.

82. A. Goldstein, pp. 128–30; quote on p. 129.

83. *NJZWH*, 2:297.

84. Instead of "mechanical overcompliance," the term used by A. Goldstein

(p. 117), the variations in mess-hall participation rates suggest that the degree of subordinate compliance varied significantly.

85. The three big cities (Beijing, Shanghai, and Tianjin) are excluded from the sample because they are predominantly urban and enjoyed special protection.

86. *NJZWH*, 2:258–70.

87. For an interesting commentary on Ke, see Wu Yu, pp. 64–65.

88. MacFarquhar, *Origins*, 2:302–3.

89. *NJZWH*, 2:254–57.

90. Goodman, *Center*, chap. 7.

91. The amount of Sichuan's grain transfer in 1960, which was apparently the largest by a provincial unit, comes from Zhao Fasheng, p. 122.

92. Sichuan Sheng Nongye, p. 10. For discussions of severe famine in a number of Sichuan counties, see pp. 501–7.

93. Goodman, *Center*, p. 136.

94. *NJZWH*, 2:286–90. This and other measures in Guizhou apparently encountered much resistance. Provincial leader Zhou Lin had this to say to the April 1960 session of the provincial party congress: "Many bad elements . . . still resist reforms. They grab every chance to destroy socialist construction. Some are still in the party, and even after education by the party, continue to resist reforms." Quoted in Goodman, *Center*, p. 115.

95. The comments of the Central Committee and of Mao are contained in *NJZWH*, 2:285–86.

96. The data for density of party membership are for 1956—the only year for which we have them. (I thus assume that the proportions indicated by these data did not change significantly over the next few years.) For levels of economic development, data for 1957 are used to filter out the impact of the leap on economic output figures.

97. The following equation is estimated: Mess-hall participation rate = $a + a_1\log$ (*Density of party membership*) + $a_2\log$(*Level of economic development*) + e.

98. It might be remarked here that my research strategy is to search out the major explanations for the variables to be explained rather than throw in many possible variables for the purpose of improving the R^2.

99. The patterns of famine severity in 1960 were of course also affected by what happened in 1960, which might to some extent interact with the relationship identified here. But the thrust of the argument remains.

100. Here famine severity is defined in relative terms. This is what Bouckaert in essence argued for, though he was more concerned about the influence of population size ("Crisis Mortality").

101. Because the central theme of this volume is rural policy, ideally the measurement of relative famine severity should rely on rural mortality data. Regrettably, I have not come across such data on a provincial basis. The calculations undertaken here thus implicitly assume that patterns of relative famine severity in Chinese provinces are representative of the provincial patterns for rural areas. For discussion on the rural-urban mortality differences in China as a whole during the Great Leap Famine, see Lardy, "Chinese Economy," pp. 372–76.

102. The following equation is estimated: Relative famine severity = $a + a_1\log$(*Density of party membership*) + $a_2\log$(*Level of economic development*) + e.

103. If we remove the income-level variable and rerun the regression, again

using logged data on density of party membership and relative famine severity, there are the following results: $N = 24$, adjusted $R^2 = 0.1988$, coefficient = -1.0861, standard error = 0.4193, and $t = -2.59$. Addition or removal of the income-level variable apparently does not change the adjusted R^2 significantly.

104. It appears that Lin misunderstands Sen when he writes: "In contrast with many other serious famines that were caused by what Sen (1981) termed an 'entitlement' to food, the estimated 30 million excess deaths in this crisis were the direct result of the crop failures (Ashton et al. 1984)" (J. Lin, "Collectivization," p. 1234).

105. Lardy, *Agriculture*, p. 42.

106. See esp. the recent account by Bo, *Ruogan*, pt. 2, chap. 26.

107. Zhao Fasheng, p. 107.

108. As will be touched upon in the next three chapters, Zhou played a vigorous role once he started to respond to the rural problems.

109. The export figures are from Zhao Fasheng, pp. 122–23.

110. Ibid., p. 108.

111. Ibid.

112. Many of those who reaffirmed the Great Leap in public were probably less convinced in private. On the distinction between private and public preferences and their implications, see Kuran, "Private."

113. Arrow, *Limits*, pp. 28–29.

114. Most post-Mao commentators on Peng Dehuai have emphasized Peng's moral uprightness. It may be pointed out, however, that one's evaluation of Peng or Mao varies significantly depending on whether one adheres to the ethics of intentions or the ethics of consequences. Both Mao and Peng came to regret the unintended consequences of their confrontation. When in 1965 Mao asked Peng to become deputy commander of the Third Front program, he ruefully told Peng: "Maybe you had the truth" on Lushan. Peng, on the other hand, commented to others that his letter to Mao on Lushan "ruined things. Without that letter, Chairman (Mao) would probably have changed for the better." See *Peng*, pp. 694–98.

3. Rural Liberalization

1. *ZGZSN*, p. 183. Much of the rural labor force was mobilized to work on huge basic construction projects.

2. *NJZWH*, 2:325–35.

3. Ibid, p. 297.

4. Ibid., p. 292.

5. See esp. ibid., pp. 287, 296, 311–17, and 318.

6. See esp. ibid., pp. 318–19. The style of this document suggests that it was written by Mao. Speaking to the Ninth Plenum of the Eighth Central Committee in January 1961, Mao claimed that information was hidden from him and others, leading to poor understanding. He did not reflect on the causes of this at the time. It was at this meeting that Mao declared 1961 to be the year for seeking truth based on facts and sent his secretaries on investigative trips immediately after the meeting (*Xuexi ziliao*, 2:427–31).

7. Pang, p. 56. While Mao was depressed about the mess China was in and was willing to share some of the blame, his admission of guilt was still a limited one.

In a speech delivered on the morning of June 18, 1960, Mao appeared to have been especially unhappy with those who were in charge of implementing rural policy (*dangshiren*). Moreover, Mao said: "The general line of our Party is correct and the actual work has basically been well done. It is inevitable that some errors have been committed" (*Xuexi ziliao*, 2: pp. 418–20, quote on p. 420).

8. Cong, pp. 259–60. Sadly, the realism regarding agriculture was not exhibited in industry. The unfolding Sino-Soviet dispute, especially the Soviet withdrawal of aid, prompted Mao and his colleagues to make steel output the yardstick for competing with the Soviet Union, and they called for a mass campaign (*lian zhengqigang*) to make (what turned out to be shoddy) steel in winter 1960–61, in order to bring credit to China and to Chairman Mao.

9. Indeed, even China's senior cadres felt the pinch of the depression by then and began to protect themselves. Beginning in August 1960, the CC authorized a special supply system to protect its own cadres in Beijing. For cadres at the deputy premier rank, each household was entitled to half a kilogram of meat per day, and three kilograms of eggs and one kilogram of sugar per month. Each ministerial level cadre (including first grade intellectuals) got two kilograms of meat, one kilogram of sugar, and one-and-a-half kilograms of eggs per month. And each cadre at the bureau director's level was entitled to one kilogram of meat, half a kilogram of sugar, and one kilogram of eggs per month. By November these rations were halved. By January 1961, a similar system, but with lower rations, was set up for cadres in the provinces. (The figures cited here are from ZGZSN, p. 185.) Ironically, a September 1960 meeting of provincial secretaries in charge of agriculture urged all cadres in rural areas, including those at the county level, to have the same low rations as the rural population and not seek special supplies (*NJZWH*, 2:345).

10. In the directive, grain rations for peasants would go directly to mess halls. This would effectively force peasants to eat at mess halls.

11. *NJZWH*, 2:336–42. In addition, the conference also approved the major measures for industry and transport in the third quarter of 1960 and a directive on launching a campaign to increase production and practice economy centered on grain and steel. It also approved a notice to party members and cadres explaining the situation of the Belgrade conference and Sino-Soviet relations.

12. Ibid., pp. 364–73.

13. Ibid., pp. 312–17.

14. Ibid., pp. 353–56. Jean C. Oi has argued that the peasant share of the harvest came after the state and collective shares (*State and Peasant*, chap. 2).

15. Zheng and Shu, p. 279.

16. *NJZWH*, 2:357–61.

17. Ibid., pp. 391–93.

18. Provincial authorities had the authority to draft and issue these documents within their own province. CC approvals of the three documents are in ibid., pp. 311–12, 352, 357. In addition, Mao, again in the name of the CC, approved the measures that had been taken by Shanxi on rural labor on October 27, 1960 (*Mao Zedong sixiang wansui* [1967], pp. 254–55).

19. Commenting on a directive by Mao in the name of the CC on October 27, 1960, MacFarquhar writes: "An interesting aspect of this directive, which went to all provincial parties, is that it sanctioned a policy that Shansi [Shanxi] had been carrying out for *three months*. . . . [It] raises the question as to how many other

278 • Notes to Pages 75–77

provinces had taken matters into their own hands; it is possible that Mao's circular was less a directive than *ex post facto* approval" (*Origins*, 2:324).

20. *SNHS*, 1:388–90.

21. The provincial directive is in *SNHS*, 1:385–86.

22. Quoted in Su and Jia, pp. 256–57.

23. Quan Yanchi suggests in a recent volume that top-secret telegrams reporting famine deaths in Anhui, Shandong, Henan, and other areas reached the center between the Lushan conference and late September in 1959. Such telegrams, according to Quan, were available to members of the standing committee of the Politburo (*Mao Zedong*, p. 208). But Quan's assertion did not have documentary support and was contradicted by Mao's own talk at the Guangzhou work conference of March 19, 1961, when he mentioned that famine deaths were not reported to the center until the summer of 1960. The December directive (*NJZWH*, 2:416–17), distributed only to provincial-level leaders, begins by saying that "you had already known something about the serious situations that had occurred in certain areas of Shandong, Henan, and Gansu" and then goes on to introduce new materials on Guizhou.

24. Huai En, p. 420; Pang, p. 56; Cong, p. 262. Those who drafted the letter came mostly from the Rural Work Department. The text of the letter, which was previously available only in summary form, is in *NJZWH*, 2:377–87. The Great Leap Forward was never ended officially, but this letter might be regarded as the "official" end of leap policies.

25. *NJZWH*, 2:388–90, quote on p. 389; emphasis added.

26. Ibid., p. 391. Judging by the wording and style, this directive was most likely written by Mao. I am not sure whether the directive of November 3, which is much longer, was also written by Mao, though he must have approved it.

27. Ibid., pp. 419–30, esp. pp. 421–22.

28. Ibid., pp. 435–36.

29. *ZGZSN*, p. 195.

30. See Chen Yun's speech to the Central Work conference on January 19, 1961 (*Chen Yun wenxuan [1956–1985]*, pp. 132–33).

31. After hearing reports from leaders of the regional bureaus (*zhongyang ju*) on December 30, 1960, Mao made the following remark: "There were both natural calamities and human errors in 1960. In addition to sabotage by enemies, we did commit mistakes in our work; the most prominent was the large-scale building of waterworks and industry, which took too much labor [out of agriculture]." Quoted in Pang Xianzhi, p. 57.

32. *Xuexi ziliao*, 4:294–96; *Mao Zedong sixiang wansui* (n.d.), pp. 359–63. Throughout the spring of 1961, Mao hammered on this theme. On March 23, Mao, in the name of the CCP CC, sent a formal letter to the party committees of regional bureaus, provinces, municipalities, and autonomous regions on the question of undertaking serious investigation work (*NJZWH*, 2:441–42).

33. The three were Chen Boda (going to Guangdong), Hu Qiaomu (Hunan), and Tian Jiaying (Zhejiang) (Pang, p. 41).

34. *NJZWH*, 2:440.

35. Relying on politically charged publications from the Cultural Revolution period, earlier studies have suggested that Deng Xiaoping planned the Sixty Articles and supervised its drafting and Mao expressed displeasure at the document

(Johnson, p. 271; P. Chang, *Power*, chap. 5, esp. p. 131; Lee, p. 120; and Ahn, "Political Economy," pp. 631–58). Similarly, Jürgen Domes writes of a Liu/Deng faction vs. Mao in the making of the Sixty Articles in his *Socialism in the Chinese Countryside* (pp. 49–51) but gives little attention to the evolution of policy over the months he covers. Interestingly, none of these authors gives much attention to Chen Yun. This view apparently needs modification now. Recent publications from the PRC indicate that Mao played *the* leading role in central policy-making on rural policy at this time. Nevertheless, as will be detailed a little later, Mao did have his limits.

36. The four main authors of the first draft of the Sixty Articles were Liao Luyan (then the minister of agriculture), Tian Jiaying, Wang Lu (unidentified), and Zhao Ziyang (second secretary of the Guangdong provincial party committee; Zhao's main portfolio before assuming this post was in agriculture in Guangdong). Tao Zhu, first secretary of the central-south region, was head of the drafting group. The other members were Chen Boda, Hu Qiaomu, Deng Liqun, Xu Liqun, Wang Li, and Pang Xianzhi. Pang, pp. 45–47; Zheng and Shu, p. 281. Note, however, that precursors to the Sixty Articles already existed at the local level. During his visit to Wuxi (Jiangsu) in late 1960, Deng Zihui helped draft a set of forty regulations on the internal affairs of people's communes for the area. This document was submitted (probably at the very end of 1960) to central leaders and might have prompted Tian Jiaying to suggest something along similar lines for the entire country. Jiang Boying, p. 340.

37. *NJZWH*, 2:452–54.

38. Ibid., pp. 455–69.

39. Pang, pp. 49–50.

40. Huai En, p. 421.

41. In his talk at the conference on March 19, 1961, Mao reflected on the sequence of events leading to the crisis:

> What about these regulations? Are there dangers? The problem of agriculture is being grasped somewhat late. This time [we must] be determined to solve the problem. The second Zhengzhou conference did not completely solve the problem. . . . The Lushan conference was intended to continue to deal with what the Zhengzhou conference did not, but an interlude [i.e., Peng Dehuai's letter] came, [we turned against] rightism, [but] actually [we] should have opposed "leftism." The Shanghai conference mentioned the rural question but focused on international issues. The Beidaihe conference also dealt mostly with international issues. The "Twelve Articles" played a significant role [in dealing with the rural situation]; but they only solved the problem of property transfers [*ping*], not that of egalitarianism [*diao*]. The Central Work Conference of December (1960) merely dealt with some problems in a fragmentary form. The rural problem had already occurred in 1959, but the antirightism of the Lushan conference exacerbated it, and it became worse in 1960. People were starved to death; this was not reported to the center until the summer of 1960.

In Pang, pp. 48–49.

42. *Xuexi ziliao*, 4:301; Pang, pp. 46, 48, and 59.

43. The travels by China's senior leaders are well known: Liu Shaoqi went to the counties of Changsha and Ningxiang in Hunan from April 1 to May 15; Zhou Enlai went to Hebei's Handan from late April to mid-May; Zhu De spent March 26–May 5 in various areas of Sichuan; Deng Xiaoping and Peng Zhen used April and early May to lead five investigative groups in two suburban counties of Beijing; Chen Yun spent fifteen days from late June to early July in Qingpu county of Shanghai. In December, the disgraced Peng Dehuai traveled in Hunan.

44. Tan Zhenlin Zhuan, pp. 328–29. It is very likely that other leaders made similar comments, which were edited out of their collected works.

45. Zhu De, p. 440 n. 318.

46. *Zhou Enlai xuanji*, 2:314–15; Zhu De, pp. 374–75; Liu Shaoqi, 2:328–34.

47. Zhu De, p. 375. Peasants in this area apparently still had things to eat and thus made better use of them when eating at home. Eating at home would not help, of course, if nothing were left.

48. *Zhou Enlai xuanji*, 2:315.

49. Wang, Chen, and Ye, p. 374.

50. *NJZWH*, 2:474–91.

51. Ibid., pp. 447–51.

52. Ibid., pp. 470–73.

53. Zheng and Shu, p. 280.

54. *NJZWH*, 2:492–97. This was based on statistical aggregations from 27 provinces.

55. Pang, p. 60.

56. *NJZWH*, 2:518.

57. Ibid., pp. 524–27.

58. Pang, p. 61.

59. Deng Hansheng, p. 23.

60. Ibid., p. 23.

61. Klein and Clark, pp. 860–62. Zeng Xisheng was elected a full member of the party Central Committee at the Eighth National Party Congress.

62. The kind of cognitive change experienced by Zeng would also apply to most cadres in the province, especially those at the lower levels.

63. Yang and Liu, p. 89.

64. Wang Lixin, p. 16.

65. The details of these cases are included in Zeng Xisheng's letter to Mao Zedong, Zhou Enlai, Deng Xiaoping, Peng Zhen, and Ke Qingshi, in *NJZWH*, 2:499.

66. More precisely, the practice was centered on what was called *dingchan daotian, zeren daoren*: first set an output target for a piece of land, then assign responsibility for producing the output to an individual. Output above the set target ensured the producer rewards, while below-target output entailed penalties.

67. *BDZX*, 1:309.

68. The conference was held from March 15 to March 23, 1961. But prior to the conference, Mao met with local leaders from different regions, who had had group discussions.

69. Wang Lixin, p. 17.

70. Zeng Xisheng letter, in *NJZWH*, 2:498–500.

71. *BDZX*, 1:309.

72. *NJZWH*, 2:503–14.

73. The conversation between Zeng Xisheng and Mao is extensively excerpted in Wang Lixin, pp. 17–18; ZGZSN, p. 204.

74. Pang, p. 65; see also Ting Wang, pp. 63–65.

75. ZGZSN, p. 205. The climate in Hunan is relatively mild during the winter, and peasants could grow winter vegetables and other crops.

76. NJZWH, 2:495. See Chao, pp. 64–65.

77. NJZWH, 2:528–32. In addition, the directive stipulated that peasants be taught that raising agricultural prices too high would not help the national economy or the true interests of peasants, which the party defined of course. It also urged peasants to fulfill grain procurement quotas, support the cities, and support state industrial construction.

78. Wang Lixin, p. 19.

79. *Xuexi ziliao*, 3:15; Liu Shaoqi, 2:349–68.

80. See Jiang Boying, p. 349. In October 1960, when Shu Tong (the party boss in Shandong) fell, Zeng Xisheng was appointed to the post of party secretary of Shandong, thus technically becoming the top cadre in both Anhui and Shandong from October 1960 to April 1961. In February 1962, Zeng was replaced by Li Baohua as first party secretary of Anhui. The severity of famine was clearly not the chief criterion for sacking provincial party secretaries. Both Sichuan and Guizhou also experienced extremely high mortality rates during the Great Leap Famine, yet the party secretaries of both provinces (Li Jingquan and Zhou Lin) kept their posts.

81. NJZWH, 2:559–66.

82. Ibid., p. 588.

83. Ibid., p. 555; bulletin is on pp. 555–57.

84. Ibid., pp. 567–76, quotes on pp. 567–68. For Deng, individual farming included household contracting and dividing land among households.

85. Pang, p. 68.

86. NJZWH, 2:562.

87. *Dangdai Zhongguo de Guizhou*, pp. 72–73.

88. "Jianbao" (Bulletin), in NJZWH, 2:556. The cadres surveyed were those attending the training meetings for making the production team the basic accounting unit. Since the sample of cadres was not selected randomly, the survey results could only be used for indicative purposes. My conjecture is that most of the cadres attending the sessions were leaders in production brigades and higher, including probably all commune party secretaries. This and the following paragraph draw on data contained in this document.

89. Ibid., p. 556.

90. Such appeals were not confined to Anhui. See, e.g., Hu Kaiming's letter to Mao Zedong (dated July 30, 1962; cover letter dated August 8, 1962). Hu was first secretary of the (Hebei) Zhangjiakou prefectural committee. He advocated contracting to small work groups within the production team. Ibid., pp. 609–16.

91. BDZX, 1:317–29. The report was dated May 1962. Because of the potentially heavy political costs involved (Qian would indeed be persecuted for many years to come), one has little reason to doubt the veracity of the claims made in such appeals except that they might be understated. Hence the conclusions that might be drawn from them are all the more convincing.

92. In Qiaoxi brigade of Xuqiao district, a typical rural community in the area, 125 of the 430 surviving persons suffered from edema.

93. The provincial leadership's conclusion rested on a tenuous foundation, even if its own data on local opinions were to be trusted. According to the resolution, "20 percent of the commune members, mostly politically conscious cadres, party and youth league members, activists, and households with difficulty in terms of labor power and farming techniques, did not like the responsibility land. 10 percent of the members were for continuing with contracting to the household and did not want the responsibility land abolished. . . . About 70 percent of the members were in the middle. Judging from the above, abolishing the responsibility land would be popular among a majority of the masses." Quoted in *BDZX*, 1:328.

94. Jiang Boying, pp. 349–50.

95. Gao Huamin, pp. 126–45. See also the other pieces in this volume.

96. Jiang Boying, p. 350.

97. *NJZWH*, 2:577–89; Jiang Boying, pp. 353–57; *ZGFS*, pp. 637–39.

98. Pang, p. 63.

99. Ibid., pp. 64–65.

100. Quoted in ibid., p. 66.

101. Ibid., p. 65; Deng Xiaoping, *Selected Works*, p. 281. As Deng Xiaoping pointed out, however, even Chen Yun did not openly object to the Great Leap Forward.

102. Pang, p. 67.

103. See, e.g., Deng's talk of July 7, 1962, in *Deng Xiaoping wenxuan (1938–1965)*, pp. 304–9, quote on p. 305.

104. This was most likely the Beijing work conference of May 7–11, 1962.

105. Ruan, p. 5.

106. Cong, p. 493.

107. The rest of this section draws on Zheng and Shu, pp. 282–85; *ZGZSN*, p. 218; Wang Renzhong, Jin, Yong, and Yu, pp. 8–9. At this time, Tao was the first party secretary of the central-south region and concurrently first party secretary of Guangdong; Wang was the second party secretary of the central-south region and also first party secretary of Hubei.

108. Zheng and Shu, p. 284.

109. Text of the report has been reprinted in *NJZWH*, 2:590–95. The report was actually drafted by Li Pu, director of the Office of Policy Research in the central-south region party bureau.

110. Compare with the case of misplaced word order in Peng Dehuai's letter to Mao during the Lushan conference of 1959.

111. *NJZWH*, 2:590–91. Needless to say, the logic in this argument does not hold water. One cannot infer from the improvement in agricultural production that people wanted to follow the socialist road, especially given the circumstances that prevailed at that time. Such was the style of political argument in China at the time.

112. Of the 30–40 percent, 10 percent of the teams adopted individual farming completely, while 20–30 percent still retained some collective elements (ibid., p. 591). In other words, Tao and Wang argued that the glass was half full, while Tian Jiaying concluded that the glass was half empty.

113. Ibid., pp. 593–95; quote on p. 594. In addition to the Tao-Wang report, Li Fuchun made a similar report to Mao on July 10, 1962, in which he called for strengthening the collective economy but stated that certain areas might adopt

measures such as Anhui's *zeren tian*. He termed this a transitional measure. Li Fuchun, *Li Fuchun*, pp. 290–97.

114. On Mao's perceptual differences from his colleagues, see Lieberthal, pp. 325–31; Zheng and Han, pp. 186–96.

115. As will be discussed in Chapter 4, this was exactly what happened in the early 1980's. Tian, however, committed suicide, from political pressure, long before the post-Mao reforms became reality.

116. Pang, p. 68.

117. Zhou Taihe, "Chen Yun," pp. 168–69. Shortly thereafter, in comments to his staff, however, Chen denied that he had advocated individual farming. Instead, his policy suggestions were merely the result of his findings from his trip to his hometown, and he wanted to encourage individual initiative. This was but an extraordinary measure in an extraordinary time. If this is to be believed, then Chen and Mao apparently had communication problems during their meeting, particularly when one recalls their strong accents (Hunan and Shanghai) and the time of the meeting.

118. Ibid.

119. Similarly, the next day, Deng Xiaoping asked Hu Yaobang to revise a speech Deng was giving. Specifically, Deng wanted his references to "black cat, yellow cat" deleted and added a paragraph on consolidating the collective economy. Xue, *Gaige*, p. 268; Ruan, p. 6. On a variety of occasions during 1964–65, Mao criticized Deng Zihui and others for advocating household contracting in 1962. Feeling the heat, Chen Yun shrewdly sent Mao a letter of self-criticism on June 18, 1965. In the letter, Chen said that his idea of household contracting was wrong and was a rightist mistake. This letter probably helped save Chen from political trouble during the Cultural Revolution. Cong, pp. 580–81.

120. This occurred at a meeting of an unspecified date. Pang suggests that the meeting was probably convened a day after Tian's report to Mao. Pang Xianzhi, p. 68.

121. Quoted in Zheng and Han, p. 200.

122. Zheng and Shu, p. 285.

123. Ibid.

124. Ibid.

125. Quoted in Zheng and Han, pp. 196–97.

126. Quoted in Zheng and Shu, p. 285; emphasis added. The East China regions include Anhui.

127. Mao gave the first speech on class struggle on August 6 at a general meeting of the conference participants. This talk was followed by six more meetings of the core group, in which he elaborated on the theme of class struggle. Wang Xueqi, Yang, Shen, and Yao, 2:326–27.

128. *Xuexi ziliao,* 3:40. For Mao and others, household contracting was equated to individual farming in this context.

129. Ibid., pp. 34, 36. The "five-guarantee households" refer to childless and infirm old persons, who were guaranteed food, clothing, medical care, housing, and burial expense by the people's commune.

130. Ibid., pp. 38–39.

131. Ibid., pp. 42–43.

132. Ibid., p. 33. For Mao, individual farming was a form of capitalism.

133. Ibid., p. 32.

134. For an English translation of this document, see *Documents of the Chinese Communist Party*, 1:719–22. The Chinese version was originally released in September 1962. It should be distinguished from the revised draft, which was internally circulated in June 1961.

135. The document on the consolidation of the collective economy called for all trades to make the support of agriculture their priority. It included a number of important measures designed to encourage agricultural development: State investment in agriculture would increase while the agricultural taxes and state procurement of agricultural products were to be stabilized at a certain level. *NJZWH*, 2:619–27.

136. The official communiqué of the plenum, which Mao had a hand in writing, explained the party's new political vigilance: "There still exist in society bourgeois influence, the force of habit of old society and the spontaneous tendency toward capitalism among part of the small producers. Therefore, among the people, a small number of persons, making up only a tiny fraction of the total population, who have not yet undergone socialist remolding, always attempt to depart from the socialist road and turn to the capitalist road whenever there is an opportunity. . . . We must remain vigilant and resolutely oppose in good time various opportunistic ideological tendencies in the Party" (*Peking Review*, quoted in Baum and Teiwes, p. 11).

137. For a catalog of the "unhealthy tendencies," see Baum and Teiwes, p. 12.

138. Cong, pp. 513–14. The reference to "big agriculture" meant the mechanization of agriculture. Needless to say, this Liu speech of September 29 and others made during the 1962–66 period cannot be found in his selected works. Ironically, during the Cultural Revolution, Liu was attacked for supporting household contracting; there was no mention of his fight against household contracting in the fall of 1962. After the plenum, the Rural Work Department of the CC, which had served as Deng Zihui's institutional base, was abolished for what Mao termed "having done not a single good deed in ten years." But Deng Zihui stood by his conclusion that household contracting in agriculture was of a collective nature and should be permitted. This was because land was still collectively owned. Jiang Boying, p. 391.

139. *NJZWH*, 2:650–55.

140. *NJZWH*, 2:656–58. On the basis of the data contained in this document, it can be estimated that 86 percent (about 261,300) of the 302,600 production teams had adopted household-based farming prior to the start of the rectification. See also Yang and Liu, p. 99; Wang Lixin, p. 20.

141. Baum and Teiwes; Baum, "Revolution," pp. 92–119. The former contains the major policy documents related to the movement. While this movement was chiefly directed at rural cadres, it had its urban counterpart in the "Five-Anti" campaign and also reached into the realms of literature and political theory.

142. This campaign was known as the "Four Cleans," which dealt with discrepancies and irregularities in accounts, granaries, properties, and work remuneration.

143. Baum and Teiwes, pp. 32–33; Baum, p. 4. For a case study, see Chan, Madsen, and Unger, esp. chap. 2.

144. Baum, *Prelude*, p. 4.

145. For examples, see *NJZWH*, 2:837–45.

146. *NJZWH*, 2:836. See also Lin Hua, "Communist China's Agriculture," p. 78.

147. For discussions of Mao's prestige among his colleagues and the populace prior to the Great Leap Forward, see Teiwes, "Mao," pp. 1–81. See also Bloodworth.

148. MacFarquhar, *Origins*, 2.

4. Cultural Revolution

1. Zweig, *Agrarian Radicalism*, p. 2. For Zweig, the radical leaders included Mao Zedong, Chen Boda, Kang Sheng, Lin Biao, Zhang Chunqiao, Jiang Qing, and Hua Guofeng (p. 16).

2. In saying so, I am not denying that agrarian radicalism had adverse consequences for rural development. Readers interested in the impact of agrarian radicalism may consult Zweig, *Agrarian Radicalism*.

3. Fitzpatrick uses extensive archival sources that have become available in recent years to portray and analyze peasants' strategies of resistance and survival in Soviet *kolkhozy* of the 1930's.

4. It should be mentioned here that, as the economy gradually recovered from the Great Leap Famine, the share of investment allocated by the state to agriculture declined in favor of heavy industry. The Third Front strategy, initiated in 1964, also contributed to the shift of resources into industry. See Lardy, "Chinese Economy," pp. 396–97.

5. For a comprehensive overview of Zhou's role during the Cultural Revolution, see Shi, chap. 19.

6. For a highly evocative treatment of Mao's perceptual changes during and immediately after the Great Leap Forward, see Zheng and Han.

7. Li Rui (1989), p. 17.

8. Quoted in Pang, p. 58.

9. *Xuexi ziliao*, 3:18–19.

10. The struggle over the direction of the socialist education movement would exacerbate intraparty discord and set the stage for the Cultural Revolution. See Baum, *Prelude*; Ahn, *Chinese Politics*, pp. 85–86.

11. On Dazhai, see the excellent historical account by Sun and Xiong; and Wu Si.

12. Chen Xuewei, p. 160. See also Li Fuchun's letter of December 31, 1962, to Mao in *Li Fuchun*, pp. 302–4.

13. Chen's report to Mao is extensively quoted in Wu Si, pp. 233–34.

14. Zhao was then in Sichuan; Tan Qilong served in Shandong during the Great Leap period and was first secretary of Zhejiang from 1972 to 1977. In addition, Zhang Chunqiao also opposed the proposal, but this was not because he did not like such institutional transitions but because he and Chen Yonggui did not get along politically. Ibid., p. 235; *ZGZSN*, p. 390. Though the Chen proposal was not officially approved, the push for the transition to brigade accounting did have some effect, because Hua Guofeng advocated building Dazhai-style counties at the first "learn-from-Dazhai" conference held in fall 1975. See Zhao Dexin, ed., 3:145–46.

15. As the data in David Zweig's book indicate, the influence of the Gang of Four's advocacy of agrarian radicalism was largely confined to the late 1970's. Even then, the actual impact was very uneven. While brigade accounting was a major goal of radical policy, it was mainly found in twelve provinces, which accounted for 86.5 percent of the total brigade accounting units in 1979. Zweig, *Agrarian Radicalism*, p. 102, table 6; see also p. 53, fig. 1.

16. This and the next paragraph draw on Tan Zhenlin Zhuan Bianji Weiyuanhui, pp. 324–44.

17. Li Rui (1993), p. 236.

18. See James C. Scott, *The Moral Economy of the Peasant*, pp. 29–32.

19. Tan Zhenlin.

20. Zheng and Shu, pp. 260–61.

21. Ibid., pp. 263, 270.

22. Li Rui (1993), p. 236.

23. Zheng and Shu, p. 236; Zeng Zhi, pp. 363–64.

24. Tan Zhenlin Zhuan Bianji Weiyuanhui, pp. 349–54; the relevant documents are collected in *NJZWH*, 2:861–70. In mid-1966, upon the recommendation of Deng Xiaoping, Mao asked Tao Zhu to work in Beijing. In early August, Mao singlehandedly gave Tao the number four rank in the party at the Eleventh Plenum of the Eighth Central Committee. For Tao's other efforts to stabilize the economy in 1966, see Zheng and Shu, pp. 312–15.

25. Zhou's talk can be found in Zhonggong zhongyang dangxiao chubanshe, p. 60.

26. Wu Si, pp. 122–24.

27. *NJZWH*, 2:869–70.

28. *JDJ*, pp. 301–2.

29. *China Quarterly*, no. 51 (July/September 1972): 584. Also in 1972, Mao and Zhou Enlai authorized the import of several fertilizer plants in an attempt to bolster agriculture. The increased availability of high-quality chemical fertilizers toward the late 1970's became a major supply factor for improved agricultural productivity under the reforms.

30. On the policy winds, see Zweig, *Agrarian Radicalism*; Zhao Dexin, ed., 3:134–36. The most obvious conflict over rural policy occurred at the Dazhai conference in fall 1975 between Deng Xiaoping and Jiang Qing; this will be discussed in Chapter 6.

31. Deng Liqun, p. 19.

32. Baum, "Cultural Revolution."

33. Hinton, *Shenfan*, p. xviii. Hinton (p. xix) mentions that it was "the general rule that the peasants of suburban communes participated more continuously and more actively in the Cultural Revolution than peasants living deep in the countryside." He thus presented the village (Long Bow) he studied as atypical.

34. Zhao Dexin, ed., 3:128; see also p. 132.

35. Bernstein, *Up to the Mountains*, p. 2.

36. Based on data in *ZGTJNJ 1991*, p. 56. For an overview of the production declines, see Zhao Dexin, ed., 3:23.

37. Walker, *Food Grain*, pp. 179–84, quote on p. 184.

38. Oi, *State and Peasant*, chap. 4, quote on p. 83.

39. Ibid., pp. 63–65.

40. Nee, p. 206.

41. For the evolution of the policy on grain reserves, see Zhao Fasheng, pp. 127–31.

42. Ibid., p. 129. In addition, the grain ministry stipulated that production teams store the grain reserves themselves and the state would store the grain reserves on behalf of the production teams only when the teams had difficulties. In the latter case, state grain agencies should charge production teams fees for storage.

43. Zhonggong zhongyang dangxiao chubanshe, p. 60.

44. *Zhongguo nongcun*, pp. 410–11. I am not saying that the burden on peasants was light, however. My point is that there was a limit on state extraction over this period.

45. Zuo and Song, p. 323.

46. Zhao Fasheng, pp. 112–13.

47. Ministry of Finance, p. 20.

48. Zuo and Song, p. 324.

49. *Dangdai Zhongguo shangye*, 1:102.

50. Zhao Fasheng, pp. 114–15.

51. Chen Yun, "Important Work," pp. 152–54.

52. Bernstein, *Up to the Mountains*, p. 2.

53. In 1971, e.g., urban grain sales exceeded planned sales by 7.7 percent, and such demands on the urban grain supply remained for the rest of the 1970's. *JDJ*, p. 318.

54. Banister, pp. 246–47.

55. *ZGZSN*, p. 377.

56. There was nevertheless much progress in rural education and health care during this period. For an overview, see Perkins and Yusuf. For overall assessments of the agricultural sector, see Lardy, *Agriculture*.

57. J. Lin, "Collectivization," pp. 1244–48, fig. on 1247; Wen, "Current Land Tenure." Lin also evaluates the validity of different estimates.

58. In addition to the backward specialization discussed in the rest of the section, stagnant agricultural procurement prices and the suppression of rural markets also contributed to agricultural stagnation. Readers interested in exploring this topic further are referred to the voluminous works on China's agricultural economy, esp. studies by Nicholas Lardy, Dwight Perkins and Shahid Yusuf, Chen Liang Yu and Allan Buckwell, and Justin Yifu Lin.

59. Liu and Wu, *Zhongguo*, p. 417. This volume is clearly deemed to reflect the official view, since it was published in an English edition by *Beijing Review* as *China's Socialist Economy: An Outline History (1949–1984)* (quote on p. 408). Liu Suinian served in a variety of posts in the State Planning Commission before he was appointed Minister of Materials and Equipment in 1988. See also Liu Zhongyi and Liu, p. 51; Xue, *Current Economic Problems*, p. 41; Xie and Luo, p. 59. Liu Zhongyi was appointed Minister of Agriculture in 1990. Before that, he served in a number of agriculture-related posts in the State Planning Commission. Xue Muqiao, one of China's most published economists, formerly served as vice-minister of the State Planning Commission and director of the State Statistical Bureau. The last volume was put together by China's various ministries to celebrate 40 years of economic development under CCP rule.

60. Oi, *State and Peasant*, p. 111. See also World Bank, 2:59.

61. Walker, "Chinese Agriculture," pp. 783–812, quote on p. 783.

62. Endicott, pp. 82–83.

63. One should not overestimate the pervasiveness of this rhetoric. For example, the national planning meeting of 1971 made agriculture and iron and steel the top priorities. The planning meeting decided on eleven specific tasks and the first item called for paying attention to agricultural diversification while promoting grain production. The planners clearly did not see just grain in agriculture (*JDJ*, p. 308). Furthermore, procurement prices for various economic crops were increased in the early 1970's despite the official rhetoric.

64. Perkins and Yusuf, pp. 36–37. Philip Huang (pp. 279–81) also came to suspect the grain-first thesis. When told by his local interviewees that agricultural policy during the Cultural Revolution was "taking grain as the key link," Huang produced local as well as national data to contradict the view, showing clearly the limits of retrospective interviews on policy issues.

65. Note here that a policy of "self-sufficiency" should not be equated with the policy of "grain first," even though for provinces with grain deficits the two are practically the same. Contrast this with Lyons, "Grain," p. 184.

66. Lyons, *Economic Integration*, pp. 40–47.

67. Ibid., p. 49, table 2.6.

68. Walker, *Food Grain*, p. 184.

69. It should be kept in mind that the original slogan was "Take grain as the key link; seek comprehensive development."

70. In the case of Fujian, Lyons's study indicates that the tendencies toward self-sufficiency were less pronounced at the county level within the province than at the provincial level within China as a whole. This suggests that "grain first" was less salient at the county level in Fujian. If this pattern holds for China, then again this implies that grain first was less important than commonly thought. Lyons, "Grain," p. 197.

71. Zhao Dexin, ed., 3:170; Liu Zhongyi and Liu, pp. 107–8.

72. For evidence about other industrial crops, see Lyons, *Economic Integration*, pp. 58–60.

73. Lyons, "Grain," p. 210.

74. More examples can be found in Zhao Dexin, ed., 3:57–58; Lardy, *Agriculture*.

75. Lyons, *Economic Integration*, p. 80.

76. This decision probably originated with Yao Yilin, who was the minister of commerce in late 1978 (as he was in the early 1960s). He was supported by Li Xiannian and Chen Yun.

77. Chen Yun, *Chen Yun wenxuan 1956–1985*, pp. 195–96, 212, quote on p. 212; see also Li Xiannian, p. 340.

78. *Dangdai Zhongguo shangye*, p. 129.

79. On reductions in grain procurement quotas, see Zhu Rong, p. 47.

80. Liu Zhongyi and Liu, p. 108.

81. Watson, "Agriculture," pp. 84–85.

82. *ZGZSN*, pp. 330–31, 335; *JDJ*, pp. 300–301, 313. See also C. Wong, "Maoist 'Model,'" pp. 183–96.

83. The findings of the American Small-Scale Industry delegation indicate that while brigade and commune enterprises at first used capital inefficiently,

they become more efficient through learning-by-doing (Perkins, *Rural Small-Scale Industry*).

84. Lu Xueyi, *Dangdai*, p. 232.

85. Sun and Xiong, p. 2.

86. On disasters becoming reference points, see Raphael, p. 306.

87. Wang Lixin, p. 13; personal interviews.

88. Wu Si, pp. 154–58.

89. For examples, see Wang Yu, p. 19; Wu Si, p. 156. Other cases are reported in the next paragraph.

90. Li Mingfu and Wu, pp. 456–62.

91. Wang Lixin, p. 22. Ou Yuanfang (p. 71) mentions a similar, but unidentified, case.

92. Zhao Dexin, ed., 3:150.

93. Wang Guichen and Wei, pp. 175–86.

94. On the effect of the Lin Biao affair on the attitudes of the youth who were sent down, see Chan, Madsen, and Unger, pp. 230–31.

95. "Quarterly Chronicle and Documentation (January–March 1974)," *China Quarterly*, no. 58 (April/June 1974): 416.

96. Wang Guichen and Wei, pp. 175–86.

97. Zhong Borong, p. 2.

98. On the succession, see Garside.

99. Domes, *Government*, p. 128. Also see MacDougall.

100. See esp. the impassioned argument in Zweig, *Agrarian Radicalism*; and Mosher, *Broken Earth*.

101. On the significance of the private plots to agricultural development, see Walker, *Planning*.

102. Gao Zhiyu, quoted in Joseph, "Tragedy," p. 423.

103. The usual portrayal of state oppression of the peasantry during the Cultural Revolution should also be put in context, since there was almost no increase in urban wages (with the exception of Shanghai). Intellectuals perhaps fared the worst as the "stinking ninth category."

104. Shue, *Reach of the State*; for a critique of Shue, see Unger, "State."

5. *Incentives for Reform*

1. My understanding of structure has benefited from Sewell, "Theory of Structure," pp. 1–29. Elster made the case against structural or functional explanations of social institutions and historical change in *Explaining Technical Change*.

2. ZGZSN, p. 377.

3. ZGZSN, p. 355.

4. Zhao Fasheng, ed., p. 143.

5. Wu Si, p. 272.

6. Quoted in Friedman, "Maoist and Post-Mao Conceptualizations," p. 78.

7. For the 1968–78 period, David Zweig sees three types of radicalism: the "hard" (Chen Boda, Gang of Four), the "soft" (Hua Guofeng, Chen Yonggui, Ji Dengkui), and the "military" (Lin Biao) (*Agrarian Radicalism*, p. 34).

8. Li Tianmin, p. 84; on the succession struggle, see Lin Qingshan, pp. 288–468. On Hua's early career, see Oksenberg and Yeung, pp. 3–53.

9. For a discussion of the relationship between Dazhai and central power

struggles among Jiang Qing, Hua Guofeng, and Deng Xiaoping, see Friedman, "Politics," pp. 873–90.

10. Wu Si, pp. 226–32; Gao and Yan, p. 550; ZGZSN, p. 390. The Jiang Qing speech surfaced in Taiwan in Zhongyao diqing huibao (Important reports on the enemy's situation), no. 183 (December 10, 1975): 12–24.

11. Hua Guofeng, pp. 42–55, quote on p. 53. As an indication of the political antagonism between Hua and the radicals, Hua's speech was not printed in the journal Hongqi, then controlled by the radical Yao Wenyuan, in 1975; neither was it propagated in Shanghai. The radicals were evidently more concerned with the distribution of political power than with ideology at this time.

12. Ibid., p. 43.

13. Chen Yonggui, pp. 56–69.

14. RMRB, August 13, 1977, p. 1.

15. RMRB, February 7, 1977, p. 1. The Chinese original is "Fanshi Mao zhuxi zuochu de juece, women dou jianjue weihu. Fanshi Mao zhuxi de zhishi, women dou shizhong buyu de zunxun!"

16. JDJ, p. 378.

17. JDJ, p. 382.

18. Hua Guofeng, "Zai Zhongguo," p. 5.

19. The central committee directive and the accompanying document may be found in NJZWH, 2:942–55, esp. p. 952.

20. JDJ, p. 387; ZGZSN, pp. 415–17; JZD, 2:576.

21. An English version of the constitution can be found in Peking Review, no. 11 (March 17, 1978): 5–14.

22. Tsou, Blecher, and Meisner, p. 91.

23. Zweig, Agrarian Radicalism, pp. 69–70; "Letter to the editor," RMRB, January 4, 1979, p. 2; RMRB, January 10, 1979, pp. 1, 4. Many other sources can be cited.

24. Two factors were especially important in Deng's return: his own stature and the growing influence of moderate forces within the Chinese leadership. The elder statesman Chen Yun led the call for Deng's return to power at the Central Work conference in March 1977. Chen Yun, Chen Yun wenxuan (1956–1985), p. 207; see also Wang Hongmo et al., pp. 51–54.

25. An, Song, and Huang, p. 2.

26. Ibid.

27. Schoenhals, "1978 Truth Criterion Controversy," pp. 243–68; Womack, pp. 768–92. See also Schram, Ideology.

28. In fact, the original version of the article was an unsolicited submission by Hu Fuming, but it was significantly reworked by Sun Changjiang and others before publication. On the organizational basis of the ideological struggle between the "whateverists" and the pragmatists, see Li Honglin, pp. 138–39, 211–12.

29. For evidence on support from other senior leaders such as Tan Zhenlin, see Tan Zhenlin Zhuan Bianji Weiyuanhui, pp. 381–82.

30. RMRB, May 12, 1978, p. 2.

31. Schoenhals, "1978 Truth Criterion Controversy," pp. 260–63.

32. Zhu Dazhai Lianhe Baodaozu, pp. 1, 4.

33. RMRB, May 13, 1978.

34. ZGZSN, p. 422; RMRB, July 5, 1978, pp. 1, 4; RMRB, July 16, 1978, pp. 1, 3; RMRB, July 28, 1978, pp. 1, 3. Contrast the Xiangxiang case with that of Shaanxi's

Xunyi county. Cadres at the latter were investigated by the provincial committee and found to have seriously damaged party-mass relations for imposing heavy burdens on peasants. As a result, a Central Committee document of July 19, 1978, held Xunyi to be a bad example. ZGZSN, p. 423.

35. RMRB, July 17, 1978, pp. 1, 4.

36. Quoted in Domes, p. 164.

37. Quoted in Lampton, *Paths*, p. 52.

38. JDJ, p. 387.

39. In July 1978, the State Council issued a directive calling on localities to refrain from offering grain to rural dwellers in exchange for the procurement of cotton, oils, and other agricultural and sideline products. JGD, p. 318.

40. JDJ, p. 402.

41. FBIS, no. 209 (October 27, 1978), cited in Zweig, "Context," p. 259.

42. RMRB special commentator, p. 2. For an interpretation of the different aspects of Mao's thought, see Tsou, "Mao Zedong," pp. 498–527.

43. The *People's Daily* article was based on Hu's speech to a State Council meeting held in July 1978 (Schram, *Ideology*, p. 5).

44. Hu Qiaomu, pp. 1–3.

45. *Lilun dongtai*, no. 93, October 25, 1978; repr. in *Lilun dongtai*, 5:16–20.

46. Li Xiannian, p. 339; emphasis added.

47. For a discussion of Deng Zihui's speech in the context of the congress, see Bachman, *Bureaucracy*, p. 70.

48. ZGNYNJ (1984 and 1985) provides the ratio of production teams that had converted to the household responsibility system for 1983 and 1984. Justin Lin reports ("Rural Reforms," p. 49) that he obtained the 1981 and 1982 ratios from the Research Center for Rural Development of the State Council. He was unable to obtain the ratios for 1978–80.

49. While the results are not presented here, for the sake of brevity, I shall be happy to supply details to those who request them.

50. Nisbett and Ross, p. 51.

51. In this context, when I refer to a province, I am referring to the collective memory of its population, including the leadership. Of course, the cognitive impact of the famine is also expected to vary among the population of a province.

52. There is a body of literature in sociology dealing with the impact of disasters on social change. This literature tends to be poorly specified and inconclusive. For an interesting discussion explicitly linking the magnitude of disasters with social change, see F. L. Bates and Peacock, "Disaster and Social Change," pp. 291–330, esp. p. 294.

53. Weber, *Economy and Society*, p. 1051; Bendix, *Max Weber*, p. 351.

54. See Donnithorne; Naughton, "Industrial Policy."

55. See, e.g., Lin Zili, p. 34.

56. Ideally, the rate of change in the brigade accounting rate should be used. However, Chinese statistical sources contain only the brigade accounting rates for 1979–81, thereby making it difficult to assess the changes from 1977 to 1979, a critical period for the reforms. Nevertheless, using the percentage change in the brigade accounting rate for 1978–81 in equation (1) presented below yields the same conclusions, though the resultant R^2 is lower.

57. It might be objected that the level of per-capita income is derived on the

292 • Notes to Pages 138–47

basis of entire provincial populations rather than the rural population alone. However, substituting these figures with data on per-capita distributed income from rural collectives for 1979 (World Bank, 1:376) does not materially alter the findings.

58. Obviously I have arbitrarily chosen 140 percent as the cut-off point for extreme famine severity. One might have chosen other points.

59. It should be noted that for rice planting rate, p occasionally hovered just above 0.05 in some of the regressions.

60. Teiwes, "Provincial Politics," p. 165.

61. I am indebted to Pei Minxin and John Londregan for reminding me of this point. Ezra Vogel showed an early concern with the "later liberated areas" in *Canton Under Communism* (esp. pp. 41–44). The dates of "liberation" may be found in Ma, Chen, Shao, and Wang, pp. 760–61.

62. Bray, *Rice Economies*; see also her "Rice Economies," pp. 193–217; and John Wong.

63. Perry, "Implications," p. 205.

64. Data on land/population ratio were calculated from *ZGNYNJ 1980*, pp. 6, 100. Commune population and acreage planted in crops were used. I must point out here that the statistical analysis pertains to provincial comparisons; hence it does not rule out the possibility that rapidly changing land/population ratios may have had the effect suggested by Perry at local levels and in specific provinces. More tests are apparently desirable if such data become available.

65. See Collier and Collier.

66. See esp. David, "Path-Dependence."

67. On the role of geography in economics, see Krugman.

6. Political Struggle over Reform

1. Lieberthal and Dickson, p. 258; Lampton, *Paths*, p. 52; for Chen Yonggui's talk during the Third Plenum, see *Issues and Studies* (May 1980): 82–84.

2. Chen would not formally assume these positions until the Third Plenum.

3. Chen Yun, *Chen Yun wenxuan (1956–1985)*, p. 212.

4. Wu Si and Liu, p. 1.

5. "Decision" in Nongyebu bangongting, pp. 1–23; "Regulations," pp. 24–49. (Translated in *Issues and Studies* 15, nos. 8 and 9 (1979): 100–112 and 104–15, respectively.) It is important to note that these were the draft versions approved at the Third Plenum. They should be differentiated from the final versions, which were approved at the Fourth Plenum in September 1979.

6. This speech is found in Deng Xiaoping, *Selected Works*, pp. 151–65.

7. Zhao Dexin, ed., 4:402.

8. Chen Yun, *Chen Yun wenxuan (1956–1985)*, p. 212; and Li Xiannian, p. 339. Li credits Yao Yilin with suggesting grain imports to support agricultural diversification.

9. Preface to the New Sixty Articles.

10. Some readers might wonder why the Great Leap Famine was not explicitly mentioned in Chinese policy debates of the late 1970's. On the basis of conversations with a number of Chinese knowledgeable about the discussions, it appears that the famine figured prominently in people's minds as comparisons between 1957 and 1978 were made, but it was still a taboo explicit political subject. While there have been a number of volumes published on the Great Leap Forward, there

has yet to be a Chinese monograph on the famine itself. Joseph, pp. 419–57, esp. 440, 448–50.

11. "Decision," p. 2. In the official version approved on September 24, 1979, this paragraph was considerably moderated by using 1978 figures. The reference to the more than 100 million people who did not have enough to eat was deleted. See *ZGNYNJ 1980*, p. 56.

12. "Decision," p. 5.

13. Editorials in *RMRB*, January 22, 1979, p. 1; January 26, 1979, p. 1. The latter editorial stipulated that all levels of rural management should practice democratic management and cadres were to be selected through elections to ensure that peasants' democratic rights were protected politically.

14. "Decision," pp. 6–15; also see *SZQH*, 1:7–8.

15. "Regulations," p. 39.

16. "Overview," in Shen and Xiang, 2:4.

17. Wang Hongmo et al., p. 181; Han, 3:23.

18. Although Anhui and Sichuan were undoubtedly leaders in pursuing rural reform, a number of other provinces, including Guizhou, Gansu, Henan, and Yunnan, were also significant contributors. As time went by, however, the contributions of Anhui and Sichuan have become the stuff of legend; they are repeated in practically every publication on rural reform. I am convinced that experiences from other provinces have been slighted, if not ignored outright, by the growing literature on rural reform. Local cadres from Anhui and Sichuan were more likely to be promoted to the center for their apparent leadership role in reform and thus had more opportunity to retell their stories.

19. Ou.

20. Wan's appointment in early 1977 as vice-minister of light industry was clearly a demotion from his position as minister of railways, to which he was appointed in 1975, and later credited with stabilizing that sector.

21. *Who's Who*, pp. 679–80.

22. Wang Lixin, pp. 23–24, 31–32, quote on p. 24.

23. Ibid., pp. 25–26.

24. Wang, like Wan, was a native of Shandong. In addition to native ties, Wang could claim to have served under Wan in the late 1940s. Wan Li was secretary general of the CCP Hebei-Shandong-Henan Area Committee in 1947–49, when Wang was deputy political instructor of the Municipal Armed Corps of Weihai in Shandong. These ties probably contributed to the trust Wan Li apparently placed in Wang from then on. *Who's Who*, pp. 662, 718.

25. Zhang Guangyou, *Lianchan*, pp. 1–5. The original essay was dated January 1978.

26. Ibid., p. 4.

27. *XSN*, p. 385.

28. Tian and Yao, pp. 1–2. Contrast this report with the Xinhua report of January 15 (*RMRB*, January 16, 1978, p. 1), which followed the official formula by attributing Anhui's economic success in 1977 to the wise leadership of Hua Guofeng and made no concrete mention of the province's new economic policies. See also Nan, Shen, and Zhang, p. 2.

29. Note Wan Li, "Talk at the Provincial Work Conference (January 3, 1979)," excerpted in *XSN*, p. 386.

30. *XSN*, p. 385.

31. Tian and Yao, pp. 1–2.

32. *RMRB*, February 15, 1978, p. 1; February 16, 1978, p. 1. Both commentaries accompanied reports on areas in Anhui. Also February 22, 1978, pp. 1, 4.

33. Zhang Guangyou and Liu, pp. 1, 3.

34. Zhang, Tian, and Duanmu, p. 2. See also *RMRB*, May 13, 1978, p. 2.

35. *RMRB*, March 23, 1978, p. 1.

36. For Sichuan, see Gu and Xu, *RMRB*, April 27, 1978, p. 2; Yang and Li, June 13, 1978, pp. 1–2; see also May 12, 1978, p. 2, and May 14, 1978, p. 2. For Guangdong, see Wang and Chen, May 13, 1978, p. 2; and May 9, 1978, p. 3 (on Gaohe county in Guangdong). For Xinjiang, see Cheng and Wang, June 30, 1978, p. 1. For Fujian, see August 15, 1978, p. 3. For Jiangxi, see August 15, 1978, p. 3. For Tibet, see October 8, 1978, p. 2.

37. Cai and Li, *RMRB*, April 19, 1978, p. 3; Yi, April 22, 1978, p. 2; for Jiangsu, June 24, 1978, p. 2.

38. *RMRB*, August 15, 1978, p. 3.

39. Wan Li, pp. 1 and 3; emphasis added.

40. Wan Li, excerpted in *XSN*, p. 386.

41. The cultivated land area for 1976 was 67.41 million *mu* in Anhui. Anhui Sheng, p. 299; Zhang Guangyou and Huang, p. 2. On the overall weather situation, see Meng and Peng, *Zhongguo zaihuangshi*, p. 106. For an evocative portrayal of the situation in Anhui, see Wang Lixin, pp. 3–6.

42. On land-clearance policies in late Imperial China, see, e.g., Perdue, esp. chap. 3.

43. Anhui Sheng, p. 291.

44. In the words of Zhou Yueli (pp. 368–76, quote on p. 368), a deputy director of the Anhui provincial agricultural commission, "In a few communes, production brigades and teams, output quotas were fixed on a household basis on the initiative of the commune members themselves." The data come from Tang Zhongxin, p. 2. This figure conflicts with the figure (400 teams) provided by Andrew Watson, but the trend is clear. I have not attempted to reconcile these different figures. The national figures on adoption of the responsibility systems are included in the last table of this chapter.

45. Weiying was then in Yangdu production brigade, Yanchen commune, Lai'an county of Chuxian prefecture, Anhui. This case study mainly draws on Zhang Guangyou, *Lianchan*, pp. 27–36.

46. *XSN*, pp. 386–89.

47. Zhang Guangyou, pp. 37–42.

48. Wu Si, p. 297; *XSN*, pp. 399–402. While the village had twenty households, only eighteen fingerprints appeared on the vow.

49. *ZGZSN*, p. 431.

50. Feixi, which then belonged to Lu'an prefecture, literally means "to the west of Hefei." Hefei is the capital of Anhui province.

51. Wang Lixin, pp. 37–40.

52. Ibid., pp. 28–29.

53. Zhang Guangyou, *Lianchan*, p. 85.

54. See the minutes of committee meetings in *XSN*, pp. 402–8.

55. Ibid., p. 406.

56. Chen Tingyuan's talk on contracting in Fengyang, May 6, 1981, excerpted in *XSN*, p. 399.

57. Mu, p. 6.

58. Ba, pp. 74–75.

59. Ibid.

60. Ibid.

61. Mu, pp. 6–9.

62. Zhou Yueli, p. 368.

63. *Dangdai Zhongguo de Guizhou*, 1:170–71.

64. Ibid.

65. *XSN*, p. 401.

66. Zhang Guangyou, *Lianchan*, p. 32.

67. *ZGZSN*, p. 431.

68. *XSN*, p. 391.

69. Wang Lixin, p. 41.

70. In light of the local initiatives, it is evidently arbitrary to make the Third Plenum the start of reforms.

71. See, e.g., Zhou Taihe, ed., p. 165.

72. *Webster's Ninth New Collegiate Dictionary* defines "experiment" as "an operation carried out under controlled conditions in order to discover an unknown effect or law, to test or establish a hypothesis, or to illustrate a known law."

73. Huang, Dai, and Yu, p. 19.

74. Du, Lin, and Dai, p. 16.

75. Timur Kuran, "East European Revolution," pp. 121–25; and "Now Out of Never," pp. 7–48.

76. Jiang Yueshao, pp. 44–45. The author of this essay was the party secretary of Changle county in Shandong province. See also *Hongqi*, nos. 2–4 (1979), for other relevant articles explicating and expanding the two central documents.

77. Zhou Chunshu, pp. 8–9.

78. Zhonggong Zhongyang Shujichu Yanjiushi Zonghezu, p. 25; Wu Si and Liu, p. 1; "Overview," in Shen and Xiang, 2:4.

79. Compare this with Wang's role in 1962 (Chapter 3).

80. Chen Yizi, *Zhongguo*, p. 34.

81. In addition, the letter was broadcast across the nation on the Central People's Broadcast Station Radio Network.

82. Zhang Hao, p. 1.

83. Xin and Lu, p. 1. Guizhou's Guanling county had a similar experience. In this case, it appeared the county authorities pushed ahead even though some provincial departments wavered. See Xiao and Xu, p. 1. In Sichuan's Leshan prefecture, the authorities were instrumental in pushing for responsibility (*RMRB*, July 18, 1979, p. 2).

84. Wu Si and Liu, p. 1.

85. Wang Lixin, pp. 33–34; Wu Si and Liu, p. 1.

86. Yang Minqing and Tian, pp. 189–92. In contrast, a witness reported that Wang and Wan allegedly had an argument about household contracting in fall 1979 on the telephone (Chen Yizi, *Zhongguo*, pp. 33–34).

87. Attacks on the Gang of Four for nearly everything undesirable were then standard fare in Chinese writings.

88. Xin and Lu; and Lu Xianqi. Both in *RMRB*, March 30, 1979, p. 1.

89. *RMRB*, April 6, 1979, p. 1.

90. On May 11, 1979, the Central Committee and the State Council had just

issued a directive saying that the state was incapable of providing more grain from the depleted reserves to cover the deficit. In the previous three years, according to the directive, the state had drawn more than 10 billion *jin* of grain reserves and could not afford to do this any more. In yet another document, issued on November 27, 1979, the Central Committee and the State Council pointed out that, despite an annual increase of 200 billion *jin* in grain output and an import of 10 million tons, the state grain situation remained tenuous. The fundamental strategic principle was to begin from within by developing production on the principle of self-reliance and economy. *ZGZSN*, pp. 435, 442.

91. Wu, Liu, and Xu, p. 2.

92. *RMRB*, July 10, 1979, p. 1; July 18, 1979, p. 2. On Sichuan, also see Mao Chaojing, September 26, 1979, p. 2; and on Sichuan's Guanghan, October 7, 1979, p. 1.

93. *RMRB*, September 17, 1979, p. 1; September 22, 1979, p. 2.

94. Xinhua News Agency Reporter, *RMRB*, July 18, 1979, p. 2.

95. Guo Chongyi. In *Dilemmas of Reform in China* (p. 33), Fewsmith writes on the basis of unattributed interviews that Hu Yaobang read Guo's report in summer 1979 and "granted permission for Feixi County to continue the household responsibility system on an experimental basis." Given that Hu had indicated his approval of the household responsibility system during the Cultural Revolution, I am not surprised that he approved of Guo's argument. But I am not sure whether Hu directly intervened in causing Feixi to rescind the decision to take land back from peasants.

96. Li Mingfu and Wu, p. 462.

97. Wu Si and Liu, p. 1. This position was thrashed out during the Huangshan conference held in July 1979.

98. *ZGNYNJ 1980*, p. 58.

99. Zhao Ziyang became candidate member of the Politburo in 1977. He was praised not only for turning around Sichuan's stagnant agriculture in the late 1970's but also for spearheading the industrial responsibility system in Sichuan. See Shambaugh, chap. 6; and Lin Zili, "Woguo," p. 5.

100. Wu Si and Liu, p. 1.

101. Watson, "Agriculture," p. 90.

102. Yang Zhongmei, p. 167. It should also be pointed out, however, that in certain areas the Third Plenum policies had not been passed on to peasants, let alone implemented.

103. Wang Lixin, p. 36. Around this time, Wan Li also visited Xiaogang, where he made the following comment: "We did not understand fully just how backward the countryside is. We never realized the people's lives were so hard and so sad. I also knew that people starved, but I didn't realize it was so many, or in such detail. The Chinese people have such great patience" (p. 59).

104. Zhang Guangyou, pp. 73–75. Originally written in February 1980.

105. Wang Lixin, p. 37. Minor changes have been made in the original translation.

106. Wang Pu, *RMRB*, January 18, 1980, p. 1. According to Li Zhuang (next note), senior editors published the commentary because they sensed the direction of policy change in China.

107. Li Zhuang, pp. 11–12.

108. Li Honglin, p. 171.

109. Wu Xiang, pp. 165–248.

110. *Dangdai Zhongguo de Sichuan*, 1:199. On February 3, 1981, Zhao, while touring Sichuan, admitted that his 1980 remark had constrained the progress of rural reforms in Sichuan during that year. Zhao became vice-premier of the State Council in April and premier in September 1980, replacing Hua Guofeng. In contrast, Unger suggests, without documentation, that Zhao Ziyang began promoting contracting production to the household in 1979 ("Decollectivization," p. 590).

111. *Dangdai Zhongguo de Sichuan*, 1:199.

112. Wang Lixin, pp. 46–48.

113. Yang Minqing and Tian, p. 194.

114. Deng Xiaoping, *Selected Works*, p. 297—the only essay on agriculture in the volume.

115. Wang Yuzhao, p. 9.

116. Wu Xiang, "Nongcun," p. 93.

117. For an account of the Yunnan debate, see Wang Songpei, pp. 28–31, 61; the Sichuan debate is alluded to in *Dangdai Zhongguo de Sichuan*, 2:438.

118. While I frame my discussion in terms of these two key questions, I do not mean to neglect the self-interest of the various participants. The State Planning Commission feared that the introduction of the household responsibility system would lead to uncertainty in the planning process. The army, which relied on recruits from the rural areas, blamed the liberal rural policies for undermining support for families of army personnel and thus demoralizing the army throughout 1979–81. Nevertheless, once the two questions were answered satisfactorily, opposition from these quarters was significantly deflected. Other things also helped. Deng Xiaoping's control over the military may not have quelled all grievances, but it perhaps ensured that the military would not do much harm. In the case of the powerful State Planning Commission, it was largely bypassed in rural policy-making at this time; the political center for making rural policy was in the recently created Secretariat of the Central Committee of the Chinese Communist Party, then headed by Hu Yaobang. It is hoped that more information will be released on these other influences to permit an independent study.

119. Chen Yizi, *Zhongguo*, p. 29. As so often happens, the political success of advocates of the household responsibility system has meant that we know more about the reformers than about their opponents, thus probably biasing the account in the reformers' favor.

120. For a sampling of the research results from the Institute of Agricultural Economics in the 1979–84 period, see Rural Development Institute, esp. vol. 2. Most of the findings from the 1980 and later research trips were first published in the three journals on agricultural economics (*Zhongguo nongcun jingji, Nongye jingji wenti*, and *Nongye jingji congkan*) and in other nonspecialist publications, especially daily newspapers such as *RMRB*. On the formation and evolution of the Rural Development Group, see Fewsmith, pp. 34–41.

121. For one such attempt, albeit for 1981, see Guo Ming, pp. 75–79.

122. Zhan, p. 6. See esp. the collection of writings on contracting output to the household in *BDZX*.

123. Chen Yizi, "Nongcun," p. 36.

124. Ibid., pp. 33–53; on the rhetorical style of reformers, see Hirschman, *Rheto-*

ric, chap. 6. Chen and other advocates of rural reform have tended to avoid discussion of the effect of the agricultural price increases on growth; the price factor is discussed in a number of articles by Terry Sicular, including "Rural Marketing," pp. 83–109.

125. Chen Yizi, "Nongcun," p. 53; and *Zhongguo*, p. 34.

126. Segal and Saich, p. 813.

127. Deng Xiaoping, *Selected Works*, pp. 302–25.

128. Wu Xiang, "Yangguandao" (internally published, November 1980), pp. 46–61, quote on p. 52.

129. Du played an important role in the land reform movement of the central-south region in the early 1950's, working under Deng Zihui. Zhao Ziyang was then the agriculture point man in Guangdong. Du and Zhao thus had close contacts. Vogel, *Canton*, pp. 99–101, 110–16.

130. Du Runsheng, p. 5.

131. Wu Si and Liu, p. 1.

132. Wu Xiang, "Yangguandao," p. 54. Wu's position as a leading advocate of household responsibility means that his comment here must be taken with a grain of salt.

133. *ZGNYNJ 1981*, pp. 409–11.

134. Du Runsheng, pp. 1–9. This was Du's explanation of the draft version of Document no. 75 during the first day of the meeting of provincial first secretaries.

135. *ZGNMB*, July 19, 1981, p. 1.

136. Ibid., August 6, 1981, p. 1; Zhu Gongjia, *ZGNMB*, September 3, 1981, p. 2.

137. Wu Si and Liu, p. 1; An, Song, and Huang, p. 2.

138. *ZGZSN*, p. 471.

139. *ZGNYNJ 1982*, pp. 1–6.

140. See Bramall, pp. 271–95.

141. Editor's note, in Wang Guichen, Zhou et al., p. 6.

142. See, e.g., commentator's article, *ZGNMB*, January 14, 1982, p. 1.

143. The strongest argument about the pressures coming from above are made by Unger, "Decollectivization," pp. 585–606. Unger argues that "the Chinese press has deliberately and consistently distorted coverage of what occurred in the countryside" (p. 586). Focusing on 1980–82, Unger collected his data from interviews with twenty-eight Chinese emigrants then working in Hong Kong in mid-1983. For a nuanced discussion of the various strategies adopted by local cadres toward the responsibility system, see Burns, "Local Cadre," pp. 607–25.

144. Needless to say, some members merely paid lip service to the new orthodoxy in what the Chinese would call "raising the flag in order to lower it."

145. Hinton, *Great Reversal*, p. 49.

146. Wu Si, p. 327.

147. On Hunan, see *Dangdai Zhongguo de Hunan*, pp. 202–4; on Zhejiang, see *Dangdai Zhongguo de Zhejiang*, p. 132. Hebei and Heilongjiang are dealt with below.

148. On Liu's career prior to the Cultural Revolution, see Klein and Clark, pp. 631–32.

149. Liu was made a deputy head of the State Planning Commission.

150. Liu's followers were either removed or transferred out of the province.

151. Yang Zhongmei, pp. 167–70.

152. Tao, Chen, and Dai, pp. 52–57. Yang in fact expressed his public support for the truth criterion debate months before Zhao Ziyang and Wan Li did.

153. For details of the conflicts over rural reforms in Heilongjiang, see Heilongjiang Nongye, pp. 425–545, esp. 484–85.

154. Ibid., p. 531.

155. Ibid., pp. 533–38.

156. Ibid., pp. 539–43, quote on p. 540.

157. Quoted in ibid., p. 544.

158. In 1983, China began a three-year crackdown on criminal activities, and Yang Yichen's emphasis on control was apparently more fitting in that area.

159. Zhonggong Heilongjiang, pp. 18–23.

160. Ibid., p. 18.

161. This "Decision" is not included in the important and comprehensive ZGZSN. Historical revisionism is in the eye of the beholder.

162. Zhou Taihe, ed., pp. 160–61, 166.

163. See Zweig, "Opposition," pp. 879–900.

164. Perry, "Casting," pp. 147–48; Daniel Kelliher, "Are Peasants?"

165. It appears to me that Unger's interesting study underestimates the regional variations in making and implementing rural policy ("Decollectivization," pp. 585–606).

166. Hall, pp. 370–75, quote on p. 375.

7. Euphoria, Myopia, and Discontent

1. This does not mean that farmers had forgotten the lessons of the famine, however. Farmers continue to stockpile far more grain than necessary in order to prepare for the worst.

2. See the essays in Nee and Mozingo.

3. Shue, *Reach*, pp. 151–52. She wrote the chapter from which I cite in 1984–85.

4. The State Statistics Bureau estimated that about 420 million people, or 60 percent of the working population, were engaged in farming in 1993. Zhongguo Tongxun She, January 19, 1994, trans. in FBIS-CHI-94-019, January 28, 1994, pp. 40–41.

5. Source of data for Fig. 9: ZGTJNJ 1992, pp. 235, 330, 390. The data for crop production are based on comparable data from the State Statistical Bureau. However, similar data for rural industry are not available. As a rough measure, I use the unadjusted rural industrial growth rates deflated by the consumer price index. Therefore, this figure is used for illustrative purposes only.

6. For the popular refrain on relying on policy, see, e.g., ZGNMB, September 10, 1981, p. 1. In his government report to the National People's Congress (November 31–December 1, 1981), then-premier Zhao Ziyang made this theme the focus of the center's strategy for rural areas: "The development of agricultural production and rural construction should continue to rely chiefly on policy and on science." See XNNWX, pp. 109–13.

7. Zhonghua Renmin, p. 56.

8. Wu Si, p. 305.

9. Based on data from ZGTJNJ 1992, pp. 221, 224. It should be pointed out that, following the drop in grain output in 1985, the center, in Central Committee Document no. 1 of 1986, called for restoring waterworks expenditures to the 1980 level (XNNWX, p. 373).

10. Besides investment in infrastructure and the problem of peasant burdens,

similar ironies may be found with regard to health care and education in rural areas. On health care, see Henderson.

11. Xia, p. 171; Huang, Dai, and Yu, pp. 142–53.

12. Jacobs, pp. 105–30; T. White, "Political Reform," pp. 38–52; Cui and Liu, p. 3.

13. Wang Zhenyao, p. 226.

14. Commentary, *ZGNMB*, February 4, 1982, p. 1, and March 25, 1982, p. 1; Henan Dengxian CCP Committee, *ZGNMB*, April 8, 1982, p. 2; July 1, 1982, p. 1.

15. Shue, "Fate," p. 273.

16. For texts of the regulations setting staff size and strengthening rural basic-level governments, see *XNNWX*, pp. 408–19.

17. *NMRB*, February 25, 1989, p. 1.

18. Robust regression was used. With 30 observations, R^2 = 0.4103, adjusted R^2 = 0.3892, p = 0.0001, coef. = 0.00515. I am indebted to Marc Blecher for discussions on this issue.

19. *Nong mu*, pp. 56–58.

20. Village cadres also collected levies of their own, usually for their own stipends, but sometimes for village projects, as well. These can be subsumed under the categories discussed here.

21. Fang Jicheng, *NMRB*, March 1, 1989, p. 1.

22. *NMRB*, March 27, 1989, p. 4.

23. Duan Zhiqiang, *NMRB*, March 17, 1989, p. 1.

24. *NMRB*, January 31, 1991, p. 1.

25. Ibid., May 25, 1988, p. 1.

26. Fan, p. 74. On wool, see Watson, Findlay, and Du, pp. 213–41. See also Jiang Jun, "Tian Jiyun on Management of Cotton Production," Xinhua, August 16, 1991; trans. in FBIS-CHI-91-160, August 19, 1991, pp. 53–54.

27. Peasant Daily Commentator, *NMRB*, January 20, 1989, p. 1.

28. Zheng Xinmin and E Xunhai, *NMRB*, February 2, 1989, p. 1; Bao Yonghui, *NMRB*, March 7, 1989, p. 3.

29. Liu Xiaojie, *NMRB*, January 4, 1989, p. 1; Niu Xiaofeng and Zhao Yipu, *NMRB*, January 17, 1989, p. 1.

30. On the patterns of popular resistance to taxes from 1840 to 1950, see Bernhardt.

31. J. C. Scott, "Everyday Forms," p. 4. Also see his *Weapons of the Weak*.

32. *NMRB*, January 9, 1989, p. 1; March 25, 1989, p. 1.

33. Wang Zenong, *NMRB*, April 19, 1988, p. 1; Chen Qi, May 2, 1989, p. 1. See also the letters January 16, 1989, p. 4; January 28, 1989, p. 4; May 8, 1989, p. 4; May 22, 1989, p. 4.

34. Ren Xianliang, *NMRB*, February 9, 1989, p. 1.

35. See, e.g., one of the letters in *NMRB*, February 13, 1989, p. 4. The other families simply say that they did not have enough grain to sell and thus fail to fulfill their quotas.

36. Jiang, Li, and Zhang, pp. 1–2.

37. Su Suining.

38. Li Qing and Wu Si, *NMRB*, April 6, 1988, p. 1.

39. Liu Shunguo, *NMRB*, September 20, 1988, p. 3. See also *NMRB*, April 22, 1988, p. 3.

40. Yang Wenliang and Huo, p. 3. The survey was conducted among 500 house-holds in four counties (Wuji, Feixiang, Zhengding, Jixian) in the spring of 1989.
41. Liu Qikun, *NMRB*, August 7, 1989, p. 4.
42. Fan Zhongting, *NMRB*, April 18, 1989, p. 3.
43. Liu Hexin, pp. 14–15.
44. Peasant Daily Commentator, *NMRB*, August 7, 1989, p. 1.
45. Xue Changlin and Li Haiyan, *NMRB*, September 8, 1988, p. 1; Liu Jingfan, September 5, 1988, p. 1; Liang Jinkai, September 8, 1988, p. 1.
46. Su Suining; Xia Bin, *NMRB*, October 26, 1989, p. 4.
47. Jiang, Li, and Zhang, pp. 1–2.
48. Liang Xuewen, *NMRB*, January 22, 1988, p. 3.
49. For a sample of such disputes that had ended in court, see Li Qianghua, Li, and Hu. Also indicative is the politically controversial movie *Qiuju da guansi* (Qiuju goes to court), directed by Zhang Yimou (1992), which portrays both the abuse of cadre power and the willingness of the powerless to seek justice through official channels.
50. Hou Peibin, *NMRB*, February 2, 1988, p. 3.
51. Fan Zhongting, *NMRB*, April 18, 1989, p. 3.
52. Zhang Zhi, *NMRB*, June 26, 1989, p. 4.
53. *NMRB*, July 7, 1988, p. 4. This letter to the editor was signed by Zhang Wenzhong, a rural cadre from Anyang, Henan province.
54. Zhong Zhushan, pp. 12–14. Conducted in late 1989, the survey sample included 1,358 village party branches in thirteen counties spread through twelve provinces (Hebei, Liaoning, Heilongjiang, Zhejiang, Anhui, Henan, Hubei, Guangdong, Sichuan, Guizhou, Shaanxi, Qinghai).
55. Liu Shunguo, p. 3.
56. Ren Weijie, *NMRB*, September 12, 1988, p. 1.
57. Ibid.
58. *NMRB*, April 13, 1988, pp. 1–2.
59. Ibid., February 15, 1989, p. 2.
60. While other civil groups such as trade associations also constitute potential sources of power competing with the party-state, my focus here is on organizations based on lineage or religion, which are far more pervasive and powerful. Also pervasive in rural China, but not dealt with here, is the practice of superstitions. For a glimpse of this, see Xu Shengbin, Wu Jiaping, and Zhang Hongwu, *NMRB*, July 4, 1989, p. 2; Hu Yongming, July 29, 1989, p. 3; and Wu Bilan, July 27, 1989, p. 4.
61. Le Roy Ladurie, pp. 29–36.
62. Groves, pp. 31–64; Wakeman; Kuhn.
63. Freedman, pp. 334–50, quote on p. 341.
64. Tang Zhongxin, p. 159.
65. Potter and Potter, p. 256.
66. For a detailed report on the establishment of one lineage, see Qiu and Xiang, *NMRB*, July 15, 1989, p. 1.
67. Gui Jicai, *NMRB*, April 27, 1989, p. 1.
68. *NMRB*, April 22, 1989, p. 6.
69. Zhou Jihua, p. 16.
70. *NMRB*, April 22, 1989, p. 6.

71. On the efforts to control religion, see Hooper, pp. 109–34.

72. Jiang Zhimin and Xu, pp. 6–9, reference is to p. 6.

73. *Economist*, August 13, 1994, p. 32.

74. Kaye, p. 13; for documentation about the growing number of people who wish to join Buddhist temples, see Luo, esp. p. 8.

75. For a report on a Christian group in a distant region of Heilongjiang, see Liu Siyu and Li Tingxuan, *NMRB*, July 15, 1989, p. 8.

76. Yang Tuoshe, *NMRB*, January 24, 1989, p. 3.

77. Jiang Zhimin and Xu, pp. 6, 9.

78. Fu Tiezhu, *NMRB*, May 2, 1989, p. 3.

79. *NMRB*, April 20, 1989, p. 4.

80. Shi Meifen, *NMRB*, February 1, 1989, p. 1. For a vivid description of a temple fair, see Chen Chaozhong, *Liaowang*, no. 15 (April 10, 1989): 29.

81. Gon Weixun, *NMRB*, October 4, 1989, p. 1.

82. The party Central Committee did call for strengthening rural ideological and political work in January 1983, but even in this case the emphasis was on not changing the newly introduced reform policies, especially the household responsibility system. See directive in *XNNWX*, pp. 185–95.

83. Chen Yun, *Chen Yun wenxuan (1956–1985)*, pp. 303–4. In a talk on June 10, 1986, Deng Xiaoping (*XNNWX*, p. 402) stated that the downturn in grain production was the top economic priority. He called for more attention to waterworks.

84. *Nong mu*, pp. 56–58.

85. *NMRB*, January 12, 1988, p. 2; Liang Xuewen, January 22, 1988, p. 3.

86. Ibid., March 12, 1988, p. 1; April 22, 1988, p. 3.

87. Ibid., March 3, 1988, p. 1.

88. *XNNWX*, pp. 358–70, esp. 359–60.

89. Ch'i, p. 251.

90. Jiang Dianguo, Li, and Zhang.

91. *XNNWX*, pp. 519–24.

92. *XNNWX*, pp. 525–29.

93. These two documents may be found in *Zhili zhengdun*, pp. 318–20 and 320–21, respectively. See also the Ministry of Finance's trial regulations on the use and management of the agricultural development fund (pp. 328–30).

94. For grain output figures, see *ZGTJNJ 1992*, p. 358.

95. Jiang Zemin. This talk was given on June 19, 1990.

96. *NMRB*, July 15, 1989, p. 1. The Ministry of Civil Affairs is the government organization in charge of rural basic-level organizations, including village residents' committees. See Guojia jigou bianzhi, pp. 48–51.

97. *NMRB*, August 17, 1989, p. 1.

98. Dai Zhou, p. 4.

99. Zhou Jihua, p. 16.

100. Chen Yun, "Guanyu," p. 1045.

101. Ibid., p. 1045n. Jiang wrote the comment on April 24, 1990, and then routed the letter to other leaders in the party center.

102. *RMRB*, overseas ed., July 13, 1991, pp. 1, 4.

103. Peasant Daily Editorial Department, *NMRB*, December 16, 1988, p. 1.

104. Yang Xiulin, *NMRB*, July 4, 1989, p. 2.

105. Fu Xingyu, "Ganbu xia jiceng yihou," pp. 32–33.

106. Peasant Daily Commentator, *NMRB*, November 15, 1989, p. 1. The top elite was not united on this campaign. Song Ping got it started and pushed for it, but in late 1991 Tian Jiyun, with the support of Wan Li, ignored it and instead emphasized the stabilization of basic rural policies.

107. For an overview of the debate about farm size, see Wang Huimin, pp. 300–330. The two tiers refer to the household and the collective. For an indication of such sentiments, see Zhonggong zhongyang zhengce yanjiushi.

108. For skewed data aggregation, see Nongcun guding, *Quanguo*, pp. 451–54. For interpretation of these data, see Nongcun guding, *Wanshan*.

109. Jiang called for "common prosperity" at the Seventh Plenum of the Thirteenth Central Committee on December 30, 1990.

110. Tian Jiyun, "Guanyu," p. 806.

111. Liu Zhongyi, p. 65; see also Tian Jiyun, "Guanyu," pp. 804–6. Many other similar statements are also available.

112. Pu Liye and Zhao Lianqing, "Minister Discusses Rural Reform," Xinhua in Chinese; trans. in FBIS-CHI-94-015, January 24, 1994, p. 61.

113. These decisions can be found in *XNNWX*, pp. 557–61, 565–73, and 574–80.

114. Liu Jiemin and Bai, pp. 111–12. Liu Fuyuan (esp. p. 106) argues that state taxes on peasants are too low, but the main problem lies with local levies and charges.

115. Liu Jiemin and Bai, pp. 109–15.

116. Data are from *ZGTJNJ 1992*, p. 276. These ratios were calculated on the basis of current prices.

117. The peasants' complaints were widely reported, especially in *NMRB*. Moreover, the Ministry of Agriculture was strongly critical of central policies, which were heavily biased in favor of urban residents in 1989–90. See Nongyebu zhengce, "Dangqian." Shifts in central policy toward the rural enterprise sector are discussed in chapter 8.

118. *XNNWX*, pp. 581–84, quote on p. 581.

119. Liu Jiemin and Bai, p. 111.

120. See esp. Chen Zhiguo, chap. 3.

121. Li Peng, "Zai quanguo," p. 1.

122. Goldstein, Kaye, and Blass, pp. 68–70. It is important to point out that protests had taken place peacefully in Renshou several months earlier and were resolved when the Sichuan provincial government ordered the county to halt its tax-raising efforts.

123. *Ming Pao*, July 26, 1993, p. 8; trans. in FBIS-CHI-93-144, July 29, 1993, pp. 26–28.

124. For a dramatic case of local despotism and peasant protest in an Anhui village, see Jan Wong; L. H. Sun. The authors suggest that there are many other villages with similar problems.

125. Cited in Goldstein, Kaye, and Blass, p. 69; Zhou Baiyi, p. 1.

126. Guowuyuan, pp. 74–75.

127. Guowuyuan, pp. 51–60; trans. in FBIS-CHI-93-147, August 3, 1993, pp. 34–38.

128. *RMRB*, overseas ed., July 29, 1994, p. 1.

129. "Liaoning Lessens Farmers' Financial Burden," Xinhua in English, March 4, 1994; trans. in FBIS-CHI-94-064, April 4, 1994, pp. 80–81.

130. Officials at the Ministry of Agriculture apparently feel the same way and have called for verification of the achievements made in 1993. Chao Wen, "Ministry Provides Measures to Ease Peasant Burdens," Xinhua in Chinese, April 2, 1994; trans. in FBIS-CHI-94-067, April 7, 1994, pp. 25–26.

131. "China's Local Governments Overtaxing Farmers, Official Newspaper Says," United Press International, July 21, 1994; *RMRB*, overseas ed., July 29, 1994, p. 1.

132. Gilley, pp. 16–17.

133. Quoted in Jan Wong; see also L. H. Sun.

134. Duara.

135. Following Albert Hirschman, this would be classified as the "voice" option, while the turn to lineages and religion would be "exit." In addition, as will be discussed in the next chapter, the turn to nonfarm sectors also belongs to the category of "exit." Hirschman, *Exit*.

136. See esp. McGregor, "As Farmers," p. 3.

137. On problems with public order, see Sun Chunying.

138. J. Parker; on the political conflicts over the passage of the Organic Law, see T. White, "Reforming the Countryside."

139. On the trial implementation, see O'Brien.

140. In this case, the leadership is caught between urban and rural interests and has therefore argued for a so-called "rational grain price"; i.e., the center will not allow grain price to rise too fast for fear of urban instability and will support grain price if it falls below a certain point to protect peasant incentives.

8. Rural Industrialization

1. That the sector is *economically* dynamic does not mean that it is "good" in all respects. Like earlier industrialization in places such as England, it must be recognized that China's rural industrialization has also been associated with a range of social problems, including child labor, poor and dangerous working conditions in many factories, industrial pollution, and ecological degradation, even though most of the problems are not exclusive to the rural enterprise sector.

2. Kingdon, esp. chap. 8; Polsby, pp. 167–72.

3. This is already the subject of a huge literature. See, e.g., Saich; and Wasserstrom and Perry.

4. The figures for 1971 and 1978 are from Byrd and Lin, p. 16; the 1989 figure is calculated from *ZGTJNJ 1990*, p. 413.

5. See, e.g., Deng Xiaoping, *Deng Xiaoping wenxuan*, 3:238–39.

6. Because of the growth in the number of people employed in private rural enterprises, the latter figure is more subject to the problem of underreporting. For a discussion of this issue, see Odgaard, pp. 29–38.

7. The comparative percentage figures are based on comparable prices. However, depending on the base year one chooses, the figures change. It should also be pointed out that the 58 percent figure for 1988 (supplied by Chinese statistics) differs significantly from that calculated from current prices (51.82 percent; *ZGNYNJ*

1989, pp. 251, 346). Despite the underlying methodological problems about data calculation, the relative scale of changes should remain apparent.

8. The figure for export earnings is from Zweig, "Rural Industry," p. 432.

9. The most pervasive problem with Chinese industrial data, including data on rural industrial output, is the double counting of intermediate goods, which inflates gross output values and growth rates. For sophisticated discussions of this and other statistical issues, see C. Wong, "Interpreting," pp. 3–30; Field, "China's Industrial Performance," pp. 577–607, esp. 582–84.

10. *RMRB*, overseas ed., September 20, 1990, p. 1.

11. Naughton, "Economic Reform," pp. 350–51. See also his "Inflation," pp. 269–72, 289–91.

12. Xun, Ye, and Fang, p. 25.

13. *RMRB*, overseas ed., March 22, 1989, p. 1.

14. On the coastal development strategy, see D. L. Yang, "China," pp. 42–64.

15. Dittmer, p. 26.

16. On Zhao Ziyang's reform strategy, see Shirk, "Political Economy," pp. 350–62, esp. 354–57.

17. Zhao Ziyang, "Zai zhongguo," pp. 6–10, quote on p. 8.

18. A small number of major joint-venture enterprises were included in the plan.

19. Naughton, "Economic Directions," p. 9. See also Chen Te-sheng, pp. 25–42.

20. In 1988, e.g., priority plans for these two sectors were not fulfilled.

21. The exception would be export-oriented rural enterprises, which would earn foreign currency at a time the government was concerned about debt repayment.

22. *RMRB*, February 9, 1989, p. 1.

23. Li Peng, "Report," pp. 11–31, at p. 18.

24. *RMRB*, overseas ed., September 21, 1989, p. 1.

25. Li Peng, "Zhengque," pp. 4–5.

26. *RMRB*, overseas ed., July 12, 1989, p. 3.

27. Li Peng, "Zhenfen jingshen," p. 4.

28. Li Peng, "Xiangzhen," pp. 6–9, quote on p. 6.

29. *RMRB*, overseas ed., February 15, 1990, p. 1.

30. He Kang, pp. 102–8.

31. People's Daily Commentator, pp. 54–55.

32. *RMRB*, overseas ed., November 9, 1990, p. 3.

33. *Zhongguo jingji*, p. VIII-115.

34. All year-end figures in this paragraph come from Zhongguo Nongye Yinhang, pp. 69–76. Regrettably, I have not found cumulative figures for the state sector.

35. Economic Daily Commentator, *Jingji ribao* (Economic daily), November 3, 1989, repr. in *Xinhua yuebao* (New China monthly digest), no. 11 (1989): 60.

36. The data cited in this paragraph are from Lu Yongjun, pp. III-10–13; *ZGTJNJ 1989*, p. 162; and *ZGTJNJ 1990*, p. 330.

37. Delfs and Bowring, p. 41.

38. Within the state sector, the industrial output of large and medium-size enterprises increased 9.6 percent, undoubtedly owing to the central policy of favoring such firms.

39. Jefferson, Rawski, and Zheng, pp. 239–66.

40. *RMRB*, overseas ed., May 11, 1990, p. 1.

41. See especially Zweig, "Internationalizing," pp. 716–41.

42. The export boom was especially strong in the coastal provinces (*RMRB*, December 1, 1989, p. 3; June 13, 1990, p. 3; June 26, 1990, p. 3). For information about preferential policies for exporting firms, see August 16, 1990, p. 3.

43. *RMRB* (June 8, 1990, p. 3) reports the 1989 export figure as $10.5 billion and the growth rate as 30.1 percent over 1988.

44. Ibid., June 26, 1990, p. 3.

45. Ibid., November 23, 1990, p. 3.

46. Byrd and Gelb, "Why Industrialize?" pp. 358–87; C. Wong, "Fiscal Reform," pp. 197–227; Naughton, "Implications," pp. 14–41, esp. pp. 33–34.

47. *RMRB*, December 1, 1989, p. 3; May 16, 1990, p. 3; Naughton, "Economic Reform," p. 359.

48. Byrd and Gelb, "Why Industrialize?"

49. *RMRB*, July 18, 1989, p. 1. Since it was a violation of discipline to use funds intended for agricultural procurement for other purposes, it was likely that those who were surveyed underreported. Thus in reality the problem was most likely greater than the official survey indicated.

50. Besides bank loans, rural enterprises could also tap into a support fund (esp. for exporters) and funds disbursed by supervisory departments (Table 31). Unfortunately, the unavailability of historical data for these categories makes it difficult for one to gauge changes in government behavior in these important areas.

51. Given China's huge size, there are clearly regional variations in this and other aspects of rural enterprise development. See D. L. Yang, "Reform."

52. For a brief summary of this approach, see Geddes, pp. 63–66. For works by Bates, see *Markets; Essays;* and *Beyond the Miracle.* For an application to China's reforms, with an emphasis on institutional incentives, see Shirk, *Political Logic.*

53. On urban bias, see Lipton.

54. See Naughton, "Implications." For a general theoretical perspective, see Hirschman, *Exit.*

55. *RMRB*, overseas ed., January 14, 1989, p. 1.

56. Bachman, *Bureaucracy*, pp. 233–35.

57. Zweig, "Internationalizing," pp. 722–23. Fewsmith argues, however, that Zhao increasingly turned away from the state industries, esp. following the launch of urban reforms in 1984.

58. *RMRB*, March 14, 1989, p.1.

59. Chen Xuesi, "One Million," p. 7; "New Headache," p. 7. On the economics of labor migration, see Stark.

60. Chen Yanhua, p. 4.

61. *RMRB*, February 25, 1989, p. 4; February 28, 1989, p. 4.

62. Ibid., October 11, 1989, p. 4.

63. *Xinhua yuebao* (New China monthly digest), no. 3 (1989): 26.

64. Solinger, "China's Transients," p. 112. For general argument, see Nelson.

65. He Xin, pp. 64–76, quote on pp. 68–69.

66. *China Daily*, March 23, 1989; quoted in A. P. L. Liu, pp. 404–5.

67. *RMRB*, April 3, 1989, p. 1. Because of their competing interests, critics and

defenders of rural enterprises are usually sharply divided, and little scholarly work has been done to assess these competing claims objectively. For a preliminary assessment, see Ody.

68. Peasant Daily Commentator [or commentators], pp. 87–88.

69. Zhang Yi, pp. 124–26.

70. Ibid., p. 124.

71. Ibid., p. 125.

72. Ibid.

73. "Zhongguo Gongchandang," pp. 2–3.

74. Chen Yaobang, pp. 108–13, quote on p. 108.

75. See Deng Xiaoping, "Zai jiejian," pp. 4–7.

76. Chen Yaobang, p. 109.

77. Ibid., p. 113. Chen's speech was made on July 25, but not published until September 11, 1989. It first appeared in *Zhongguo xiangzhen qiye bao* (Bulletin of Chinese rural enterprises) and was then reprinted in other places.

78. *RMRB*, September 15, 1989, p. 1.

79. Official permission for the establishment of CARE was granted in May 1989, and it was officially founded in early January 1990.

80. *NMRB*, January 15, 1990, p. 1.

81. Bo, "Fazhan," pp. 101–2.

82. For discussions of corporatism in the Chinese context, see Anita Chan, "Revolution?" pp. 31–61.

83. C. Wong, "Central-Local Relations," p. 696.

84. Naughton, "Implications."

85. The data used here are based on C. Wong, "Central-Local Relations," p. 715.

86. Chen Yuan, pp. 18–26, quote on p. 18.

87. *ZGTJNJ 1990*, p. 232.

88. *ZGTJNJ 1990*, p. 237.

89. Zhang Guorong, pp. 39–41.

90. McGregor, "China's Conundrum," pp. 1, 14.

91. The first draft of this chapter was written in 1990. Since then, a number of Chinese documents suggest that this argument is very likely to have been used to make the case for rural enterprises in 1989–90. See, e.g., (Vice-Premier) Tian Jiyun, "Jiefang sixiang," p. 91.

92. Ibid.

93. This is not to deny that the leadership had some policy choice. One reader suggested that two other possible alternatives would have been: (*a*) Concentrate on the state sector, and (*b*) privilege rural enterprises through measures such as tax concessions. I believe that these alternatives would have involved much higher potential political costs than return to the *status quo ante*. Space limitations do not permit me to elaborate.

94. Li Peng, "Zhenfen jingshen," p. 7.

95. "AFP Interviews Ruan Chongwu on Labor Reform," May 15, 1991; trans. in FBIS-CHI-91-094, May 15, 1991, p. 21. Emphasis added.

96. Heclo, pp. 298, 310–11.

Conclusions and Reflections

1. Ross and Nisbett, p. 60.

2. For a general discussion of the relevant issues, see Elster, *Nuts and Bolts*.

3. For an important exception, see M. Taylor. Jon Elster's many works provide nuanced refinements of the rational choice approach.

4. Simon, "Rational Choice," p. 129.

5. North, *Structure*, chap. 3.

6. Needless to say, Mao was also concerned about social distribution and, in launching the Great Leap Forward, competition with Khrushchev. But these were secondary considerations compared with the argument that collectivization would boost productivity.

7. North, *Institutions*, p. 7.

8. *Deng Xiaoping wenxuan*, 3:29; see also pp. 78, 81–82.

9. On contracting in the industrial sector, see Shirk, *Political Logic*, chaps. 11–13; for a provincial experience, see Guizhou, p. 92.

10. Lin Zili, *Lun*, pp. 212–14.

11. For theoretical justification, see Kiser and Hechter, pp. 1–30.

12. There is now an extensive literature on how past events affected later decisions, especially among national leaders. See May; Neustadt and May; and Khong.

13. Hirschman, *Shifting Involvements*, p. 133.

14. *NJZWH*, 2:556.

15. The same pattern holds for crop production as well. Despite the government slogan about taking grain as the key link, cash crops received greater attention. Growth for most cash crops surpassed that for grain between 1957 and 1980. Perkins and Yusuf, p. 36.

16. W. S. Robinson, pp. 351–57. On strategies for dealing with the effect of the "ecological fallacy," see King, Keohane, and Verba, pp. 30–31.

17. Lewis, "Social Limits," p. 33.

18. Nolan, p. 400. That China could have increased its agricultural production at respectable rates is supported by a cross-national study by Pryor. Comparing cross-section estimates from sixteen Marxist and eighteen non-Marxist countries for 1970–87, Pryor found that there was no statistically significant difference in the aggregate growth of agriculture between the two sets of countries. Pryor, "Performance," pp. 95–126.

19. On leadership transition and policy innovation, see Bunce.

20. See Kuran, "Private and Public Preferences," for a theoretical discussion of this duality.

21. For an interesting discussion of the historical and theoretical issues related to agrarian change, with an emphasis on the role of the state in the making of the peasantry, see R. H. Bates, "Some Conventional Orthodoxies," pp. 234–54.

22. Even though rural residents had no formal power over the choice of national leaders, they did have access to a variety of formal (and often manipulated) channels of local participation. See Burns, *Political Participation*.

23. R. H. Bates, "Some Conventional Orthodoxies," pp. 234–54, quote on p. 234.

24. Wolf, p. 290.

25. Ibid., p. 297. See also Shanin, pp. 214–18.

26. On the logic of why individuals not resorting to collective action may still have a collective impact, see Schelling.

27. For a discussion of the former Soviet Union, see Wegren.

28. For comparative perspective, see Migdal, pp. 31–32.

29. Ma Zhongchen, pp. 43–44.

30. J. R. Taylor, "Rural Employment," pp. 736–66; J. R. Taylor and Banister, pp. 87–120.

31. On grain imports, see Perkins, "Prospects," pp. 33–34.

32. For an update on France, see "French Farmers," pp. 21–24. See also K. Anderson. Anderson takes a long-term look at the "de-agriculturalization" in China.

33. Hu Xiao, pp. 291–306.

34. Rogowski. For a recent application and critique with reference to East Europe and the Soviet Union, see Brada, pp. 211–38, esp. pp. 232–37.

35. Stolper and Samuelson, pp. 58–73.

36. Rogowski, p. 3.

37. Zhang Mengyi, p. 3; Guo Shutian and Liu; Cheung, pp. 18–20.

38. Note Murrell, pp. 1–11.

39. North, *Institutions*.

40. A good collection on evolutionary theories and their implications for social sciences is Somit and Peterson.

41. Stinchcombe, pp. 153ff. The difficulty of major transformations in institutional structures appears to be supported by a growing literature on the borderline of economics and psychology. This literature directs its attention to phenomena variously called endowment effect, status-quo bias, and loss aversion (such as people's often demanding much more to give up an object than they would be willing to pay to acquire it). For an overview, see Kahneman, Knetsch, and Thaler, pp. 193–206.

42. David, "Understanding," p. 30.

43. For summary discussions, see Ikenberry, pp. 223–36; Collier and Collier, pp. 27–39.

44. Haggard, p. 3; see also Gourevitch.

45. Weir.

46. For an interesting discussion on the theoretical foundations of hysteresis, see Cross, pp. 53–74.

47. Bates, *Beyond the Miracle*, p. 153.

48. Krasner, "Approaches" and "Sovereignty"; Collier and Collier.

49. Watkins and Menken, pp. 665–68.

50. The following account draws on Guinnane; and O'Rourke.

51. O'Rourke, p. 309.

52. Ibid., p. 312.

53. See Guinnane, p. 304, fig. 1. Guinnane (p. 305) states that the number of Irish emigrants for 1850–1910 was 4.2 million according to official figures, and the true number was probably still higher. He also discusses other factors contributing to the population decline.

54. Guinnane, p. 307.

55. The Great Leap Famine also poses a similar contrast with the Chinese famine of the 1930's, when both human and physical capital fled rural areas. Hu Naitsui.

56. Hirschman, "Search," pp. 329–43; repr. in his *Bias for Hopes*.

57. Arrow, "Methodological Individualism," p. 3.

58. Popper, p. 160.

59. This poses a stark contrast with India, where, in the presence of active opposition, it would be hard for the government to ignore a tragedy of such proportions. Sen, "Indian Development," pp. 382–85.

60. For a more comprehensive statement to this effect, see Hayek, "Competition."

Bibliography

For the sake of space, with some exceptions, the titles of numerous CCP documents and newspaper articles are not listed in the bibliography.

Advisory Committee on Economic and Social Development Strategy and Planning of Henan Province and Office of Investigation and Study of the Henan People's Government. *Henan shengqing* (Henan provincial situation). Zhengzhou: Henan renmin chubanshe, 1987.

Ahn, Byung-joon. *Chinese Politics and the Cultural Revolution*. Seattle: University of Washington Press, 1976.

———. "The Political Economy of the People's Commune in China: Changes and Continuities." *Journal of Asian Studies* 34, no. 3 (May 1975).

Aird, John S. "Population Studies and Population Policy in China." *Population and Development Review* 8, no. 2 (June 1982).

An Gang, Song Cheng, and Huang Yuejun. "Zhonghua nongye zhenxing youwang" (There is hope for the vigorous development of Chinese agriculture). *RMRB*, July 9, 1981.

Anderson, Craig, Mark Lepper, and Lee Ross. "Perseverance of Social Theories: The Role of Explanation in the Persistence of Discredited Information." *Journal of Personality and Social Psychology* 39, no. 6 (1980).

Anderson, Kym. *Changing Comparative Advantages in China: Effects on Food, Feed and Fibre Markets*. Paris: Organization for Economic Cooperation and Development, Development Center, 1990.

Anhui Sheng Renmin Zhengfu Bangongting. *Anhui shengqing* (Information Anhui). Hefei: Anhui renmin chubanshe, 1985.

Arnold, David. *Famine: Social Crisis and Historical Change*. New York: Blackwell, 1988.

Arrow, Kenneth. "Methodological Individualism and Social Knowledge." *American Economic Review* 84, no. 2 (May 1994).

———. *The Limits of Organization*. New York: Norton, 1974.

———. *Social Choice and Individual Values*. 2d ed. New Haven, CT: Yale University Press, 1963.

Arthur, Brian. "Designing Economic Agents That Act like Human Agents: A Behavioral Approach to Bounded Rationality." *American Economic Review* 81, no. 2 (May 1991).

Ashton, Basil, Kenneth Hill, Alan Piazza, and Robin Zeitz. "Famine in China, 1958–1961." *Population and Development Review* 10, no. 4 (December 1984).

Ba Shan. *Ji'e de guodu: Zhongguo liangshi weiji* (Land of hunger: China's grain crisis). Hong Kong: Baixing wenhua shiye youxian gongsi, 1991.

Bachman, David. *Bureaucracy, Economy, and Leadership in China: The Institutional Origins of the Great Leap Forward*. Cambridge: Cambridge University Press, 1991.

———. *Chen Yun and the Chinese Political System*. Center Research Monograph no. 29. Berkeley: University of California, Institute of East Asian Studies, 1985.

———. "Review of *China and the Challenge of the Future*." *Pacific Affairs* 64, no. 2 (Summer 1991).

Bacon, Francis. *The New Organon and Related Writings*. New York: Liberal Arts, [1620] 1960.

Banister, Judith. *China's Changing Population*. Stanford, CA: Stanford University Press, 1987.

Barnett, A. Doak, ed. *Chinese Communist Politics in Action*. Seattle: University of Washington Press, 1969.

Bates, Frederick L., and Walter G. Peacock, "Disaster and Social Change." In Dynes, Marchi, and Pelanda.

Bates, Robert H. *Beyond the Miracle of the Market*. Cambridge: Cambridge University Press, 1989.

———. *Essays on the Political Economy of Rural Africa*. Cambridge: Cambridge University Press, 1983.

———. *Markets and States in Tropical Africa: The Political Basis of Agricultural Policies*. Berkeley: University of California Press, 1981.

———. "Some Conventional Orthodoxies in the Study of Agrarian Change." *World Politics* 36, no. 2 (January 1984).

Baum, Richard. "The Cultural Revolution in the Countryside: Anatomy of a Limited Rebellion." In T. W. Robinson.

———. *Prelude to Revolution: Mao, the Party, and the Peasant Question, 1962–66*. New York: Columbia University Press, 1975.

———. "Revolution and Reaction in the Chinese Countryside: The Socialist Education Movement in Cultural Revolution Perspective." *China Quarterly*, no. 38 (April–June, 1969).

Baum, Richard, and Frederick C. Teiwes. *Ssu-Ch'ing: The Socialist Education Movement of 1962–1966*. China Research Monograph no. 2. Berkeley: University of California, Center for Chinese Studies, 1968.

Bendix, Reinhard. *Max Weber: An Intellectual Portrait*. Berkeley: University of California Press, 1977.

Berlin, Isaiah. *Russian Thinkers*. Harmondsworth: Penguin, 1978.

Bernhardt, Kathryn. *Rents, Taxes, and Peasant Resistance: The Lower Yangzi Region, 1840–1950.* Stanford, CA: Stanford University Press, 1992.

Bernstein, Thomas P. "Cadre and Peasant Behavior Under Conditions of Insecurity and Deprivation: The Grain Supply Crisis of the Spring of 1955." In Barnett.

———. "Keeping the Revolution Going: Problems of Village Leadership After Land Reform." In Lewis, ed.

———. "Stalinism, Famine, and Chinese Peasants: Grain Procurement During the Great Leap Forward." *Theory and Society* 13, no. 3 (May 1984).

———. *Up to the Mountains and Down to the Villages: The Transfer of Youth from Urban to Rural China.* New Haven, CT: Yale University Press, 1977.

Bian Luqun and Han Sheng. "'*Ting, suo, fa' fangzhen yu nongye hezuohua de yichang bianlun*" (The principle of "pause, reduction, and development" and the debate on agricultural collectivization). In Zhongguo geming bowuguan dangshi yanjiushi, ed.

Bloodworth, Dennis. *The Messiah and the Mandarins: Mao Tsetung and the Ironies of Power.* New York: Athenaeum, 1982.

Bo Yibo. "Fazhan xiangzhen qiye shi yixiang juyou zhanlue yiyi de renwu" (The development of rural enterprises is a strategic task). *RMRB*, January 21, 1990; *Xinhua yuebao*, no. 1 (1990).

———. *Ruogan zhongda juece yu shijian de huigu* (A look back at various important policy decisions and events). 2 pts. Beijing: Zhonggong zhongyang dangxiao chubanshe, 1991, 1993.

Booth, William, Patrick James, and Hudson Meadwell, eds. *Rationality and Politics.* Cambridge: Cambridge University Press, 1993.

Borgida, E., and R. E. Nisbett. "The Differential Impact of Abstract vs. Concrete Information on Decisions." *Journal of Applied Social Psychology* 7, no. 3 (July–September 1977).

Bouckaert, Andre. "Crisis Mortality: Extinction and Near-Extinction of Human Populations." In Ruzicka, Wunsch, and Kane.

Brada, Josef C. "The Political Economy of Communist Foreign Trade Institutions and Policies." *Journal of Comparative Economics* 15, no. 2 (June 1991).

Bramall, Chris. "The Role of Decollectivization in China's Agricultural Miracle, 1978–90." *Journal of Peasant Studies* 20, no. 2 (January 1993).

Braudel, Fernand. *The Identity of France.* Vol. 2: *People and Production.* New York: Harper, 1992.

Bray, Francesca. *The Rice Economies: Technology and Development in Asian Societies.* Oxford: Blackwell, 1986.

———. "Rice Economies: The Rise and Fall of China's Communes in East Asian Perspective." In Breman and Mundle.

Breman, Jan, and Sudipto Mundle, eds. *Rural Transformation in Asia.* Delhi: Oxford University Press, 1991.

Bromley, Daniel W. *Economic Interests and Institutions: The Conceptual Foundations of Public Policy.* Oxford: Blackwell, 1989.

Bunce, Valerie. *Do New Leaders Make a Difference? Executive Succession and Public Policy Under Capitalism and Socialism.* Princeton, NJ: Princeton University Press, 1981.

Burns, John P. "Local Cadre Accommodation to the 'Responsibility System' in Rural China." *Pacific Affairs* 58, no. 4 (Winter 1985–86).

————. *Political Participation in Rural China*. Berkeley: University of California Press, 1988.

Byrd, William A., and Alan Gelb. "Why Industrialize? The Incentives for Rural Community Governments." In Byrd and Lin.

Byrd, William A., and Lin Qingsong, eds. *China's Rural Industry: Structure, Development, and Reform*. New York: Oxford University Press, for the World Bank, 1990.

Center for Population Research of the Chinese Academy of Social Sciences and the Editorial Office of China Population Yearbook. *Zhongguo renkou nianjian 1985* (China population yearbook 1985). Beijing: Zhongguo shehui kexue chubanshe, 1986.

Chan, Alfred L. "The Campaign for Agricultural Development in the Great Leap Forward: A Study of Policy-Making and Implementation in Liaoning," *China Quarterly*, no. 129 (March 1992).

Chan, Anita. "Revolution or Corporatism?" *Australian Journal of Chinese Affairs*, no. 29 (January 1993).

Chan, Anita, Richard Madsen, and Jonathan Unger. *Chen Village*. Berkeley: University of California Press, 1984.

Chang, Jung. *Wild Swans: Three Daughters of China*. New York: Simon & Schuster, 1991.

Chang Naiguang, Song Chuansheng, and Chen Xinhui, eds. *Zhongguo renkou: Ningxia fence* (China's population: Ningxia volume). Beijing: Zhongguo caizheng jingji chubanshe, 1988.

Chang, Parris H. "Political Reform in China." In Kim and Zacek.

————. *Power and Policy in China*. 2d ed. University Park: Pennsylvania State University Press, 1978.

Chao, Kang. *Agricultural Production in Communist China, 1949–1965*. Madison: University of Wisconsin Press, 1970.

Chen Liang Yu and Allan Buckwell. *Chinese Grain Economy and Policy*. Wallingford: CAB International, 1991.

Chen Te-sheng. "Mainland China's Economic Reform Policies in the Wake of the Fifth Plenum of the CCP's Thirteenth Central Committee." *Issues and Studies* 26, no. 3 (March 1990).

Chen Xuesi. "A New Headache: Human Deluge." *Beijing Review* 32, no. 12 (March 20–26, 1989).

————. "One Million Job Seekers." *Beijing Review* 32, no. 11 (March 13–19, 1989).

Chen Xuewei. "Jingji jianshe de tingzhi, daotui jiqi lishi jiaoxun" (The stagnation and retrogression of economic construction and their historical lessons). In Tan Zongji et al.

Chen Yanhua. "'Mingong langchao' zhixiang hefang?" (Where is the wave of laborers pointed toward?), *RMRB*, overseas ed., March 3, 1989.

Chen Yaobang. "Renzhen guanche dang de shisan jie si zhong quanhui jingshen he Deng Xiaoping jianghua, cujin xiangzhen qiye chixu, xietiao, jiankang de fazhan" (Conscientiously put into effect the spirit of the fourth plenum of the thirteenth central committee of the party and the talks of Deng Xiaoping, promote the sustained, balanced, and healthy development of rural enterprises). *Xinhua yuebao* (New China monthly digest), no. 9 (1989).

Chen Yizi. "Nongcun de shuguang, Zhongguo de xiwang" (The dawn in the countryside, the hope of China). In *Nongcun, Jingji, Shehui*.

————. *Zhongguo: Shinian gaige yu bajiu minyun* (China: ten years of reform and the democracy movement of 1989). Taiwan: Lianjing chuban shiye gongsi, 1990.

Chen Yonggui. "Chedi pipan 'sirenbang,' xianqi puji Dazhai xian yundong de xin gaochao" (Thoroughly criticize the 'gang of four' and bring about a new upsurge in the movement to build Dazhai-type counties throughout the country). *Hongqi* (Red flag), no. 1 (1977).

Chen Yuan. "Woguo jingji de shenceng wenti he xuanze (gangyao)" (The deep problems and choices of our country's economy). *JJYJ*, no. 4 (1991).

Chen Yun. *Chen Yun wenxuan (1949–1956)* (Selected writings of Chen Yun, 1949–1956). Beijing: Renmin chubanshe, 1984.

————. *Chen Yun wenxuan (1956–1985)* (Selected writings of Chen Yun, 1956–1985) Beijing: Renmin chubanshe, 1986.

————. "Guanyu gaodu zhongshi zongjiao shentou wenti de xin" (Letter calling for taking extremely seriously the issue of religious infiltration). In Zhonggong zhongyang wenxian yianjiushi.

————. "An Important Work That Relates to the Overall Situation (May 1961)." In Lardy and Lieberthal.

Chen Yun yu xin Zhongguo jingji jianshe bianji zu, ed. *Chen Yun yu xin Zhongguo jingji jianshe* (Chen Yun and the economic construction of New China). Beijing: Zhongyang wenxian chubanshe, 1991.

Chen Zhiguo, ed. *Zhongguo nongmin wenti da puguang* (Exposed: China's peasant problems). Beijing: Jincheng chubanshe, 1993.

Cheng, J. Chester, ed. *The Politics of the Chinese Red Army.* Stanford, CA: Hoover Institution Press, 1966.

Cheung, Henry. "Freedom of the City: Urban-Rural Segregation Policy to Be Phased Out." *Window,* February 25, 1994.

Ch'i, Hsi-Sheng. *Politics of Disillusionment: The Chinese Communist Party Under Deng Xiaoping, 1978–1989.* Armonk, NY: M. E. Sharpe, 1991.

Christiansen, Flemming. "Social Division and Peasant Mobility in Mainland China: The Implications of the *Hu-k'ou* System." *Issues and Studies* 26, no. 4 (April 1990).

Coale, Ansley J. "Population Trends, Population Policy, and Population Studies in China." *Population and Development Review* 7, no. 1 (March 1981).

Cohn, Norman. *The Pursuit of the Millennium: Revolutionary Messianism in Medieval and Reformation Europe and Its Bearing on Modern Totalitarian Movements.* 2d ed. New York: Harper, 1961.

Colburn, Forrest D., ed. *Everyday Forms of Peasant Resistance.* Armonk, NY: M. E. Sharpe, 1989.

Collier, Ruth Berins, and David Collier. *Shaping the Political Arena: Critical Junctures, the Labor Movement, and Regime Dynamics in Latin America.* Princeton, NJ: Princeton University Press, 1991.

Communist China, 1955–1959: Policy Documents with Analysis. Cambridge, MA: Harvard University Press, 1965.

Cong Jin. *Quzhe fazhan de suiyue* (Years of tortuous development). Zhengzhou: Henan renmin chubanshe, 1989.

Conquest, Robert. *The Harvest of Sorrow: Soviet Collectivization and the Terror-Famine.* Oxford: Oxford University Press, 1986.

Cross, Rod. "On the Foundations of Hysteresis in Economic Systems." *Economics and Philosophy* 9, no. 1 (April 1993).

Crotty, William, ed. *Political Science: Looking to the Future*, vol. 2. Evanston, IL: Northwestern University Press, 1991.

Cui Chuanyi and Liu Zhenwei. "Nongcun shinian gaige de lilun tupo ji mianlin de wenti" (Theoretical breakthrough during ten years of rural reforms and the problems that lie ahead). *NMRB*, November 16, 1988.

Dai Zhou. "Jiaqiang dang de nongcun sixiang zhengzhi gongzuo de jidian sikao" (Several reflections on strengthening the party's rural ideological political work). *NMRB*, September 28, 1989.

Dangdai Zhongguo de Guizhou (Contemporary China: Guizhou). Beijing: Zhongguo shehui kexue chubanshe, 1989.

Dangdai Zhongguo de Hunan (Contemporary China: Hunan). Beijing: Zhongguo shehui kexue chubanshe, 1990.

Dangdai Zhongguo de Sichuan (Contemporary China: Sichuan). 2 vols. Beijing: Zhongguo shehui kexue chubanshe, 1990.

Dangdai Zhongguo de tongji shiye (Contemporary China's statistical undertakings). Beijing: Zhongguo shehui kexue chubanshe, 1990.

Dangdai Zhongguo de Zhejiang (Contemporary China: Zhejiang). Beijing: Zhongguo shehui kexue chubanshe, 1989.

Dangdai Zhongguo shangye (Contemporary China's commerce). 2 vols. Beijing: Zhongguo shehui kexue chubanshe, 1988.

David, Paul A. "Path-Dependence." Technical Report no. 533. Stanford, CA: Stanford University, Institute for Mathematical Studies in the Social Sciences, August 1988.

———. "Understanding the Economics of QWERTY: The Necessity of History." In Parker.

Davis, Deborah, and Ezra F. Vogel, eds. *Chinese Society on the Eve of Tiananmen: The Impact of Reform*. Cambridge, MA: Harvard University, Council on East Asian Studies, 1990.

Delfs, Robert, and Philip Bowring. "China's Credit Gamble." *Far Eastern Economic Review*, December 6, 1990.

Deng Hansheng. "Liushi niandai nongye shengchan zerenzhi de chuxian jiqi cuozhe" (The appearance of the production responsibility system in agriculture and its setbacks in the 1960's). *Dangshi yanjiu* (Party history research), no. 6 (December 1981).

Deng Liqun. "Tantan jihua tiaojie he shichang tiaojie" (On regulation by plan and regulation through the market). *Diaocha he yanjiu* (Investigation and study) (for internal use), September 30, 1979. In *Diaocha he yanjiu (1979/1980)*.

Deng Xiaoping. *Deng Xiaoping wenxuan* (Selected works of Deng Xiaoping), vol. 3. Beijing: Renmin chubanshe, 1993.

———. *Deng Xiaoping wenxuan (1938–1965)* (Selected works of Deng Xiaoping, 1938–1965). Beijing: Renmin chubanshe, 1989.

———. *Selected Works of Deng Xiaoping (1975–1982)*. Beijing: Foreign Languages, 1984.

———. "Zai jiejian shoudu jieyan budui jun yishang ganbu shi de jianghua" (Talk at reception for martial law troop cadres of army level and above in the Capital). *Qiushi* (Seek truth), no. 13 (1989).

Deng Zihui. "Zai quanguo disanci nongcun gongzuo huiyi shang de kaimuci" (Opening remarks at the third national rural work conference). *Dangshi yanjiu* (Party history research), no. 1 (Feburary 1981).

Deng Zihui nongye hezuo sixiang xueshu taolunhui lunwenji (Proceedings of the symposium on Deng Zihui's thought on agricultural cooperativization). Beijing: Nongye chubanshe, 1989.

Development Research Institute. *Gaige mianlin zhidu chuangxin* (Reform faces system innovation). Shanghai: Sanlian shudian, 1988.

Dittmer, Lowell. "China in 1989." *Asian Survey* 30, no. 1 (January 1990).

Documents of the Chinese Communist Party Central Committee, September 1956–April 1969, vol. 1. Hong Kong: Union Research Institute, 1971.

Domes, Jürgen. *The Government and Politics of the PRC: A Time of Transition*. Boulder, CO: Westview, 1985.

———. *Socialism in the Chinese Countryside*. Trans. Margitta Wendling. London: C. Hurst, 1980.

Dong Bian, Tan Deshan, and Zeng Zhi, eds. *Mao Zedong he ta de mishu Tian Jiaying* (Mao Zedong and his secretary Tian Jiaying). Beijing: Zhongyang wenxian chubanshe, 1989.

Dong Fureng. "Development Theory and Problems of Socialist Developing Economies." In Ranis and Schultz.

———. *Jingji fazhan zhanlue yanjiu* (Studies of economic development strategy). Beijing: Jingji kexue chubanshe, 1988.

Dong, Xiao-Yuan, and Gregory K. Dow. "Does Free Exit Reduce Shirking in Production Teams?" *Journal of Comparative Economics* 17, no. 2 (June 1993).

Donnithorne, Audrey. "China's Cellular Economy: Some Economic Trends Since the Cultural Revolution." *China Quarterly*, no. 52 (1972).

Downing, Brian M. *The Military Revolution and Political Change: Origins of Democracy and Autocracy in Early Modern Europe*. Princeton, NJ: Princeton University Press, 1992.

Du Daozheng, Lin Tian, and Dai Huang. "Long shang chen xi" (The sun rises in Gansu). *Liaowang*, no. 5 (August 1981).

Du Runsheng. *Zhongguo nongcun jingji gaige* (The reform of China's rural economy). Beijing: Zhongguo shehui kexue chubanshe, 1985.

Du Runsheng et al. *Sikao yu xuanze* (Reflections and choices). Beijing: Zhonggong zhongyang dangxiao chubanshe, 1990.

Du Wenzhen and Gu Jirui, eds. *Zhongguo renkou: Jiangsu fence* (China's population: Jiangsu volume). Beijing: Zhongguo caizheng jingji chubanshe, 1987.

Duara, Prasenjit. *Culture, Power, and the State: Rural North China, 1900–1942*. Stanford, CA: Stanford University Press, 1988.

Dynes, Russell, Bruna de Marchi, and Carlo Pelanda, eds. *Sociology of Disasters*. Milan: Franco Angeli, 1987.

Eckstein, Harry. "Case Study and Theory in Political Science." In Greenstein and Polsby.

Eggertsson, Thráinn. *Economic Behavior and Institutions*. Cambridge: Cambridge University Press, 1990.

———. "The Economics of Institutions: Avoiding the Open-Field Syndrome and the Perils of Path Dependence." *Acta Sociologica* 36, no. 3 (1993).

Ellis, Frank. *Peasant Economics: Farm Households and Agrarian Development*. Cambridge: Cambridge University Press, 1988.

Elster, Jon. *Explaining Technical Change*. Cambridge: Cambridge University Press, 1983.

———. *Nuts and Bolts for the Social Sciences*. Cambridge: Cambridge University Press, 1989.

———. *Political Psychology*. Cambridge: Cambridge University Press, 1993.

Endicott, Stephen. *Red Earth: Revolution in a Sichuan Village*. Toronto: NC Press, 1989.

Fan Zhengping. "Jihua jinrong he shichang jinrong xiang jiehe de ruogan lilun wenti" (Several theoretical questions concerning the combination of planned and market-oriented finances). *JJYJ*, no. 4 (1991).

Feher, Ferenc, Agnes Heller, and Gyorgy Markus. *Dictatorship over Needs: An Analysis of Soviet Societies*. Oxford: Blackwell, 1983.

Fewsmith, Joseph. *Dilemmas of Reform in China: Political Conflict and Economic Debate*. Armonk, NY: M. E. Sharpe, 1994.

Field, Robert Michael. "China's Industrial Performance Since 1978," *China Quarterly*, no. 131 (September 1992).

———. "The Performance of Industry During the Cultural Revolution: Second Thoughts." *China Quarterly*, no. 108 (December 1986).

Findlay, Christopher, and Jiang Shu, "Interest Group Conflicts in a Reforming Economy." In Watson, ed.

Fiske, Susan, and Shelley Taylor. *Social Cognition*. Reading, MA: Addison-Wesley, 1984.

Fitzpatrick, Sheila. *Stalin's Peasants: Resistance and Survival in the Russian Village After Collectivization*. New York: Oxford University Press, 1994.

Freedman, Maurice. *The Study of Chinese Society: Essays*. Stanford, CA: Stanford University Press, 1979.

"French Farmers: Trouble in the Fields of Elysium." *Economist*, September 19, 1992.

Friedman, Edward. "Maoist and Post-Mao Conceptualization of World Capitalism." In Kim, ed.

———. "The Politics of Local Models, Social Transformation and State Power Struggles in the People's Republic of China: Tachai and Teng Hsiao-P'ing." *China Quarterly*, no. 76 (December 1978).

Friedman, Edward, Paul G. Pickowicz, and Mark Selden. *Chinese Village, Socialist State*. New Haven, CT: Yale University Press, 1991.

Fu Xingyu. "Ganbu xia jiceng yihou . . ." (After cadres are sent down to the basic level . . .). *Banyuetan* (Fortnightly discussion), no. 7 (April 1991).

Fujian Province Bureau of Statistics and Bureau of Public Security. *Fujian sheng renkou tongji ziliao huibian, 1949–1988* (Collection of statistical materials on the population of Fujian province, 1949–1988). Beijing: Zhongguo tongji chubanshe, 1989.

Gansu Province Statistical Bureau. *Gansu tongji nianjian 1988* (Statistical yearbook of Gansu 1988). Beijing: Zhongguo tongji chubanshe, 1988.

Gao Gao and Yan Jiaqi. *"Wenhua dageming" shinian shi* (A history of the ten-year "great cultural revolution"). Tianjin: Tianjin renmin chubanshe, 1986.

Gao Huamin. "Deng Zihui tongzhi dui woguo nongye hezuohua de shensui jianjie" (Comrade Deng Zihui's profound understanding of our country's agricultural cooperativization). In *Deng Zihui nongye*.

Gao Yi. "Yijiu wujiu nian de nongye shengchan zerenzhi" (The agricultural production responsibility system of 1959). *Dangshi yanjiu* (Party history research), no. 1 (February 1983).

Gao Zhiyu and Li Yanqi. *Deng Xiaoping yu dangdai Zhongguo gaige* (Deng Xiaoping and contemporary China's reforms). Beijing: Zhongguo renmin daxue chubanshe, 1990.

Garside, Roger. *Coming Alive: China After Mao*. New York: McGraw-Hill, 1981.

Geddes, Barbara. "Paradigms and Sand Castles in the Comparative Politics of Developing Areas." In Crotty.

Gilley, Bruce. "Beijing Considers Single Tax on Peasants." *Eastern Express*, April 14, 1994; FBIS-CHI-94-072, April 14, 1994.

Goldstein, Avery. *From Bandwagon to Balance-of-Power Politics: Structural Constraints and Politics in China, 1949–1978*. Stanford, CA: Stanford University Press, 1991.

Goldstein, Carl, Lincoln Kaye, and Anthony Blass. "Get Off Our Backs." *Far Eastern Economic Review*, July 15, 1993.

Goldstone, Jack. *Revolution and Rebellion in the Early Modern World*. Berkeley, CA: University of California Press, 1991.

Goodman, David G. *Center and Province in the People's Republic of China, 1955–1965*. Cambridge: Cambridge University Press, 1986.

———. "Provincial Party First Secretaries in National Politics: A Categoric or a Political Group?" In Goodman, ed.

———, ed. *Groups and Politics in the People's Republic of China*. Armonk, NY: M. E. Sharpe, 1984.

Gould, Stephen Jay. *Wonderful Life: The Burgess Shale and the Nature of History*. New York: Norton, 1989.

Gourevitch, Peter. *Politics in Hard Times: Comparative Responses to International Economic Crises*. Ithaca, NY: Cornell University Press, 1986.

Grindle, Merilee, and John W. Thomas. "Policy Makers, Policy Choices, and Policy Outcomes: The Political Economy of Reform in Developing Countries." *Policy Sciences* 22, nos. 3–4 (1989).

Groves, Robert G. "Militia, Market and Lineage." *Journal of the Hong Kong Branch of the Royal Asiatic Society* 9 (1969).

Guinnane, Timothy W. "The Great Irish Famine and Population: The Long View." *American Economic Review* 84, no. 2 (May 1994).

Guizhou shengqing bianweihui. *Guizhou shengqing* (Information Guizhou). Guiyang: Guizhou renmin chubanshe, 1986.

Guo Chongyi. "Zeren daohu de xingzhi jiqi youguan wenti" (The nature of household responsibility and related issues). August 1979. In Zhongguo fazhan wenti yanjiu zu.

Guo Ming. "Yinian lai guanyu nongye shengchan zerenzhi wenti taolun zongshu" (A summary of the discussion concerning the production responsibility systems in agriculture in the past year). *JJYJ*, no. 3 (1982).

Guo Shutian, Liu Chunbin, et al. *Shiheng de Zhongguo* (Unbalanced China). Shijiazhuang: Hebei renmin chubanshe, 1990.

Guojia jigou bianzhi weiyuanhui bangongshi (The office of the state commision on organizational establishment). *Zhonghua Renmin Gongheguo Guowuyuan zuzhi jigou gaiyao (1988)* (Outline of the organizational structure of the state council of the People's Republic of China). Shenyang: Dongbei gongxueyuan chubanshe, 1989.

Guojia Nongye Weiyuanhui Bangongting (General office of the state agriculture commission). *Nongye jitihua zhongyao wenjian huibian* (Compendium of important documents on agricultural collectivization). 2 vols. (vol. 1: 1949–57; vol. 2: 1958–81). Beijing: Zhongyang dangxiao chubanshe, 1981.

Guowuyuan fazhiju fagui bianzuan shi. *Jianqing nongmin fudan wenjian huibian* (Compendium of documents on reducing peasant burdens). Beijing: Zhongguo fazhi chubanshe, 1993.

Gupta, S. P., Nicholas Stern, Athar Hussain, and William Byrd, eds. *Development Experiences in China and India: Reforms and Modernization.* New Delhi: Allied, 1991.

Haggard, Stephan. *Pathways from the Periphery: The Politics of Growth in the Newly Industrializing Countries.* Ithaca, NY: Cornell University Press, 1990.

Hall, Peter A. "Conclusion: The Politics of Keynesian Ideas." In Hall, ed.

———, ed. *The Political Power of Economic Ideas: Keynesianism Across Nations.* Princeton, NJ: Princeton University Press, 1989.

Han Shanbi. *Deng Xiaoping.* Vol. 3: *Deng Xiaoping shidai* (1978–1988) (The era of Deng Xiaoping). Hong Kong: Dongxi wenhua shiye gongsi, 1988.

Hansen, John M. "The Political Economy of Group Membership." *American Political Science Review* 79, no. 1 (March 1985).

Harberger, Arnold. "Secrets of Success: A Handful of Heroes." *American Economic Review* 83, no. 2 (May 1993).

Hardin, Garrett. "The Tragedy of the Commons." *Science* 162 (December 13, 1968).

Hardin, Russell. *Collective Action.* Baltimore: Johns Hopkins University Press, for Resources for the Future, 1982.

Harding, Harry. *China's Second Revolution: Reform After Mao.* Washington, DC: Brookings Institution, 1987.

Hayek, Friedrich von. "Competition as a Discovery Procedure." In Nishiyama and Leube.

———. "The Use of Knowledge in Society." In Nishiyama and Leube.

He Kang. "Renzhen guanche dang de shisan jie wuzhong quanhui jingshen, jiji yindao xiangzhen qiye jiankang fazhan" (Conscientiously carry out the spirit of the fifth plenum of the thirteenth party central committee and actively guide rural enterprises to healthy development). *Xinhua yuebao,* no. 2 (1990).

He Xin. "Analysis of the Current Student Protests and Forecasts Concerning the Situation." *Australian Journal of Chinese Affairs,* no. 23 (January 1990).

Heclo, Hugh. *Modern Social Politics in Britain and Sweden.* New Haven, CT: Yale University Press, 1974.

Heilongjiang Nongye Hezuoshi Bianweihui. *Heilongjiang nongye hezuoshi* (A history of agricultural cooperativization in Heilongjiang). Beijing: Zhonggong dangshi ziliao chubanshe, 1990.

Heilongjiang Province Statistical Bureau. *Heilongjiang tongji nianjian 1987* (Statistical yearbook of Heilongjiang, 1987). Beijing: Zhongguo tongji chubanshe, 1987.

Henderson, Gail. "Increased Inequality in Health Care." In Davis and Vogel.

Hinton, William. *The Great Reversal: The Privatization of China, 1978–1989.* New York: Monthly Review, 1990.

———. *Shenfan: The Continuing Revolution in a Chinese Village.* New York: Vintage, 1984.

Hirschman, Albert O. *A Bias for Hope: Essays on Development and Latin America.* Boulder, CO: Westview, 1985.

———. *Exit, Voice, and Loyalty: Response to Decline in Firms, Organizations, and States.* Cambridge, MA: Harvard University Press, 1970.

———. *The Rhetoric of Reaction: Perversity, Futility, Jeopardy.* Cambridge, MA: Belknap Press, 1991.

———. "The Search for Paradigms as a Hindrance to Understanding." *World Politics* 22, no. 3 (March 1970).

———. *Shifting Involvements: Private Interest and Public Action.* Princeton, NJ: Princeton University Press, 1982.

Hogarth, Robin. *Judgement and Choice: The Psychology of Decision.* 2d ed. New York: Wiley, 1987.

Hooper, Beverley. *China Stands Up: Ending the Western Presence, 1948–1950.* North Sydney: Allen & Unwin, 1986.

Hu, Nai-tsui. "The Problem of the Peasant Exodus in China." In Research Staff of the Secretariat.

Hu Qiaomu. "Anzhao jingji guilü banshi, jiakuai shixian sige xiandaihua" (Observe economic laws, speed up the four modernizations). *RMRB*, October 6, 1978.

Hu Xiao, ed. *Shiji zhijiao de xiangtu Zhongguo* (Rural China at century's end). Changsha: Hunan chubanshe, 1991.

Hua Guofeng. "Quandang dongyuan, daban nongye, wei puji Dazhai xian er fendou" (Mobilize the whole party, make greater efforts to develop agriculture, and strive to build Dazhai-type counties throughout the country." *Hongqi* (Red flag), no. 1 (1977).

———. "Zai Zhongguo Gongchandang di shiyi ci quanguo daibiao dahui shang de zhengzhi baogao" (Political report delivered at the eleventh national congress of the Chinese communist party). *RMRB*, August 23, 1977.

Huai En (pseud.). *Zhou zongli shengping dashiji* (A chronology of major events in the life of premier Zhou). Chengdu: Sichuan renmin chubanshe, 1986.

"Huainian Zhou Enlai" bianji xiaozu. *Huainian Zhou Enlai* (Cherish the memory of Zhou Enlai). Beijing: Renmin chubanshe, 1986.

Huang Daoxia, Dai Zhou, and Yu Zhan, eds. *Jidang Zhongguo nongcun de biange* (The changes that have animated China's rural areas). Beijing: Guangming ribao chubanshe, 1988.

Huang, Philip C. C. *The Peasant Family and Rural Development in the Yangzi Delta, 1350–1988.* Stanford, CA: Stanford University Press, 1990.

Huang Xianlin and Mo Datong, chief eds. *Zhongguo renkou: Guangxi fence* (China's population: Guangxi volume). Beijing: Zhongguo caizheng jingji chubanshe, 1988.

Ikenberry, G. John. "Conclusion: An Institutional Approach to American Foreign Economic Policy." In Ikenberry, Lake, and Mastanduno.

Ikenberry, G. John, David A. Lake, and Michael Mastanduno, eds. *The State and American Foreign Economic Policy.* Ithaca, NY: Cornell University Press, 1988.

Jacobs, J. Bruce. "Political and Economic Institutional Changes and Continuities in Six Rural Chinese Localities." *Australian Journal of Chinese Affairs*, no. 14 (July 1985).

Jefferson, Gary, Thomas Rawski, and Yuxin Zheng. "Growth, Efficiency, and Convergence in China's State and Collective Industry." *Economic Development and Cultural Change* 40, no. 2 (January 1992).

Jiang Boying. *Deng Zihui zhuan* (A biography of Deng Zihui). Shanghai: Shanghai renmin chubanshe, 1986.

Jiang Dianguo, Li Zhanhui, and Zhang Xiaochun. "Burong huibi de 'redian'" (The unavoidable hot spot). *NMRB*, August 30, 1988.

Jiang Yueshao. "Rang yibufen sheyuan xian fu qilai" (Let some commune members become prosperous first). *Hongqi* (Red flag), no. 4 (1979).

Jiang Zemin. "Zai nongcun gongzuo zuotanhui shang de jianghua" (Talk at the forum on rural work). In *XNNWX*, pp. 594–603.

Jiang Zhimin and Xu Zugen. "Miandui shizijia de sikao" (Reflections before the Cross). *Liaowang* (Outlook), no. 5 (January 30, 1989).

Jin Yu and Chen Xiankui. *Dangdai Zhongguo da silu: Deng Xiaoping de lilun yu shijian* (The strategic thinking for contemporary China: the thought and practice of Deng Xiaoping). Beijing: Zhongguo renmin daxue chubanshe, 1989.

Johnson, Chalmers, ed. *Ideology and Politics in Contemporary China*. Seattle: University of Washington Press, 1973.

Johnson, D. Gale. "Economic Reforms in the People's Republic of China." *Economic Development and Cultural Change* 36, no. 3 (Supp.) (April 1988).

———. *The People's Republic of China, 1978–1990*. San Francisco: ICS Press, 1990.

Joint Economic Committee. *China's Economic Dilemmas in the 1990s: The Problem of Reforms, Modernization, and Interdependence*. Washington, DC: Government Printing Office, 1991.

Joseph, William W. "A Tragedy of Good Intentions: Post-Mao Views of the Great Leap Forward." *Modern China* 12, no. 4 (October 1986).

Joseph, William, Christine Wong, and David Zweig, eds. *New Perspectives on the Cultural Revolution*. Harvard Contemporary China Series no. 8. Cambridge, MA: Harvard University, Council on East Asian Studies, 1991.

Kahneman, Daniel, and Amos Tversky. "On the Psychology of Prediction." *Psychological Review* 80, no. 4 (July 1973).

———. "Subjective Probability: A Judgment of Representativeness." *Cognitive Psychology* 3, no. 3 (July 1972).

Kahneman, Daniel, Jack L. Knetsch, and Richard H. Thaler. "Anomalies: The Endowment Effect, Loss Aversion, and Status Quo Bias." *Journal of Economic Perspectives* 5, no. 5 (Winter 1991).

Kahneman, Daniel, Paul Slovic, and Amos Tversky, eds. *Judgment Under Uncertainty: Heuristics and Biases*. New York: Cambridge University Press, 1982.

Kai Di. "Wenzhou zongjiao qingkuang de diaocha yu sikao" (A survey of and reflections on the religious situation in Wenzhou). *Shehuixue yanjiu* (Sociological research), no. 2 (1989).

Kane, Anthony J. *China Briefing, 1990*. Boulder, CO: Westview, 1990.

Kane, Penny. *Famine in China, 1959–61*. New York: St Martin's, 1988.

Kau, Michael Y. M., and John K. Leung, eds. *The Writings of Mao Zedong, 1949–1976*. Vol. 1: *September 1949–December 1955*. Armonk, NY: M. E. Sharpe, 1986.

Kaye, Lincoln. "Religious Groundswell: Underground Churches Lead Christian Revival." *Far Eastern Economic Review* 156, no. 3 (January 21, 1993).

Kelliher, Daniel. "Are Peasants the Enemy of Democracy and Progress? Why Chinese Politicians (No Matter What Kind) Don't Like Peasants." Paper presented to the Colloquium of the Program in Agrarian Studies, Yale University, 1991.

———. *Peasant Power in China: The Era of Rural Reform, 1979–1989*. New Haven, CT: Yale University Press, 1992.

Khong, Yuen Foong. *Analogies at War: Korea, Munich, Dien Bien Phu, and the Vietnam Decisions of 1965*. Princeton, NJ: Princeton University Press, 1992.

Kim, Ilpyong J., and Jane S. Zacek, eds. *Reform and Transformation in Communist Systems*. New York: Paragon House, 1991.

Kim, Samuel S., ed. *China and the World: New Directions in Chinese Foreign Relations*. 2d ed. Boulder, CO: Westview, 1989.

King, Gary, Robert O. Keohane, and Sidney Verba. *Designing Social Inquiry: Scientific Inference in Qualitative Research*. Princeton, NJ: Princeton University Press, 1994.

Kingdon, John W. *Agendas, Alternatives, and Public Policies*. New York: Harper Collins, 1984.

Kiser, Edgar, and Michael Hechter. "The Role of General Theory in Comparative-Historical Sociology." *American Journal of Sociology* 97, no. 1 (July 1991).

Klein, Donald W., and Anne B. Clark, eds. *Biographic Dictionary of Chinese Communism, 1921–1965*. Cambridge, MA: Harvard University Press, 1971.

Knight, Jack. *Institutions and Social Conflict*. Cambridge: Cambridge University Press, 1992.

Krasner, Stephen D. "Approaches to the State: Alternative Conceptions and Historical Dynamics." *Comparative Politics* 16, no. 2 (January 1984).

———. "Sovereignty: An Institutional Approach." *Comparative Political Studies* 21, no. 4 (April 1988).

Krugman, Paul R. *Geography and Trade*. Cambridge, MA: MIT Press, 1991.

Kueh, Y. Y., and Robert F. Ash, eds. *Economic Trends in Chinese Agriculture: The Impact of Post-Mao Reforms*. Oxford: Clarendon Press, 1993.

Kuhn, Philip A. *Rebellion and Its Enemies in Late Imperial China: Militarization and Social Structure, 1796–1864*. Harvard East Asian Series no. 49. Cambridge, MA: Harvard University Press, 1970.

Kung, James Kaising. "Transaction Costs and Peasants' Choice of Institutions: Did the Right to Exit Really Solve the Free Rider Problem in Chinese Collective Agriculture?" *Journal of Comparative Economics* 17, no. 2 (June 1993).

Kuran, Timur. "The East European Revolution of 1989: Is It Surprising That We Were Surprised?" *American Economic Review* 81, no. 2 (May 1991).

———. "Now Out of Never: The Element of Surprise in the East European Revolution of 1989." *World Politics* 44, no. 1 (October 1991).

———. "Private and Public Preferences." *Economics and Philosophy* 6, no. 1 (April 1990).

———. "The Tenacious Past: Theories of Personal and Collective Conservatism." *Journal of Economic Behavior and Organization* 10, no. 2 (September 1988).

Lampton, David M. *Paths to Power: Elite Mobility in Contemporary China*. Michigan Monograph in Chinese Studies no. 55. Ann Arbor: University of Michigan, Center for Chinese Studies, 1986.

———, ed. *Policy Implementation in Post-Mao China*. Berkeley: University of California Press, 1987.

Lardy, Nicholas R. *Agriculture in China's Modern Economic Development.* Cambridge: Cambridge University Press, 1983.

———. "The Chinese Economy Under Stress, 1958–1965." In MacFarquhar and Fairbank, vol. 14.

———. "Economic Recovery and the 1st Five-Year Plan." In MacFarquhar and Fairbank, vol. 14.

Lardy, Nicholas R., and Kenneth Lieberthal, eds. *Chen Yun's Strategy for China's Development: A Non-Maoist Alternative.* Armonk, NY: M. E. Sharpe, 1983.

Larson, Deborah. *Origins of Containment.* Princeton, NJ: Princeton University Press, 1985.

Lee, Ching Hua. *Deng Xiaoping: The Marxist Road to the Forbidden City.* Princeton, NJ: Kingston, 1985.

Le Roy Ladurie, Emmanuel. *The Peasants of Languedoc.* Trans. John Day. Urbana: University of Illinois Press, [1966] 1974.

Levine, Ross, and Sara Zervos. "What We Have Learned About Policy and Growth from Cross-Country Regressions," *American Economic Review* 83, no. 2 (May 1992).

Lewis, John W. "The Social Limits of Politically Induced Change." In Morse.

———, ed. *Party Leadership and Revolutionary Power in China.* Cambridge: Cambridge University Press, 1970.

Li Debin, Lin Shunbao, Jin Bihua, He Fengqin, and Jin Shiying. *Xin Zhongguo nongcun jingji jishi 1949.10:1984.9* (Major events of new China's rural economy, October 1949–September 1984). Beijing: Beijing daxue chubanshe, 1989.

Li Fuchun. *Li Fuchuan xuanji* (Selected works of Li Fuchun). Beijing: Zhongguo jihua chubanshe, 1992.

———. "Report on the First Five-Year Plan for Development of the National Economy of the People's Republic of China in 1953–1957." In *Communist China.*

Li Honglin. *Mingyun: Li Honglin zizhuan* (Fate: the autobiography of Li Honglin). Taibei: Wentong tushu, 1993.

Li Jingneng, Wang Qiang, and He Ziqiang, eds. *Zhongguo renkou: Tianjin fence* (China's population: Tianjin volume). Beijing: Zhongguo caizheng jingji chubanshe, 1987.

Li Mingfu and Wu Shaofu. "Baochan daohu shi nongmin de xinyuan" (Household contracting is the peasants' dream). In Zhang Xiaoli.

Li Peng. "Report on the Work of Government." Beijing Domestic Service, March 20, 1989; FBIS-CHI-89-053, March 21, 1989.

———. "Xiangzhen qiye yaozai zhili zhengdun, shenhua gaige zhong jixu qianjin" (Rural enterprises should continue to advance amid 'improvement, rectification, and the deepening of reforms'). *Qiushi* (Seek truth), no. 6 (1990).

———. "Zai quanguo jingji gongzuo huiyi shang de jianghua" (Talk at the national economic conference) (December 24, 1992). *RMRB*, overseas ed., January 30, 1993.

———. "Zhenfen jingshen, zengqiang xinxin, nuli zuohao 1990 nian de jingji gongzuo" (Inspire enthusiasm and confidence, strive to do well the economic work of 1990). *Qiushi* (Seek truth), no. 1 (1990).

———. "Zhengque renshi dangqian de jingji xingshi, jinyibu gaohao zhili zhengdun" (Correctly understand the present economic situation and further do a good job of rectification and readjustment). *Qiushi* (Seek truth), no. 21 (1989).

Li Qianghua, Li Weizhou, and Hu Yijin, eds. *Nongcun chengbao hetong anli xi* (A case analysis of rural responsibility contracts). Chongqing: Chongqing chuban-she, 1991.

Li Rui. *Lushan huiyi shilu* (A factual record of the Lushan conference). Beijing: Chunqiu chubanshe, 1989; Hong Kong: Tiandi tushu youxian gongsi, 1993.

Li Tianmin. *Hua Guofeng yu Hua Guofeng zhengquan* (Hua Guofeng and the Hua Guofeng regime). Taibei: Youshi wenhua shiye gongsi, 1982.

Li Xiannian. *Li Xiannian wenxuan (1935–1988)* (Selected writings of Li Xiannian, 1935–1988). Beijing: Renmin chubanshe, 1989.

Li Zhuang. *Wo zai renmin ribao sishi nian* (My forty years at the *People's Daily*). Beijing: Renmin ribao chubanshe, 1990.

Liao Gailong, Ding Xiaochun, and Li Zhongzhi, eds. *Zhongguo gongchan dang fazhan shidian* (Chronicle of events of the Chinese communist party's development). Shenyang: Liaoning jiaoyu chubanshe, 1991.

Liao Gailong, Zhao Baoxu, and Du Qinglin, eds. *Zhongguo zhengzhi dashi dian* (Encyclopedia of major events in Chinese politics). Changchun: Jilin wenshi chubanshe, 1991.

Lieberthal, Kenneth G. "The Great Leap Forward and the Split in the Yenan Leadership." In MacFarquhar and Fairbank, vol. 14.

Lieberthal, Kenneth G., and Bruce J. Dickson. *A Research Guide to Central Party and Government Meetings in China, 1949–1986*. Rev. ed. Armonk, NY: M. E. Sharpe, 1989.

Lilun dongtai. Vol. 5. Beijing: Renmin chubanshe, 1979.

Lin, Justin Yifu. "Collectivization and China's Agricultural Crisis in 1959–1961." *Journal of Political Economy* 98, no. 6 (1990).

———. "Exit Rights, Exit Costs, and Shirking in Agricultural Cooperative: A Reply." *Journal of Comparative Economics* 17, no. 2 (June 1993).

———. "The Household Responsibility System in China's Agricultural Reform: A Theoretical and Empirical Study." *Economic Development and Cultural Change* 36, no. 3 (Supp.) (April 1988).

———. "Rural Reforms and Agricultural Growth in China." *American Economic Review* 82, no. 1 (March 1992).

Lin Lishan, ed. *Jinggao gongheguo* (Warnings to the republic). Beijing: Tuanjie chubanshe, 1993.

Lin Qingshan. *Fengyun shinian yu Deng Xiaoping* (The tumultuous ten years and Deng Xiaoping). Beijing: Jiefangjun chubanshe, 1989.

Lin Yunhui, Fan Shouxin, and Zhang Gong. *Kaige xingjin de shiqi* (The period of triumphant advance). Zhengzhou: Henan renmin chubanshe, 1989.

Lin Zili. *Lun lianchan chengbao zhi* (On the output contracting system). Shanghai: Shanghai renmin chubanshe, 1983.

———. "Woguo jingji tizhi gaige de kaiduan: Sichuan, Anhui, Zhejiang kuoda qiye zizhuquan shidian kaocha" (The beginning of economic system reform in our country: An investigation of the experiments in expanding enterprise rights in Sichuan, Anhui, and Zhejiang). *RMRB*, April 4, 1980.

Lindbeck, John M. H., ed. *China: Management of a Revolutionary Society*. Seattle: University of Washington Press, 1971.

Lindqvist, Sven. *China in Crisis*. Trans. Sylvia Clayton. New York: Crowell, 1963.

Ling Xin, ed. *Lu manman qi xiuyuan: Zhongguo gaige dachao jishi* (The long journey: Chronicle of China's big wave of reforms). Hong Kong: Tiandi tushu, 1993.

Lippit, Victor. *Land Reform and Economic Development in China*. White Plains, NY: International Arts and Sciences, 1974.

Lipton, Michael. *Why Poor People Stay Poor: A Study of Urban Bias in World Development*. Cambridge, MA: Harvard University Press, 1977.

Little, Daniel. "Rational-Choice Models and Asian Studies." *Journal of Asian Studies* 50, no. 1 (Feburary 1991).

———. *Understanding Peasant China: Case Studies in the Philosophy of Social Science*. New Haven, CT: Yale University Press, 1989.

Liu, Alan P. L. "Economic Reform, Mobility Strategies, and National Integration in China." *Asian Survey* 31, no. 5 (May 1991).

Liu Fuyuan. *Nongcun gaige de xin fanglue* (New strategies for rural reform). Beijing: Zhongguo caizheng jingji chubanshe, 1992.

Liu Hexin. "Analysis of Abrupt Incidents in Rural Areas." *RMRB*, April 28, 1992; FBIS-CHI-92-095, May 15, 1992.

Liu Jiemin, and Bai Tianshan. "Nongye fengshou nongmin shouru xiajiang wenti yingdang gaodu zhongshi" (Great importance should be attached to the issue of peasant income declines amid agricultural bumper harvests). In Nongyebu zhengce tigai fagui si.

Liu, Minquan. "Exit Right, Retaliatory Shirking, and the Agricultural Crisis in China." *Journal of Comparative Economics* 17, no. 2 (June 1993).

Liu Shaoqi. *Liu Shaoqi xuanji* (Selected works of Liu Shaoqi), vol. 2. Beijing: Renmin chubanshe, 1985.

Liu Shaoqi yanjiu lunwenji (Studies on Liu Shaoqi: A collection of papers). Beijing: Zhongyang wenxian chubanshe, 1989.

Liu Shunguo. "Nongcun dang zuzhi jianshe jidai jiaqiang" (The building of rural party organizations urgently needs strengthening). *NMRB*, January 31, 1989.

Liu Suinian and Wu Qungan, eds. *China's Socialist Economy: An Outline History (1949–1984)* (English ed. of next item). Beijing: Beijing Review, 1986.

———. *Zhongguo shehuizhuyi jingji jianshe* (An outline history of China's Socialist Construction). Harbin: Heilongjiang renmin chubanshe, 1985.

Liu Xianjun and Tian Weiben. *Lijie zongli fuzongli xiaozuan* (Biographies of premiers and vice-premiers). Jilin: Jilin renmin chubanshe, 1993.

Liu Zhideng and Huang Peimin, eds. *Zhongguo liangshi zhi yanjiu* (A study of grain in China). Beijing: Zhongguo nongye keji chubanshe, 1989.

———. *Zhongguo nongye zhi yanjiu* (A study of China's agriculture). Beijing: Zhongguo nongye keji chubanshe, 1989.

Liu Zhongyi "Guanyu wending fazhan nongye shengchan he nongcun jingji de yijian" (Suggestions on the stable development of agricultural production and rural economy). *Xinhua yuebao* (New China monthly digest), no. 2 (1991).

Liu Zhongyi and Liu Yaochuan. *Zhongguo nongye jiegou yanjiu* (A study in the structure of Chinese agriculture). Taiyuan: Shanxi jingji chubanshe, 1986.

Livi-Bacci, Massimo. "On the Human Costs of Collectivization in the Soviet Union." *Population and Development Review* 19, no. 4 (December 1993).

Lu Fanzhi. *Zhongguo jingji fazhan lun* (A treatise on economic development in China). Taibei: Nanfang congshu chubanshe, 1988 [Hong Kong, 1986].

Lu Wenfu. "Huanzhai" (Paying a debt). In *Lu Wenfu*.

———. *Lu Wenfu*. Beijing: Renmin wenxue chubanshe, 1991.

Lu Xianqi. "Shengchandui zhege jichu buneng dongyao" (The team as the foundation should not be undermined). *RMRB*, March 30, 1979.

Lu Xueyi. *Dangdai zhongguo nongcun yu dangdai zhongguo nongmin* (Rural areas and peasants in contemporary China). Beijing: Zhishi chubanshe, 1991.

———. *Lianchan chengbao zerenzhi yanjiu* (A study of the output-linked contract responsibility system). Shanghai: Shanghai renmin chubanshe, 1986.

Lu Yongjun. "Xiangzhen qiye fazhan qingkuang" (The situation of rural enterprises). In *Zhongguo jingji nianjian 1990*.

Luo Guoming. *Putishu xia de youhuo* (The Buddhist temptation). Guangzhou: Huacheng chubanshe, 1993.

Lupher, Mark. "Power Restructuring in China and the Soviet Union." *Theory and Society* 21, no. 5 (1992).

Lyons, Thomas. *Economic Integration and Planning in Maoist China*. New York: Columbia University Press, 1987.

———. "Grain in Fujian: Intra-provincial Patterns of Production and Trade, 1952–1988." *China Quarterly*, no. 129 (March 1992).

Ma Juxian, Shi Yuan, and Yi Yiqu, eds. *Zhongguo renkou: Jiangxi fence* (China's population: Jiangxi volume). Beijing: Zhongguo caizheng jingji chubanshe, 1989.

Ma Qibin, Chen Wenbin, Lin Yunhui, Cong Jin, Wang Nianyi, Zhang Tianrong, and Pu Weihua, eds. *Zhongguo gongchandang zhizheng sishi nian (1949–1989)* (The Chinese communist party's forty years in power, 1949–1989). Rev. ed. Beijing: Zhonggong dangshi chubanshe, 1991.

Ma Qibin, Chen Wenbin, Shao Weizheng, and Wang Qilai, eds. *Zhongguo gongchandang chuangye sanshinian (1919–1949)* (Thirty years of building the Chinese communist party, 1919–1949). Beijing: Zhonggong dangshi chubanshe, 1991.

Ma Zhongchen. "Agricultural Development and Population." *RMRB*, overseas ed., September 7, 1991, p. 4; FBIS-CHI-91-181, September 18, 1991, pp. 43–44.

MacDougall, Colina. "The Chinese Economy in 1976," *China Quarterly*, no. 70 (June 1977).

MacFarquhar, Roderick. *The Origins of the Cultural Revolution*. Vol. 1: *Contradictions Among the People, 1956–1957*. New York: Columbia University Press, 1974.

———. *The Origins of the Cultural Revolution*. Vol. 2: *The Great Leap Forward, 1958–1960*. New York: Columbia University Press, 1983.

———. "The Succession to Mao and the End of Maoism." In MacFarquhar and Fairbank, vol. 15.

MacFarquhar, Roderick, and John K. Fairbank, eds. *The Cambridge History of China*. Vol. 14: *The People's Republic*. Part 1: *The Emergence of Revolutionary China, 1949–1965*. Cambridge: Cambridge University Press, 1987.

———. *The Cambridge History of China*. Vol. 15: *The People's Republic*. Part 2: *Revolutions Within the Chinese Revolution, 1966–1982*. Cambridge: Cambridge University Press, 1991.

McGregor, James. "As Farmers Fall Further Behind Urban Dwellers, Chinese Government Displays Growing Anxiety." *Asian Wall Street Journal Weekly*, February 22, 1993.

———. "China's Conundrum." *Wall Street Journal*, September 24, 1991.

MacLeod, W. Bentley. "The Role of Exit Costs in the Theory of Cooperative Teams: A Theoretical Perspective." *Journal of Comparative Economics* 17, no. 2 (June 1993).

McMillan, John, John Whalley, and Lijing Zhu. "The Impact of China's Economic Reforms on Agricultural Productivity Growth." *Journal of Political Economy* 97, no. 4 (August 1989).

Madsen, Richard. "The Countryside Under Communism." In MacFarquhar and Fairbank, vol. 15.

Mao Kuangsheng, ed. *Zhongguo renkou: Hunan fence* (China's population: Hunan volume). Beijing: Zhongguo caizheng jingji chubanshe, 1987.

Mao Zedong. *Selected Works of Mao Tsetung*, vol. 5. Beijing: Foreign Languages, 1977.

Mao Zedong sixiang wansui (Long live the thought of Mao Zedong). N.p., n.d.

Mao Zedong sixiang wansui (Long live the thought of Mao Zedong). N.p., 1967.

March, James G., ed. *Handbook of Organizations*. Chicago: Rand McNally, 1965.

Martin, Michael F. "Defining China's Rural Population." *China Quarterly*, no. 130 (June 1992).

Martin, Roberta. *Party Recruitment in China: Patterns and Prospects*. New York: Columbia University, East Asian Institute, 1981.

Marx, Karl. "The Eighteenth Brumaire of Louis Bonaparte." In Tucker.

Maxwell, Neville, and Bruce McFarlane, eds. *China's Changed Road to Development*. Oxford: Pergamon, 1984.

May, Ernest. *"Lessons" of the Past: The Use and Misuse of History in American Foreign Policy*. New York: Oxford University Press, 1973.

Meng Shaohua and Peng Chuanrong. *Zhongguo zaihuang cidian* (A dictionary of famines in China). Harbin: Heilongjiang kexue jishu chubanshe, 1989.

———. *Zhongguo zaihuangshi, 1949–1989* (A history of disasters and famines in China, 1949–1989). Beijing: Shuili dianli chubanshe, 1989.

Migdal, Joel S. *Strong Societies and Weak States: State-Society Relations and State Capabilities in the Third World*. Princeton, NJ: Princeton University Press, 1988.

Milgrom, Paul, Yingyi Qian, and John Roberts. "Complementaries, Momentum, and the Evolution of Modern Manufacturing." *American Economic Review* 81, no. 2 (May 1991).

Ministry of Finance. "Weida zhuanbian shike yi zongli" (Remembering the premier at a moment of great transition). *Hongqi* (Red flag), no. 3 (1979).

Miscellany of Mao Tse-tung Thought (1949–1968). Arlington, VA: Joint Publications Research Service, 61269-1, 1974.

Morse, Chandler, ed. *Modernization by Design: Social Change in the Twentieth Century*. Ithaca, NY: Cornell University Press, 1969.

Mosher, Steven W. *Broken Earth: The Rural Chinese*. New York: Free Press, 1983.

———. *China Misperceived*. New York: Basic, 1990.

Mu Qing. "Er'shi nianjian" (In twenty years). *Liaowang* (Outlook), no. 5 (August 1981).

Murrell, Peter. "'Big Bang' Versus Evolution: East European Economic Reforms in the Light of Recent Economic History." *PlanEcon Report* 6, no. 26 (June 29, 1990).

Nan Zhenzhong, Shen Zurun, and Zhang Guangyou. "Luoshi dang de zhengce fei pi jiazuo zhenyou buke" ([We] must criticize false leftism but real rightism in implementing the party's policies). *RMRB*, July 6, 1978.

Naughton, Barry. "Economic Directions for the '90s." *China Business Review* 18, no. 3 (May–June 1991).

————. "Economic Reform and the Chinese Political Crisis of 1989." *Journal of Asian Economics* 1, no. 2 (1990).

————. "Implications of the State Monopoly over Industry and Its Relaxation." *Modern China* 18, no. 1 (January 1992).

————. "Industrial Policy During the Cultural Revolution: Military Preparation, Decentralization, and Leaps Forward." In Joseph, Wong, and Zweig.

————. "Inflation and Economic Reform in China." *Current History* 88 (September 1989).

Nee, Victor. Review of *State and Peasant in Contemporary China. Contemporary Sociology* 20, no. 3 (March 1991).

Nee, Victor, and David Mozingo, eds. *State and Society in Contemporary China*. Ithaca, NY: Cornell University Press, 1983.

Nee, Victor, and David Stark, eds. *Remaking the Economic Institutions of Socialism: China and Eastern Europe*. Stanford, CA: Stanford University Press, 1989.

Nelson, Joan. *Access to Power: Politics and the Urban Poor in Developing Nations*. Princeton, NJ: Princeton University Press, 1979.

Neustadt, Richard, and Ernest May. *Thinking in Time: The Uses of History for Decision-Makers*. New York: Free Press, 1986.

Newell, Allen, and Herbert A. Simon. *Human Problem Solving*. Englewood Cliffs, NJ: Prentice-Hall, 1972.

Ning Yuan, ed. *Gongheguo bu xiangxin yanlei* (The republic does not believe in tears). Beijing: Tuanjie chubanshe, 1993.

Nisbett, Richard, and Lee Ross. *Human Inference: Strategies and Shortcomings of Social Judgment*. Englewood Cliffs, NJ: Prentice-Hall, 1980.

Nishiyama, Chiaki, and Kurt R. Leube, eds. *The Essence of Hayek*. Stanford, CA: Hoover Institution Press, 1984.

Niu Deming, ed. *Zhongyao juece shijian yu sikao* (The practice of and reflections on the making of important decisions). Beijing: Shehui kexue wenxian chubanshe, 1992.

Nolan, Peter. "Decollectivization of Agriculture in China, 1979–1982: A Long-term Perspective." *Cambridge Journal of Economics* 7, nos. 3/4 (1983).

Nong mu yu ye fagui huibian (1949–1986) (A compendium of laws and regulations on agriculture, animal husbandry, and fishing, 1949–1986). Beijing: Nongye chubanshe, 1989.

Nongcun guding guanchadian bangongshi. *Quanguo nongcun shehui jingji dianxing diaocha shuju huibian* (Compendium of survey data on China's rural socioeconomic typical cases). Beijing: Zhonggong zhongyang dangxiao chubanshe, 1992.

————. *Wanshan zhong de nongcun shuangceng jingying tizhi* (The improving rural two-tiered operational system). Beijing: Zhonggong zhongyang dangxiao chubanshe, 1992.

Nongcun, Jingji, Shehui (Countryside, economy, society), vol. 1. Beijing: Zhishi chubanshe, 1985.

Nongcun jingji yu shehui bianjibu. *Zhongguo nongcun jingji gaige yu fazhan de taolun (1978–1990)* (Debates on China's rural economic reform and development). Beijing: Shehui kexue wenxian chubanshe, 1993.

Nongyebu bangongting, ed. *Zhonghua Renmin Gongheguo nongye zhengce fagui* xuanbian (1979) (Selected agricultural policies and regulations of the People's Republic of China, 1979). Beijing: Falü chubanshe, 1983.

Nongyebu zhengce tigai fagui si. "Dangqian nongye, nongmin ruogan wenti fenxi" (An analysis of various issues concerning agriculture and peasants). In Nongyebu zhengce tigai faui si, Zhongguo nongcun.

———. Zhongguo nongcun: Zhengce yanjiu beiwanglu (Rural China: policy research memoranda), vol. 3. Beijing: Gaige chubanshe, 1992.

North, Douglass C. "Economic Performance Through Time." American Economic Review 84, no. 3 (June 1994).

———. "Institutional Change: A Framework of Analysis." In Sjöstrand, ed.

———. "Institutions." Journal of Economic Perspectives 5, no. 1 (Winter 1991).

———. Institutions, Institutional Change and Economic Performance. Cambridge: Cambridge University Press, 1990.

———. Structure and Change in Economic History. New York: Norton, 1981.

North, Douglass C., and Robert Thomas. The Rise of the Western World: A New Economic History. Cambridge: Cambridge University Press, 1973.

Nove, Alec. An Economic History of the U.S.S.R. Harmondsworth: Penguin, 1989.

O'Brien, Kevin J. "Implementing Political Reform in China's Villages." Australian Journal of Chinese Affairs, no. 32 (July 1994).

Odgaard, Ole. "Inadequate and Inaccurate Chinese Statistics: The Case of Private Rural Enterprises." China Information 5, no. 3 (Winter 1990/91).

Ody, Anthony. Rural Enterprise Development in China, 1986–90. World Bank Discussion Papers no. 162. Washington, DC: World Bank, 1992.

Oi, Jean C. "The Chinese Village Incorporated." In Reynolds.

———. State and Peasant in Contemporary China: The Political Economy of Village Government. Berkeley: University of California Press, 1989.

Oksenberg, Michel C. "Policy Formulation in Communist China: The Case of the Mass Irrigation Campaign, 1957–58." Ph.D. diss. Columbia University, 1959.

Oksenberg, Michel C., and Sai-cheung Yeung. "Hua Kuo-feng's Pre-Cultural Revolution Hunan Years, 1949–66: The Making of a Political Generalist." China Quarterly, no. 69 (March 1977).

Oksenberg, Michel C., and Gail Henderson, eds. Research Guide to "People's Daily" Editorials, 1949–1975. Ann Arbor: University of Michigan, Center for Chinese Studies, 1982.

O'Leary, Greg, and Andrew Watson. "The Production Responsibility System and the Future of Collective Farming." Australian Journal of Chinese Affairs, no. 8 (1982).

Olson, Mancur. The Logic of Collective Action: Public Goods and the Theory of Groups. Cambridge, MA: Harvard University Press, 1965.

———. The Rise and Decline of Nations: Economic Growth, Stagflation, and Social Rigidities. New Haven, CT: Yale University Press, 1982.

O'Rourke, Kevin. "The Economic Impact of the Famine in the Short and Long Run." American Economic Review 84, no. 2 (May 1994).

Ou Yuanfang. Anhui baogan daohu yanjiu (A study of contracting everything to the household in Anhui). Hefei: Anhui renmin chubanshe, 1982.

Pan, Lynn. The New Chinese Revolution. Chicago: Contemporary, 1988.

Pan Zhifu, Zhang Zhengdong, Chen Yongxiao, and Lü Zuo, eds. Zhongguo renkou:

Guizhou fence (China's population: Guizhou volume). Beijing: Zhongguo cai-zheng jingji chubanshe, 1988.

Pang Xianzhi. "Mao Zedong he ta de mishu Tian Jiaying" (Mao Zedong and his secretary Tian Jiaying). In Dong, Tan, and Zeng.

Parish, William L., ed. *Chinese Rural Development: The Great Transformation.* Armonk, NY: M. E. Sharpe, 1985.

Parish, William L., and Martin King Whyte. *Village and Family in Contemporary China.* Chicago: University of Chicago Press, 1978.

Parker, Jeffrey. "China Tries Rural Democracy to Curb Warlords." Reuters, May 6, 1994.

Parker, William N., ed. *Economic History and the Modern Economist.* Oxford: Blackwell, 1986.

Peasant Daily Commentator. "Jianli shehui zhuyi laodongli liutong xinzhixu" (Build a new order of socialist labor circulation). *NMRB*, May 31, 1989; *Xinhua yuebao* (New China monthly digest), no. 6 (1989).

Peasant Daily Editorial Department. "Jianchi sanzhong quanhui fazhan nongye he nongcun gaige de jiben sixiang" (Adhere to the basic thinking of the third plenum on developing agricultural and rural reforms). *NMRB*, December 16, 1988.

Peng Dehuai. *Peng Dehuai zishu* (Peng Dehuai's autobiography). Beijing: Renmin chubanshe, 1981.

Peng Dehuai zhuan (A biography of Peng Dehuai). Beijing: Dangdai Zhongguo chubanshe, 1993.

Peng, Xizhe. "China's Population Control and the Reform in the 1980s." In Gupta, Stern, Hussain, and Byrd.

———. "Demographic Consequences of the Great Leap Forward in China's Provinces," *Population and Development Review* 13, no. 4 (December 1987).

Pennell, W. V. "The Long March Back," *Current Scene* 2, no. 9 (February 15, 1963).

People's Daily Commentator. "Have Correct Understanding About Strategic Position of Township and Town Enterprises." *RMRB*, May 7, 1991, p. 2; FBIS-CHI-91-093, May 14, 1991.

Perdue, Peter C. *Exhausting the Earth: State and Peasant in Hunan, 1500–1850.* Cambridge, MA: Harvard University, Council on East Asian Studies, 1987.

Perkins, Dwight H. *Agricultural Development in China, 1368–1969.* Chicago: Aldine, 1969.

———. "China's Economic Policy and Performance." In MacFarquhar and Fairbank, vol. 15.

———. *Market Control and Planning in Communist China.* Cambridge, MA: Harvard University Press, 1966.

———. "The Prospects for China's Economic Reforms." In A. J. Kane.

———, ed. *Rural Small-Scale Industry in the People's Republic of China.* Berkeley: University of California Press, 1977.

Perkins, Dwight H., and Shahid Yusuf. *Rural Development in China.* Baltimore: Johns Hopkins University Press, for the World Bank, 1984.

Perry, Elizabeth J. "Casting a Chinese 'Democracy' Movement: The Roles of Students, Workers, and Entrepreneurs." In Wasserstrom and Perry.

———. "Implications of Household Contracting in China: The Case of Fengyang County." In Rhee.

Perry, Elizabeth J., and Christine Wong, eds. *The Political Economy of Reform in Post-Mao China*. Cambridge, MA: Harvard University, Council on East Asian Studies, 1985.

Polsby, Nelson. *Political Innovation in America: The Politics of Policy Initiation*. New Haven, CT: Yale University Press, 1984.

Popper, Karl R. *The Poverty of Historicism*. London: Routledge & Kegan Paul, 1957.

Potter, Sulamith Heins, and Jack M. Potter. *China's Peasants: The Anthropology of a Revolution*. Cambridge: Cambridge University Press, 1990.

Pryor, Frederic L. "The Performance of Agricultural Production in Marxist and Non-Marxist Nations." *Comparative Economic Studies* 33, no. 3 (Fall 1991).

———. *The Red and the Green: The Rise and Fall of Collectivized Agriculture in Marxist Regimes*. Princeton, NJ: Princeton University Press, 1992.

Putterman, Louis, and Gilbert L. Skillman. "Collectivization and China's Agricultural Crisis." *Journal of Comparative Economics* 17, no. 2 (June 1993).

Pye, Lucian W. "On Chinese Pragmatism in the 1980s." *China Quarterly*, no. 106 (June 1986).

———. "Reassessing the Cultural Revolution." *China Quarterly*, no. 108 (December 1986).

Qiang Yuanxin and Lin Bangguang. "Shilun yijiu wuwu nian dangnei guanyu nongye hezuohua wenti de zhenglun" (A preliminary discussion on the 1955 intraparty debate about agricultural collectivization). *Dangshi yanjiu* (Party history research), no. 1 (February 1981).

Qiu Yizhong. "Shisheng qingyi qiangiu song" (The celebrated bonds of friendship between teacher and student). *RMRB*, overseas ed., January 7, 1994.

Qu Kunqiang. "Sichuan sheng baochan daohu de zuizao tichuze jiqi zaoyu" (The person who was the first to devise the household contracting system in Sichuan and his bitter experience). In Zhang Xiaoli.

Quan Yanchi. *Mao Zedong yu Heluxiaofu* (Mao Zedong and Khrushchev). Changchun: Jilin renmin chubanshe, 1989.

———. *Zouxia shentan de Mao Zedong* (Mao Zedong off the shrine). Hong Kong: Nanyue chubanshe, 1990.

———. *Zouxia shentan de Zhou Enlai* (Zhou Enlai in real life). Hong Kong: Tandi tushu, 1993.

Ranis, Gustav, and T. Paul Schultz, eds. *The State of Development Economics: Progress and Perspectives*. Oxford: Blackwell, 1988.

Raphael, Beverley. *When Disaster Strikes: How Individuals and Communities Cope with Catastrophe*. New York: Basic, 1986.

Research Staff of the Secretariat, Institute of the Pacific, comp. and trans. *Agrarian China: Selected Source Materials from Chinese Authors*. London: Allen & Unwin, 1939.

"Renqing nongcun dahao xingshi, jixu jianchi luoshi zhengce" (Recognize the excellent situation in rural areas, continue to insist on the implementation of policies). *RMRB*, September 17, 1979.

Reynolds, Bruce, ed. *Chinese Economic Policy*. New York: Paragon House, 1988.

Rhee, Sang-Woo, ed. *China's Reform Politics: Policies and Their Implications*. Seoul: Sogang University Press, 1986.

Riskin, Carl. *China's Political Economy: The Quest for Development Since 1949*. Oxford: Oxford University Press, 1987.

RMRB Commentator. "Jizhong liliang zhuahao dangqian nongye shengchan" (Concentrate efforts and grasp well the agricultural production of the moment). *RMRB*, April 6, 1979.

RMRB Special Commentator. "Tantan luoshi nongcun jingji zhengce zhong de jige renshi wenti" (On several epistemological questions concerning the implementation of rural economic policies). *RMRB*, July 29, 1978.

Robinson, Thomas W., ed. *The Cultural Revolution in China.* Berkeley: University of California Press, 1971.

Robinson, W. S. "Ecological Correlations and the Behavior of Individuals." *American Sociological Review* 15, no. 3 (June 1950).

Rogowski, Ronald. *Commerce and Coalitions: How Trade Affects Domestic Political Alignments.* Princeton, NJ: Princeton University Press, 1989.

Ross, Lee, and Richard Nisbett. *The Person and the Situation: Perspectives of Social Psychology.* New York: McGraw-Hill, 1991.

Ruan Ming. *Deng Xiaoping diguo* (The Deng Xiaoping empire). Taibei: Shibao wenhua chuban qiye youxian gongsi, 1992.

Rummel, R. J. *China's Bloody Century: Genocide and Mass Murder Since 1900.* New Brunswick, NJ: Transaction, 1991.

Rural Development Institute. *Nongye jingji yanjiu wenji* (Collected studies on the rural economy). 3 vols. Shanghai: Xuelin chubanshe, 1986.

Ruttan, Vernon W., and Yujiro Hayami. "Strategies for Agricultural Development." *Food Research Institute Studies in Agricultural Economics, Trade and Development* 9, no. 2 (1972).

———. "Toward a Theory of Induced Institutional Innovation." *Journal of Development Studies* 20, no. 4 (July 1984).

Ruzicka, Lado, Guillaume Wunsch, and Penny Kane, eds. *Differential Mortality: Methodological Issues and Biosocial Factors.* Oxford: Clarendon Press, 1989.

Saich, Tony, ed. *The Chinese People's Movement: Perspectives on Spring 1989.* Armonk, NY: M. E. Sharpe, 1990.

Samuelson, William, and Richard Zeckhauser. "Status Quo Bias in Decision Making." *Journal of Risk and Uncertainty* 1, no. 1 (March 1988).

Schelling, Thomas C. *Micromotives and Macrobehavior.* New York: Norton, 1978.

Schoenhals, Michael. "The 1978 Truth Criterion Controversy." *China Quarterly*, no. 126 (June 1991).

———. *Saltationist Socialism: Mao Zedong and the Great Leap Forward, 1958.* Stockholm: University of Stockholm, Institutionen for Orientaliska Sprak, 1987.

Schram, Stuart R. "Chairman Hua Edits Mao's Literary Heritage: 'On the 10 Great Relationships.'" *China Quarterly*, no. 69 (March 1977).

———. "China After the 13th Congress." *China Quarterly*, no. 114 (June 1988).

———. *Ideology and Policy in China Since the Third Plenum, 1978–84.* Research Notes and Studies no. 6. London: School of Oriental and African Studies, Contemporary China Institute, 1984.

———. *The Thought of Mao Tse-Tung.* Cambridge: Cambridge University Press, 1989.

Schultz, Theodore W. "Institutions and the Rising Economic Value of Man." *American Journal of Agricultural Economics* 50, no. 5 (1968).

———*Transforming Traditional Agriculture.* Chicago: University of Chicago Press, [1964] 1983.

Schurmann, Franz. *Ideology and Organization in Communist China*. 2d ed. Berkeley: University of California Press, 1968.

Scott, James C. "Everyday Forms of Resistance." In Colburn.

———. *The Moral Economy of the Peasant*. New Haven, CT: Yale University Press, 1976.

———. *Weapons of the Weak*. New Haven, CT: Yale University Press, 1985.

Scott, W. Richard. "The Adolescence of Institutional Theory." *Administrative Science Quarterly* 32, no. 4 (December 1987).

Segal, Gerald, and Tony Saich. "Quarterly Chronicle and Documentation (July–September 1980)." *China Quarterly*, no. 84 (December 1980).

Selden, Mark. "Cooperation and Conflict: Cooperative and Collective Formation in China's Countryside." In Selden and Lippit.

Selden, Mark, and Victor Lippit, eds. *The Transition to Socialism in China*. Armonk, NY: M. E. Sharpe, 1982.

Sen, Amartya. "Indian Development: Lessons and Non-Lessons." *Daedalus* 118, no. 4 (Fall 1989).

———. *Poverty and Famines: An Essay on Entitlement and Deprivation*. Oxford: Clarendon Press, 1981.

Sewell, William, Jr. "A Theory of Structure: Duality, Agency, and Transformation." *American Journal of Sociology* 98, no. 1 (July 1992).

Shambaugh, David L. *The Making of a Premier: Zhao Ziyang's Provincial Career*. Boulder, CO: Westview, 1984.

Shandong sheng nongye hezuohua shiliaoji (A compendium of historical materials on agricultural collectivization in Shandong province). 2 vols. Jinan: Shandong renmin chubanshe, 1989.

Shanin, Teodor. *The Awkward Class: Political Sociology of Peasantry in a Developing Society: Russia, 1910–1925*. Oxford: Clarendon Press, 1972.

Shanxi sishi nian bianji weiyuanhui. *Shanxi sishi nian 1949–1989* (Shanxi's forty years, 1949–1989). Beijing: Zhongguo tongji chubanshe, 1989.

Shen Chong and Xiang Xiyang, eds. *Shinian lai: lilun, zhengce, shijian—ziliao xuanbian* (For the last ten years: theory, policy, and practice—selected documents), vol. 2. Beijing: Qiushi chubanshe, 1988.

Shi Zhongquan. *Zhou Enlai de zhuoyue gongxian* (Zhou Enlai's outstanding contributions). Beijing: Zhonggong zhongyang dangxiao chubanshe, 1993.

Shirk, Susan. "The Political Economy of Chinese Industrial Reform." In Nee and Stark.

———. *The Political Logic of Economic Reform in China*. Berkeley: University of California Press, 1993.

Shue, Vivienne. "China: Transition Postponed?" *Problems of Communism* 41, nos. 1–2 (January–April 1992).

———. "The Fate of the Commune." *Modern China* 10, no. 3 (July 1984).

———. *Peasant China in Transition: The Dynamics of Development Toward Socialism, 1949–1956*. Berkeley: University of California Press, 1980.

———. *The Reach of the State: Sketches of the Chinese Body Politic*. Stanford, CA: Stanford University Press, 1988.

Sichuan Sheng Nongye Hezuo Jingji Shiliao Bianjizu. "Sichuan sheng nongye hezuo jingji fazhan de huigu yu fansi" (Review and reflections on the development of the agricultural cooperative economy in Sichuan). In Zhang Xiaoli.

Sicular, Terry. "Rural Marketing and Exchange in the Wake of Recent Reforms." In Perry and Wong.

Simon, Herbert A. "Human Nature in Politics: The Dialogue of Psychology with Political Science." *American Political Science Review* 79, no. 2 (June 1985).

———. *Models of Bounded Rationality.* Vols. 1–2. Cambridge, MA: MIT Press, 1982.

———. "Rational Choice and the Structure of the Environment." *Psychological Review* 63, no. 2 (1956).

Simon, Herbert A., et al. "Decision Making and Problem Solving." In Zey.

Sjöstrand, Sven Erik. "On Institutional Thought in the Social and Economic Sciences." In Sjöstrand, ed.

———, ed. *Institutional Change: Theory and Empirical Findings.* Armonk, NY: M. E. Sharpe, 1993.

Solinger, Dorothy J. "China's Transients and the State." *Politics and Society* 21, no. 1 (March 1993).

———. *From Lathes to Looms: China's Industrial Policy in Comparative Perspective, 1979–1982.* Stanford, CA: Stanford University Press, 1991.

Solow, Robert M. "Economic History and Economics." *American Economic Review* 75, no. 2 (May 1985).

Somit, Albert, and Steven A. Peterson, eds. *The Dynamics of Evolution: The Punctuated Equilibrium Debate in the Natural and Social Sciences.* Ithaca, NY: Cornell University Press, 1992.

Song Xigong, Zhang Zengzhi, Wang Mingzhong, and Mao Zhaohui, eds. *Zhongguo renkou: Neimenggu fence* (China's population: Inner Mongolia volume). Beijing: Zhongguo caizheng jingji chubanshe, 1987.

Stark, Oded. *The Migration of Labor.* Cambridge, MA: Blackwell, 1991.

State Statistical Bureau. *Guanghui de sanshiwu nian* (The glorious thirty-five years). Beijing: Zhongguo tongji chubanshe, 1984.

———. *Quanguo gesheng zizhiqu zhixiashi lishi tongji ziliao huibian 1949–1989* (Compendium of historical statistics for Chinese provincial-level units, 1949–1989). Beijing: Zhongguo tongji chubanshe, 1990.

———. *Zhongguo guding zichan touzi tongji ziliao 1950–1985* (China fixed asset investment statistics, 1950–1985). Beijing: Zhongguo tongji chubanshe, 1987.

———. *Zhongguo nongcun tongji nianjian* (China rural statistics yearbook). Beijing: Zhongguo tongji chubanshe, various years.

———. *Zhongguo tongji nianjian* (Statistical yearbook of China). Beijing: Zhongguo tonji chubanshe, various years; Hong Kong: Jingji daobao she, various years.

Statistical Bureau of Shanghai. *Shanghai tongji nianjian 1989* (Statistical yearbook of Shanghai, 1989). Beijing: Zhongguo tongji chubanshe, 1989.

Steinmo, Sven, Kathleen Thelen, and Frank Longstreth, eds. *Structuring Politics: Historical Institutionalism in Comparative Analysis.* Cambridge: Cambridge University Press, 1992.

Stinchcombe, Arthur. "Social Structure and Organizations." In March, ed.

Stolper, Wolfgang Friedrich, and Paul A. Samuelson. "Protection and Real Wages." *Review of Economic Studies* 9, no.1 (Winter 1941).

Su Suining. "Nongcun ganqun guanxi jinzhang de yuanyin shi duo fangmian de" (The strained rural cadre-mass relations have many causes). *NMRB*, September 26, 1988, p. 1.

Su Xiaokang, Luo Shixu, and Zhen Zheng. *Wutuobang ji* (Sacrifice to utopia). Hong Kong: Cunzhenshe, 1988.

Su Ya and Jia Lusheng. *Shui lai chengbao?* (Who contracts [for China]?). Guangzhou: Huacheng chubanshe, 1990.

Suedfeld, Peter, and Philip E. Tetlock. "Psychological Advice About Political Decision Making: Heuristics, Biases, and Cognitive Defects." In Suedfeld and Tetlock.

————, eds. *Psychology and Social Policy*. New York: Hemisphere, 1992.

Sun, Lena H. "China's Villagers Vent Hatred at Leaders They Say Are Corrupt; Party Braces for Trouble As Peasant Protests Mount." *Washington Post*, April 28, 1994.

Sun Qitai and Xiong Zhiyong. *Dazhai hongqi de shengqi yu zhuiluo* (The rise and fall of the red banner of Dazhai). Zhengzhou: Henan renmin chubanshe, 1990.

Sun Yefang Jingji Kexue Jiangli Jijin Weiyuanhui Bangongshi. *Sun Yefang jingji kexue jijin huojiang wenji* (A collection of award-winning writings from the Sun Yefang economic science fund). Beijing: Zhongguo shehui kexue chubanshe, 1991.

Tainter, Joseph. *The Collapse of Complex Societies*. Cambridge: Cambridge University Press, 1988.

Tan Zhenlin. "Jicheng he fazhan Mao Zedong sixiang" (Carry on and develop Mao Zedong's thought). *RMRB*, December 7, 1983; repr. in Tan Zhenlin Zhuan Bianji Weiyuanhui.

Tan Zhenlin Zhuan Bianji Weiyuanhui. *Tan Zhenlin zhuan* (A biography of Tan Zhenlin). Hangzhou: Zhejiang renmin chubanshe, 1992.

Tan Zhenqiu, ed. *Mao Zedong wai xun ji* (Mao Zedong's provincial tours). Changsha: Hunan wenyi chubanshe, 1993.

Tan Zongji et al. *Shinian hou de pingshuo* (Comments in the aftermath of the cultural revolution). Beijing: Zhonggong dangshi ziliao chubanshe, 1987.

Tan Zongtai, Cheng Du, and Liang Wenda, eds. *Zhongguo renkou: Hubei fence* (China's population: Hubei volume). Beijing: Zhongguo caizheng jingji chubanshe, 1988.

Tang, Anthony M. *An Analytical and Empirical Investigation of Agriculture in Mainland China, 1952–1980*. Taibei: Chung-Hua Institution for Economic Research, 1984.

Tang Zhongxin. *Nongcun liangchu le huangpai* (The yellow card flashes for the countryside). Beijing: Zhongguo funü chubanshe, 1989.

Tao Kai, Chen Yide, and Dai Qing. "Zouchu xiandai mixin" (Beyond modern superstition). In Ling Xin.

Taylor, Jeffrey R. "Rural Employment Trends and the Legacy of Surplus Labor, 1978–1986." *China Quarterly*, no. 116 (December 1988).

Taylor, Jeffrey R., and Judith Banister. "Surplus Rural Labor in the People's Republic of China." In Veeck.

Taylor, Michael. "Structure, Culture, and Action in the Explanation of Social Change." In Booth, James, and Meadwell.

Teiwes, Frederick C. "Establishment and Consolidation of the New Regime." In MacFarquhar and Fairbank, vol. 14.

————. "Mao and His Lieutenants." *Australian Journal of Chinese Affairs*, nos. 19–20 (1988).

————. "Provincial Politics in China: Themes and Variations." In Lindbeck.

Thelen, Kathleen, and Sven Steinmo. "Historical Institutionalism in Comparative Politics." In Steinmo, Thelen, and Longstreth.

Thurston, Anne. "The Dragon Stirs." *Wilson Quarterly* 17, no. 2 (Spring 1993).

Tian Jiyun. "Guanyu wending nongcun jiben zhengce de jige wenti" (Several issues concerning the stabilization of rural basic policy). In *XNNWX*.

————. "Jiefang sixiang, zhuazhu jiyu, jiakuai zhongxibu xiangzhen qiye de fazhan" (Emancipate thinking, seize the opportunity, and accelerate rural enterprise development in central and western regions). *Xinhua yuebao* (New China monthly digest), no. 11 (1992).

Tian Wenxi, and Yao Liwen. "Yifen shengwei wenjian de dansheng" (The birth of a provincial [party] committee document). *RMRB*, February 3, 1978.

Ting Wang. *Chairman Hua: Leader of the Chinese Communists.* Montreal: McGill-Queen's University Press, 1980.

Treadgold, Donald, ed. *Soviet and Chinese Communism: Similarities and Differences.* Seattle: University of Washington Press, 1967.

Tsou, Tang. *The Cultural Revolution and Post-Mao Reforms: A Historical Perspective.* Chicago: University of Chicago Press, 1986.

————. "Mao Zedong Thought, the Last Struggle for Succession, and the Post-Mao Era." *China Quarterly*, no. 71 (September 1977).

Tsou, Tang, Marc Blecher, and Mitch Meisner. "The Responsibility System in Agriculture: Its Implementation in Xiyang and Dazhai." *Modern China* 8, no. 1 (January 1982).

Tucker, Robert C., ed. *The Marx-Engels Reader.* 2d ed. New York: Norton, 1978.

Tversky, Amos. "Features of Similarity." *Psychological Review* 84, no. 4 (July 1977).

Tversky, Amos, and Daniel Kahneman. "Availability: A Heuristic for Judging Frequency and Probability." *Cognitive Psychology* 5, no. 2 (September 1973).

Unger, Jonathan. "The Decollectivization of the Chinese Countryside: A Survey of Twenty-eight Villages." *Pacific Affairs* 58, no. 4 (Winter 1985–86).

————. "State and Peasant in Post-Revolution China." *Journal of Peasant Studies* 17, no. 1 (October 1989).

Veeck, Gregory, ed. *The Uneven Landscape: Geographic Studies in Post-Reform China.* Geoscience and Man: no. 30. Baton Rouge, LA: Geoscience, 1991.

Vogel, Ezra F. *Canton Under Communism: Programs and Politics in a Provincial Capital, 1949–1968.* Cambridge, MA: Harvard University Press, 1969.

————. "China and the East Asian Modernization Model." In Reynolds.

Wakeman, Frederic, Jr. *Strangers at the Gate: Social Disorder in South China, 1839–1861.* Berkeley: University of California Press, 1966.

Walker, Kenneth R. "Chinese Agriculture During the Period of the Readjustment, 1978–83." *China Quarterly*, no. 100 (December 1984).

————. "Collectivization in Retrospect: The 'Socialist High Tide' of Autumn 1955–Spring 1956." *China Quarterly*, no. 26 (April–June 1966).

————. *Food Grain Procurement and Consumption in China.* Cambridge: Cambridge University Press, 1984.

————. *Planning in Chinese Agriculture.* London: Cass, 1965.

Wan Li. "Renzhen luoshi dang de nongcun jingji zhengce" (Conscientiously carry out the party's rural economic policy). *RMRB*, March 17, 1978.

Wang Gengjin, Yang Xun, Wang Ziping, Liang Xiaodong, and Yang Guansan, eds.

Xiangcun sanshi nian: Fengyang nongcun shehui jingji fazhan shilu (1949–1983 nian) (The countryside over three decades: A veritable record of rural socio-economic development in Fengyang, 1949–1983). 2 pts. Beijing: Nongcun duwu chubanshe, 1989.

Wang Guichen and Wei Daonan. "Lianxi chanliang de shengchan zerenzhi shi yizhong hao banfa" (Output-linked production responsibility system is a good method). In Sun Yefang Jingji Kexue Jiangli Jijin Weiyuanhui Bangongshi.

Wang Guichen, Wei Daonan, and Qin Qiming. *Nongye shengchan zerenzhi de jianli he fazhan* (The establishment and development of the production responsibility system in agriculture). Hebei: Hebei renmin chubanshe, 1984.

Wang Guichen, Zhou Qiren, et al. *Smashing the Communal Pot: Formulation and Development of China's Rural Responsibility System.* Beijing: New World, 1985.

Wang Hongmo, Huang Jianqiu, Sun Dali, Wei Xinsheng, and Zhang Zhanbin. *Gaige kaifang de licheng* (The course of reform and opening up). Zhengzhou: Henan renmin chubanshe, 1989.

Wang Huimin. "Nongye shidu guimo jingying" (Appropriate scale operations in agriculture." In Nongcun jingji yu shehui bianjibu.

Wang Lixin. "Life After Mao Zedong: A Report on Implementation of and Consequences of Major Chinese Agricultural Policies in Anhui Villages." *Kunlun*, no. 6 (December 1988); JPRS-CAR-89-079, July 28, 1989.

Wang Mingyuan, ed. *Zhongguo renkou: Hebei fence* (China's population: Hebei volume). Beijing: Zhongguo caizheng jingji chubanshe, 1987.

Wang Pu. "Silu geng guang xie geng huo xie" ([Make our] thinking broader and more flexible). *RMRB*, January 18, 1980.

Wang Renzhong, Jin Ming, Yong Wentao, and Yu Mingtao. "Songshu de fengge changcun" (Long live the pine tree's [upright] style). In Zheng and Shu.

Wang Sijun and Wang Ruizi, eds. *Zhongguo renkou: Zhejiang fence* (China's population: Zhejiang volume). Beijing: Zhongguo caizheng jingji chubanshe, 1988.

Wang Songpei. "Yunnan shanqu jingji lilun taolunhui xueshu guandian zongshu" (A summary of academic viewpoints presented at the Yunnan theoretical forum on the economy of mountainous areas). *NYJJWT*, no. 8 (1980).

Wang Xueqi, Yang Shubiao, Shen Jiashan, and Yao Hongrui. *Zhongguo shehui zhuyi shigao* (A history of China's socialist period), vol. 2. Hangzhou: Zhejiang renmin chubanshe, 1988.

Wang Yu. *Dazhuanbian shiqi* (The era of great transformation). Shijiazhuang: Hebei renmin chubanshe, 1987.

Wang Yuzhao. "Woguo jingji tizhi gaige de yi xiang lishixing juece" (A historic decision is reforming the economic system of our country). In Niu.

Wang Zhenmin. "Anhui Fengyang nongcun xinmao" (The new look of rural Fengyang in Anhui). *Nongye jingji wenti* (Problems in agricultural economy), no. 9 (1982).

Wang Zhenyao. "Nongcun jiceng zhengquan jiegou de yanbian yu zhengce xuanze" (The evolution of rural basic level political structure and policy choices). In Development Research Institute.

Wang Zhongjie, Chen Qinglin, and Ye Jianjun. "Shixi 1961 nian Liu Shaoqi Hunan dundian diaocha" (A preliminary analysis of Liu Shaoqi's on-the-spot investigation in Hunan in 1961). In *Liu Shaoqi yanjiu lunwenji.*

Wasserstrom, Jeffrey N., and Elizabeth J. Perry, eds. *Popular Protest and Political Culture in Modern China: Learning from 1989.* Boulder, CO: Westview, 1992.

Watkins, Susan Cotts, and Jane Menken. "Famines in Historical Perspective." *Population and Development Review* 11, no. 4 (December 1985).

Watson, Andrew. "Agriculture Looks for 'Shoes That Fit': The Production Responsibility System and Its Implications." In Maxwell and McFarlane.

———. "The Family Farm, Land Use and Accumulation in Agriculture." *Australian Journal of Chinese Affairs*, no. 17 (January 1987).

———, ed. *Economic Reform and Social Change in China*. London: Routledge, 1992.

Watson, Andrew, Christopher Findlay, and Du Yintang. "Who Won the 'Wool War'?" *China Quarterly*, no. 118 (June 1989).

Weber, Max. *Economy and Society*. Ed. Guenther Roth and Claus Wittich. Berkeley: University of California Press, 1978.

Wegren, Stephen K. "Dilemmas of Agrarian Reform." *Soviet Studies* 44, no. 1 (1992).

Weir, Margaret. "Ideas and the Politics of Bounded Innovation." In Steinmo, Thelen, and Longstreth.

Wen, G. James. "The Current Land Tenure System and Its Impact on Long Term Performance of Farming Sector: The Case of Modern China." Ph.D. diss. University of Chicago, 1989.

White, Lynn T. III. *Policies of Chaos: The Organizational Causes of Violence in China's Cultural Revolution*. Princeton, NJ: Princeton University Press, 1989.

White, Tyrene. "From Cadres to Personnel: The Impact of Reform on Rural Administration in China." Paper presented at the Annual Meeting of the Association for Asian Studies, New Orleans, LA, April 11–14, 1991.

———. "Political Reform and Rural Government." In Davis and Vogel.

———. "Postrevolutionary Mobilization in China: The One-Child Policy Reconsidered." *World Politics* 43, no. 1 (October 1990).

———. "Reforming the Countryside." *Current History* 91 (September 1992).

Who's Who in China: Current Leaders. Beijing: Foreign Languages, 1989.

Whyte, Martin K. "Family Change in China." *Issues and Studies* 15, no. 7 (July 1979).

Wolf, Eric R. *Peasant Wars of the Twentieth Century*. New York: Harper & Row, 1969.

Womack, Brantly. "Politics and Epistemology in China Since Mao." *China Quarterly*, no. 80 (December 1979).

Wong, Christine. "Central-Local Relations in an Era of Fiscal Decline." *China Quarterly*, no. 128 (December 1991).

———. "Fiscal Reform and Local Industrialization." *Modern China* 18, no. 2 (April 1992).

———. "Interpreting Rural Industrial Growth in the Post-Mao Period." *Modern China* 14, no. 1 (January 1988).

———. "The Maoist 'Model' Reconsidered: Local Self-Reliance and the Financing of Rural Industrialization." In Joseph, Wong, and Zweig.

Wong, Jan. "Petty Local Communist Party Cadres, Oppressors of the Peasants." *Globe and Mail*, April 18, 1994.

Wong, John. *Labor Mobilization in the Chinese Commune System: A Perspective from Guangdong*. Bangkok: ILO-ARTEP, 1982.

World Bank. *China: Socialist Economic Development*. Vol. 1: *The Economy, Statistical System, and Basic Data*; Vol. 2: *The Economic Sectors: Agriculture, Industry, Energy, Transport, and External Trade and Finance*. Washington, DC: World Bank, 1983.

Wu Si. *Chen Yonggui chenfu Zhongnanhai: Gaizao Zhongguo de shiyan* (The rise and fall of Chen Yonggui in Chinese politics: an experiment for transforming China). Guangzhou: Huacheng chubanshe, 1993.

Wu Si and Liu Qing. "Lishi xing de wenjian he wenjian de lishi" (Historic documents and the history of documents). *NMRB*, December 22, 1988.

Wu Xiang. "Nongcun gaige de lishi huigu" (A historical review of the rural reforms). In Du Runsheng et al.

———. *Woguo nongcun weida xiwang zhi suozai* (The great hope of the countryside in our country). Beijing: Jingji kexue chubanshe, 1984.

———. "Yangguandao yu dumuqiao" (The open road and the single-log bridge). In Wu Xiang, *Woguo nongcun.*

Wu Xiang, Liu Jiarui, and Xu Zhongying. "Xiyue he xiwang" (Happiness and hope). *RMRB*, October 10, 1979.

Wu Yu. "Bo Yibo lun Ke Qingshi" (Bo Yibo on Ke Qingshi). *Zhongguo shibao zhoukan* (China times weekly), April 3, 1994.

Wu Yulin and Chen Longfei, eds. *Zhongguo renkou: Shandong fence* (China's population: Shandong volume). Beijing: Zhongguo caizheng jingji chubanshe, 1989.

Xia Hai. "Lun jiceng xiang zhengquan jianshe zhong de jige wenti" (On several problems in building basic-level township political power). In Zhang Yunlun.

Xiao Shimao and Xu Xiji. "Guanche baogong daozu zeren zhi yao pi jizuo" (In implementing the responsibility system of contracting work to the group, [we] must criticize extreme leftism). *RMRB*, April 29, 1979.

Xie Chuntao. *Dayuejin kuanglan* (The raging tide of the great leap forward). Henan: Henan renmin chubanshe, 1990.

Xie Minggan and Luo Yuanming, eds. *Zhongguo jingji fazhan sishinian* (Forty years of Chinese economic development). Beijing: Renmin chubanshe, 1990.

Xin Sheng and Lu Jiafeng. "Zhengque kandai lianxi chanliang de zeren zhi" (Treat the output-linked responsibility system correctly). *RMRB*, March 30, 1979, p. 1.

Xinshiqi nongye he nongcun gongzuo zhongyao wenxian xuanbian (Compendium of important documents on agriculture and rural work in the new era). Beijing: Zhongyang wenxian chubanshe, 1992.

Xue Muqiao. *Current Economic Problems in China.* Ed. and trans. K. K. Fung. Boulder, CO: Westview, 1982.

———. *Gaige yu lilun shang de tupo* (The breakthrough in reform and theory). Beijing: Renmin chubanshe, 1988.

———. "Zai Zhou Enlai tongzhi lingdao xia gongzuo de huiyi" (A recollection of my work under Zhou Enlai). In "Huainian Zhou Enlai."

———, ed. *Almanac of China's Economy, 1981.* Hong Kong: Modern Cultural Co., 1982.

Xuexi ziliao (Study materials), vols. 2–3. N.p., n.d.

Xun Dazhi, Ye Baishou, and Fang Xiangdong. "Dangqian jingji xingshi: Maodun fenxi yu zouchu kunjing de xuanze" (The current economic situation: an analysis of contradictions and the strategies for getting out of the straits). *Jingji yanjiu* (Economic research), no. 4 (1992).

Yang, Dali. "China Adjusts to the World Economy: The Political Economy of China's Coastal Development Strategy." *Pacific Affairs* 64, no. 1 (Spring 1991).

———. "Reform and Intra-Provincial Inequality in China" (in Chinese translation). *Zhongguo gongye jingji* (China's industrial economy), no. 1 (January 1995). [English version available from the author upon request.]

Yang Jianwen, Ge Zhengliang, Peng Jinguan, Zhang Zuguo, and Chen Wei, eds. *Zhongguo dangdai jingji sichao* (Trends of economic thought in contemporary China). Shanghai: Sanlian shudian, 1991.

Yang Minqing and Tian Xuexiang. "Cong Xiaogang heihui dao Wan Li bianfa" (From the secret meeting of Xiaogang to Wan Li's reforms). In Ning Yuan.

Yang Wenliang and Huo Guoming. "Jinnian wancheng liangshi dinggou renwu nandu zengda" (The difficulty of fulfilling this year's grain procurement task has increased). *NMRB*, June 14, 1989.

Yang Xun and Liu Jiarui. *Zhongguo nongcun gaige de daolu* (The path of Chinese rural reforms). Beijing: Beijing daxue chubanshe, 1987.

Yang Zhongmei. *Hu Yaobang*. Hunan: Hunan renmin chubanshe, 1989.

Yeh, K. C. "Soviet and Communist Chinese Industrialization Strategies." In Treadgold.

Yu Zuyao. "Nongye shixing baogan daohu shi woguo jingji tizhi gaige de qianzou" (The adoption of contracting everything to the household is a prelude to the economic system reform of our country). *JJYJ*, no. 3 (1983).

Yuan Yongsong and Wang Junwei. *Zuoqing ershi nian 1957–1976* (Twenty years of leftism, 1957–1976). Beijing: Nongcun duwu chubanshe, 1993.

Zeng Zhi. "Tao Zhu zai zuihou de suiyue li" (Tao Zhu's last days). In Zheng and Shu.

Zey, Mary, ed. *Decision Making: Alternatives to Rational Choice Models*. Newbury Park, CA: Sage, 1992.

Zhan Wu. "Fazhan nongye de zhengque juece" (Correct policies for developing agriculture). *NYJJWT*, no. 8 (1980).

Zhang Guangyou. *Lianchan chengbao zerenzhi de youlai yu fazhan* (The origins and development of the output-linked contract responsibility system). Henan: Henan renmin chubanshe, 1983.

Zhang Guangyou and Huang Zhenggen. "Zhongzai zhihou fang Anhui" (Visiting Anhui after the severe drought). *RMRB*, January 23, 1979.

Zhang Guangyou and Liu Zongtang. "Shengchandui you le zizhuquan nongye bi zengchan" (Agricultural output will increase once the production teams are given their autonomy). *RMRB*, February 16, 1978.

Zhang Guangyou, Tian Wenxi, and Duanmu Laidi. "Zhengce diaodong le qianjun wanma" ([Good] policy has motivated the masses). *RMRB*, April 18, 1978.

Zhang Guorong. "Face Up to Problems, Forge Ahead by Doing Pioneering Work." *RMRB*, July 21, 1991, p. 2; FBIS-CHI-91-147, July 31, 1991.

Zhang Hao. "Sanji suoyou, dui wei jichu' yinggai wending," ([The system of] three-tiered ownership with the team as the foundation should be stabilized). *RMRB*, March 15, 1979.

Zhang Mengyi. "Wei shixian nongcun laodongli zhuanyi, shehuixuejia fenfen xianji xiance" (Sociologists suggest strategies for realizing the transfer of the rural labor force). *RMRB*, overseas ed., August 14, 1991.

Zhang Qingwu. "Basic Facts on the Household Registration System." Ed. and trans. Michael Dutton. *Chinese Economic Studies* 22, no. 1 (Fall 1988).

Zhang Weixuan, Liu Wuyi, and Xiao Xing, eds. *Gongheguo fengyun sishinian 1949–1989* (The republic's forty stormy years, 1949–1989). Beijing: Zhongguo zhengfa daxue chubanshe, 1989.

Zhang Wentian. *Zhang Wentian xuanji* (Selected works of Zhang Wentian). Beijing: Renmin chubanshe, 1985.

Zhang Xiaoli, ed. *Sichuan sheng nongye hezuo jingji shiliao* (Historical materials on the agricultural cooperative economy in Sichuan province). Chengdu: Sichuan kexue jishu chubanshe, 1989.

Zhang Yi. "Xin xingshi xia dui xiangzhen qiye de jidian renshi" (A few items of understanding on rural enterprises under the new situation). *Jingji ribao* (Economic daily), June 6, 1989; repr. in *Xinhua yuebao* (New China monthly digest), no. 6 (1989).

Zhang Yunlun, ed. *Zhongguo jigou de yange* (The evolution of organizations in China). Beijing: Zhongguo jingji chubanshe, 1988.

Zhao Dexin, comp. *Zhonghua Renmin Gongheguo jingji zhuanti dashiji* (A chronology of major economic events in the People's Republic of China, arranged by subject). Vol. 1: *1949–1966*; Vol. 2: *1967–1984*. Zhengzhou: Henan renmin chubanshe, 1989.

———, ed. *Zhonghua Renmin Gongheguo jingjishi* (An economic history of the People's Republic of China). 4 vols. Vol. 1: *1949–1956*; Vol. 2: *1957–1966*; Vol. 3: *1967–1976*; Vol. 4: *1977–1984*. Zhengzhou: Henan renmin chubanshe, 1989.

Zhao Fasheng, ed. *Dangdai Zhongguo de liangshi gongzuo* (Contemporary China's grain work). Beijing: Zhongguo shehui kexue chubanshe, 1988.

Zhao Wei. *Zhao Ziyang zhuan* (A biography of Zhao Ziyang). Hong Kong: Wenhua jiaoyu chubanshe, 1988.

Zhao Ziyang. "Fangkai nongchanpin jiage, cujin nongcun chanye jiegou de tiaozheng" (Free up the prices of agricultural products and promote the adjustment of rural production structure). *Hongqi* (Red flag), no. 3 (Feburary 1985).

———. "Zai zhongguo gongchandang di shisan jie zhongyang weiyuanhui di san ci quanti huiyi shang de baogao" (Report at the third plenary session of the thirteenth central committee of the Chinese communist party). *Xinhua yuebao*, no. 10 (1988).

Zheng Qian and Han Gang. *Mao Zedong zhi lu: Wannian suiyue—1956 nian hou de Mao Zedong* (Mao Zedong's road: the last years—Mao Zedong after 1956). Vol. 4 of *Mao Zedong zhi lu*. Beijing: Zhongguo qingnian chubanshe, 1993.

Zheng Xiaofeng and Shu Ling. *Tao Zhu zhuan* (A biography of Tao Zhu). Beijing: Zhongguo qingnian chubanshe, 1992.

Zhili zhengdun shenhua gaige zhengce fagui xuanbian (Selected policies, laws, and regulations on rectifying and consolidating [the economic order] and deepening reform). Beijing: Zhongguo caizheng jingji chubanshe, 1990.

Zhong Borong. "Ji jiaqiang zerenzhi, you wending suoyouzhi" (Stabilize the ownership system while strengthening the responsibility system). *RMRB*, May 5, 1979.

Zhong Zhushan. "Nongcun jiceng dang zuzhi xianzhuang tanxi" (An investigation and analysis of rural basic-level party organizations). *Liaowang* (Outlook), no. 1 (January 1, 1990).

Zhonggong Heilongjiang sheng weiyuanhui (CCP Heilongjiang Provincial Committee). "Zuohao tuixing jiating lianchan chengbao zerenzhi gongzuo" (Do well the job of spreading the household output-linked contract responsibility system). *NYJJWT*, no. 2 (1984).

Zhonggong zhongyang dangxiao chubanshe, ed. *"Wenhua dageming" zhong de Zhou Enlai* (Zhou Enlai during the Cultural Revolution). Beijing: Zhonggong zhongyang dangxiao chubanshe, 1991.

Zhonggong zhongyang dangxiao dangshi jiaoyanshi, ed. *Zhonggong dangshi cankao ziliao* (Reference materials on CCP party history), vol. 8. Beijing: Renmin chubanshe, 1980.

Zhonggong Zhongyang Shujichu Yanjiushi Zonghezu. *Dang de shiyi jie sanzhong quanhui yilai dashiji* (A chronology of major events since the party's third plenum of the eleventh central committee). Beijing: Hongqi chubanshe, 1987.

Zhonggong zhongyang wenxian yanjiushi. *Sanzhong quanhui yilai zhongyao wenxian xuanbian* (A selected compilation of important documents since the third plenum). 2 vols. Beijing: Renmin chubanshe, 1982.

———. *Shisanda yilai zhongyao wenxian xuanbian* (Selected important documents since the thirteenth party congress), vol. 2. Beijing: Renmin chubanshe, 1991.

Zhonggong zhongyang zhengce yanjiushi. *Zhongguo nongmin de weida shijian: nongcun gaige he fazhan dianxing jingyan.* (The great practices of Chinese peasants: typical experiences in rural reform and development). Beijing: Zhonggong zhongyang dangxiao chubanshe, 1991.

Zhongguo dituce (Atlas of China). Pocket ed. Beijing: Ditu chubanshe, 1978.

Zhongguo fazhan wenti yanjiu zu. *Baochan daohu ziliao xuan* (Selected materials on fixing farm output quotas for each household). 2 vols. Beijing: N.p., 1981.

Zhongguo geming bowuguan dangshi yanjiushi, ed. *Dangshi yanjiu ziliao* (Party history research materials), vol. 3. Chengdu: Sichuan renmin chubanshe, 1982.

"Zhongguo Gongchandang di shisan jie zhongyang weiyuanhui disici quanti huiyi gongbao" (Communiqué of the fourth plenary session of the thirteenth central committee of the Chinese communist party). *Qiushi* (Seek truth), no. 13 (1989).

Zhongguo jingji nianjian 1990 (China economic almanac 1990). Beijing: Jingji guanli chubanshe, 1990.

Zhongguo lüyou (China tourism), no. 19 (January 1982).

Zhongguo nongcun jingji tongji daquan (1949–1986) (Complete statistics on China's rural economy, 1949–1986). Beijing: Nongye chubanshe, 1989.

Zhongguo nongye nianjian (Agriculture yearbook of China), 1980–90. Beijing: Nongye chubanshe, 1981–91.

Zhongguo Nongye Yinhang. *Zhongguo nongcun jinrong tongji* (Rural financial statistics of China). Beijing: Zhongguo tongji chubanshe, 1991.

Zhongguo Shehui Zhuyi Jianshe Bianxie Zu. *Zhongguo shehui zhuyi jianshe* (China's socialist construction). Shenyang: Liaoning renmin chubanshe, 1986.

Zhongguo xiangzhen qiye nianjian (Yearbook of China's rural enterprises). Beijing: Nongye chubanshe, various years.

Zhonghua Renmin Gongheguo guomin jingji he shehui fazhan jihua dashi jiyao (1949–1985) (A summary of major events in national economic and social development planning of the People's Republic of China, 1949–1985). Beijing: Hongqi chubanshe, 1987.

Zhonghua Renmin Gongheguo jingji guanli dashiji (A chronology of major events in economic management of the People's Republic of China). Beijing: Zhongguo jingji chubanshe, 1987.

Zhonghua Renmin Gonheguo Nongyebu Zhengce Fagui Si. *Zhongguo nongcun 40 nian* (Four decades of Chinese countryside). Henan: Zhongyuan nongmin chubanshe, 1989.

Zhou Baiyi. "Laizi nongcun diyixian de zuixin baodao" (The latest report from the rural front). In Lin Lishan.

Zhou Chunshu. "Zunzhong shengchandui zizhuquan bushi buyao dang de ling-dao" (Respect for the rights of production teams does not mean the abandon-ment of party leadership). *Qunzhong* (Masses), no. 4 (1979).

Zhou Enlai xuanji (Selected works of Zhou Enlai), vol. 2. Beijing: Renmin chuban-she, 1984.

Zhou Jihua. "Xiuzhi yu xupu" (Writing annals and extending genealogies). *Liaowang*, no. 28 (July 10, 1989).

Zhou Taihe. "Chen Yun tongzhi sixia nongcun diaocha de qianhou" (Comrade Chen Yun's four rural investigations). In Chen Yun yu xin Zhongguo.

———, ed. *Dangdai Zhongguo de jingji tizhi gaige* (Contemporary China's economic system reforms). Beijing: Zhongguo shehui kexue chubanshe, 1984.

Zhou Xiaozhou zhuanji bianxie zu. *Zhou Xiaozhou zhuan* (A biography of Zhou Xiaozhou). Changsha: Hunan renmin chubanshe, 1985.

Zhou Yueli. "The System of Responsibility in Agricultural Production in Anhui Province." In Xue Muqiao, ed.

Zhu Chuzhu, ed. *Zhongguo renkou: Shaanxi fence* (China's population: Shaanxi vol-ume). Beijing: Zhongguo caizheng jingji chubanshe, 1988.

Zhu Dazhai Lianhe Baodaozu. "Xiyang diaodong nongmin shehui zhuyi jijixing de jingyan hao" (The experiences of Xiyang in mobilizing the socialist enthusi-asm of peasants are good). *RMRB*, May 13, 1978.

Zhu De. *Zhu De xuanji* (Selected works of Zhu De). Beijing: Renmin chubanshe, 1983.

Zhu Gongjia. "Ruhe xiaochu qunzhong 'pabian' de gulü" (How to soothe the masses' worries of 'policy shifts'). *ZGNMB*, September 3, 1981.

Zhu Rong, ed. *Dangdai Zhongguo de nongzuowu ye* (Crop production in contempo-rary China). Beijing: Zhongguo shehui kexue chubanshe, 1988.

Zhu Yuncheng, Chen Haoguang, and Lu Datong, eds. *Zhongguo renkou: Guangdong fence* (China's population: Guangdong volume). Beijing: Zhongguo caizheng jingji chubanshe, 1988.

Zong Jun. *Zong shejishi* (The general architect). Beijing: Zhonggong zhongyang dangxiao chubanshe, 1993.

Zou Qiyu and Miao Wenjun, eds. *Zhongguo renkou: Yunnan fence* (China's popula-tion: Yunnan volume). Beijing: Zhongguo caizheng jingji chubanshe, 1989.

Zuo Chuntai and Song Xinzhong, eds. *Zhongguo shehui zhuyi caizheng jianshi* (An outline history of China's socialist finance). Beijing: Zhongguo caizheng jingji chubanshe, 1988.

Zweig, David. *Agrarian Radicalism in China, 1968–1981*. Cambridge, MA: Harvard University Press, 1989.

———. "Context and Content in Policy Implementation: Household Contracts and Decollectivization, 1977–1983." In Lampton, ed.

———. "Internationalizing China's Countryside: The Political Economy of Exports from Rural Industry." *China Quarterly*, no. 128 (December 1991).

———. "Opposition to Change in Rural China: The System of Responsibility and People's Communes." *Asian Survey* 23, no. 7 (July 1983).

———. "Rural Industry: Constraining the Leading Growth Sector in China's Economy." In Joint Economic Committee.

Index

• • ● • •

In this index an "f" after a number indicates a separate reference on the next page, and an "ff" indicates separate references on the next two pages. A continuous discussion over two or more pages is indicated by a span of page numbers, e.g., "pp. 57–58." *Passim* is used for a cluster of references in close but not continuous sequence.

Bias, 12, 238–39, 252. *See also* Cognitive psychology
Bo Yibo, 34, 232
Bray, Francesca, 142
Brigade accounting, *see* Basic accounting unit, brigade as
Brigades, *see* Production brigades
Bulletin of Assorted News, 44
Bureaucracy, 185–91 *passim*, 202, 210–11, 247

Cash crops, 65, 110–14, 123, 126. *See also individual crops by name*
CCP, *see* Chinese Communist Party
Central Committee (CC), 4, 52, 71, 103, 186, 190, 202, 206, 209; and collectivization, 25, 28, 44, 47, 52, 77; and agrarian reforms, 75, 101, 125, 128, 149, 169; plenums, 144–48 *passim*, 163, 176, 185, 201, 216, 230
Central-local relations, 67, 75, 162–67 *passim*, 178, 183–84, 202–3, 212, 228
Central Military Commission, 109, 122, 146
Central Party School, 130
Chang Guangnan, 157
Chang Zhenying, 155
Chen Boda, 44
Chen Jungsheng, 175f
Chen Tingyuan, 156–57
Chen Yaobang, 231
Chen Yizi, 168–69
Chen Yonggui, 101, 103, 123–29 *passim*, 146, 150, 152f
Chen Yuan, 233
Chen Yun, 30, 33–34, 124, 146f, 150, 171, 179, 204; and grain, 26, 77f, 114, 144, 201
Chinese Academy of Sciences, 46, 168, 227
Chinese Association of Rural Enterprises (CARE), 231–32
Chinese Communist Party (CCP), 3, 21, 35, 59, 135, 141, 200, 204; membership and leadership of, 62–64, 140, 143, 197–98
Coale, Ansley J., 37
Cognitive psychology, 2, 9, 11–14, 99, 106, 134, 237. *See also* Bias
Cohn, Norman, 40
Collective action, 243–44
Collectivization, 22–27 *passim*, 33, 40, 142, 199, 206; motivation and support, 14, 166, 170, 238. *See also* Agricultural Producers' Cooperatives; Decollectivization
Communes, 2, 23, 36, 45, 52–55 *passim*, 73,

77, 125, 160; Xinmin commune, 50; Tonghaikou, 74; Chayashan, 76; Huaminglou, 79; Yuanzhou, 118; Jiacun, 119; Mahu, 154–59 *passim*; Xinjie, 155; Jinyu, 157; Sanshui, 157; Dingyun, 158; Qingjiang, 159–60; Nanweizi, 161; Ruidan, 163. *See also* Mess halls; Tragedy of the commons
Communist Party, *see* Chinese Communist Party
Communist wind, 43, 72, 75f, 101
Comparative advantage, 112, 120. *See also* Trade, interprovincial
Cong Jin, 37
Constitution, Chinese, 126, 200, 229
Contracting: output to the group, 154–61, 167, 176. *See also* Household contracting
Contract workers, 47
Cotton, 28, 32, 112–14 *passim*, 129, 147f, 155, 192. *See also* Cash crops
Credit, *see* Loans
Cui Naifu, 204
Cultural Revolution, 6, 98, 102, 104, 121, 123; influence of on rural reform, 1, 4–5, 129, 131, 243

Dai Zhou, 204
David, Paul, 249
Dazhai, 101, 117f, 129, 148, 169, 173, 185; lessons of, 103, 124–28 *passim*, 146, 150, 152, 165
Decollectivization, 2–3
Deficit, government, 65, 232–33
Deng Liqun, 104, 169
Deng Xiaoping, 34, 78, 101f, 127, 144, 146–47, 179, 244, 255; and reforms, 5–6, 117, 124f, 150, 166, 171, 203, 205, 209, 216, 230–31, 239
Deng Zihui, 34, 37, 46, 130, 170; and collectivization, 25–31 *passim*, 99
Document no. 1, 172, 174f, 184
Domes, Jürgen, 43, 119
Drought, 153–54, 159
Du Runsheng, 168–71 *passim*, 175

Economic crops, *see* Cash crops
Economic Daily, 229
Economic News, 44
Economic System Reform Institute, 169
Edema, 44, 75, 79
Egalitarianism, 45, 77, 118f, 127f, 148, 156, 163, 175
Elster, Jon, 15

Emulation, political, 158–59
Endowment effect, *see* Bias
Enterprises, rural, 213–33 *passim. See also* Industry, rural
Enterprises, state, 217–26 *passim*
Exports, 222, 233. *See also individual exports by name*
Externalities, 239

Fertilizers, 109, 115f, 148, 172, 188f, 193
Field, Robert M., 4
Five winds, 43
Foreign currency reserves, 129
Four Modernizations, 129, 147
Fujian, 114, 153; Putian municipality, 191

Gang of Four, 99, 124–25, 150, 162
Gansu, 38–39, 43, 56, 75, 119, 131, 138; reform in, 50, 153, 159, 164, 170; Huining county, 159–60
Gao Yang, 174
Geng Qichang, 49, 58
Goldstein, Avery, 39–40, 56, 59, 67
Grain, 44ff, 53, 55, 65, 72, 74, 106, 192, 202; national output of, 25–29 *passim*, 53, 111, 129, 201, 203, 207; prices and rationing of, 26, 75f, 79, 212, 239; procurement and extraction of, 26–29 *passim*, 43, 58, 65, 98f, 105–8 *passim*, 119, 122, 148–53 *passim*, 198; import/export of, 42, 66f, 77, 108, 113f, 129, 144, 147; local output of, 102, 124, 160, 162–63
"Grain first" policy, 109–12
Great Irish Famine, 17, 250–52
Great Leap Famine, 6–7, 37–42 *passim*, 54–56, 65, 240, 252; effects of, 1, 73, 119, 121f, 143, 159, 177, 241; and institutional change, 14, 138, 183, 242, 249
Great Leap Forward, 33f, 36f, 49, 51f, 65, 73, 102, 238, 240
Gu Zhuoxin, 150
Guangdong, 32, 43, 74–79 *passim*, 102, 128, 153, 159, 161, 219, 226–28; Dongguan county, 114; Gaozhou county, 118; Boluo county, 118
Guangxi, 32, 38–39, 75, 131, 138, 168, 240
Guangzhou, 77
Guinnane, Timothy, 251
Guizhou, 56, 58, 131, 138, 145; Guanling county, 158; reform in, 158ff, 164, 167, 170f, 178
Guizhou Daily, 158
Guomindang (KMT), 1

Haggard, Stephan, 250
Hainan, 226
Hall, Peter, 179
Harding, Harry, 5
Hayami, Yujiro, 10
He Kang, 228, 232
He Xin, 227
Hebei, 32, 52, 113f, 149, 161, 165; Changli county, 46; agrarian radicalism in, 60, 79, 131, 142, 174; Daming county, 174; Chongyi township, Wu'an county, 195
Heilongjiang, 56, 131, 142, 149, 165f, 170–76 *passim*; Nenjiang prefecture, 175
Henan: collectivization in, 28–29, 44–52 *passim*, 58, 113f, 171, 176, 201, 226–27; reform in, 32, 131, 143, 159; Xiping county, 36; Great Leap in, 38–39, 56, 75–76, 79, 101f, 138; Xinyang prefecture, 48, 49–50, 75–76, 153; Luoyang prefecture, 50; Suiping county, 76; Qiliying, 78; Beijie village, Neihuang county, 202; Nanyang county, 202
Hill, Kenneth, 37
Hinton, William, 104, 173
Hirschman, Albert, 240, 252
Household contracting, 49, 52, 73, 130, 149–58 *passim*, 164f, 240; leaders on, 16, 102, 167, 174
Household farming, 54, 99, 117–21 *passim*, 156, 161, 240, 243f
Household responsibility system, 131, 149, 163–72 *passim*, 177, 179, 206, 246; adoption of, 2, 157–59, 174, 239, 241
Hsi-Sheng Ch'i, 202–3
Hu Jiwei, 128, 166
Hu Qiaomu, 78, 129–30
Hu Yaobang, 127, 130, 146, 171, 179, 185; and other leaders, 117, 164, 169, 174, 216, 225
Hua Guofeng, 5, 101, 127–29, 146–53 *passim*, 162, 179, 244
Hubei, 28–29, 43f, 75, 102, 142, 192f, 226–27; Mianyang county, 74f; Jingmen municipality, 197
Hysteresis, *see* Path dependency

Illumination Daily, 127–28, 129
Imperial China, 135, 199
Incentives, *see* Peasant incentives
Income, 135, 221. *See also under* Peasants
Individual farming, *see* Household farming
Industry, heavy, 35f, 53, 216

State Council, 51–53, 65, 109, 122, 171, 186, 190, 202–9 *passim*, 227
State Planning Commission (SPC), 22
State Science and Technology Commission, 228
State Statistical Bureau, 218
Status quo bias, *see* Bias
Steel, 34, 116
Stinchcombe, Arthur, 11, 14, 249
Stolper-Samuelson theorem, 248
Structure, 121–22
Succession struggle (post-Mao), 119, 121f
Sugar, 112, 129
Sugar beets, 112, 123, 148. *See also* Cash crops

Tan Qilong, 101
Tan Zhenlin, 37, 48, 55, 78, 99–103 *passim*
Tang Junying, 159–60
Tang Maolin, 155–56
Tao Zhu, 43, 74–75, 78, 99, 101–2
Taxes, 106–7, 148, 190–94, 201, 207, 210, 222, 233. *See also* Levies
Teams, *see* Production teams
Teiwes, Frederick, 140
Three-fix policy, 33, 51
Three red banners, 74
Thurston, Anne, 6
Tian Jiaying, 77
Tian Jiyun, 219
Tiananmen Incident (1976), 119
Tiananmen Incident (1989), 203–4, 213, 227
Tianjin, 65–66, 72, 131, 142, 227
Tibet, 153
Tobacco, 112. *See also* Cash crops
Trade, interprovincial, 112–13, 115
Tragedy of the commons, 42, 55, 67
Trends in Propaganda and Education, 44
Truth criterion: debate over, 127–28, 129, 145, 174
Tsou, Tang, 126
Tversky, Amos, 11
TVE sector, *see* Enterprises, rural
Twelve Articles, 76
Two whatevers, 125, 159

Urban bias, 224–25
Urban supplies, 51, 108f, 122
USSR, *see* Soviet Union

Vogel, Ezra, 4

Walker, Kenneth, 105, 110, 113
Wan Li, 150–56 *passim*, 162–73 *passim*, 178f, 244
Wang Dongxing, 39
Wang Guangyu, 150
Wang Guichen, 168
Wang Huizhi, 50, 58
Wang Renzhong, 102, 161–62, 164f
Wang Xiaoqiang, 168
Wang Xuezhou, 163
Wang Yusheng, 175
Wang Yuzhao, 151
Waterworks, 52–53, 74, 101, 130, 184–85, 191, 207
Watson, Andrew, 3
Weber, Max, 134
Wei Daonan, 168
Wei Jingsheng, 40
Wei Qichang, 203
Wen, James, 109
Whateverism, 125, 159
Wheat, 111. *See also* Grain
White, Tyrene, 186
White slips, *see* IOUs
Wolf, Eric, 245–46
Wong, Christine, 4
"Work Regulations on Rural Communes," *see* Sixty Articles
Wu Lengxi, 100
Wu Xiang, 168
Wu Zhipu, 48, 58

Xiao Yang, 210
Xinhua News Agency, 163
Xinjiang, 50, 131, 142, 153, 201
Xue Muqiao, 4, 129

Yan Hongchang, 155
Yang Yichen, 174–76
Yao Yilin, 114, 147, 216
Yiping erdiao, 103
Yu Guangyuan, 129
Yuan Mu, 225
Yunnan, 36, 44, 56, 58, 131
Yusuf, Shahid, 110

Zechauser, Richard, 12
Zeitz, Robin, 37
Zeng Xisheng, 58, 151, 172
Zeren tian, 118, 149–50
Zhan Wu, 168
Zhang Hao letter, 161–63

Library of Congress Cataloging-in-Publication Data
Yang, Dali L.
  Calamity and reform in China : state; rural society, and
institutional change since the Great Leap Famine / Dali L.
Yang.
      p.   cm.
  Includes bibliographical references and index.
  ISBN 0-8047-2557-8 (cl.)   :   ISBN 0-8047-3470-4 (pbk.)
  1. Rural development—China. 2. Agriculture and state—
China. 3. Famines—China. 4. China—Politics and
government—1949–
  I. Title
  HN740.Z9C685   1996
  307.1'412'0951—dc20   95-30871
                                                          CIP

Original printing 1996
Last figure below indicates year of this printing:

05   04   03   02   01   00   99   98